INTERNATIC
BUSINESS 9
Seventh Edition

Editor

Dr. Fred Maidment
Park College

Dr. Fred Maidment is associate professor and department chair of the Department of Business Education at Park College. He received his bachelor's degree from New York University in 1970 and his master's degree from Bernard M. Baruch College of the City University of New York. In 1983 he received his doctorate from the University of South Carolina. His research interests include training and development in industry. He resides in Kansas City, Missouri, with his wife and children.

Annual Editions
A Library of Information from the Public Press
Dushkin/McGraw·Hill
Sluice Dock, Guilford, Connecticut 06437

Visit us on the Internet—http://www.dushkin.com/

The Annual Editions Series

ANNUAL EDITIONS, including GLOBAL STUDIES, consist of over 70 volumes designed to provide the reader with convenient, low-cost access to a wide range of current, carefully selected articles from some of the most important magazines, newspapers, and journals published today. ANNUAL EDITIONS are updated on an annual basis through a continuous monitoring of over 300 periodical sources. All ANNUAL EDITIONS have a number of features that are designed to make them particularly useful, including topic guides, annotated tables of contents, unit overviews, and indexes. For the teacher using ANNUAL EDITIONS in the classroom, an Instructor's Resource Guide with test questions is available for each volume. GLOBAL STUDIES titles provide comprehensive background information and selected world press articles on the regions and countries of the world.

VOLUMES AVAILABLE

ANNUAL EDITIONS
Abnormal Psychology
Accounting
Adolescent Psychology
Aging
American Foreign Policy
American Government
American History, Pre-Civil War
American History, Post-Civil War
American Public Policy
Anthropology
Archaeology
Astronomy
Biopsychology
Business Ethics
Child Growth and Development
Comparative Politics
Computers in Education
Computers in Society
Criminal Justice
Criminology
Developing World
Deviant Behavior
Drugs, Society, and Behavior
Dying, Death, and Bereavement
Early Childhood Education

Economics
Educating Exceptional Children
Education
Educational Psychology
Environment
Geography
Geology
Global Issues
Health
Human Development
Human Resources
Human Sexuality
International Business
Macroeconomics
Management
Marketing
Marriage and Family
Mass Media
Microeconomics
Multicultural Education
Nutrition
Personal Growth and Behavior
Physical Anthropology
Psychology
Public Administration
Race and Ethnic Relations

Social Problems
Social Psychology
Sociology
State and Local Government
Teaching English as a Second
  Language
Urban Society
Violence and Terrorism
Western Civilization,
  Pre-Reformation
Western Civilization,
  Post-Reformation
Women's Health
World History, Pre-Modern
World History, Modern
World Politics

GLOBAL STUDIES
Africa
China
India and South Asia
Japan and the Pacific Rim
Latin America
Middle East
Russia, the Eurasian Republics,
  and Central/Eastern Europe
Western Europe

Cataloging in Publication Data
Main entry under title: Annual Editions: International Business. 1998/99.
    1. International business enterprises—Periodicals. 2. Business—
Periodicals. I. Maidment, Fred, *comp.* II. Title: International business.
ISBN 0–697–39182–5   338.88'05   ISSN 1091–1731

Seventh Edition

Cover image ©1998 PhotoDisc, Inc.

Printed in the United States of America

Printed on Recycled Paper

Editors/Advisory Board

Members of the Advisory Board are instrumental in the final selection of articles for each edition of ANNUAL EDITIONS. Their review of articles for content, level, currency, and appropriateness provides critical direction to the editor and staff. We think that you will find their careful consideration well reflected in this volume.

EDITOR

Fred Maidment
Park College

ADVISORY BOARD

Staff

Ian A. Nielsen, Publisher

To the Reader

In publishing ANNUAL EDITIONS we recognize the enormous role played by the magazines, newspapers, and journals of the *public press* in providing current, first-rate educational information in a broad spectrum of interest areas. Many of these articles are appropriate for students, researchers, and professionals seeking accurate, current material to help bridge the gap between principles and theories and the real world. These articles, however, become more useful for study when those of lasting value are carefully *collected, organized, indexed,* and *reproduced* in a *low-cost format,* which provides easy and permanent access when the material is needed. That is the role played by ANNUAL EDITIONS. Under the direction of each volume's *academic editor,* who is an expert in the subject area, and with the guidance of an *Advisory Board,* each year we seek to provide in each ANNUAL EDITION a current, well-balanced, carefully selected collection of the best of the public press for your study and enjoyment. We think that you will find this volume useful, and we hope that you will take a moment to let us know what you think.

When the first edition of *Annual Editions: International Business* was being compiled a few years ago, the world was extremely unstable. Power in the Soviet Union was very much in question, and hardliners had conducted a coup against the reform government. On August 19, 1991, Russian president Boris Yeltsin jumped on a tank outside the Russian parliament building and denounced the coup leaders, galvanizing the people to take back their government. On that same day, I was writing the introductory essay for the section of this book that included articles on the Soviet Union. In fact, I was typing the essay at the very moment when the news bulletin reporting Yeltsin's act came over the radio. Needless to say, I had to rewrite the essay.

With the subsequent dissolution of the Soviet Union and the turn to capitalism by its newly independent states, many new opportunities for international business have opened. In the future, virtually all countries and all organizations will be engaged in doing business with other organizations outside of their home countries. Students of business administration and, indeed, all people involved in business need to be aware of the new international environment. They need to recognize the opportunities and the problems associated with doing business outside of their home markets. They need to understand that the same types of opportunities await all who engage in business.

Business must respond to this change in the environment by keeping an open mind about the opportunities available to it on a global basis. The articles that have been chosen for *Annual Editions: International Business 98/99* comprise a cross section of the current literature on the subject. The collection addresses the various aspects of international business, with emphasis on the foundations and environment of international trade and on how corporations respond to and deal with this environment. To this editor, the general tone of the articles seems to be growing more optimistic than it was a few years ago. This trend has been borne out in this latest edition. No one claims that all the news is good (because it is not) or that all the problems have been solved (because they never will be), but there has been a change. Most of the literature seems to be more hopeful and less bleak and foreboding than it was at the start of the decade. There is more talk about opportunity and success and less talk about problems and failure. A new era seems to be dawning.

This anthology contains a number of features designed to make it useful for people interested in international business. These features include a *topic guide* for locating articles on specific subjects and a *table of contents* with abstracts that summarize each article and draw attention to key words in bold italics. The volume is organized into four units dealing with specific interrelated topics in international business. Each unit begins with an overview that provides the necessary background information to allow the reader to place a selection in the context of the book. Important topics are emphasized, and challenge questions address major themes.

New to this edition are *World Wide Web* sites that can be used to further explore the topics. These sites are cross-referenced by number in the topic guide.

We would like to know what you think about our book. Please take a few minutes to complete and return the postage-paid *article rating form* in the back of the volume. We need your advice and assistance to help to improve future editions of *Annual Editions: International Business.*

Fred Maidment

Fred Maidment
Editor

Contents

UNIT 1

The Nature of International Business

Eight selections describe the dynamics of today's international business community.

The concepts in bold italics are developed in the article. For further expansion please refer to the Topic Guide and the Index.

UNIT 2

The International Environment: Organizations and Monetary Systems

Four articles examine international organizations, the international monetary system, and the finance of international businesses.

UNIT 3

Foreign Environment

Fourteen selections discuss how international markets are influenced by the common pressures of financing, the economy, sociocultural dynamics, politics, the legal system, labor relations, and other forces.

The concepts in bold italics are developed in the article. For further expansion please refer to the Topic Guide and the Index.

UNIT 4

How Management Deals with Environmental Forces

Twenty-two articles discuss
challenging aspects of
managing in the
international business
community.

The concepts in bold italics are developed in the article. For further expansion please refer to the Topic Guide and the Index.

ix

The concepts in bold italics are developed in the article. For further expansion please refer to the Topic Guide and the Index.

The concepts in bold italics are developed in the article. For further expansion please refer to the Topic Guide and the Index.

1

Topic Guide

This topic guide suggests how the selections in this book relate to topics of traditional concern to students and professionals involved with international business. It is useful for locating articles that relate to each other for reading and research. The guide is arranged alphabetically according to topic. Articles may, of course, treat topics that do not appear in the topic guide. In turn, entries in the topic guide do not necessarily constitute a comprehensive listing of all the contents of each selection. **In addition, relevant Web sites, which are annotated on the next two pages, are noted in bold italics under the topic articles.**

TOPIC AREA	TREATED IN	TOPIC AREA	TREATED IN
Communication	2. American Isolationism versus the Global Economy 6. Education and the Wealth of Nations 10. Challenges in Managing Technology 16. Global Transfer of Critical Capabilities 28. Crafting Strategies for Global Marketing 44. Asia's Bamboo Network 45. When Sexual Harassment Is a Foreign Affair 46. HR Pioneers Explore the Road Less Traveled 47. One Assignment, Two Lives 48. Toward Global Convergence *(1, 2, 7, 16, 18, 20, 21, 25, 26, 27, 28, 32)*	**Economic Trends**	1. Growth through Global Sustainability 2. American Isolationism versus the Global Economy 3. "Globalization and the International Division of Labor" 6. Education and the Wealth of Nations 7. World Education League: Who's Top? 8. Balancing Act 11. Great Escape 15. Africa's New Dawn 16. Global Transfer of Critical Capabilities 24. Global Economy, Local Mayhem? 27. Shock Therapy 30. Troubles Ahead in Emerging Markets 48. Toward Global Convergence *(1, 5, 6, 15, 18, 19, 21, 23, 29)*
Developing Countries	1. Growth through Global Sustainability 2. American Isolationism versus the Global Economy 5. Back to the Land 9. Riding the Dragon 11. Great Escape 13. International Monetary Arrangements 14. Ignored Warnings 15. Africa's New Dawn 16. Global Transfer of Critical Capabilities 18. Keeping Up on Chinese Culture 19. American Involvement in Vietnam, Part II 20. Political Risk Analysis 21. Scourge of Global Counterfeiting 22. Rule by Law 23. Wanted: Muscle 24. Global Economy, Local Mayhem? 26. Investing in India 27. Shock Therapy 29. Asia's Next Tiger? 30. Troubles Ahead in Emerging Markets 31. Maquiladora-ville 32. Myth of the China Market 34. "Compromise Increases Risk of War" 35. Doing Business in China 36. Doing Business in Vietnam 39. Discreet Charm of Provincial Asia 42. Getting What You Pay For 43. Company without a Country 44. Asia's Bamboo Network *(1, 3, 5, 9, 10, 11, 12, 14, 15, 16, 18, 21, 22, 23, 24, 25, 26, 29, 32, 33)*	**European Union (European Community)** **Finance**	3. "Globalization and the International Division of Labor" 4. Building Effective R&D Capabilities Abroad 6. Education and the Wealth of Nations 7. World Education League: Who's Top? 8. Balancing Act 10. Challenges in Managing Technology 12. International Banking 25. Global Deregulation 28. Crafting Strategies for Global Marketing 33. Ship It! 38. Europe in the Global Financial World 45. When Sexual Harassment Is a Foreign Affair 48. Toward Global Convergence *(5, 9, 10, 12, 14, 15, 16, 18, 20, 24, 26)* 1. Growth through Global Sustainability 5. Back to the Land 8. Balancing Act 9. Riding the Dragon 11. Great Escape 12. International Banking 13. International Monetary Arrangements 14. Ignored Warnings 15. Africa's New Dawn 24. Global Economy, Local Mayhem? 25. Global Deregulation 26. Investing in India 37. Earn 20% Investing Abroad 38. Europe in the Global Financial World *(1, 2, 5, 12, 13, 14, 15, 17, 19, 22)*

TOPIC AREA	TREATED IN	TOPIC AREA	TREATED IN
Management	1. Growth through Global Sustainability 3. "Globalization and the International Division of Labor" 4. Building Effective R&D Capabilities Abroad 8. Balancing Act 10. Challenges in Managing Technology 12. International Banking 16. Global Transfer of Critical Capabilities 17. Put Your Ethics to a Global Test 20. Political Risk Analysis 21. Scourge of Global Counterfeiting 23. Wanted: Muscle 25. Global Deregulation 39. Discreet Charm of Provincial Asia 40. From Major to Minor 41. Are Expats Getting Lost in the Translation? 42. Getting What You Pay For 43. Company without a Country? 44. Asia's Bamboo Network 45. When Sexual Harassment Is a Foreign Affair 46. HR Pioneers Explore the Road Less Traveled 47. One Assignment, Two Lives 48. Toward Global Convergence *(1, 4, 6, 11, 21, 25, 26, 32, 33)*	**Marketing**	2. American Isolationism versus the Global Economy 9. Riding the Dragon 15. Africa's New Dawn 19. American Involvement in Vietnam, Part II 20. Political Risk Analysis 21. Scourge of Global Counterfeiting 22. Rule by Law 27. Shock Therapy 28. Crafting Strategies for Global Marketing 29. Asia's Next Tiger? 30. Troubles Ahead in Emerging Markets 31. Maquiladora-ville 32. Myth of the China Market 33. Ship It! 43. Company without a Country? 44. Asia's Bamboo Network 48. Toward Global Convergence *(1, 3, 7, 10, 16, 18, 21, 22, 23, 27, 30)*
Manufacturing	1. Growth through Global Sustainability 3. "Globalization and the International Division of Labor" 4. Building Effective R&D Capabilities Abroad 6. Education and the Wealth of Nations 7. World Education League: Who's Top? 9. Riding the Dragon 10. Challenges in Managing Technology 15. Africa's New Dawn 16. Global Transfer of Critical Capabilities 21. Scourge of Global Counterfeiting 22. Rule by Law 23. Wanted: Muscle 24. Global Economy, Local Mayhem? 25. Global Deregulation 26. Investing In India 31. Maquiladora-ville 32. Myth of the China Market 39. Discreet Charm of Provincial Asia 40. From Major to Minor 43. Company without a Country? 44. Asia's Bamboo Network *(1, 3, 5, 8, 10, 11, 13, 14, 16, 18, 21, 22, 31)*	**Political Trends**	2. American Isolationism versus the Global Economy 6. Education and the Wealth of Nations 7. World Education League: Who's Top? 15. Africa's New Dawn 17. Put Your Ethics to a Global Test 19. American Involvement in Vietnam, Part II 20. Political Risk Analysis 22. Rule by Law 30. Troubles Ahead in Emerging Markets 34. "Compromise Increases the Risk of War" 35. Doing Business in China 36. Doing Business in Vietnam 43. Company without a Country? *(1, 9, 11, 15, 17, 18, 20, 21, 22, 26)*
		Technology	1. Growth through Global Sustainability 2. American Isolationism versus Global Economy 4. Building Effective R&D Capabilities Abroad 6. Education and the Wealth of Nations 7. World Education League: Who's Top? 10. Challenges in Managing Technology 15. Africa's New Dawn 16. Global Transfer of Critical Capabilities 23. Wanted: Muscle 24. Global Economy, Local Mayhem? 25. Global Deregulation 26. Investing in India 30. Troubles Ahead in Emerging Markets 31. Maquiladora-ville 39. Discreet Charm of Provincial Asia 40. From Major to Minor *(1, 5, 10, 11, 14, 16, 21, 22, 26, 31)*

Selected World Wide Web Sites for
Annual Editions: International Business

All of these Web sites are hot-linked through the *Annual Editions* home page:
http://www.dushkin.com/annualeditions (just click on a book). In addition, these sites are referenced
by number and appear where relevant in the Topic Guide on the previous two pages.

Some Web sites are continually changing their structure and content, so the information listed may not always be available.

General Sources

1. Internet Resources for International Economics & Business—*http://dylee.keel.econ.ship.edu/intntl/int_home.htm*—Dr. Daniel Y. Lee of the College of Business at Shippensburg University maintains this site, which lists Internet resources related to economics and business in general; references; and specific international business topics, such as international development.

2. NewsPage—*http://pnp1.individual.com/*—This site from Individual, Inc. provides daily business briefings and more in-depth stories related to such fields as computing and media, banking and finance, health care, insurance, and transportation and distribution.

3. STAT-USA—*http://www.stat-usa.gov/stat-usa.html*—This essential site, a service of the U.S. Department of Commerce, contains daily economic news, frequently requested statistical releases, information on export and international trade, domestic economic news and statistical series, and databases.

The Nature of International Business

4. Business Policy and Strategy—*http://comsp.com.latrobe.edu.au/bps.html*—This site, the home page of the Business Policy and Strategy Division of the U.S. Academy of Management, is packed with information about the theory and practice of international business. The division is interested in "the roles and problems of general managers."

5. OECD/FDI Statistics—*http://www.oecd.org/daf/cmis/fdi/statist.htm*—Explore foreign direct investment trends and statistics on this site from the Organization for Economic Cooperation and Development. It provides links to many related topics and addresses the issues on a country-by-country basis.

6. Harvard Business School—*http://www.hbs.edu/*—This Web site of the Harvard Business School provides useful links to library and research resources, to the Harvard Business Review, and to information regarding executive education as well as other topics.

7. Sales & Marketing Executives International—*http://www.smei.org/*—Visit this home page of Sales & Marketing Executives (SME), a worldwide association of sales and marketing management. Through this "Digital Resource Mall," you can access research and useful articles on sales and management. You can even listen in as marketing leaders discuss their latest strategies and ideas.

8. World Trade Centers Association—*http://www.wtca.org/*—WTCA On-Line presents this site as a news and information service. Members can access the *Dun & Bradstreet Exporters' Encyclopaedia* and other valuable sources, but guests to the site can also gain entry to interesting trade-related information.

9. Legal Material Organized by Topic—*http://www.law.cornell.edu/topical.html*—Explore this site's extensive searchable index to learn about a myriad of international legal subjects. It provides useful topic summaries with links to key primary source material and off-Net references.

10. MSU-Ciber—*http://ciber.bus.msu.edu/busres.htm*—Michigan State University's Center for International Business Education and Research provides this invaluable site, which allows a keyword search and points you to a great deal of trade information and leads, government resources, and related periodicals. It also provides general and specific country and regional information.

The International Environment: Organizations and Monetary Systems

11. International Labour Organization—*http://www.ilo.org/*—ILO's home page leads to links that describe the goals of the organization and summarizes international labor standards and human rights. Its official UN Web site locator can point you to many other useful resources.

12. Resources for Economists on the Internet—*http://coba.shsu.edu/EconFAQ/node76.html*—This site and its links are essential reading for those interested in learning about the Organization for Economic Cooperation and Development, the World Bank, the International Monetary Fund, and other important international organizations.

13. Finance (and Banking) Related Links—*http://ananse.irv.uit.no/trade_law/frames/body-finance.html*—Surf this site for information on international banking and finance. It provides links to popular sites for finance, stock research, and electronic banking.

14. International Trade Law Monitor—*http://ananse.irv.uit.no/trade_law/nav/trade.html*—Use this valuable site to access a wealth of resources related to international trade, including data on the European Union and the International Monetary Fund. Among its many links, it addresses such topics as Principles of International Commercial Contracts and UN Arbitration Laws.

15. RefLaw: The Virtual Law Library Reference Desk—*http://law.wuacc.edu/washlaw/reflaw/refgatt.html*—This site from the Washburn University School of Law Library can direct you to primary documents related to GATT and other information about the Agreement. It also reproduces world constitutions and the text of NAFTA and other major treaties.

16. Center for International Business Education and Research—*http://www.cob.ohio-state.edu/ciberweb/*—Surf this site for information about international business/trade organizations and emerging markets, and for news links to related topics.

17. Institute of International Bankers—*http://www.IIB.org/*—Examine this site for information on the Institute of International Bankers, IBB events, and publications in order to become familiar with trends in international banking.

Foreign Environment

18. CIBERWeb—*http://www3.mgmt.purdue.edu/ciber/*—The Centers for International Business Education and Research work to increase and promote Americans' capacity for international understanding and economic enterprise. This site is useful for exploring issues of doing business in a global market.

19. Charts and Tables Related to Foreign Direct Investment in Japan—*http://www.jef.or.jp/news/jp/index.html*—This site from the Japan Economic Foundation presents charts illustrating trends of foreign direct investment in Japan.

20. Chambers of Commerce World Network—*http://worldchambers.net/*—This site of the World Network of Chambers of Commerce and Industry describes itself as "The world's first, oldest, and largest business network." Access a global index of Chambers of Commerce & Industry and Chambers for International Business, as well as information on "Strategic Alliance Partners" such as G7.

21. United States Trade Representative—*http://www.ustr.gov/*—This home page of the U.S. Trade Representative provides links to many other U.S. government resources of value to those interested in international business. It notes important trade-related speeches and agreements and describes the mission of the USTR.

22. Facilities and Incentives for Foreign Investment in India—*http://india-times.com/frinvest/fr_inv.html*—India Times summarizes salient features of the foreign-investment climate in India, one of the largest markets in the world. It discusses technology transfer, industrial licensing, capital market investment, and other topics.

23. WWW Virtual Library Demography & Population Studies—*http://coombs.anu.edu.au/ResFacilities/DemographyPage.html*—Through this Internet Guide to Demography and Population Studies via the World Wide Web Virtual Library, you can learn of leading information facilities of value and/or significance to researchers in the field of demography. The site is provided by Australian National University.

24. International Economic Law Web Site—*http://www.tufts.edu/fletcher/inter_econ_law/index.htm*—This site of the International Economic Law Group of the American Society of International Law contains valuable research tools and links to Web resources regarding international law.

How Management Deals with Environmental Forces

25. STAT-USA/Internet—*http://www.stat-usa.gov/stat-usa.html*—This site, a service of the U.S. Department of Commerce, presents daily economic news; a myriad of links to databases, statistical releases, and selected publications; and general information on export and international trade as well as business leads and procurement opportunities.

26. IR-Net—*http://www.ir-net.co.za/*—Examine this site of South Africa's Industrial-Relations Network as a sample of how different countries address labor issues. It provides information on mediation and conciliation, discusses the International Labour Organization, and notes many library and resource links.

27. International Marketing Review—*http://www.mcb.co.uk/cgi-bin/journal1/imr/*—Visit this home page of the journal *International Marketing Review* to gather leads to a number of resources and articles. It also provides for interactive discussion and an "International Meeting Place."

28. Fr. Oswald Mascarenhas (S.J.) Web Site Links—*http://www.udmercy.edu/htmls/personal/parasuba/ozzie.htm*—Fr. Oswald Mascarenhas of University of Detroit Mercy maintains this useful site of links to marketing Web sites: journals, magazines, departments, and associations.

29. International Agribusiness Marketing and Trade—*http://mail.ipt.com/intlagmktg*—This site of the Texas Agricultural Extension Service provides links to international agribusiness marketing and trade resources. Those who want to see an example of international business at work will enjoy surfing this site.

30. MELNET—*http://www.bradford.ac.uk/acad/mancen/melnet/index.html*—MELNET, self-described as a "World Class Business Network," is a virtual cooperative for people looking to improve the way they do business. Through this interactive site, you can learn about such important topics as branding.

31. Kitchener Business Self-Help Office: Seven Steps to Exporting—*http://www.city.kitchener.on.ca/kitchener_import_export.html*—This site describes seven steps to exporting, from selecting an export market to actually beginning to export. It addresses such critical topics as distribution, pricing, and subsidiaries.

32. Telecommuting as an Investment: The Big Picture-John Wolf—*http://www.svi.org/telework/forums/messages5/48.html*—This page deals with the many issues related to telecommuting, including its potential role in reducing environmental pollution. The site discusses such topics as dealing with unions, employment-law concerns, and the impact of telecommuting on businesses and employees.

33. Research and Reference (Library of Congress)—*http://lcweb.loc.gov/rr*—This research and reference site of the Library of Congress will lead you to invaluable information on different countries. It provides links to numerous publications, bibliographies, and guides in area studies that can be of great help to the international businessperson.

We highly recommend that you review our Web site for expanded information and our other product lines. We are continually updating and adding links to our Web site in order to offer you the most usable and useful information that will support and expand the value of your book. You can reach us at: *http://www.dushkin.com/*.

The Nature of International Business

- Introduction to International Business (Articles 1–3)
- International Trade and Foreign Investment (Articles 4 and 5)
- Economic Theories on International Trade, Development, and Investment (Articles 6–8)

The world is growing smaller each day. Communication and transportation have made planet Earth more closely knit for the people who live on it.

Global growth is accelerating, especially in the developing countries of the Pacific Rim, and it is starting to increase in Latin America. In the first unit article, "Growth through Global Sustainability," Robert Shapiro, the CEO of Monsanto, discusses how his company plans to deal with global growth. Industrialized countries, such as the United States, Japan, and Germany, will continue to grow, but at a much slower rate than the emerging "tigers" of the Pacific Rim. China, in particular, with over 1 billion people, is a country with tremendous potential. It is, however, a nation with huge needs. The infrastructure needs to be built. Railroads, roads, bridges, sewer systems, and electrification are all desperately needed, and this is where much of China's growth will take place. It will not be easy, and there are risks, especially political risks, but the Chinese prize is so attractive that many Western organizations will willingly accept those risks.

While international trade continues to grow, it continues to become more and more complex. It is a simple equation. The more countries, the more trading blocs, and the more people involved, the more complicated trade becomes. Rules can be set, such as those associated with the General Agreement on Tariffs and Trade (GATT) and the World Trade Organization (WTO). But the more rules there are, the greater is the potential for gray areas between them. Not only is international trade becoming more complicated, but it is also becoming more competitive. The developing countries of the world are challenging the established countries in a variety of areas. Software is being developed in India; electronics manufacture is leaving Japan and going to other countries in Asia; and textiles, the traditional first step on the road to industrialization, have become major industries in many emerging countries.

The United States, faced with such complexity and competition, must not revert to isolationism and abandon world trade. Rather, it must embrace it, as Murray Weidenbaum suggests in "American Isolationism versus the Global Economy."

In the next essay, "Globalization and the International Division of Labor: The Role of Europe and the Response of European Companies," Jürgen Schrempp examines the inevitability of the world to transform into a single economy. Preparing for this dynamic presents a real challenge as well as a great opportunity.

Theories of trade are also changing, and the resources necessary to engage in international trade are reflecting this change. In the past, utilitarians talked about the four factors of production—land, the entrepreneur, labor, and capital—and how each country had certain advantages over other countries in these areas. Today, that old analysis does not necessarily work. Transportation and communication have made the relative advantages in the four factors of production less important. The factor of land, or raw material, has been made less imposing by the transportation system. Japan, for example, has virtually no natural resources, yet few would argue with the success of the Japanese economy. Education is likely to be the fifth factor of production, as discussed in "Education and the Wealth of Nations" and how various countries stack-up in the "World Education League: Who's on Top?"

The entrepreneurial factor can be seen everywhere. It is not just North Americans who start new ventures, but Chinese, South Americans, and Europeans. The former Soviet bloc more than demonstrates the ability of former communists to become entrepreneurs, as do developments in mainland China over the past 10 years. Even in Bangladesh, local financing is being used to help small entrepreneurs. True, these new beehives of entrepreneurial activity may have their problems learning to negotiate the world of business, just as infants have difficulty learning to walk. But eventually, just like small children, they will be on their feet and running everywhere.

Even labor, perhaps the most sedentary of all the factors of production, has shown signs of movement. Labor has always been willing to move, but historians have tended to view these movements as migrations of peoples, not as the movement of a mundane factor of production. Emigrations from Europe to Australia, South Africa, and North and South America have been made by people seeking a better life for themselves and their families. This same kind of movement goes on today. Australia is still gaining population through immigration; Europe is experiencing waves of new workers from former colonies, whether they are Algerians in France or Indians and Pakistanis in Great Britain; and the United States continues to receive immigrants, both legal and illegal, from all over the world, especially from Latin America. Whatever the reason for immigrating, these people certainly represent potential labor, at least, and they are all seeking better lives.

Finally, capital, or the means of production, has shown an ability to go global. Ever since the start of the industrial revolution, there have been countries that were "developed" (with the means of production) and countries that were "less" or "least" developed (generally without the means of production). But that is starting to change. Because of the global transportation and communications system, the location of production facilities is not as important as it once was. In addition, real and potential growth is now to be found in these developing countries. Any organization that is looking to grow will find it much easier to do so in an economy that is rapidly expanding than in one that is saturated and growing only as fast as the population. Capital and the division of production are global at last and will be even more so in the future.

Looking Ahead: Challenge Questions

The world is growing smaller. How have improvements in transportation and communication affected international trade?

Economies are growing all over the world, but the most rapid growth is in the emerging countries of the Pacific Rim. How is this important to business people in the strategic planning of their businesses?

How has the mobility of production factors changed their importance when considering theories of international trade?

GROWTH THROUGH GLOBAL SUSTAINABILITY

An Interview with Monsanto's CEO, Robert B. Shapiro

by Joan Magretta

Robert B. Shapiro, chairman and CEO of Monsanto Company, based in St. Louis, Missouri, sees the conundrum facing his company this way. On the one hand, if a business doesn't grow, it will die. And the world economy must grow to keep pace with the needs of population growth. On the other hand, how does a company face the prospect that growing and being profitable could require intolerable abuse of the natural world? In Shapiro's words, "It's the kind of question that people who choose to spend their lives working in business can't shrug off or avoid easily. And it has important implications for business strategy."

Sustainable development is the term for the dual imperative – economic growth and environmental sustainability – that has been gaining ground among business leaders since the 1992 United Nations Earth Summit in Rio de Janeiro. As Shapiro puts it, "We can't expect the rest of the world to abandon their economic aspirations just so we can continue to enjoy clean air and water. That is neither ethically correct nor likely to be permitted by the billions of people in the developing world who expect the quality of their lives to improve."

Monsanto – with its history in the chemicals industry – may seem an unlikely company to lead the way on an emerging environmental issue. But a number of resource- and energy-intensive companies criticized as environmental offenders in the 1980s have been the first to grasp the strategic implications of sustainability.

Monsanto, in fact, is seeking growth through sustainability, betting on a strategic discontinuity from which few businesses will be immune. To borrow Stuart L. Hart's phrase, Monsanto is moving "beyond greening." (See "Beyond Greening: Strategies for a Sustainable World" in HBR. January–February 1997). In the following interview with HBR editor-at-large Joan Magretta, the 58-year-old Shapiro discusses how Monsanto has moved from a decade of progress in pollution prevention and clean-up to spotting opportunities for revenue growth in environmentally sustainable new products and technologies.

HBR: Why is sustainability becoming an important component of your strategic thinking?

Robert B. Shapiro: Today there are about 5.8 billion people in the world. About 1.5 billion of them live in conditions of abject poverty – a subsistence life that simply can't be romanticized as some form of simpler, preindustrial lifestyle. These people spend their days trying to get food and firewood so that they can make it to the next day. As many as 800 million people are so severely malnourished that they can neither work nor participate in family life. That's where we are today. And, as far as I know, no demographer questions that the world population will just about double by sometime around 2030.

Without radical change, the kind of world implied by those numbers is unthinkable. It's a world of mass migrations and environmental degradation on an unimaginable scale. At best, it means the preservation of a few islands of privilege and prosperity in a sea of misery and violence.

Our nation's economic system evolved in an era of cheap energy and careless waste disposal, when limits seemed irrelevant. None of us today, whether we're managing a house or running a business, is living in a sustainable way. It's not a question of good guys and bad guys. There is no point in saying, If only those bad guys would go out of business, then the world would be fine. The whole system has to change; there's a huge opportunity for reinvention.

We're entering a time of perhaps unprecedented discontinuity. Businesses grounded in the old model will become obsolete and die. At Monsanto, we're trying to invent some new businesses around the concept of environmental sustainability. We may not yet know exactly what those businesses will look like, but we're willing to place some bets because the world cannot avoid needing sustainability in the long run.

Can you explain how what you're describing is a discontinuity?

Years ago, we would approach strategic planning by considering "the environment" – that is, the eco-nomic, technological, and competitive context of the business – and we'd forecast how it would change over the planning horizon. Forecasting usually meant extrapolating recent trends. So we almost never predicted the critical discontinuities in which the real money was made and lost – the changes that really determined the future of the business. Niels Bohr was right when he said it is difficult to make predictions – especially about the future. But every consumer marketer knows that you can rely on demographics. Many market discontinuities were predictable – and future ones can still be predicted – based on observable, incontrovertible facts such as baby booms and busts, life expectancies, and immigration patterns. Sustainable development is one of those discontinuities. Far from being a soft issue grounded in emotion or ethics, sustainable development involves cold, rational business logic.

This discontinuity is occurring because we are encountering physical limits. You can see it coming arithmetically. Sustainability involves the laws of nature—physics, chemistry, and biology—and the recognition that the world is a closed system. What we thought was boundless has limits, and we're beginning to hit them. That's going to change a lot of today's fundamental economics, it's going to change prices, and it's going to change what's socially acceptable.

Is sustainability an immediate issue today in any of Monsanto's businesses?

In some businesses, it's probably less apparent why sustainability is so critical. But in our agricultural business, we can't avoid it. In the twentieth century, we have been able to feed people by bringing more acreage into production and by increasing productivity through fertilizers, pesticides, and irrigation. But current agricultural practice isn't sustainable: we've lost something on the order of 15% of our topsoil over the last 20 years or so, irrigation is increasing the salinity of soil, and the petrochemicals we rely on aren't renewable.

Most arable land is already under cultivation. Attempts to open new farmland are causing severe ecological damage. So in the best case, we have the same amount of land to work with and twice as many people to feed. It comes down to resource productivity. You have to get twice the yield from every acre of land just to maintain current levels of poverty and malnutrition.

Now, even if you wanted to do it in an unsustainable way, no technology today would let you double productivity. With current best practices applied to all the acreage in the world, you'd get about a third of the way toward feeding the whole population.

If companies genetically code a plant to repel pests, farmers don't have to spray with pesticides. That's what's meant by "replacing stuff with information."

The conclusion is that new technology is the only alternative to one of two disasters: not feeding people – letting the Malthusian process work its magic on the population – or ecological catastrophe.

What new technology are you talking about?

We don't have 100 years to figure that out; at best, we have decades. In that time frame, I know of only two viable candidates: biotechnology and information technology. I'm treating them as though they're separate, but biotechnology is really a subset of information technology because it is about DNA-encoded information.

Using information is one of the ways to increase productivity without abusing nature. A closed system like the earth's can't withstand a systematic increase of material things, but it can support exponential increases of information and knowledge. If economic development means using more stuff, then those who argue that growth and environmental sustainability are incompatible are right. And if we grow by using more stuff, I'm afraid we'd better start looking for a new planet.

But sustainability and development might be compatible if you could create value and satisfy people's needs by increasing the information com-

DRAWING BY GARISON WEILAND

Monsanto's Smarter Products

Scientists at Monsanto are designing products that use information at the genetic or molecular level to increase productivity. Here are three that are on the market today.

The NewLeaf Potato. The NewLeaf potato, bioengineered to defend itself against the destructive Colorado potato beetle, is already in use on farms. Monsanto also is working on the NewLeaf Plus potato with inherent resistance to leaf virus, another common scourge. Widespread adoption of the product could eliminate the manufacture, transportation, distribution, and aerial application of millions of pounds of chemicals and residues yearly.

B.t. Cotton. In ordinary soil, microbes known as B.t. microbes occur naturally and produce a special pro-

tein that, although toxic to certain pests, are harmless to other insects, wildlife, and people. If the destructive cotton budworm, for example, eats B.t. bacteria, it will die.

Some cotton farmers control budworms by applying to their cotton plants a powder containing B.t. But the powder often blows or washes away, and reapplying it is expensive. The alternative is for farmers to spray the field with a chemical insecticide as many as 10 or 12 times per season.

But Monsanto's scientists had an idea. They identified the gene that tells the B.t. bacteria to make the special protein. Then they inserted the gene in the cotton plant to enable it to produce the protein on its own while remaining unchanged in other respects. Now

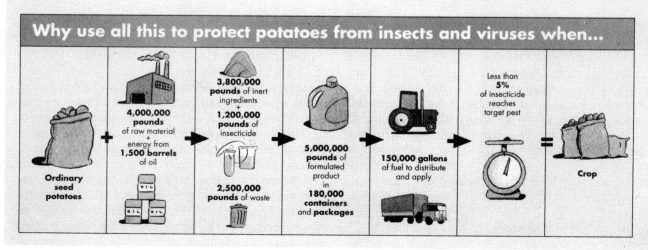

Why use all this to protect potatoes from insects and viruses when...

Ordinary seed potatoes + 4,000,000 pounds of raw material + energy from 1,500 barrels of oil → 3,800,000 pounds of inert ingredients + 1,200,000 pounds of insecticide / 2,500,000 pounds of waste → 5,000,000 pounds of formulated product in 180,000 containers and packages → 150,000 gallons of fuel to distribute and apply → Less than 5% of insecticide reaches target pest = Crop

ponent of what's produced and diminishing the amount of stuff.

How does biotechnology replace stuff with information in agriculture?

We can genetically code a plant, for example, to repel or destroy harmful insects. That means we don't have to spray the plant with pesticides – with stuff. Up to 90% of what's sprayed on crops today is wasted. Most of it ends up on the soil. If we put the right information in the plant, we waste less stuff and increase productivity. With biotechnology, we can accomplish that. It's not that chemicals are inherently bad. But they are less efficient than biology because you have to manufacture and distribute and apply them.

I offer a prediction: the early twenty-first century is going to see a struggle between information technology and biotechnology on the one hand and environmental degradation on the other. Information technology is going to be our most powerful tool. It will let us miniaturize things, avoid waste, and produce more value without producing and processing more stuff. The substitution of information for stuff is essential to sustainability. (See the insert "Monsanto's Smarter Products.") Substituting services for products is another.

Explain what you mean by substituting services for products.

Bill McDonough, dean of the University of Virginia's School of Architecture in Charlottesville, made this come clear for me. He points out that we often buy things not because we want the things themselves but because we want what they can do. Television sets are an obvious example. No one says, "Gee, I'd love to put a cathode-ray tube and a lot of printed circuit boards in my living room." People *might* say, "I'd like to watch the ball game" or "Let's turn on the soaps." Another example: Monsanto makes nylon fiber, much of which goes

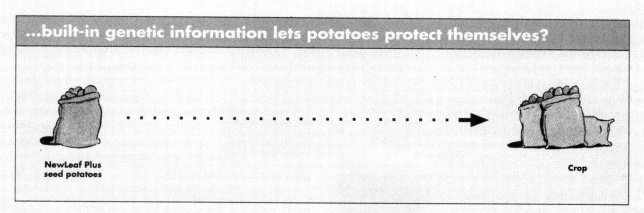

...built-in genetic information lets potatoes protect themselves?

NewLeaf Plus
seed potatoes

Crop

when budworms attack, they are either repelled or killed by the B.t.

With products like B.t. cotton, farmers avoid having to buy and apply insecticides. And the environment is spared chemicals that are persistent in the soil or that run off into the groundwater.

Roundup Herbicide and No-Till Farming. Sustainability has become an important design criterion in Monsanto's chemically based products as well as in its bioengineered products. Building the right information into molecules, for example, can render them more durable or enhance their recyclability.

Roundup herbicide is a molecule designed to address a major problem for farmers: topsoil erosion. Topsoil is necessary for root systems because of its organic matter, friability in structure, and water-holding capabilities. The subsoil underneath is incapable of supporting root systems. Historically, farmers have tilled their soil primarily for weed control and only

to a minor extent for seed preparation. But plowing loosens soil structure and exposes soil to erosion.

By replacing plowing with application of herbicides like Roundup – a practice called *conservation tillage* – farmers end up with better soil quality and less topsoil erosion. When sprayed onto a field before crop planting, Roundup kills the weeds, eliminating the need for plowing. And because the Roundup molecule has been designed to kill only what is growing at the time of its initial application, the farmer can come back a few days after spraying and begin planting; the herbicide will have no effect on the emerging seeds.

The Roundup molecule has other smart features that contribute to sustainability. It is degraded by soil microbes into natural products such as nitrogen, carbon dioxide, and water. It is nontoxic to animals because its mode of action is specific to plants. Once sprayed, it sticks to soil particles; it doesn't move into the groundwater. Like a smart tool, it seeks out its work.

into carpeting. Each year, nearly 2 million tons of old carpeting go into landfills, where they constitute about 1% of the entire U.S. municipal solid-waste load. Nobody really wants to own carpet; they just want to walk on it. What would happen if Monsanto or the carpet manufacturer owned that carpet and promised to come in and remove it when it required replacing? What would the economics of that look like? One of our customers is exploring that possibility today. It might be that if we got the carpet back, we could afford to put more cost into it in the first place in ways that would make it easier for us to recycle. Maybe then it wouldn't end up in a landfill.

We're starting to look at all our products and ask, What is it people really need to buy? Do they need the stuff or just its function? What would be the economic impact of our selling a carpet service instead of a carpet?

Can you cite other examples of how we can replace stuff with information?

Sure. Information technology, whether it's telecommunications or virtual reality–whatever that turns out to be – can eliminate the need to move people and things around. In the past, if you wanted to send a document from one place to another, it involved a lot of trains and planes and trucks. Sending a fax eliminates all that motion. Sending E-mail also eliminates the paper.

I have to add that any powerful new technology is going to create ethical problems – problems of privacy, fairness, ethics, power, or control. With any major change in the technological substrate, society has to solve those inherent issues.

You referred earlier to using information to miniaturize things. How does that work?

Miniaturization is another piece of sustainability because it reduces the amount of stuff we use. There are enormous potential savings in moving from very crude, massive designs to smaller and more elegant ones. Microelectronics is one example: the computing power you have in your PC would have required an enormous installation not many years ago.

We've designed things bigger than they need to be because it's easier and because we thought we had unlimited space and material. Now that we know we don't, there's going to be a premium on smaller, smarter design. I think of miniaturization as a way to buy time. Ultimately, we'd love to figure out how to replace chemical processing plants with fields of growing plants–literally, green plants capable of producing chemicals. We have some

leads: we can already produce polymers in soybeans, for example. But I think a big commercial breakthrough is a long way off.

Today, by developing more efficient catalysts, for example, we can at least make chemical plants smaller. There will be a number of feasible alternatives if we can really learn to think differently and set design criteria other than reducing immediate capital costs. One way is to design chemical plants differently. If you looked at life-cycle costs such as energy consumption, for instance, you would design a plant so that processes needing heat were placed next to processes generating heat; you wouldn't install as many heaters and coolers that waste energy. We think that if you really dig into your costs, you can accomplish a lot by simplifying and shrinking.

Some people are talking about breakthroughs in mechanical devices comparable to what's being done with electronic devices. Maybe the next wave will come through nanotechnology, but probably in 10 or 20 years, not tomorrow.

The key to sustainability, then, lies in technology?

I am not one of those techno-utopians who just assume that technology is going to take care of everyone. But I don't see an alternative to giving it our best shot.

Business leaders tend to trust technology and markets and to be optimistic about the natural unfolding of events. But at a visceral level, people know we are headed for trouble and would love to find a way to do something about it. The market is going to want sustainable systems, and if Monsanto provides them, we will do quite well for ourselves and our shareowners. Sustainable development is going to be one of the organizing principles around which Monsanto and a lot of other institutions will probably define themselves in the years to come.

Describe how you go about infusing this way of thinking into the company?

It's not hard. You talk for three minutes, and people light up and say, "Where do we start?" And I say, "I don't know. And good luck."

Maybe some context would help. We've been grappling with sustainability issues here long before we had a term for the concept. Part of our history as a chemical company is that environmental issues have been in our face to a greater extent than they've been in many other industries.

My predecessor, Dick Mahoney, understood that the way we were doing things had to change. Dick grew up, as I did not, in the chemical industry, so he tended to look at what was coming out of the

Substituting services for products is one solution. Selling a carpet service instead of a carpet could be more sustainable.

plants. The publication of our first toxic-release inventory in 1988 galvanized attention around the magnitude of plant emissions.

Dick got way out ahead of the traditional culture in Monsanto and in the rest of the chemical industry. He set incredibly aggressive quantitative targets and deadlines. The first reaction to them was, My God, he must be out of his mind. But it was an effective technique. In six years, we reduced our toxic air emissions by 90%.

Not having "grown up in the chemical industry," as you put it, do you think differently about environmental issues?

Somewhat. Dick put us on the right path. We have to reduce—and ultimately eliminate—the negative impacts we have on the world. There is no argument on that subject. But even if Monsanto reached its goal of zero impact next Tuesday, that wouldn't solve the world's problem. Several years ago, I sensed that there was something more required of us than doing no harm, but I couldn't articulate what that was.

So I did what you always do. I got some smart people together – a group of about 25 critical thinkers, some of the company's up-and-coming leaders – and sent them off to think about it. We selected a good cross-section – some business-unit leaders, a couple from the management board, and people from planning, manufacturing, policy, and safety and health. And we brought in some non-traditional outsiders to challenge our underlying assumptions about the world. My request to this group was, "Go off, think about what's happening to the world, and come back with some recommendations about what it means for Monsanto. Do we have a role to play? If so, what is it?"

That off-site meeting in 1994 led to an emerging insight that we couldn't ignore the changing global environmental conditions. The focus around sustainable development became obvious. I should have been able to come up with that in about 15 minutes. But it took a group of very good people quite a while to think it through, to determine what was real and what was just puff, to understand the data, and to convince themselves that this wasn't a fluffy issue—and that we ought to be engaged in it.

People came away from that meeting emotionally fired up. It wasn't just a matter of Okay, you threw me an interesting business problem, I have done the analysis, here is the answer, and now can I go back to work. People came away saying, "Damn it, we've got to get going on this. This is important." When some of your best people care intensely, their excitement is contagious.

So now we have a bunch of folks engaged, recognizing that we have no idea where we're going to end up. No one—not the most sophisticated thinker in the world—can describe a sustainable world with 10 billion to 12 billion people, living in conditions that aren't disgusting and morally impermissible. But we can't sit around waiting for the finished blueprint. We have to start moving in directions that make us less unsustainable.

How are you doing that?

There's a quote of Peter Drucker's – which I will mangle here – to the effect that at some point strategy has to degenerate into work. At Monsanto, there was a flurry of E-mail around the world, and in a matter of four months a group of about 80 coalesced. Some were chosen; many others just heard about the project and volunteered. They met for the first time in October 1995 and decided to organize into seven teams: three focused on developing tools to help us make better decisions, three focused externally on meeting world needs, and one focused on education and communication. (See the insert "Monsanto's Seven Sustainability Teams.")

We realized that many of the things we were already doing were part of a sustainability strategy even if we didn't call it that. We'd been working on pollution prevention and investing in biotechnology for years before we thought about the concept of sustainability. As we made more progress in pollution prevention, it became easier for everyone to grasp how pollution – or waste – actually represents a resource that's lost. When you translate that understanding into how you run a business, it leads to cost reduction. You can ask, did we do it because it reduces our costs or because of sustainability? That would be hard to answer because optimizing resources has become part of the way we think. But having the sustainability framework has made a difference, especially in how we weigh new business opportunities.

Can you give me some examples?

One of the seven sustainability teams is discussing how to gain a deeper understanding of global water needs and whether we at Monsanto might meet some of those needs with our existing capabilities. That is an example of a conversation that might not have occurred – or might have occurred much later – if we weren't focused on sustainability. Agricultural water is becoming scarcer, and the salination of soils is an increasing problem. In California, for example, they do a lot of irrigation, and when the water evaporates or flushes through the soil, it leaves small amounts of minerals and salts. Over time, the build-up is going to affect the soil's productivity.

Should we address the water side of the problem? Or can we approach the issue from the plant side? Can we develop plants that will thrive in salty soil? Or can we create less thirsty plants suited to a drier environment? If we had plants that could adapt, maybe semidesert areas could become productive.

Another problem is drinking water. Roughly 40% of the people on earth don't have an adequate supply of fresh water. In the United States, we have a big infrastructure for cleaning water. But in developing countries that lack the infrastructure, there might be a business opportunity for in-home water-purification systems.

I realize this is still early in the process, but how do you know that you're moving forward?

One interesting measure is that we keep drawing in more people. We started off with 80; now we have almost 140. And a lot of this response is just one person after another saying, "I want to be involved, and this is the team I want to be involved in." It's infectious. That's the way most good business processes work. To give people a script and tell them, "Your part is on page 17; just memorize it" is an archaic way to run institutions that have to regenerate and re-create themselves. It's a dead end.

Today, in most fields I know, the struggle is about creativity and innovation. There is no script. You have some ideas, some activities, some exhortations, and some invitations, and you try to align what people believe and what people care about with what they're free to do. And you hope that you can coordinate them in ways that aren't too wasteful – or, better still, that they can self-coordinate. If an institution wants to be adaptive, it has to let go of some control and trust that people will work on the right things in the right ways. That has some obvious implications for the ways you select people, train them, and support them.

Would it be accurate to say that all of your sustainability teams have been self-created and self-coordinated?

Someone asked me recently whether this was a top-down exercise or a bottom-up exercise. Those don't sound like very helpful concepts to me. This is about *us*. What do *we* want to do? Companies aren't machines anymore. We have thousands of independent agents trying to self-coordinate because it is in their interest to do so.

There is no top or bottom. That's just a metaphor and not a helpful one. People say, Here is what I think. What do you think? Does that make sense to you? Would you like to try it? I believe we must see what ideas really win people's hearts and trust that those ideas will turn out to be the most productive.

People in large numbers won't give their all for protracted periods of time – with a cost in their overall lives – for an abstraction called a corporation or an idea called profit. People can give only to people. They can give to their coworkers if they believe that they're engaged together in an enterprise of some importance. They can give to society, which is just another way of saying they can give to their children. They can give if they believe that their work is in some way integrated into a whole life.

Historically, there has been a bifurcation between who we are and the work we do, as if who we are is outside our work. That's unhealthy, and most people yearn to integrate their two sides. Because of Monsanto's history as a chemical company, we have a lot of employees – good people – with a recurrent experience like this: their kids or their neighbors' kids or somebody at a cocktail party asks them what kind of work they do and then reacts in a disapproving way because of what they *think* we are at Monsanto. And that hurts. People don't want to be made to feel ashamed of what they do.

I don't mean to disparage economic motives – they're obviously important. But working on sustainability offers a huge hope for healing the rift between our economic activity and our total human activity. Instead of seeing the two in Marxist opposition, we see them as the same thing. Economics is part of human activity.

What are the organizational implications of that?

Part of the design and structure of any successful institution is going to be giving people permission to select tasks and goals that they care about. Those tasks have to pass some kind of economic screen; but much of what people care about will pass because economic gain comes from meeting people's needs. That's what economies are based on.

The people who have been working on sustainability here have done an incredible job, not because there has been one presiding genius who has organized it all and told them what to do but because they want to get it done. They care intensely about it and they organize themselves to do it.

I don't mean to romanticize it, but, by and large, self-regulating systems are probably going to be more productive than those based primarily on control loops. There are some institutions that for a short period can succeed as a reflection of the will and ego of a single person. But they're unlikely to survive unless other people resonate with what that person represents.

We're going to have to figure out how to organize people in ways that enable them to coor-

---

Monsanto's Seven Sustainability Teams

Three of Monsanto's sustainability teams are working on tools and methodologies to assess, measure, and provide direction for internal management.

The Eco-efficiency Team. Because you can't manage what you don't measure, this team is mapping and measuring the ecological efficiency of Monsanto's processes. Team members must ask, In relation to the value produced, what inputs are consumed, and what outputs are generated? Managers have historically optimized raw material inputs, for example, but they have tended to take energy and water for granted because there is little financial incentive today to do otherwise. And although companies such as Monsanto have focused on toxic waste in the past, true eco-efficiency will require better measures of all waste. Carbon dioxide, for instance, may not be toxic, but it can produce negative environmental effects. Ultimately, Monsanto's goal is to pursue eco-efficiency in all its interactions with suppliers and customers.

The Full-Cost Accounting Team. This team is developing a methodology to account for the total cost of making and using a product during the product's life cycle, including the true environmental costs associated with producing, using, recycling, and disposing of it. The goal is to keep score in a way that doesn't eliminate from consideration all the environmental costs of what the company does. With better data, it will be possible to make smarter decisions today and as the underlying economics change in the future.

The Index Team. This team is developing criteria by which business units can measure whether or not they're moving toward sustainability. They are working on a set of metrics that balance economic, social, and environmental factors. Units will be able to track the sustainability of individual products and of whole businesses. These sustainability metrics

People come to us and say, "I want to be involved, and this is the team I want to be involved in."

WATER TEAM

will, in turn, be integrated into Monsanto's balanced-scorecard approach to the management of its businesses. The scorecard links and sets objectives for financial targets, customer satisfaction, internal processes, and organizational learning.

Three teams are looking externally to identify sustainability needs that Monsanto might address.

The New Business/New Products Team. This team is examining what will be valued in a marketplace that increasingly selects products and services that support sustainability. It is looking at areas of stress in natural systems and imagining how Monsanto's technological skills could meet human needs with new products that don't aggravate – that perhaps even repair – ecological damage.

The Water Team. The water team is looking at global water needs – a huge and growing problem. Many people don't have access to clean drinking water, and there is a worsening shortage of water for irrigation as well.

The Global Hunger Team. This team is studying how Monsanto might develop and deliver technologies to alleviate world hunger. That goal has been a core focus for the company for a number of years. For example, Monsanto had been studying how it might use its agricultural skills to meet people's nutritional needs in developing countries.

The final team develops materials and training programs.

The Communication and Education Team. This team's contribution is to develop the training to give Monsanto's 29,000 employees a common perspective. It offers a framework for understanding what sustainability means, how employees can play a role, and how they can take their knowledge to key audiences outside the company.

DRAWINGS BY GARISON WEILAND

15

dinate their activities without wasteful and intrusive systems of control and without too much predefinition of what a job is. My own view is that as long as you have a concept called a job, you're asking people to behave inauthentically; you're asking people to perform to a set of expectations that someone else created. People give more if they can figure out how to control themselves, how to regulate themselves, how to contribute what they can contribute out of their own authentic abilities and beliefs, not out of somebody else's predetermination of what they're going to do all day.

How will you measure your progress toward sustainability? Do you have milestones?

For something at this early level of exploration, you probably want to rely for at least a year on a subjective sense of momentum. People usually know when they're going someplace, when they're making progress. There's a pace to it that says, yes, we're on the right track. After that, I would like to see some quantitative goals with dates and very macro budgets. As the teams begin to come to some conclusions, we will be able to ignite the next phase by setting some specific targets.

This is so big and complicated that I don't think we're going to end up with a neat and tidy document. I don't think environmental sustainability lends itself to that.

As your activities globalize, does the issue of sustainability lead you to think differently about your business strategy in different countries or regions of the world?

The developing economies can grow by brute force, by putting steel in the ground and depleting natural resources and burning a lot of hydrocarbons. But a far better way to go would be for companies like Monsanto to transfer their knowledge and help those countries avoid the mistakes of the past. If emerging economies have to relive the entire industrial revolution with all its waste, its energy use, and its pollution, I think it's all over.

Can we help the Chinese, for example, leapfrog from preindustrial to postindustrial systems without having to pass through that destructive middle? At the moment, the signs aren't encouraging. One that is, however, is China's adoption of cellular phones instead of tons of stuff: telephone poles and copper wire.

The fact that India is one of the largest software-writing countries in the world is encouraging. You'd like to see tens of millions of people in India employed in information technology rather than in

making more stuff. But there's an important hurdle for companies like Monsanto to overcome. To make money through the transfer of information, we depend on intellectual property rights, which let us reconcile environmental and economic goals. As the headlines tell you, that's a little problematic in Asia. And yet it's critically important to our being able to figure out how to be helpful while making money. Knowledge transfer will happen a lot faster if people get paid for it.

Will individual companies put themselves at risk if they follow sustainable practices and their competitors don't?

I can see that somebody could get short-term advantage by cutting corners. At a matter of fact, the world economy *has* seized such an advantage – short-term in the sense of 500 years – by cutting corners on some basic laws of physics and thermodynamics. But it's like asking if you can gain an advantage by violating laws. Yes, I suppose you can – until they catch you. I don't think it is a good idea to build a business or an economy around the "until-they-catch-you principle." It can't be the right way to build something that is going to endure.

The multinational corporation is an impressive invention for dealing with the tension between the application of broadly interesting ideas on the one hand and economic and cultural differences on the other. Companies like ours have gotten pretty good at figuring out how to operate in places where we can make a living while remaining true to some fundamental rules. As more countries enter the world economy, they are accepting – with greater or lesser enthusiasm – that they are going to have to play by some rules that are new for them. My guess is that, over time, sustainability is going to be one of those rules.

Doesn't all this seem far away for managers? Far enough in the future for them to think, "It won't happen on my watch"?

The tension between the short term and the long term is one of the fundamental issues of business – and of life – and it isn't going to go away. Many chief executives have gotten where they are in part because they have a time horizon longer than next month. You don't stop caring about next month, but you also have to think further ahead. What's going to happen next in my world? If your world is soft drinks, for example, you have to ask where your clean water will come from.

How do you react to the prospect of the world population doubling over the next few decades?

"If emerging economies have to relive the entire industrial revolution... I think it's all over."

First you may say, Great, 5 billion more customers. That is what economic development is all about. That's part of it. Now, keep going. Think about all the physical implications of serving that many new customers. And ask yourself the hard question, How exactly are we going to do that and still live here? That's what sustainability is about.

I'm fascinated with the concept of distinctions that transform people. Once you learn certain things – once you learn to ride a bike, say – your life has changed forever. You can't unlearn it. For me, sustainability is one of those distinctions. Once you get it, it changes how you think. A lot of our people have been infected by this way of seeing the world. It's becoming automatic. It's just part of who you are.

American Isolationism Versus The Global Economy

THE ABILITY TO IDENTIFY WITH CHANGE

Address by MURRAY WEIDENBAUM, *Mallinckrodt Distinguished University Professor and Chairman of the Center for the Study of American Business, Washington University*

Delivered to the Fourteenth Annual Monetary and Trade Conference in Philadelphia, Pennsylvania, November 13, 1995

A growing paradox faces the United States. It is the simultaneous rise of a new spirit of isolationism amid the increasing globalization of business and economic activity. Viewed independently, each of the two trends possesses a certain logic. In juxtaposition, however, isolationism amid globalization is simply unachievable. Some explanation may help.

The end of the Cold War brought on a widespread expectation that the United States could safely and substantially cut back its military establishment. The threat from a powerful Soviet Union was a fear of the past. Moreover, government leaders could shift their attention from foreign policy to the host of domestic problems that face the American people. Surely, there is no shortage of urgent national issues to occupy our attention, and they are all inwardly oriented - welfare reform, health care, immigration, environmental cleanup, crime control, deficit reduction, and tax reform. The isolationist tendency is visible and apparent.

But, in a far less dramatic way, it is also becoming clear that the rest of the world is not content with going its separate way. Overseas forces, institutions, and people increasingly affect the workers and managers of America's business and their families. The global marketplace has rapidly shifted from just being a simple minded buzzword to complex reality. International trade is growing far more rapidly than domestic production. That's true all around the globe. It is hardly a matter of a company or an investor deciding to participate or not. The days of agonizing over whether to go global are over. Eight basic points illustrate the changing external environment for public sector and private sector decisionmakers.

1.   Americans do not have to do anything or change anything to be part of the global marketplace. Even if a business does not export a thing and has no overseas locations, its owners, managers, and employees are still part of the world economy. The same goes for the many companies and individuals that supply it with goods and services. The issue has been decided by technology. The combination of fax machines, universal telephone service (including cellular), low-cost, high-speed copiers and computers, and speedy jet airline service enables money, goods, services, and people to cross most borders rapidly and often instantly. And that goes especially for what is the most strategic resource - information.

A dramatic example of the ease of business crossing national borders occurred during the Gulf War. On the first day of the Iraqi attack on Kuwait, a savvy Kuwaiti bank manager began faxing his key records to his subsidiary in Bahrain. Every once in a while the shooting got close and transmission was interrupted. By the end of the day, however, all of the key records had been transferred out of Kuwait. The next morning, the bank opened as a Bahraini institution, beyond the reach of the Iraqis - and also not subject to the U.S. freeze on Kuwaiti assets. Literally, a bank was moved from one country to another via a fax machine.

No American business of any consequence remains insulated from foreign producers because of vast distances. Every American is subject to competition from overseas. If that force has not hit a region yet, it probably is on its way.

2.   Employees, customers, suppliers, and investors in U.S. companies are increasingly participating in the international economy. That is not just a matter of sales or even earnings originating from foreign operations. Increasingly, U.S. firms are establishing factories, warehouses, laboratories, and offices in other countries. As a result, one-half of Xerox's employees work on foreign soil. The pharmaceutical firm Pfizer is exceedingly blunt on this subject:

Pfizer does not have a choice about whether to manufacture in the EC or not.

` If we are going to sell to Europe, we have to manufacture there.

Surprisingly large numbers of American companies have already deployed a majority of their assets overseas. Here are a few important examples: Citicorp (51 percent), Bankers Trust (52 percent), Chevron (55 percent), Exxon (56 percent), Digital Equipment (61 percent), Mobil (63 percent), Gillette (66 percent), and Manpower Inc. (72 percent). To underscore the point, a recent Conference Board survey of American manufacturing companies shows that becoming an internationally oriented company usually pays off. Sales by firms with foreign activities grow at twice the rate of those with no foreign operations. Firms with international activities grow faster in every industry - and profits are higher. Geographic diversification is especially important for profitability. Companies with factories in North America, Europe, and the Asian rim outperform companies that stay in one region.

 From *Vital Speeches of the Day,* January 15, 1996, pp. 212-215.

3.   The transnational enterprise is on the rise. It is far more than merely a matter of which country to choose to locate a manufacturing or marketing operation. For the dominant companies, the locus of executive decision-making is shifting. "Think global but act local" is not just a slogan. It is a competitive necessity. The larger business firms operating in several regions of the world have been setting up multiple locations for decision-making. For those domestic firms that sell goods or services to other American companies, increasingly their customers are located in one or more decentralized divisions, some of which are now based overseas. That works two ways for Americans. DuPont has shifted the headquarters of its electronic operation to Japan. Germany's Siemens has moved its ultrasound equipment division to the United States.

Moreover, cross-border alliances have become commnon place. It is the rare business of any considerable size that has not entered into some form of cooperative arrangement with one or more companies located overseas - companies that they still often compete against in many markets. The concept of strategic alliances has moved from the classroom to the boardroom. A new set of international business relationships has arisen: joint ventures, production sharing, cross-licensing agreements, technology swaps, and joint research projects.

Increasingly, the successful business looks upon its entire operation in a global context. It hires people, buys inputs, and locates production, marketing, and decision-making centers worldwide. An example helps to convert theory to reality. Here is a shipping label used by an American electronics company:

Made in one or more of the following countries: Korea, Hong Kong, Malaysia, Singapore, Taiwan, Mauritius, Thailand, Indonesia, Mexico, Philippines. The exact country of origin is unknown.

Any comprehensive and balanced analysis also tells us that not every aspect of the international economy has a positive impact on Americans. Of course, a similar warning applies to the business environment here at home.

4.   Some overseas markets are more profitable than domestic sales, but high risk and high rewards tend to go together. The attraction of overseas locations is increasing. Southeast Asia is the faster growing part of the world. Any observant visitor to Hong Kong, Singapore, Malaysia, or Thailand will see that the 8 percent real growth they have been reporting is no statistical mirage. Each of those economies is booming. Mainland China has been experiencing double-digit expansion year after year. Only the most modest slowdown is in sight. Of course, starting off from a small base makes it easier to achieve large percentage gains than is the case for an advanced industrialized country like the United States. But far more than that is involved.

Government policy in each of those countries welcomes foreign investment. With the inevitable exceptions, they encourage the formation of new private enterprises. The contrast with the United States is striking — and ironic. While these present or former communist and totalitarian countries are moving toward capitalism and trying to reduce the role of the public sector, we have been moving in the opposite direction. Despite efforts by the House of Representatives, the United States is still expanding government regulation of business. The result is to make it more difficult and certainly more costly for private enterprise to prosper. Under these circumstances, it is not surprising that so many American companies are doing their expansion overseas.

Take the energy company that explores in faraway Kazakhstan, or the mining enterprise that moves to Bolivia, or the medical devices firm that sets up a laboratory in the Netherlands, or the manufacturing corporation that builds a new factory in Guangdong. To a very considerable extent, these companies are responding to adverse domestic policies as much as to the attractions of overseas markets. The villains of the piece are the government officials in the United States who lock up much of the nation's natural and labor resources in fear that somebody somewhere may make a profit.

Nevertheless, the risks overseas may be great. Over the years, many companies have suffered the expropriation of their foreign assets. You do not have to go farther than Mexico to recall a vivid, although not recent, instance. Iran furnishes a more current and dramatic example. The dangers are not just political. Wars and insurrections are more likely in the regions of the world with less strongly established political institutions. There is no shortage of examples - Croatia, Bosnia, Armenia, Azerbaijan and Chechnya currently make the headlines. Civil wars and large scale violence occurred in recent decades in Indonesia, Malaysia, Thailand, Sri Lanka (Ceylon), and Myanmar (Burma).

Less dramatic but still noteworthy are the difficulties experienced by some Western enterprises in collecting on their debts in China. Moreover, many companies operating in that region report that the special expenses of doing business there make it difficult to convert sales into profits. One large American law firm expects to show its first profit only after six years of doing business on the mainland.

The special risks are numerous. Differences in language, culture, and business practices are pervasive. Our notions of personal honesty are not exactly universal. My purpose is not to scare anyone away from foreign markets, but to emphasize the often painfully close relationship between high profits and high risk. But there is a new positive side to all this.

5.   The rise of the global market place provides vast new opportunity for Americans to diversify their investments and — of course — to broaden business risk. The last half dozen years provide a cogent example in terms of the global business cycle. At first, the AngloSaxon economies lost momentum. Remember when our friends in continental Europe needled us about the odd phenomenon of an English-speaking recession? That was the time when the economies of the United States, the United Kingdom, Canada, Australia, and New Zealand all were in decline simultaneously.

But, as we were coming out of recession, Japan and most of Western Europe started to experience slowdowns and then downturns in their economies. The American economy has been coming off a cyclical peak and is now slowing down. At the same time, Western Europe has turned the corner and is on an expansion path once again.

In the case of the developing countries, it is hazardous to forecast which one of them will get unglued. There is no certainty that any of them will. But the odds are that at least one of those rapidly growing nations will be derailed from the path of continued progress. Military coups and domestic insurrections do occur. The biggest uncertainties are what will happen to China after Deng Xiaoping dies and how well will the integration of Hong Kong go.

6.   The rise of China and Southeast Asia is a new and durable force in the world economy that Americans will have to recognize. Depending how you measure national economies, China is in the top 10 or top three, or top two. That is an interesting range of variation.

Even the most experienced Asia experts candidly tell you that they do not know what will happen after Deng. There is already considerable pressure in China to reverse course, to move back to a more authoritarian society with less opportunity for private ownership. China also has a history of internal dissension, of splitting up into several regions each of which is the size of several major Western European countries. So far, the ability of the economic reforms to create tremendous amounts of income and wealth is the best guarantee of their being continued. But, the many misunderstandings between China and the United States constitute a very real dark cloud on the political as well as economic horizon.

The economies of several other countries in Southeast Asia are also growing rapidly at about 8 percent a year, compared to China's 10-12 percent. They seem to be welcoming American and other Western businesses with more enthusiasm than the Chinese.

Malaysia is a good example of a fairly stable nation with a sound economic policy notably a balanced budget - and an 8 percent overall growth rate. Other opportunities for geographic diversification exist in Thailand, Indonesia, and now the Philippines, whose economy has turned around. To the surprise of some, Vietnam welcomes American businesses as well as tourists.

A decade from now, Southeast Asia will be one of the major economic regions of the globe - along with Japan, North America, and Western Europe. Americans must face the fact that the economies of Southeast Asia are potentially both customers and competitors for our companies. To think of that area as just low-cost labor is misleading. The level of technology is high in Taiwan, Singapore, and Malaysia. The amount of education is also impressive. Intelligent and productive work forces are available in substantial quantities - and they also constitute a substantial and rapidly rising consumer base.

The 1 1/2 billion people in Southeast Asia constitute the major new market area of the world. A noteworthy although not particularly welcome trend is for the nations of Southeast Asia increasingly to trade with each other. That is not surprising when you examine the investment patterns. Who are the major investors in China, Malaysia, Indonesia, Thailand, and Vietnam? The answer is neither the United States nor Western Europe. It is Hong Kong, Taiwan, South Korea, and Japan.

As a result, the major sources of imports into Southeast Asia are Hong Kong, Taiwan, South Korea, and Japan. Likewise, those same four nations are the major markets for Southeast Asia's products. As Southeast Asia continues to grow rapidly, it will be a major challenge to Western businesses to participate in that key market.

7. *Despite the military and political issues that divide Western Europe, the economic unification is continuing full bore.* With a minimum of fanfare, Sweden, Finland, and Austria are entering the European Union. Note the successive changes in terminology as the nations of Western Europe move closer together while increasing their membership. The six-nation European Common Market became the 12-nation European Community. Now we have the 15 member European Union.

As in every major change, there are winners and losers - for Americans as well as for Europeans. With the elimination of internal trade barriers, the stronger European companies can now compete in a continent-wide market. They enjoy considerable economies of scale. American companies well established in Western Europe - such as Ford - are included in that category. The losers are the high-cost European producers who were accustomed to the protections afforded by a restricted national market. The loser category also contains those American producers who have been taken by surprise by the reinvigorated European competition.

Fifteen member nations are not going to be the end of the line for the European Union. The entrance of Austria is a strategic move because Vienna is a major gateway to Eastern Europe. Hungary, Poland, and the Czech Republic are anxious to develop closer economic and business relations with Western Europe. They can become low-cost suppliers or low-cost competitors - likely both.

Perhaps the most important positive development in that continent in the coming decade will be the new economic strength of the largest member, Germany. It is taking more time than expected to fully consummate the integration of the "new provinces (neuer Under), as East Germany is now referred to. Any visitor is struck by the substantial amount of physical investment that the national government is making in the East. That is bound to result in a strong and newly competitive region. All in all, we should not forget Europe in our attention to the Orient.

Let us end on an upbeat and realistic note.

8. *The American economy is still the strongest in the world and our prospects are impressive.* We are not a weak or declining nation in the world marketplace. Legislation and political pressures to "buy local" may be popular, but they fly in the face of economic reality.

Our concern for the losers in the domestic marketplace requires a constructive response; make the United States a more attractive place to hire people and to do business.

After all, in a great many important industries, American firms are still the leaders. U.S. firms rank number one (in sales volume in 13 major industries - aerospace, apparel, beverages, chemicals, computers, food products, motor vehicles, paper products, petroleum, pharmaceuticals, photographic and scientific equipment, soap and cosmetics, and tobacco.

What about the future? Recall that the first of these eight points began with an illustration of the awesome power of technology. Nobody can forecast which specific technologies will succeed in the coming decade. But the prospects for American companies being in the lead are very bright. There is a special reason for optimism.

Although in the 1990s, America will be benefiting from the upsurge of industrial research and development (R&D) during the 1980s. A key but undramatic crossover occurred in the early 1980s. For the first time in over a half century, the magnitude of companysponsored R&D exceeded the total of government-financed R&D. That primary reliance on private R&D continues to this day.

Few people appreciate the long-term impact of that strategic crossover. The new and continued dominance of the private sector in the choice of investments in advanced technology makes it more likely that there will be an accelerated flow of new and improved civilian products and production processes in the years ahead. A progression of innovation may be forthcoming comparable to the advent of missiles and space vehicles following the massive growth of military R&D in the

1950s and 1960s. Just consider how the fax machine has altered our customary work practices.

There is a positive macroeconomic aspect to continued technological progress. When the persistent trade deficit of the United States is disaggregated, we find some surprisingly good news: our exports of high-tech products steadily exceed our high-tech imports. We more than hold our own. This country does indeed enjoy a comparative advantage in the production and sales of goods and services that embody large proportions of new technology.

Of course, these are not laurels to rest on. The point is that there is no need to take the low road of economic isolationism - which is protectionism - to deal with foreign competition. We should take the necessary actions, in both the public and private sectors, which make American business and labor more productive and hence more competitive in what is increasingly a globalized marketplace. The ingredients are well known - tax reform, regulatory reform, and a modern labor policy.

Perhaps the most basic development since the end of the Cold War has been missed by all observers and analysts because it is so subtle. During the Cold War, the two military superpowers dominated the world stage. It is currently fashionable to say that in the post-Cold War period, three economic superpowers have taken their place - the United States, Japan, and Germany. That is technically accurate but very misleading.

During the Cold War, government was the pace-setting player on the global stage. Governments made the strategic decisions. Businesses were important, but they were respond-ing to government orders, supplying armaments to the super-powers. In the process, of course, business created substantial economic wealth. But the shift from military to economic competition is fundamental. It means that the business firm is now the key to global economic competition. Governments, to be sure, can help or hinder, and in a major way. But they are supporting players, at best.

The basic initiative in the global marketplace has shifted to private enterprise. Individual entrepreneurs and individual business firms now make the key decisions that will determine the size, composition, and growth of the international economy. That makes for an extremely challenging external environment for the competitive American enterprise of the 1990s. It also requires greater degrees of understanding and fore-bearance on the part of U.S. public policymakers.

The rapidly growing business-oriented global marketplace is a source of great actual and potential benefit to American entrepreneurs, workers, and consumers. Because the international economy is changing so rapidly, Americans face both threats and opportunities.

Those who identify with the change are likely to be the winners; those who resist will be among the losers.

History tells us that trying to shut ourselves off from these "foreign" influences just does not work. When imperial China tried to do that some 500 years ago, it fairly quickly went from being the world's most advanced and powerful nation to becoming a very poor backwater of the globe.

One thing is certain; it is futile to say, "Stop the world, I want to get off!"

"Globalization and the International Division of Labor: the Role of Europe and the Response of European Companies"

Jürgen E. Schrempp

In the whole of Europe, there's probably nowhere more appropriate than Luxembourg for addressing the kind of topics on your agenda today and tomorrow.

This small country has shown how to handle structural change efficiently. It has demonstrated how to make the transition from steel to innovative financial services as the pillar of the national economy.

And there are other areas where the Grand Duchy can teach its neighbors a thing or two: for example, how to live in a monetary union.

A New Order of Globalization

Ladies and gentlemen, an entire analysis—and a whole speech—could be dedicated to the question of why the topic of globalization is so unpopular in Europe as a whole and in Germany in particular. Books on "the pitfalls of globalization" are high on the bestseller lists at the moment. Globalization, such works instruct us, kills jobs, unravels the fabric of society, and leads to ecological and social dumping. Indeed, globalization goes so far as to pension off democracy—or so warns the U. S. political scientist Benjamin R. Parker. Many people are thus already very frightened of globalization.

And yet we are only at the beginning of an upheaval which will fundamentally alter our way of living and of doing business. In the words of Robert Reich, former U.S. Secretary of Labor, "We are currently undergoing a period of transformation out of which new forms of politics and business will emerge in the next century. There will no longer be any national products and national technologies, national companies and national industries. It will be the end of national economies".

How does he arrive at such conclusions? And what constitutes this process?

In the *first* place, we see world trade expanding. Since 1985, it has grown by more than 10 percent annually.

Second, more and more countries are rushing towards economic integration on the global level. In Southeast Asia, for example, countries such as Malaysia or Thailand have been quick to follow the lead of the four "Asian Tigers," so that the entire region is undergoing a huge boom.

In Eastern Europe, many countries are toeing the starting line.

In South America, too, a region beset by despair just a few years ago, a similar process is unfolding.

And even Africa, long the big loser according to many, is showing early signs of a new dynamism. As democracy and free-market economics gain an ever stronger foothold, encouraging trends are to be observed first and foremost in South Africa and in 11 of

From *Financial Market Forum*, October 15, 1997, pp. 3-15. Reprinted by permission of the Luxembourg Financial Market Forum (Daimler-Benz AG Corporate Communications).

its northerly neighbors, all of whom have joined to form the Southern African Development Community. Regional integration of this new growth market is progressing well, while trade barriers are being dismantled. All in all, chances for the region to better integrate itself into the global market are looking good.

In fact, precisely what years of developmental aid tried and failed to bring about is now happening: more and more countries are participating in the wave of economic development—and therefore reaping the benefits of social progress, too.

Such changes dramatically alter the economic balance among the individual economic zones. New competitors emerge, for example, but so do new markets with opportunities for additional growth. As a consequence, companies here must position themselves there today if they are to fully exploit the growth markets in tomorrow's boom regions. The next few years will see companies like Daimler-Benz substantially boost the proportion of value-added operations in Asia.

Third, the increasing pace of globalization is evident from the growing interdependence of investment activity. Cross-border direct investments, for example, have grown over the last 10 years by around 18 percent per year—in other words, almost twice as fast as world trade. In many cases, countries previously served by exports are now calling for customized products fully oriented toward local demand. In short, to secure such markets, you must invest right on the spot. "Go where the markets are" was why we set up our new M-Class plant in Tuscaloosa in the U.S.A. And it goes without saying that in whatever country we operate, we do so as good corporate citizens. This, too, is a strategy which pays off: the M-Class, recently launched on the U.S. market, is seen as a national brand—which casts a very positive light on our passenger car range as a whole.

Market access restrictions or local content requirements also force a company to invest locally, as another example illustrates. Since the early 1950s, we have been manufacturing commercial vehicles in Brazil and Argentina. Today, we are the unchallenged market leader in Latin America.

Further reasons for relocating value-added activities abroad include the ability to avoid exchange-rate swings and to balance out local market fluctuations. And, of course, through direct investment, one can tap all the advantages of local manufacturing locations—an absolute must, given cutthroat competition.

Does this mean that by transferring production halls to low-wage countries, we will kill European jobs? No, we can—still—reassure people that this is not the case.

Companies are primarily interested in making the best use of market potential. For instance, around 65 percent of all cross-border investments today flow into the industrial Triad nations. If the remaining 35 percent, some two-thirds go to the Asian growth regions. Now, these investments also create jobs at home. At Daimler-Benz, for example, for every three jobs we create abroad, a supplementary one is generated in Germany. Along these lines, our plant in Tuscaloosa, which I mentioned earlier, imports its engines from Bad Cannstatt near Stuttgart, where we have invested DM 700 million to build a new plant. Bad Cannstatt employs 1,200 people directly, and indirectly generates jobs for 5,000 more in the region.

As to my *fourth* point, globalization impacts not merely trade in products, but also, and especially, financial markets. In recent years, the volume of international financial transactions has skyrocketed, and is pursuing a growth course independent of trade in goods. In 1995, on the foreign exchange markets alone, turnover reached a volume of $ 1.6 trillion— 1,600 billion—a day. That's more than the entire world currency reserves.

The *fifth* aspect of globalization is the growth in the number of multinational companies, which has increased sixfold in the last 20 years. There are some 39,000 multinationals plus 270,000 subsidiaries active around the globe today. These firms account for three-quarters of all goods traded worldwide. This figure includes that from intra-corporate trade, which now amounts to a third of all world trade.

What spurs on such development? Obviously, it is innovation—new products, new processes, new technologies. Here, mobility plays a particularly important role. The development of new ways of transporting people, goods, services and information over great distances has reduced time and space. Today, you can get in touch with anyone else in real time and at an acceptable cost. And knowledge itself is no longer available to only a privileged few, but increasingly on open markets the world over.

This process has already revolutionized the world, and is by no means over. It is an upheaval as dramatic as the Industrial Revolution, but with one significant difference: its speed. There's no avoiding it, and anyone trying to work around the international division of labor will end up in the backwaters of business life.

Yet there is no need to fear these developments. History is full of similar processes, such as the invention of the printing press or the steam locomotive.

In fact, globalization itself is not a new phenomenon: trade and business were already internationally meshed before World War I. However, today's version runs at a higher speed, and is of a different nature. And this is what worries many people in Europe.

The industrial nations have never had any problems with the "international division of labor." During the age of colonialism, a comfortable living could be made by adhering to the principle of high-tech products plus skilled, well-paid jobs in the rich countries;

and low-tech and bottom-of-the-barrel jobs in the poor ones. Today's unlimited mobility of capital and knowledge, however, has changed the rules of the game. Now, labor markets are no longer defined in geographic terms, but according to one's qualifications, ideas, commitment, and speed. What's more, wage policy no longer devolves on national criteria regulating the division of labor, but instead moves in line with company competitiveness and the advances achieved in productivity.

Today, knowledge is accessible the world over. A powerful illustration of this fact is the research center opened last year by Daimler-Benz in the Indian city of Bangalore. Along with Palo Alto and Portland in the U.S.A. and Shanghai in China, it is our fourth research center outside of Europe. Here, we conduct research in information technology—a field in which India is a world leader. Naturally, with 20,000 computer scientists graduating from Indian universities each year, we want to ensure that the best come work for our company so that we can continue to develop innovative products and capture new markets and consumer groups in the future.

What are the lessons to be learned here?

Quite simply, that we in Europe don't have the monopoly on knowledge, education, or the cleverest thinkers. As a consequence, European educational policy and attitude face a gigantic challenge.

Why Europe?

Since there is no stopping globalization, why do we still need Europe?

First of all, a market undergoing globalization also requires an institutional infrastructure.

Second, only a unified Europe has sufficient geopolitical weight to help shape this framework. Today's world is marked not only by growing globalization. But, paradoxically, by increasing regionalization as well. Think of APEC, ASEAN, or the plans to institute a Free Trade Area of the Americas, which will stretch from Alaska to Tierra del Fuego and unite Nafta with the growth regions of South America.

We in Europe are blessed with a history in which this process of regional integration is more advanced than anywhere else. And this is fortunate, since otherwise, we could not maintain our interests against those other regional alliances. As it is, no single European country today can hold its own against nations such as China or the U.S.A., which already have continental proportions.

We also need Europe for corporate reasons; an economically powerful Europe. In his book, *Competitiveness of Nations,* Michael Porter provides sound empirical proof of the relationship between a strong domestic market and global competitiveness. Now, al-

though we try—in fact, must try—to establish an insider position in foreign markets, our geographical and cultural proximity in Europe to customers, suppliers, and research and scientific centers provides us with a tremendous competitive edge. It also gives us an easier lead market.

Who else, for example, could seriously challenge Boeing if it were not for the European consortium Airbus Industrie?

In summary: what we in Europe need to do, ladies and gentlemen, is to put faith in our own strengths. That this entails the rejection of all forms of protectionism, is something we owe both our credibility and our cause.

The Role of Europe in a Global Economy

Just what are Europe's strengths?

My answer will surprise you, because it is one generally given by opponents of a united Europe: Europe's strengths arise precisely out of its heterogeneity—out of the fact that the individual countries are at various levels of industrial development and play different roles in the international division of labor.

The reason for this lies in the laws governing structural transition. It can be empirically demonstrated, for example, that national economies or individual industrial sectors all pass though various, relatively predetermined phases.

Countries in an early phase of industrialization, for instance, are characterized by a rapidly growing population, low standards of education, and a very fragmentary infrastructure. They possess neither product nor process know-how of their own, but rather manufacture cheap products for their own use according to foreign specifications.

By contrast, the second phase is typified by a deceleration in population growth. Certain standard products are developed and manufactured indigenously—some even for export. Educational standards rise and there is heavy investment in infrastructure.

In the third phase, the development and manufacture of various types of products begins. In addition, plant construction commences, and services become more important. Direct investment in foreign markets supplants export activity.

Finally, in the fourth phase, standard products are completely replaced by complex specialized products, both for export and domestic demand. A country in this phase is an undisputed leader in the fields of technology and innovation and has accomplished the transition from an industrial to a services society.

In each of these phases, a national economy has specific opportunities peculiar to that stage. Properly exploited, these will lead to growth and prosperity. At the same time, a law of globalization says that value added is to be attained precisely where the conditions are optimal at a particular time.

This is also valid for the countries of Europe. The principles governing the global division of labor must be applied in Europe itself, too. We must systematically exploit our various strengths—those advantages stemming from having different locations in various European countries undergoing different stages of development and structural transition.

Hence, globalization in Europe initially means, above all, Europeanization. The more we optimize the intra-European division of labor and thereby strengthen Europe itself from within, the better. And that goes for Eastern Europe as well.

The Europeanization of Europe

What are the pre-requisites for the further Europeanization of Europe?

Of *the highest priority* is the common European currency. Its critics should reflect on the amount of resources that are wasted when an economic zone with 370 million inhabitants has 15 different currencies, which hinders a common standard of evaluation. Transaction costs alone for European companies amount to DM 100 billion annually. That's a heavy burden for any enterprise trying to negotiate the hurdle toward a profitable next century! The European economy needs the euro, and it needs it on schedule.

At Daimler-Benz, we are preparing to move the entire company completely over to the euro on January 1, 1999. We're confident that the currency will be introduced on time and that's why we've invested more than a few German marks in the conversion process.

It's worth mentioning the positive effects already yielded by the euro today. For example, preparations for the new currency are helping hone the competitive edge of many European countries. Just look at Italy, which now has the lowest inflation rate in 50 years.

Second, meeting the prerequisites for Europeanization includes achieving greater harmonization on economic policy so that the forces of growth can flourish. Because a common currency will also result in greater competition in Europe—between our companies, between different industrial locations, and also between competing economic policies. We therefore need comparable regulations to organize Europe better as an industrial location. But no measure leading to smoother coordination must be allowed to thwart the European Central Bank's independence in fiscal policy!

Third, the European Union of today is not the sum total of Europe. Europe is not just a collection of countries on the map, but rather a shared history, endured and lived together; a civilization that has arisen from great traditions. The countries of Central and Eastern

Europe are part of this European tradition, too. So how do things stand with their integration?

Reunifying the arbitrarily divorced eastern and western halves of Europe is not only a moral obligation, but also in our own best interest. The east abounds with attractive production and investment locations with a willing and well-educated workforce. The region, which encompasses more than 110 million inhabitants with growing incomes, is characterized by a burgeoning demand for higher-value goods. Already, France and Germany export more, in monetary terms, to Central and Eastern Europe than to the U.S.A.

I am aware that EU entry for some of these countries lies in the distant future. But once the requisite framework is in place in Eastern and Central Europe, I see no reason to argue against their entry—on the contrary.

Fourth, Europe needs a lean administration capable of taking rapid decisions. This entails as few laws as possible, but ones which can be strictly upheld. Europe does not need additional, national laws leading to over-regulation! Europe has no lack of areas of growth where new job opportunities could arise; the problem is the bureaucratic barriers. Our basic problem is that during times of upheaval, we tend to cling to comfortable, outdated regulations, or even introduce additional ones.

Perhaps the European administrative apparatus could follow the example of European business. Most companies have already sped up their administrative procedures through lean management, less bureaucracy, and decentralization wherever possible.

At Daimler-Benz, for example, we introduced a new group structure at the beginning of the year. This has eliminated certain management levels and given much more entrepreneurial freedom to our operative units. This, too, is one of the lessons of globalization: large companies can react dynamically only when they are decentrally organized.

We have examined our processes within the group and made them more efficient. Planning, for example, is now 50 percent faster—and without, let me assure you, any loss of quality. All in all, we've boosted the efficiency of our main administrative processes by some 30 percent. Product development has also become significantly faster:

In the past, we launched three new cars within every 10 years; today, it's 10 within every three years. At Adtranz, our joint venture with ABB and the world's largest supplier of rail transportation systems, the entire product range has been revamped in the last 18 months. And, in the last five years, Daimler-Benz Aerospace—Dasa—has brought 15 new aircraft and helicopters to the maiden flight stage—compared with 10 in the previous 10 years. But we're not resting on our laurels, for we know that speed is of the essence in practically every market.

In addition to the above four points, I could also mention competition law, or European policy on research and technology. However the gist is clear: Europe's strengths can be further improved.

Making Full Use of Europe's Strengths on the Global Market: Growth Through Innovation

To what end can we Europeans use our strengths on the global market?

My answer is: for growth through innovation—meaning innovation throughout the entire value-added chain.

Admittedly, given the current mood in my country, which is more concerned with protecting vested interests than with fostering a spirit of change, such remarks sound daring and perhaps to some, even foolhardy.

But it is precisely because of this backdrop that I am happy to see the topic of innovation gain popularity in all the German political parties.

It goes without saying that commercial success hinges, among other things, on keeping your costs competitive. But that's not the whole story. On the contrary, I find it very dangerous to pursue this route only and at all costs. For, valuable as reengineering, cost cutting, value analysis, and process optimization are, they do not help bring about a quantum lead for a company. Costs and productivity are but one side of the coin. The other is innovation: the ability to rapidly transform trailblazing ideas into marketable products. Rather than continually optimizing the old, the primary task of the entrepreneur is to discover and exploit the new.

Let me give you an example: our new A-class, which has just been launched onto the market, contains a total of 20 technical innovations. These include the sandwich concept, which sets completely new standards of passive safety for an automobile of this class. Market response tells us that were on the right track: our order books are full until mid-1998. Or, look at what the retractable steel roof has done for sales of our ELK roadster. The order books are full there, too.

At Daimler-Benz, the bottom line is to beat the competition to market with innovative products offering a high degree of customer utility in return for the premium price tag.

Naturally, we have cut costs across the board in the company. But it was the dual strategy of cost reduction plus innovation that finally led us back into profitable territory, and it's also thanks to this two-track approach that we've not only safeguarded jobs, but also created new ones. In this year alone, some 4,300 new jobs will have been generated throughout the

Group as a whole. Incidentally, 1,500 of these are at our services subsidiary, debis, which is capturing many new markets with new services. Last but not least, 3,000 new apprentices mean that we are 10 percent up on last year's already impressive trainee numbers.

The chances look good for Europe to profit from innovation-led growth and thereby re-attain its economic prowess of old. Europe has always been fertile ground for innovation, thanks precisely to its national and regional diversity and its pluralistic society. After all, uniformity rarely engenders anything genuinely new. The new arises where ideas compete, where demands are varied; out of the rich variety and tough competition on the supply side, paired with technological competence and entrepreneurial spirit.

Ladies and gentlemen, companies in Europe have not managed the process of globalization any less successfully than their competitors in other countries and regions. They have cut costs and are now leaner, faster, and more efficient. We have caught up, for we had no other choice than to do so. However, our real competitive edge today is based on sophisticated, individualized solutions.

In the past, individual production would have led to unwarrantably high costs; today, such an approach creates a competitive advantage. Why? Because the global markets are not mass markets. The individualization of demand on a global scale is resulting in highly differentiated markets. That's one reason why Daimler-Benz has doubled the number of models in the automobile sector within just four years, and has opened up completely new market segments with the launch of innovative products.

And we in Europe are still at the top of many growth sectors:

• Take the performance of European companies in automotive technology. Consider, for example, the efforts made to improve existing propulsion concepts or to develop completely new ones. In the first category is common rail direct-injection technology—new fuel-injection system for diesel engines. As to new propulsion developments, the hydrogen-powered, emission-free fuel cell is leading the way. Even here, however, patents are only the first step. The key factor is time-to-market.

• Europe is also performing well in the area of new materials. For instance, there are the new aluminum alloys used in civil aircraft construction; they are distinguished by properties formerly thought utterly incompatible. Combining minimal density with high plasticity and strength, they can be welded instead of riveted. They're a dream come true for aircraft designers!

• Excellent chances for Europe also exist with regard to intelligent product and service combinations which offer customers an innovative, tailor-made package. Traffic management systems such as the Intelligent Traffic Guidance System are good examples. In fact we recently installed the world's first dynamic traffic control system in high-tech Japan for the Tokyo police force.

• Naturally Europe will continue to produce and export for the foreseeable future, not the least because of the diversity of its different countries. However, services associated with industrial products will increasingly come to the fore. In fact, this area represents an especially dynamic environment for innovation.

Finally, thanks to its unique international infrastructure, Europe is in an ideal position to develop completely new types of services—such as in the area of preventive health care and rehabilitation in less developed countries. Sophisticated research and development projects or the development of training programs for people from countries with poorer standards of education are other areas where much can be achieved.

This brings me to a topic that is very important to me and which is central to maintaining Europe's competitive strength: our educational and research system.

Early this year, the largest international study ever on the quality of educational systems, the third International Maths and Science Study, was published. More than 500,000 schoolchildren in 41 countries were tested in mathematics and the natural sciences. The results should give Europe cause for concern. At the top were the countries of eastern Asia, with children in Eastern European countries outperforming by far their rivals in the rich neighboring states to the West.

It is, of course, always possible to dispute such tests. Nevertheless, they should at least prompt us to ask this critical question: Does our education system impart the skills required by the Europe of the 21st century? For example, the ability to filter relevant items out of a flood of information and then properly organize and process them? And do today's children still know how to learn? Do they learn, for instance, how to react to the rapid pace of change that characterizes our times—or how to shape and control these changes despite their rapidity?

We should be alarmed that foreign students and researchers tend to avoid all but a very few of our universities. This signals danger for European companies as well, who will have more difficulty forging international business contacts.

What is worse, Europe lags far behind the U.S.A. in the number of companies being founded. This is not merely a matter of the availability of venture capital; it is also a question of attitude. With a total of around three million, Germany has the lowest proportion of self-employed in its population of any EU country. Moreover, an average of 400,000 companies founded each year is offset by 300,000 liquidations. Nobody in the U.S.A. would ever dream of saying that the less successful of these company founders were flops.

At the same time, our national economy depends heavily on the small and medium-sized companies which such people set up in order to secure their own livelihoods. These companies not only contribute strongly to the overall performance of the national economy, they have also—particularly in recent times—created a great many jobs. In Germany today, a tradesperson is better prepared to manage his or her own company than a university graduate. Why is entrepreneurship not taught at our universities?

Now is the Time for Action

Permit me to summarize: we need to promote innovation-led growth to strengthen our economic base, instead of harping on the disadvantages of doing business in Europe. Yes, we do have worrying levels of unemployment here in Europe. We do have rigid labor markets along with over-regulation and excess capacity. We also must tackle our educational, academic, and research systems. But simply recognizing these deficits in no way absolves us from the obligation to act—and to encourage all those capable of action to start shaping the future.

We must succeed in this mission if we are to hold our own in the global market. And here I am an incorrigible optimist.

All foreign R&D sites fall into one of two categories,
and each type has different needs.

Building Effective R&D Capabilities Abroad

by Walter Kuemmerle

An increasing number of companies in technologically intensive industries such as pharmaceuticals and electronics have abandoned the traditional approach to managing research and development and are establishing global R&D networks in a noteworthy new way. For example, Canon is now carrying out R&D activities in 8 dedicated facilities in 5 countries, Motorola in 14 facilities in 7 countries, and Bristol-Myers Squibb in 12 facilities in 6 countries. In the past, most companies – even those with a considerable international presence in terms of sales and manufacturing – carried out the majority of their R&D activity in their home countries. Conventional wisdom held that strategy development and R&D had to be kept in close geographical proximity. Because strategic decisions were made primarily at corporate headquarters, the thinking went, R&D facilities should be close to home.

But such a centralized approach to R&D will no longer suffice – for two reasons. First, as more and more sources of potentially relevant knowledge emerge across the globe, companies must establish a presence at an increasing number of locations to access new knowledge and to absorb new research results from foreign universities and competitors into their own organizations. Second, companies competing around the world must move new products from development to market at an ever more rapid pace. Consequently, companies must build R&D networks that excel at tapping new centers of knowledge and at commercializing products in foreign markets with the speed required to remain competitive. And more and more, superior manufacturers are doing just that. (See the exhibit "Laboratory Sites Abroad in 1995.")

In an ongoing study on corporate strategy and the geographical dispersion of R&D sites, I have been examining the creation of global research networks by 32 U.S., Japanese, and European multinational companies.[1] The most successful companies in my study brought each new site's research productivity up to full speed within a few years and quickly transformed knowledge created there into innovative products. I found that establishing networks of such sites poses a number of new, complex managerial challenges. According to my research, managers of the most successful R&D networks under-

Walter Kuemmerle is an assistant professor at the Harvard Business School in Boston, Massachusetts, where he teaches technology and operations management, as well as entrepreneurial finance. His research focuses on the technology strategies of multinational companies, patterns of strategic interaction between small and large companies, and foreign direct investment.

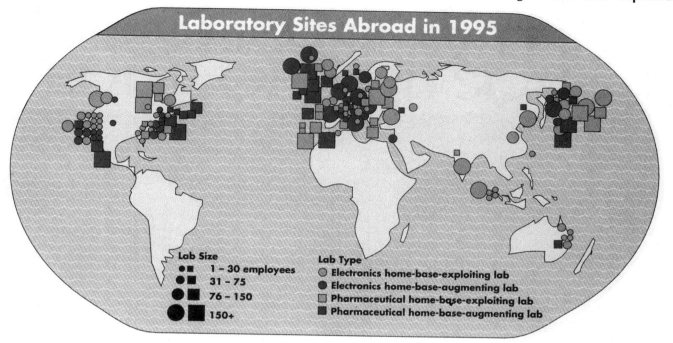

Laboratory Sites Abroad in 1995

Lab Size
● ■ 1 – 30 employees
● ■ 31 – 75
● ■ 76 – 150
● ■ 150+

Lab Type
○ Electronics home-base-exploiting lab
● Electronics home-base-augmenting lab
□ Pharmaceutical home-base-exploiting lab
■ Pharmaceutical home-base-augmenting lab

stand the new dynamics of global R&D, link corporate strategy to R&D strategy, pick the appropriate sites, staff them with the right people, supervise the sites during start-up, and integrate the activities of the different foreign sites so that the entire network is a coordinated whole.

Adopting a Global Approach to R&D

Adopting a global approach to R&D requires linking R&D strategy to a company's overall business strategy. And that requires the involvement of managers at the highest levels of a company.

Creating a Technology Steering Committee. The first step in creating a global R&D network is to build a team that will lead the initiative. To establish a global R&D network, the CEOs and top-level managers of a number of successful companies that I studied assembled a small team of senior managers who had both technical expertise and in-depth organizational knowledge. The technology steering committees reported directly to the CEOs of their respective companies. They were generally small – five to eight members – and included managers with outstanding managerial and scientific records and a range of educational backgrounds and managerial responsibilities. The committees I studied included as members a former bench scientist who had transferred into manufacturing and had eventually become the head of manufacturing for the company's most important category of therapeutic drugs; a head of marketing for memory chips who had worked before in product develop-

ment in the same electronics company; and an engineer who had started out in product development, had moved to research, and eventually had become the vice president of R&D. Members of these committees were sufficiently senior to be able to mobilize resources at short notice; and they were actively involved in the management and supervision of R&D programs. In many cases, members included the heads of major existing R&D sites.

Categorizing New R&D Sites. In selecting new sites, companies find it helpful first to articulate each site's primary objective. (See the exhibit "Establishing New R&D Sites.") R&D sites have one of two missions. The first type of site – what I call a *home-base-augmenting site* – is established in order to tap knowledge from competitors and universities around the globe; in that type of site, information flows *from* the foreign laboratory *to* the central lab at home. The second type of site – what I call a *home-base-exploiting site* – is established to support manufacturing facilities in foreign countries or to adapt standard products to the demand there; in that type of site, information flows *to* the foreign laboratory *from* the central lab at home. (See the exhibit "How Information Flows Between Home-Base and Foreign R&D Sites.")

The overwhelming majority of the 238 foreign R&D sites I studied fell clearly into one of the two categories. Approximately 45% of all laboratory sites were home-base-augmenting sites, and 55% were home-base-exploiting sites. The two types of sites were of the same average size: about 100 employees. But they differed distinctly in their strategic purpose and leadership style.[2] (See the insert "Home-Base-Augmenting and Home-Base-Exploiting Sites: Xerox and Eli Lilly.")

Choosing a Location for the Site. Home-base-augmenting sites should be located in regional clusters of scientific excellence in order to tap new sources of knowledge. Central to the success of corporate R&D strategy is the ability of senior researchers to recognize and combine scientific advancements from different areas of science and technology. Absorbing the new knowledge can happen in a number of ways: through participation in formal or informal meeting circles that exist within a geographic area containing useful knowledge (a knowledge cluster), through hiring employees from competitors, or through sourcing laboratory equipment and research services from the same suppliers that competitors use.

For example, the Silicon Valley knowledge cluster boasts a large number of informal gatherings of experts as well as more formal ways for high-tech companies to exchange information with adjacent universities, such as industrial liaison programs with Stanford University and the University of California at Berkeley. In the field of communication technology, Siemens, NEC, Matsushita, and Toshiba all operate laboratory sites near Princeton University and Bell Labs (now a part of Lucent Technologies) to take advantage of the expertise located there. For similar reasons, a number of companies

in the same industry have established sites in the Kanto area surrounding Tokyo. Texas Instruments operates a facility in Tsukuba Science City, and Hewlett-Packard operates one in Tokyo.

After a company has picked and established its major R&D sites, it might want to branch out. It might selectively set up secondary sites when a leading competitor or a university succeeds in building a critical mass of research expertise in a more narrowly defined area of science and technology outside the primary cluster. In order to benefit from the resulting miniclusters of expertise, companies sometimes establish additional facilities. For that reason, NEC operates a small telecommunications-oriented R&D facility close to a university laboratory in London, and Canon operates an R&D facility in Rennes, France, close to one of France Telecom's major sites.

Home-base-exploiting sites, in contrast, should be located close to large markets and manufacturing facilities in order to commercialize new products rapidly in foreign markets. In the past, companies from industrialized countries located manufacturing facilities abroad primarily to benefit from lower wages or to overcome trade barriers. Over time, however, many of those plants have taken on increasingly complex manufacturing tasks that require having an R&D facility nearby in order to ensure the speedy transfer of technology from research to manufacturing. A silicon-wafer plant, for

Establishing New R&D Sites

Types of R&D Sites	Phase 1 Location Decision	Phase 2 Ramp-Up Period	Phase 3 Maximizing Lab Impact
Home-Base-Augmenting Laboratory Site Objective of establishment: absorbing knowledge from the local scientific community, creating new knowledge, and transferring it *to* the company's central R&D site	–Select a location for its scientific excellence –Promote cooperation between the company's senior scientists and managers	–Choose as first laboratory leader a renowned local scientist with international experience – one who understands the dynamics of R&D at the new location –Ensure enough critical mass	–Ensure the laboratory's active participation in the local scientific community –Exchange researchers with local university laboratories and with the home-base lab
Home-Base-Exploiting Laboratory Site Objective of establishment: commercializing knowledge by transferring it *from* the company's home base to the laboratory site abroad and from there to local manufacturing and marketing	–Select a location for its proximity to the company's existing manufacturing and marketing locations –Involve middle managers from other functional areas in start-up decisions	–Choose as first laboratory leader an experienced product-development engineer with a strong companywide reputation, international experience, and knowledge of marketing and manufacturing	–Emphasize smooth relations with the home-base lab –Encourage employees to seek interaction with other corporate units beyond the manufacturing and marketing units that originally sponsored the lab

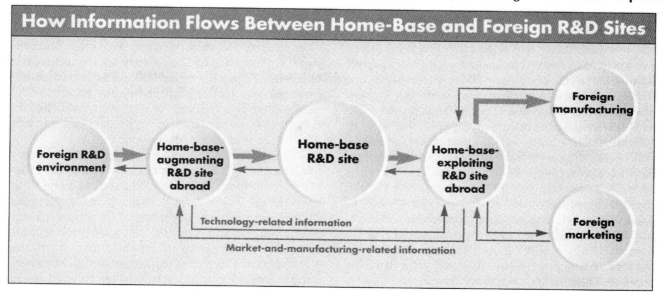

How Information Flows Between Home-Base and Foreign R&D Sites

example, has to interact closely with product development engineers during trial runs of a new generation of microchips. The same is true for the manufacture of disk drives and other complex hardware. For that reason, Hewlett-Packard and Texas Instruments both operate laboratories in Singapore, close to manufacturing facilities.

The more complex and varied a manufacturing process is, the more often manufacturing engineers will have to interact with product development engineers. For example, in the case of one of Toshiba's laptop-computer-manufacturing plants, a new model is introduced to the manufacturing line every two weeks. The introduction has to happen seamlessly, without disturbing the production of existing models on the same line. In order to predict and remedy bugs during initial production runs, development engineers and manufacturing engineers meet several times a week. The proximity of Toshiba's laptop-development laboratory to its manufacturing plant greatly facilitates the interaction.

Establishing a New R&D Facility

Whether establishing a home-base-augmenting or a home-base-exploiting facility, companies must use the same three-stage process: selecting the best laboratory leader, determining the optimal size for the new laboratory site, and keeping close watch over the lab during its start-up period in order to ensure that it is merged into the company's existing global R&D network and contributes sufficiently to the company's product portfolio and its economic performance.

Selecting the Best Site Leader. Identifying the best leader for a new R&D site is one of the most important decisions a company faces in its quest to establish a successful global R&D network. My research shows that the initial leader of an R&D site has a powerful impact not only on the culture of the site but also on its long-term research agenda and performance. The two types of sites require different types of leaders, and each type of leader confronts a particular set of challenges.

The initial leaders of home-base-augmenting sites should be prominent local scientists so that they will be able to fulfill their primary responsibility: to nurture ties between the new site and the local scientific community. If the site does not succeed in becoming part of the local scientific community quickly, it will not be able to generate new knowledge for the company. In addition to hiring a local scientist, there are a variety of other ways to establish local ties. For example, Toshiba used its memory-chip joint venture with Siemens to develop local ties at its new R&D site in Regensburg, Germany. The venture allowed Toshiba to tap into Siemens's dense network of associations with local universities. In addition, it helped Toshiba develop a better understanding of the compensation packages required to hire first-class German engineering graduates. Finally, it let the company gain useful insights into how to establish effective contract-research relationships with government-funded research institutions in Germany.

In contrast, the initial leaders of home-base-exploiting sites should be highly regarded managers from within the company – managers who are intimately familiar with the company's culture and systems. Such leaders will be able to fulfill their primary responsibility: to forge close ties between the new lab's engineers and the foreign community's manufacturing and marketing facilities. Then the transfer of knowledge from the company's home base to the R&D site will have the maximum impact on manufacturing and marketing located near that site. When one U.S. pharmaceutical company established a home-base-exploiting site in Great Britain, executives appointed as the initial site leader a manager who had been with the company for several years. He had started his career as a bench scientist first in exploratory research, then in the development of one of the company's blockbuster drugs. He had worked closely with marketing, and he had spent two years as supervisor of manufacturing quality at one of the company's U.S. manufacturing sites. With such a background, he was able to lead the new site effectively.

However, the best candidates for both home-base-augmenting and home-base-exploiting sites share four qualities: they are at once respected scientists or engineers and skilled managers; they are able to integrate the new site into the company's existing R&D network; they have a comprehensive understanding of technology trends; and they are able to overcome formal barriers when they seek access to new ideas in local universities and scientific communities.

Appointing an outstanding scientist or engineer who has no management experience can be disastrous. In one case, a leading U.S. electronics company decided to establish a home-base-augmenting site in the United Kingdom. The engineer who was appointed as the first site leader was an outstanding researcher but had little management experience outside the company's central laboratory environment. The leader had difficulties marshaling the necessary resources to expand the laboratory beyond its starting size of 14 researchers. Furthermore, he had a tough time mediating between the research laboratory and the company's product development area. Eleven of the 14 researchers had been hired locally and therefore lacked deep ties to the company. They needed a savvy corporate advocate who could understand company politics and could promote their research results within the company. One reason they didn't have such an advocate was that two of the three managers at the company's home base – people who had promoted the establishment of the new R&D lab – had quit about six months after the lab had opened because they disagreed about the company's overall R&D strategy. The third manager had moved to a different department.

In an effort to improve the situation, the company appointed a U.S. engineer as liaison to the U.K. site. He realized that few ideas were flowing from the site to the home base; but he attributed the problem to an inherently slow scientific-discovery process rather than to organizational barriers within the company. After about two years, senior management finally replaced the initial laboratory leader and the U.S. liaison engineer with two managers – one from the United Kingdom and one from the United States. The managers had experience overseeing one of the company's U.S. joint ventures in technology, and they also had good track records as researchers. Finally, under their leadership, the site dramatically increased its impact on the company's product portfolio. In conjunction with the increase in scientific output, the site grew to its projected size of 225 employees and is now highly productive.

In the case of both types of sites, the ideal leader has in-depth knowledge of both the home-base culture and the foreign culture. Consider Sharp's experience. In Japan, fewer corporate scientists have Ph.D.'s than their counterparts in the United Kingdom; instead they have picked up their knowledge and skills on the job. That difference presented a management challenge for Sharp when it established a home-base-augmenting facility in the United Kingdom. In order to cope with that challenge, the company hired a British laboratory leader who had previously worked as a science attaché at the British embassy in Japan. In that position, he had developed a good understanding of the Japanese higher-education system. He was well aware that British and Japanese engineers with different aca-

The best managers of foreign R&D sites are respected scientists or engineers and, at the same time, skilled managers.

demic degrees might have similar levels of expertise, and, as a result, he could manage them better.

The pioneer who heads a newly established home-base-augmenting or home-base-exploiting site also must have a broad perspective and a deep understanding of technology trends. R&D sites abroad are often particularly good at combining knowledge from different scientific fields into new ideas and products. Because those sites start with a clean slate far from the company's powerful central laboratory, they are less plagued by the "not-invented-here" syndrome. For example, Canon's home-base-augmenting laboratory in the United Kingdom developed an innovative loudspeaker that is now being manufactured in Europe for a worldwide market. Senior researchers at Canon in Japan acknowledge that it would have been much more difficult for a new research team located in Japan to come up with the product. As one Canon manager puts it, "Although the new loudspeaker was partially based on knowledge that existed within Canon already, Canon's research management in Japan was too focused on existing product lines and would probably not have tolerated the pioneering loudspeaker project."

Finally, leaders of new R&D sites need to be aware of the considerable formal barriers they might confront when they seek access to local universities and scientific communities. These barriers are often created by lawmakers who want to protect a nation's intellectual capital. Although foreign companies do indeed absorb local knowledge and transfer it to their home bases – particularly in the case of home-base-augmenting sites – they also create important positive economic effects for the host nation. The laboratory leader of a new R&D site needs to communicate that fact locally in order to reduce existing barriers and prevent the formation of new ones.

Determining the Optimal Size of the New R&D Site. My research indicates that the optimal size for a new foreign R&D facility during the start-up phase is usually 30 to 40 employees, and the best size for a site after the ramp-up period is about 235 employees, including support staff. The optimal size of a site depends mainly on a company's track record in international management. Companies that already operate several sites abroad tend to be more successful at establishing larger new sites.

Companies can run into problems if their foreign sites are either too small or too large. If the site is too small, the resulting lack of critical mass produces an environment in which there is little cross-fertilization of ideas among researchers. And a small R&D site generally does not command a sufficient level of respect in the scientific community surrounding the laboratory. As a result, its researchers have a harder time gaining access to informal networks and to scientific meetings that provide opportunities for an exchange of knowledge. In contrast, if the laboratory site is too large, its culture quickly becomes anonymous, researchers become isolated, and the benefits of spreading fixed costs over a larger number of researchers are out-

weighed by the lack of cross-fertilization of ideas. According to one manager at such a lab, "Once people stopped getting to know one another on an informal basis in the lunchroom of our site, they became afraid of deliberately walking into one another's laboratory rooms to talk about research and to ask questions. Researchers who do not know each other on an informal basis are often hesitant to ask their colleagues for advice: they are afraid to reveal any of their own knowledge gaps. We realized that we had crossed a critical threshold in size. We subsequently scaled back somewhat and made an increased effort to reduce the isolation of individual researchers within the site through communication tools and through rotating researchers among different lab units at the site."

Supervising the Start-Up Period. During the initial growth period of an R&D site, which typically lasts anywhere from one to three years, the culture is formed and the groundwork for the site's future productivity is laid. During that period, senior management in the home country has to be in particularly close contact with the new site. Although it is important that the new laboratory develop its own identity and stake out its fields of expertise, it also has to be closely connected to the company's existing R&D structure. Newly hired scientists must be aware of the resources that exist within the company as a whole, and scientists at home and at other locations must be aware of the opportunities the new site creates for the company as a whole. Particularly during the start-up period, senior R&D managers at the corporate level have to walk a fine line and decide whether to devote the most resources to connecting the new site to the company or to supporting ties between the new site and its local environment.

To integrate a new site into the company as a whole, managers must pay close attention to the site's research agenda and create mechanisms to integrate it into the company's overall strategic goals. Because of the high degree of uncertainty of R&D outcomes, continuous adjustments to research agendas are the rule. What matters most is speed, both in terms of terminating research projects that go nowhere and in terms of pushing projects that bring unexpectedly good results.

The rapid exchange of information is essential to integrating a site into the overall company during the start-up phase. Companies use a number of mechanisms to create a cohesive research community in spite of geographic distance. Hewlett-Packard regularly organizes an in-house science fair at which teams of researchers can present projects and prototypes to one another. Canon has a program that lets researchers from home-base-augmenting sites request a temporary transfer to home-base-exploiting sites. At Xerox, most sites are linked by a sophisticated information system that allows senior R&D managers to determine

Managers must integrate a site's research agenda into the company's overall goals.

within minutes the current state of research projects and the number of researchers working on those projects. But nothing can replace face-to-face contact between active researchers. Maintaining a

global R&D network requires personal meetings, and therefore many researchers and R&D managers have to spend time visiting not only other R&D sites but also specialized suppliers and local universities affiliated with those sites.

Failing to establish sufficient ties with the company's existing R&D structure during the start-up phase can hamper the success of a new foreign R&D site. For example, in 1986, a large foreign pharmaceutical company established a biotechnology research site in Boston, Massachusetts. In order to recruit outstanding scientists and maintain a high level of creative output, the company's R&D management decided to give the new laboratory considerable leeway in its research agenda and in determining what to do with the results – although the company did reserve the right of first refusal for the commercialization of the lab's inventions. The new site was staffed exclusively with scientists handpicked by a newly hired laboratory leader. A

Home-Base-Augmenting and Home-Base-Exploiting Sites:

The particular type of foreign R&D site determines the specific challenges managers will face. Setting up a *home-base-augmenting site* – one designed to gather new knowledge for a company – involves certain skills. And launching a *home-base-exploiting site* – one established to help a company efficiently commercialize its R&D in foreign markets – involves others. The cases of Xerox and Eli Lilly present an instructive contrast.

Xerox established a home-base-augmenting laboratory in Grenoble, France. Its objective: to tap new knowledge from the local scientific community and to transfer it back to its home base. Having already established, in 1986, a home-base-augmenting site in Cambridge, England, Xerox realized in 1992 that the research culture in continental Western Europe was sufficiently different and complementary to Great Britain's to justify another site. Moreover, understanding the most advanced research in France or Germany was very difficult from a base in Great Britain because of language and cultural barriers. One senior R&D manager in the United States notes, "We wanted to learn firsthand what was going on in centers of scientific excellence in Europe. Being present at a center of scientific excellence is like reading poetry in the original language."

It was essential that managers from the highest levels of the company be involved in the decision-making process from the start. Senior scientists met with

high-level managers and entered into a long series of discussions. Their first decision: to locate the new laboratory at a center of scientific excellence. Xerox also realized that it had to hire a renowned local scientist as the initial laboratory leader. The leader needed to be able to understand the local scientific community, attract junior scientists with high potential, and target the right university institutes and scholars for joint research projects. Finally, Xerox knew that the laboratory would have an impact on the company's economic performance only if it had the critical mass to become an accepted member of the local scientific community. At the same time, it could not become isolated from the larger Xerox culture.

Xerox considered a number of locations and carefully evaluated such aspects as their scientific excellence and relevance, university liaison programs, licensing programs, and university recruiting programs. The company came up with four potential locations: Paris, Grenoble, Barcelona, and Munich. At that point, Xerox also identified potential laboratory leaders. The company chose Grenoble on the basis of its demonstrated scientific excellence and hired as the initial laboratory leader a highly regarded French scientist with good connections to local universities. Xerox designed a facility for 40 researchers and made plans for further expansion. In order to integrate the new laboratory's scientists into the Xerox community, senior R&D management in Palo Alto, California, allocated renowned local biochemist, he had been employed for many years by a major U.S. university, where he had carried out contract research for the company. During the start-up phase, few of the company's veteran scientists were involved in joint research projects with the site's scientists – an arrangement that hindered the transfer of ideas between the new lab and the company's other R&D sites. Although the academic community now recognizes the lab as an important contributor to the field, few of its inventions have been patented by the company, fewer have been targeted for commercialization, and none have reached the commercial stage yet. One senior scientist working in the lab commented that ten years after its creation, the lab had become so much of an "independent animal" that it would take a lot of carefully balanced guidance from the company to instill a stronger sense of commercial orientation without a risk of losing the most creative scientists.

There is no magic formula that senior managers can follow to ensure the success of a foreign R&D site during its start-up phase. Managing an R&D network, particularly in its early stages, is delicate and complex. It requires constant tinkering—evaluation and reevaluation. Senior R&D managers have to decide how much of the research should be initiated by the company and how much by the scientist, determine the appropriate incentive structures and employment contracts, establish policies for the temporary transfer of researchers to the company's other R&D or manufacturing sites, and choose universities from which to hire scientists and engineers.

Flexibility and experimentation during a site's start-up phase can ensure its future productivity. For example, Fujitsu established a software-research laboratory site in San Jose, California, in 1992. The company was seriously thinking of establishing a second site in Boston but eventually re-

Xerox and Eli Lilly

a considerable part of the initial laboratory budget to travel to other Xerox sites and started a program for the temporary transfer of newly hired researchers from Grenoble to other R&D sites. At the same time, the Grenoble site set out to integrate itself within the local research community.

In 1989, Eli Lilly considered establishing a home-base-exploiting laboratory in East Asia. The company's objective was to commercialize its R&D more effectively in foreign markets. Until then, Eli Lilly had operated one home-base-augmenting laboratory site abroad and some small sites in industrialized countries for clinical testing and drug approval procedures. But in order to exploit Lilly's R&D capabilities and product portfolio, the company needed a dedicated laboratory site in East Asia. The new site would support efforts to manufacture and market pharmaceuticals by adapting products to local needs. To that end, the management team decided that the new laboratory would have to be located close to relevant markets and existing corporate facilities. It also determined that the initial laboratory leader would have to be an experienced manager from Lilly's home base – a manager with a deep understanding of both the company's local operations and its overall R&D network.

The team considered Singapore as a potential location because of its proximity to a planned Lilly manufacturing site in Malaysia. But ultimately it decided that the new home-base-exploiting laboratory would

have the strongest impact on Lilly's sales if it was located in Kōbe, Japan. By establishing a site in the Kōbe-Osaka region – the second-largest regional market in Japan and one that offered educational institutions with high-quality scientists – Lilly would send a signal to the medical community there that the company was committed to the needs of the Japanese market. Kōbe had another advantage: Lilly's corporate headquarters for Japan were located there, and the company was already running some of its drug approval operations for the Japanese market out of Kōbe. The city therefore was the logical choice.

The team assigned an experienced Lilly researcher and manager to be the initial leader of the new site. Because he knew the company inside and out – from central research and development to international marketing – the team reasoned that he would be able to bring the new laboratory up to speed quickly by drawing on resources from various divisions within Lilly. In order to integrate the new site into the overall company, some researchers from other Lilly R&D sites received temporary transfers of up to two years to Kōbe, and some locally hired researchers were temporarily transferred to other Lilly sites. It took about 30 months to activate fully the Kōbe operation – a relatively short period. Today the site is very productive in transferring knowledge from Lilly's home base to Kōbe and in commercializing that knowledge throughout Japan and Asia.

considered. Fujitsu realized that the effort that had gone into establishing the San Jose site had been greater than expected. Once the site was up and running, however, its productive output also had been higher than expected. Furthermore, Fujitsu found that its R&D managers had gained an excellent understanding of the R&D community that created advanced software-development tools. Although initially leaning toward establishing a second site, the managers were flexible. They decided to enlarge the existing site because of its better-than-expected performance as well as the limited potential benefits of a second site. The San Jose site has had a major impact on Fujitsu's software development and sales – particularly in Japan but in the United States, too. Similarly, at Alcatel's first foreign R&D site in Germany, senior managers were flexible. After several months, they realized that the travel-and-communications budget would have to be increased substantially beyond initial projections in order to improve the flow of knowledge from the French home base. For instance, in the case of a telephone switchboard project, the actual number of business trips between the two sites was nearly twice as high as originally projected.

Integrating the Global R&D Network

As the number of companies' R&D sites at home and abroad grows, R&D managers will increasingly face the challenging task of coordinating the network. That will require a fundamental shift in the role of senior managers at the central lab. Managers of R&D networks must be global coordinators, not local administrators. More than being managers of people and processes, they must be managers of knowledge. And not all managers that a company has in place will be up to the task.

Consider Matsushita's R&D management. A number of technically competent managers became obsolete at the company once it launched a global approach to R&D. Today managers at Matsushita's central R&D site in Hirakata, Japan, continue to play an important role in the research and development of core processes for manufacturing. But the responsibility of an increasing number of senior managers at the central site is overseeing Matsushita's network of 15 dedicated R&D sites. That responsibility includes setting research agendas, monitoring results, and creating direct ties between sites.

How does the new breed of R&D manager coordinate global knowledge? Look again to Matsushita's central R&D site. First, high-level corporate managers in close cooperation with senior R&D managers develop an overall research agenda and assign different parts of it to individual sites. The process is quite tricky. It requires that the managers in charge have a good understanding of not only the technological capabilities that Matsushita will need to develop in the future but also the stock of technological capabilities already available to it.

Managing an R&D network is both delicate and complex. It requires constant tinkering—evaluation and reevaluation.

Matsushita's central lab organizes two or three yearly off-site meetings devoted to informing R&D scientists and engineers about the entire company's current state of technical knowledge and capabilities. At the same meetings, engineers who have moved from R&D to take over manufacturing and marketing responsibilities inform R&D members about trends in Matsushita's current and potential future markets. Under the guidance of senior project managers, members from R&D, manufacturing, and marketing determine timelines and resource requirements for specific home-base-augmenting and home-base-exploiting projects. One R&D manager notes, "We discuss not only why a specific scientific insight might be interesting for Matsushita but also how we can turn this insight into a product quickly. We usually seek to develop a prototype early. Prototypes are a good basis for a discussion with marketing and manufacturing. Most of our efforts are targeted at delivering the prototype of a slightly better mousetrap early rather than delivering the blueprint of a much better mousetrap late."

To stimulate the exchange of information, R&D managers at Matsushita's central lab create direct links among researchers across different sites. They promote the use of videoconferencing and frequent face-to-face contact to forge those ties. Reducing the instances in which the central lab must act as mediator means that existing knowledge travels more quickly through the company and new ideas percolate more easily. For example, a researcher at a home-base-exploiting site in Singapore can communicate with another researcher at a home-base-exploiting site in Franklin Park, Illinois, about potential new research projects much more readily now that central R&D fosters informal and formal direct links.

Finally, managers at Matsushita's central lab constantly monitor new regional pockets of knowledge as well as the company's expanding network of manufacturing sites to determine whether the company will need additional R&D locations. With 15 major sites around the world, Matsushita has decided that the number of sites is sufficient at this point. But the company is ever vigilant about surveying the landscape and knows that as the landscape changes, its decision could, too.

As more pockets of knowledge emerge worldwide and competition in foreign markets mounts, the imperative to create global R&D networks will grow all the more pressing. Only those companies that embrace a global approach to R&D will meet the competitive challenges of the new dynamic. And only those managers who embrace their fundamentally new role as global coordinators and managers of knowledge will be able to tap the full potential of their R&D networks.

1. In a systematic effort to analyze the relationship of global strategy and R&D investments in technologically intensive industries, I have been collecting detailed data on all dedicated laboratory sites operated by 32 leading multinational companies. The sample consists of 10 U.S., 12 Japanese, and 10 European companies. Thirteen of the companies are in the pharmaceutical industry, and 19 are in the electronics industry. Data collection includes archival research, a detailed questionnaire, and in-depth interviews with several senior R&D managers in each company. Overall, these companies operate 238 dedicated R&D sites, 156 of them abroad. About 60% of the laboratory sites abroad were established after 1984. I have used this sample, which is the most complete of its kind, as a basis for a number of quantitative and qualitative investigations into global strategy, competitive interaction, and R&D management.

2. My research on global R&D strategies builds on earlier research on the competitiveness of nations and on research on foreign direct investment, including Michael E. Porter, *The Competitive Advantage of Nations* (New York: The Free Press, 1990), and Thomas J. Wesson, "An Alternative Motivation for Foreign Direct Investment" (Ph.D. dissertation, Harvard University, 1993). My research also builds on an existing body of knowledge about the management of multinational companies. See, for example, Christopher A. Bartlett and Sumantra Ghoshal, *Managing Across Borders* (New York: The Free Press, 1989).

INVESTING

Back to the Land

Asian investors move in on Tokyo's property bargains
but plenty of obstacles await them.

By Peter Landers in Tokyo

To Hong Kong's Richard Li it's all very simple. Punching a few figures into his calculator, he declares that when he paid ¥86.9 billion ($710 million) for a sliver of choice Tokyo property, it was just good business.

He's not alone. Major property players in Hong Kong, Singapore and Taiwan agree that quality Japanese real estate—whose value has plunged by up to 85% since 1991—has finally reached rock bottom and is an attractive overseas play. A joint venture between Singapore's government and Hong Kong firm HKR International headed by Payson Cha, for example, recently won an auction for part of a large plot near Tokyo's prestigious Ginza shopping area, as part of a group bid with Japanese companies totalling ¥138.2 billion.

To a nation starved for news of a real-estate recovery, it looks like the bandwagon is rolling. Japan's corporate chieftains certainly hope so: If overseas money jacks up local land prices, banks can at last shed their bad-loan problems and free Japan's economy of its biggest burden.

But for foreign investors, Japan often doesn't play by the rules to which they are accustomed elsewhere—and that applies to real estate as much as any other industry. On paper, the nation's store of property looks like a supermarket packed

with bargains, yet many Asian shoppers may never get to the checkout line.

To see why, imagine a wealthy investor with a few hundred million dollars to put into property. He calls up a real-estate agent in Tokyo and asks for data on a few properties in that price range. Yasuo Kawakami, managing director at real-estate agent Richard Ellis in Tokyo, has been on the other end of such calls, and he always has to explain that Japanese sellers will only divulge information when they feel the potential buyer is serious. The seller wants to be sure of the buyer's liquidity, reputation and discretion, and often asks for a formal letter of interest. Foreign companies, other than a few multinationals, are just not known to the local players. The investors may well ask for brochures, says Kawakami, "but that's not how business is done here. They'll never get those."

Another reason Asian investors have run up against a wall, says Kawakami, is the "sense of shame and guilt" Japanese feel about selling property. In the most prestigious business district, the Marunouchi-Otemachi next to Tokyo Station, property almost never goes on the market. Yet Asian investors often aren't interested in buying lesser-quality real estate. They feel that top-notch

property values will outpace the rest whether the market recovers or not.

Simply put, buying is heavily weighted against outsiders. "The whole machinery is catered to self-sufficiency without the need for foreign participation," concurs Li, the 30-year-old son of Hong Kong tycoon Li Ka-shing. The current business troubles of Japanese companies, he adds, are "the only reason there's a window for foreigners to play, and there may not be a window five to six years from now."

Li was looking for a year at Tokyo property before he found an opportunity that interested him: auctions of land by the company settling the debts of the former national railway. After two unsuccessful bids, he landed a 5,000-square-metre site right next to Tokyo Station, the central terminal for Japan's major rail lines. His Pacific Century company will put up a 28-storey building on the former railway offices site. Only a handful of other Asians, however, have had similar success. As Li's Tokyo representative, Andrew Reilly, puts it: "You could put all the Asians who have bought real estate in Japan into a taxi, and still have room to sit in the front seat."

If real-estate investors are finding Japan less than hospitable, they are only reach-

 From *Far Eastern Economic Review,* April 17, 1997, pp. 52-53. © 1997 by Review Publishing Company Limited. Reprinted by permission.

ing the same conclusion that foreign companies in other sectors came to long ago. Direct foreign investment in Japan amounted to just $3.8 billion in the year ending March 1996, most of it by American and European companies. Compare that to the $50.7 billion in Japanese investment abroad, most of which was in industry and real estate. Much of it goes to Asia, which accounted for 24% of Japan's total foreign direct investment in fiscal 1995.

Now, Japanese officials insist, Asian interest in Japan is growing, and there are some indications to support that. South Korea's Samsung conglomerate has bought half of an office building in Tokyo and stepped up marketing investment to sell its TV sets in Japan. And an investment arm of Malaysia's government last year bought a stake in Nichiei Seiki, a medium-sized tool-and-die manufacturer, although the purchase was such a novelty it drew widespread media attention.

Officially Japan would like to see a lot more foreign investment, but many Japanese admit popular sentiment is not as welcoming. Minoru Mori, the president and CEO of major developer Mori Building Co., says there's a "feeling of resistance against investment from abroad," even though it would help Japan's economy recover more quickly.

"Money from abroad is the best reinforcement we could have. We ought to welcome it with open arms," says Mori. "But Japanese have a kind of fear that the small land area [of Japan] will be taken over by foreigners." Japanese know well the resentment that can be generated by foreign investment, having themselves been subject to opposition in the United States in the 1980s and early 1990s.

Mori estimates that commercial property in Tokyo now goes for about one-sixth of the peak in the late 1980s, a collapse that led to piles of bad loans at

Japanese banks and a five-year economic slowdown. But for all its concern about an economic recovery the Japanese government has done little to invigorate the market. Anyone buying real estate, for instance, has to pay both national and regional purchase taxes, plus a registration tax and a fee for the revenue stamp that must be affixed to the contract.

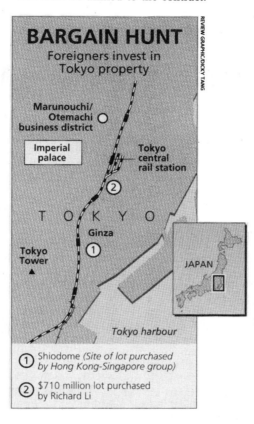

BARGAIN HUNT
Foreigners invest in Tokyo property

Marunouchi/ Otemachi business district

Imperial palace

Tokyo central rail station

②

T O K Y O

Ginza

Tokyo Tower ▲

①

JAPAN

Tokyo harbour

① Shiodome (Site of lot purchased by Hong Kong-Singapore group)

② $710 million lot purchased by Richard Li

REVIEW GRAPHIC/DICKY TANG

The government also doesn't look kindly on real-estate investors taking quick profits when prices go up, something that comes naturally to those used to Hong Kong's fast-and-loose property market. A confiscatory tax of up to 76% is levied on

any capital gains within two years of a property purchase. Japanese developers know the tax system but foreigners often overlook its complexities and added costs, say property professionals.

And it is not just the tax system that can leave foreigners puzzled—not being clued-in about underhand business practices can leave outsiders exposed. Cosy relations between construction companies, for example, mean that they routinely confer and fix bids for developing sites to keep costs artificially high.

Li says he had to be wary when discussing his bidding plans with Japanese because he was afraid they might leak details to his competitors. "You never know who is friend or foe," he says. "There are no secrets in this town."

The fact that foreign investors are still interested in Japan despite all those difficulties illustrates just how attractive prices are. Li anticipates a 5%–6% return on his investment, well above the 2.2% yield on Japanese government bonds. While 5%–6% may not sound much for more hot-blooded bulls, the figure is regarded as a minimum return. If the market takes off, much more is expected. Property analysts also point out that conservative investors like the Singapore government are not buying Tokyo property for speculation, but for good, secure returns.

"If you compare on a global basis, Japan is a very good opportunity," says Kohei Ogawa, managing director for a Hong Kong property company, the Far East Consortium. "We can buy very cheaply." Far East took a 24.8% stake on April 1 in Mori Denki, a publicly traded manufacturer of industrial illumination equipment, hoping that real-estate investment would be easier through a listed vehicle.

Ogawa admits Japan is "to a certain extent a closed society," but he adds: "Japan is changing. I think we'll see many more deals in the next couple of years."

Education and the wealth of nations

THE politics of education is in a confused and peculiar state. All over the world it is taken for granted that educational achievement and economic success are closely linked—that the struggle to raise a nation's living standards is fought first and foremost in the classroom. What has established this idea so unshakeably in people's minds is a recent, and to many a rather alarming, phenomenon: the new intensity of global economic rivalry. The idea of competition among nations is now familiar (albeit often misunderstood). But the idea of international competition among schools—that is, among educational methods and systems—has so far made only a dull impression on people's thinking.

Up to now, education professionals have tended to resist comparisons even of apparently similar schools within neighbourhoods. Such are the subtleties of their craft, they say, that exercises of that sort are meaningless. In Britain, where the government has begun to publish league tables of schools' results, teachers and local-authority bureaucrats remain intensely sceptical of such information. To go further, and compare a school in Manchester with one in Tampa, say, or Seoul, would strike them as simply ridiculous. But the very changes that are concentrating people's attention on education are obliging everyone to be more outward-looking, and to judge their ways of doing things by the yardstick of the best in the world. Education should not be exempt.

Introduction to comparative studies

Certainly, no one any longer needs convincing that education matters. Not long ago a fashionable anxiety in many western countries was that youngsters were being over-educated—that is, schooled beyond society's needs. Machines were taking all the jobs that required basic skills, it was argued. In future only a handful of brain-workers would be needed. To teach cleaners and nightwatchmen advanced mathematics (such as adding up without a calculator) seemed pretty wasteful, and apt to breed discontent.

How quaint that seems now. In the advanced economies of America and Europe, today's chief economic worry is that jobs and industries will be lost to new competition from Asia, Latin America and Eastern Europe. It is a commonplace that, among these emerging economies, the most successful are the ones that have educated most of their workers up to, and in many cases well beyond, levels typically achieved in the West.

In the rich economies too the mix of jobs is changing rapidly, away from manufacturing and towards services, ancient and modern. But what many of the new activities have in common is that they too are based to a greater extent than before on information. One of the world's most conspicuously successful centres of enterprise lies in that bit of California known as Silicon Valley: computing is today's knowledge-based industry *par excellence*. The new jobs in tomorrow's industries, in manufacturing and services alike, will call for more than button-pressing automatons. They will require workers that are literate, numerate, adaptable, and trainable—in a word, educated.

When teachers and educational policymakers start, like everybody else, to seek out best practice by looking around the world, what will they find? The first thing is a surprisingly large—and therefore potentially informative—variation in performance. The next is that this variation has little to do with things you might suppose would explain it: class sizes, hours of study per subject, and spending per pupil.

The biggest piece of international research on educational standards, involving schools in 41 countries, was published recently. It compared scores of 13-year-olds in maths and science tests, calibrating the scores so that a mark of 500 was equal to the international average. In maths, as it happens, America's score was 500, placing it 28th in the league. England's score was 506, giving a rank of 25. The Czech Republic, with 564, achieved Europe's highest score and a rank of 6. Top of the table was Singapore, with 643, followed by South Korea, Japan and Hong Kong (see next article).

The Czech Republic spent a third as much per pupil as America. Many of the most generous spenders achieved results that were mediocre or worse. Pupils per teacher and hours devoted to study in each subject were no more closely linked to results. The East Asian tigers scored well (without spending more than other countries), suggesting "Asian values" as the secret of success. But this too is misleading. English students scored almost as well in science as their Japanese counterparts. If "culture" is the key, why should this be so?

Academics are starting to ask why countries as culturally different as Japan and Switzerland do so well. The evidence suggests that teaching methods are the key. In teaching maths, for instance, both those countries spend more time on basic arithmetic than on deeper mathematical ideas, emphasise mental arithmetic, rely on standard teaching manuals and favour whole-class (as opposed to group) teaching.

Nobody, least of all their authors, is claiming that such studies are conclusive. So far they are proving much better at saying what doesn't work than what does. But it should be beyond doubt that more, and more detailed, comparisons of this sort are the way to advance the debate on education beyond tiresome quarrels over how much governments should be spending. This just doesn't matter very much. The argument, in Britain at least, has begun to shift to teachers' methods in the classroom. Henceforth it should concentrate squarely on that issue.

Further research will be needed before it is possible to say with confidence what works best. Many teachers and most local education officials will treat such inquiries with suspicion, of course: in most rich countries, unlike the pupils they turn out into the world, they have been sheltered from competition since they left college. Everybody else is part of the new global economy. It's time the schools joined in.

WORLD EDUCATION LEAGUE

Who's top?

Some countries seem to educate their children much better than others. Why? No comprehensive answer has emerged yet but plenty of lessons are being learnt from the tests which reveal the educational discrepancies

A CLASS has 28 students and the ratio of girls to boys is 4:3. How many girls are there? Which of the following is made using bacteria: yogurt, cream, soap or cooking oil? Simple enough questions in any language (the answers, by the way, are 16 and yogurt). But when half a million pupils from around the world were set questions like these, some countries, just like some pupils, did very well and some very badly.

The tests were set for the largest-ever piece of international education research, the Third International Maths and Science Study (TIMSS). Of the 41 nations participating in this first phase, Singapore was teacher's pet: the average scores of its pupils were almost twice those of South Africa, bottom of the class (see table 1).

East Asian countries have overtaken nations such as America and Britain which have had universal schooling for much longer. America came 17th in science and 28th in mathematics. England came 25th in maths and Scotland (whose pupils were tested separately) came 29th. The four richest East Asian economies took the first four places in maths.

Some former communist countries, notably the Czech Republic, Slovakia, Slovenia and Bulgaria, also did significantly better than their richer western neighbours, even though they spend much less on education. Six of the top 15 places in both maths and science went to East Europeans. It seems that how much a country can afford to spend has less than you might think to do with how well educated its children are. American children have three times as much money spent on their schooling as young South Koreans, who nevertheless beat them hands down in tests.

International educational comparisons like the TIMSS study have been subjects of growing academic enthusiasm and criticism since the 1960s (for the controversies, see box on next page). Teachers, though, have been almost entirely

hostile and most governments have held themselves aloof from the arguments, fearing embarrassment. A poor showing in the league table would give political opponents ammunition, while the studies might be used to accuse ministers of starving their education system (or, possibly, of wasting taxpayers' money on a grand scale).

Now, attitudes are changing, at least among politicians. Over the past ten years or so, governments' desire to know more about how their schools compare with others, and what lessons can be learned from the comparison, have begun to outweigh fear of embarrassment. More countries took part in TIMSS than in its predecessors, and the attention paid to its findings by the world's politicians, educators and the news media was much greater than for previous studies.

Politicians do their homework

President Clinton described the test in his state-of-the-union message in February, as one "that reflects the world-class standards our children must meet for the new era." America's poor overall showing has sparked calls for the adoption of a national curriculum and national standards for school tests—including from Mr Clinton himself. These calls are based on the observation that the countries which did best in the study tended to have national frameworks of this kind.

In a television interview in December, the French president, Jacques Chirac, described as "shameful" a decision by his education ministry to pull out of an international study of adult literacy which was showing that the French were doing badly. And in Britain last year, Michael Heseltine, the deputy prime minister, brushed aside objections from officials in the Department for Education and Employment, and published the unflattering results of a study he had commissioned comparing British workers with those in France, America, Singapore and Germany—chosen as key economic competitors.

The Germans, in turn, were shocked by their pupils' mediocre performance in the TIMSS tests. Their pupils did only slightly better than the English at maths, coming 23rd out of 41 countries. In science, the English surged ahead (though not the Scots) while the Germans were beaten by, among others, the Dutch, the Russians—and even the Americans. A television network ran a special report called "Education Emergency in Ger-

2+2=?			**1**
13-year-olds' average score in TIMSS* (Int average =500)			
Maths		**Science**	
1 Singapore	643	Singapore	607
2 South Korea	607	Czech Republic	574
3 Japan	605	Japan	571
4 Hong Kong	588	South Korea	565
5 Belgium (F†)	565	Bulgaria	565
6 Czech Republic	564	Netherlands	560
7 Slovakia	547	Slovenia	560
8 Switzerland	545	Austria	558
9 Netherlands	541	Hungary	554
10 Slovenia	541	England	552
11 Bulgaria	540	Belgium (F†)	550
12 Austria	539	Australia	545
13 France	538	Slovakia	544
14 Hungary	537	Russia	538
15 Russia	535	Ireland	538
16 Australia	530	Sweden	535
17 Ireland	527	United States	534
18 Canada	527	Canada	531
19 Belgium (W‡)	526	Germany	531
20 Thailand	522	Norway	527
21 Israel	522	Thailand	525
22 Sweden	519	New Zealand	525
23 Germany	509	Israel	524
24 New Zealand	508	Hong Kong	522
25 England	506	Switzerland	522
26 Norway	503	Scotland	517
27 Denmark	502	Spain	517
28 United States	500	France	498
29 Scotland	498	Greece	497
30 Latvia	493	Iceland	494
31 Spain	487	Romania	486
32 Iceland	487	Latvia	485
33 Greece	484	Portugal	480
34 Romania	482	Denmark	478
35 Lithuania	477	Lithuania	476
36 Cyprus	474	Belgium (W‡)	471
37 Portugal	454	Iran	470
38 Iran	428	Cyprus	463
39 Kuwait	392	Kuwait	430
40 Colombia	385	Colombia	411
41 South Africa	354	South Africa	326

*Third International Maths and Science Study †Flanders ‡Wallonia
Source: TIMSS

many"; industrialists accused politicians of ignoring repeated warnings about declining standards in schools.

There are more studies to come. In December the Organisation for Economic Co-operation and Development (OECD), a club of 29 of the world's richest countries, launched its own series of annual reports. The OECD already collects data on how the governments spend their combined $1 trillion annual education budgets, and what proportion of each nation's population reaches a given level of education. The new studies will go much further, comparing how schools, colleges and universities are run in each country and analysing the implications for policymakers.

In some countries, international comparisons are already being used as a catalyst for educational reform. The poor performance of Swedish children in maths, in one study in the mid 1980s, led to the setting up of a new programme of in-service training for teachers. The initial results from TIMSS suggest that Sweden has since pulled itself up to slightly above the international average.

Although Japanese children have repeatedly gained high overall marks in maths tests, some studies have suggested that they are not as advanced in other things, such as analysing data, as they are in basic arithmetic. The Japanese government has started using such findings to reform its national curriculum. Hungary, discovering in early studies that its children were among the world's best in maths and sci-

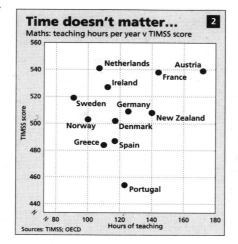

Time doesn't matter... 2
Maths: teaching hours per year v TIMSS score

Sources: TIMSS; OECD

ence but among the least literate, ordered its teachers to spend more time on reading.

Knowledge workers

Leaving aside the results of the tests, two main factors lie behind governments' increasing willingness to take part in international education studies to begin with. The first is the growing consensus that education is the key to getting rich—for countries as well as for individuals. It is widely believed that one of the main reasons why tiger economies like Singapore and South Korea have grown so quickly is that their governments have made determined and successful efforts to raise educational standards.

The other factor is value for money. Governments everywhere have woken up to the full economic significance of education just as they are making desperate attempts to rein in public spending. OECD countries already spend about 6% of national income on education; given the pressure to trim budgets there is no prospect that governments will chuck money at schools without checking to see whether standards are improving. Hence the enthusiasm for comparisons. If governments could discover what it is about their education system that helps growth, then perhaps, they hope, they could do better without spending more.

So do the tests help? They do not provide a sure-fire formula of exactly how much should be spent on schools, how schools should be managed and precisely how each subject should be taught.

All the same, the tests are already proving useful, especially for exposing myths. A popularly-held view has it that "opportunity to learn" is the key to educational success—ie, the more time children spend on a subject, the better they do at it. Alas, the evidence so far is not encouraging for the proponents of this theory. Taking the twelve countries which both took part in TIMSS and also had their average teaching hours measured in the OECD's recent study of school management, there seems little correlation between time spent on a subject and performance of pupils in tests (see chart 2). Young Austrians spend exceptionally long hours on maths and science les-

Answering the critics

CROSS-COUNTRY comparisons have long been controversial. Among the doubts: Do tests put an unwarranted premium on certain qualities—speed of recall, mental arithmetic—while ignoring hard-to-measure ones like creative thinking? Were pupils from different countries really comparable? (For instance, in countries where children are made to repeat a year of their education if they fail to reach a certain standard, tests for, say, 13-year-olds may exclude those who have been sent to join a class of 12-year-olds.) Were pupils in some countries told that the tests were extremely important, while others were not? Did the tests give an unfair advantage to countries whose curriculum for 13-year-olds happens to include more of the topics included in them?

Wendy Keys of Britain's National Foundation for Educational Research, one of the bodies that organised the TIMSS project, says that a number of measures

were taken to answer such criticisms. The score for each country was adjusted to take account of any pupils who were held back a year. Teachers everywhere were given precise instructions on how to explain the tests to pupils, and independent monitors were sent to schools chosen at random. After the results were in, experts in each country looked at how their pupils had done on those questions which most closely matched the curriculum for children of their age.

The results? Broadly, the new study confirmed the relative positions of countries which had taken part in earlier studies. That consistency suggested the original criticisms may have been exaggerated. However, the refinements made in the recent study may overturn one of the theories that has been used to explain why America and Britain, in spite of having had universal education for longer than most nations, do so poorly. This is that

they contain an unusually large proportion of pupils who perform very badly. The comforting implication would be that ordinary pupils do reasonably well but that average scores are dragged down by a so-called "long tail of low achievers".

This explanation was given a colour of plausibility by earlier tests. In those, mediocre scores in Britain and America could be explained away by the failure of the tests to take account of countries where pupils are held back a year. The new version of the test puts that problem right—and the two countries are still doing poorly. Though the mass of results from TIMSS is still being analysed, Dr Keys says there is no sign so far of the "long tail". The implication would be that the average scores of American and British pupils are mediocre because average performance is mediocre, and not because of some peculiarity at the very bottom of the class.

selection of students?

sons; for them, it pays off in higher test scores. But so do New Zealand's teenagers—and they do not do any better than, say, Norwegians, who spend an unusually short time on lessons in both subjects.

Next—and of particular interest to cash-strapped governments—there appears to be little evidence to support the argument, often heard from teachers' unions, that the main cause of educational under-achievement is under-funding. Low-spending countries such as South Korea and the Czech Republic are at the top of the TIMSS league table. High-spenders such as America and Denmark do much worse (see chart 3). Obviously, there are dozens of reasons other than spending why one country does well, another badly, but the success of the low-spending Czechs and Koreans does show that spending more on schools is not a prerequisite for improving standards.

Another article of faith among the teaching profession—that children are bound to do better in small classes—is also being undermined by educational research. As with other studies, TIMSS found that France, America and Britain, where children are usually taught in classes of twenty-odd, do significantly worse than East Asian countries where almost twice as many pupils are crammed into each class. Again, there may be social reasons why some countries can cope better with large classes than others. All the same, the comparison refutes the argument that larger is necessarily worse.

Further, the tests even cast some doubt over the cultural explanation for the greater success of East Asia: that there is some hard-to-define Asian culture, connected with parental authority and a strong social value on education, which makes children more eager to learn and easier to teach. Those who make this argument say it would of course be impossible to replicate such oriental magic in the West.

Yet the results of TIMSS suggest that this is, to put it mildly, exaggerated. If "culture" makes English children so poor at maths,

then why have they done so well at science (not far behind the Japanese and South Koreans)? And why do English pupils do well at science and badly at maths, while in France it is the other way around? A less mystical, more mundane explanation suggests itself: English schools teach science well and maths badly; French schools teach maths better than science; East Asian schools teach both subjects well.

Apart from casting doubt on some widely-held beliefs, do international comparisons have anything constructive to say? So far, the conclusions are tentative, but some answers are emerging.

Teaching the teachers

As well as getting pupils to sit tests, the TIMSS researchers monitored the way lessons were taught in each country. Eventually this should point to which teaching method tends to be most successful, though the data are still being worked on. Meanwhile, other researchers have been searching for common factors among those countries whose schools seem to turn out well-educated pupils.

...nor does money 3
State spending per pupil*, $'000 PPP 1993

	TIMSS ranking Maths	Science
Switzerland	8	25
United States	28	17
Germany	23	18
Denmark	27	34
France	13	28
England †	25	10
Japan	3	3
South Korea	2	2
Czech Rep.	6	2
Hungary	14	9

Sources: TIMSS; OECD *Secondary †Average for whole of Britain

Julia Whitburn of Britain's National Institute of Economic and Social Research has studied the way maths is taught in Japan and Switzerland, two countries which are different in many ways but whose pupils seem to do consistently well at in the subject. She noted a number of common factors:
• Much more time is spent on the basics of arithmetic than on more general mathematical topics such as handling data;
• Pupils learn to do sums in their heads before they are taught to do them on paper; calculators are usually banned;
• Standardised teaching manuals, which are tested extensively in schools before being published, are used widely;
• A method known as "whole-class interactive teaching" is used widely. The teacher addresses the whole class at once, posing questions to pupils in turn, to ensure they are following the lesson. American and British schools have been criticised for letting pupils spend much of their time working in small groups, with the teacher rushing from one group to the next to see how they are doing. Ms Whitburn notes that in Japan and Switzerland this method is only used in teaching arts and crafts;
• Finally, great efforts are made to ensure that pupils do not fall behind. Those that do are given extra coaching.

Learning, though, is not a one-way street. Just as western countries are busy seeking to emulate Japanese schools, schools and universities in Japan are coming under pressure from employers to turn out workers with the sort of creativity and individuality that the Japanese associate with western education. And just as American and British politicians are demanding that schools copy their more successful oriental counterparts and set their pupils more homework, the South Korean government is telling schools to give pupils regular homework-free days, so they can spend more time with their families—just like western children. Perhaps in education there is such a thing as a happy medium.

Balancing act

How might the worldwide boom in foreign direct investment affect international trade flows—and the political tensions those movements cause?

TRADE figures are among the most politically sensitive statistics around. In the late 1980s and early 1990s Japan's colossal trade surpluses were regularly paraded as evidence of Japanese economic ascendancy. America's unbroken 21-year string of trade deficits is routinely presented as evidence of the country's economic weakness.

Many critics expected the worldwide growth in foreign direct investment to aggravate these "problems". Total flows of direct investment doubled, to $315 billion, between 1991 and 1995. In the United States, opponents of the North American Free-Trade Agreement, signed in 1994, feared a "giant sucking sound" as domestic manufacturers served American customers from new plants in low-wage Mexico. Politicians in many developed countries worried that the sharp rise in investment in China would trigger a flood of imported consumer goods.

So far, the critics have been wrong. As foreign direct investment has soared, trade has become more balanced, not less so (see chart). Although America's trade deficit is much the same in dollar terms as it was in the late 1980s, it is only 2.5% of GDP, compared with 3.4% in 1987. But Japan's trade surplus, which peaked at 4.7% of GDP in 1986, is now less than 2%. Why is trade seemingly moving closer to balance? One important reason, according to an article in the OECD's *Economic Outlook*, published last month, is a change in the ways in which companies make investments in foreign countries.

The OECD's economists studied the behaviour of American and Japanese companies that invest in factory equipment and property or take large stakes in existing businesses outside their home countries. They found basic differences in the way those different nations' companies have planned their strategies. Those differences, it turns out, account for much of the recent change in the flow of trade.

American companies invest abroad mainly to serve foreign markets, rather than to produce finished or partly finished goods to ship back home. In 1992, about two-thirds of the sales of American companies' foreign subsidiaries took place in the regions in which they were based. In Europe, this share has been pretty static since the early 1980s. American companies' affiliates in Asia increasingly serve that region's markets. Asia ac-

ECONOMICS FOCUS

counted for 62% of those affiliates' sales in 1992, up from 41% in 1982.

Only in Canada and Mexico is there much evidence that American companies are investing to serve the American market. American-owned factories in these countries made 26% of their sales in the United States in 1992, up from 18% in 1982. That ratio may have increased further since the North American free-trade deal took effect in 1995.

Japanese companies, by contrast, are increasingly looking homeward as they

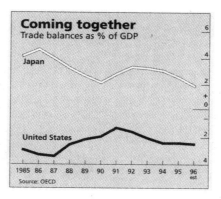

Coming together
Trade balances as % of GDP

Japan

United States

1985 86 87 88 89 90 91 92 93 94 95 96 est
Source: OECD

expand overseas. About 10% of Japanese-owned companies' total output took place outside Japan in 1995, compared with only 4% in 1986. Almost everything that Japanese companies make in America is sold there. But the Asian subsidiaries of Japanese companies have been exporting a growing proportion of their wares to Japan. Japanese sales accounted for 16% of the total turnover of Asian affiliates in 1992, compared with only 11% a decade before.

The OECD's economists argue that this shift in the nature of Japanese foreign investment will have durable effects on the country's trade patterns. Imports from foreign subsidiaries now account for 14% of all Japanese imports; in 1992, they were worth only 4%. As a proportion of GDP, imports of goods and services have risen from 9% in mid-1992 to 12% in mid-1996. Imports of consumer goods from Japanese-owned factories in Asia account for much of the increase.

How does all this translate into trade statistics? In principle, foreign investment can affect exports and imports in a

number of ways, depending on the precise circumstances. Suppose, for instance, that a firm builds a factory abroad from which it will serve local markets. Sales from that factory could supplant exports from the home country, cutting the trade surplus or increasing the deficit. Or the sales could be entirely new, and therefore have no direct effect on the trade balance.

Trade's tricky arithmetic

There are other complications. Firms often rely on home-country partners to build their overseas factories, so construction of the foreign factory might raise exports of construction materials or machinery. And once the factory is up and running, some components or half-finished goods may be exported from home for assembly abroad. Or investment might not be in a factory, but in a distribution system. If the system is a successful one, exports to the foreign market will increase.

But foreign investment can also be a base for production for the home market. It may simply be cheaper to produce overseas than at home: wages may be lower, after taking differences in productivity into account; or foreign governments may levy lower taxes or provide investment incentives. Such investment is far more likely to increase the home country's imports and reduce its exports, because foreign production is a substitute for producing at home. The migration of Japanese factories to South-East Asia, whence goods are sent to Japan as well as the rest of the world, is an example of exactly this.

The OECD's economists reckon that this change in the nature of Japanese foreign investment appears to have made Japanese imports more responsive to changes in import prices. Thus smaller increases in the value of the yen should be needed to bring about a given increase in imports. This means that large Japanese trade surpluses may be less persistent than they have been in the past.

Whether the changes in the pattern of Japanese foreign direct investment are permanent, of course, remains to be seen. A weaker yen, for instance, might eventually shift some Japanese production from South-East Asia back to Japan—just as a strong yen made foreign production attractive in the first place. But even if changing investment patterns do rein in trade imbalances, they are unlikely to calm politicians' nerves about trade disputes for good.

The International Environment: Organizations and Monetary Systems

- International Organizations (Articles 9 and 10)
- International Monetary System and Balance of Payments (Articles 11 and 12)

One of the most obvious features of international trade has been the development of international trade organizations. Some of these organizations have existed for several decades, while others are very new. They all have several things in common. The first is that while there have been some global agreements, such as the General Agreement on Tariffs and Trade (GATT) and the World Trade Organization (WTO), most of the trade organizations tend to be regional. The European Union (EU), which was known as the European Economic Community or Common Market until 1994, the North American Free Trade Agreement (NAFTA), and the Asia Pacific Economic Cooperation forum (APEC) are three of the more obvious examples.

The second common bond is that trade organizations involve nations in a sort of customs union, which tends to lower and/or remove trade barriers among its members while maintaining, at a somewhat higher level, trade restrictions for products and services from outside the association.

A few trade organizations, such as the EU, also have political ambitions of uniting the member countries into a political union. The headquarters of EU is located in Brussels, Belgium. One of the problems that EU has had over the years has been the struggle over sovereignty among the countries making up the union and its centralized government in Brussels.

One recently developed trade organization is the North American Free Trade Agreement (NAFTA), a trading agreement between the United States, Canada, and Mexico that took effect in January 1994. NAFTA was built on an agreement that was in force for several years between the United States and Canada. That agreement essentially removed the vast majority of trade barriers between these two countries. NAFTA included Mexico in the deal. This was not accomplished without great struggle in the U.S. Congress or without second thoughts, especially when the Mexican economy crashed shortly after U.S. ratification of the agreement in late 1993.

NAFTA does broaden opportunities for all businesses involved. However, one major problem is going to be the integrating of Mexico, a country that for decades has seemed to be on the verge of joining the developed world, into a union with Canada and the United States. Integrating the Canadian and U.S. economies is a relatively simple task: The legal systems are based on the same philosophy of law; the most-used language is the same; the political systems are very similar; many U.S. and Canadian firms are already doing substantial business in each other's countries; and the standard of living, while not exactly the same, is certainly comparable. Mexico, however, is a very different story: The legal system is based on a whole different philosophy of law; the language is different; it has one-party rule; the standard of living is very different; and in Mexico, much of the business activity is aimed at export to the United States. Still, economically, geographically, or politically, it does not make sense to exclude Mexico from economic integration with the rest of North America. The difficulty arises in how to do it.

Another recent development in world trade has been the creation of the World Trade Organization (WTO). The WTO was created as a result of the Uruguay Round (1986–1993) of the GATT talks and in many ways supersedes GATT. Many challenges face the WTO. One of the first challenges is the trading conflict between the United States and Japan over automobiles. This conflict has been going on for over 25 years, and it is part of a larger balance of trade problem between the two countries. Much of the conflict is not to be found in official gov-

ernment policy, but in the way individual firms do business, something that has always been difficult to control and will surely prove a thorny problem for the WTO.

Financial markets have always been a major cause of concern for organizations engaged in world trade. Financial markets, along with the International Monetary Fund (IMF) and the World Bank, were the major focus of the Bretton Woods Agreement at the end of World War II. But the financial markets aspect of the agreement failed, and while the IMF and the World Bank have continued in their missions, the value of currencies has been unhitched and been allowed to float. This has led banks and other international financial institutions to seek greater cooperation and stability in the world monetary markets. It also led to the recognition that world trade conditions were fluid and subject to change, and that a mechanism was needed to help deal with the inherent risks associated with that change. Such a mechanism was found in the international market for currencies and the associated markets, such as derivatives, that have developed over the years. It is difficult to say what will happen in the future concerning the international monetary systems. Some possible solutions are outlined in the articles "The Great Escape" and "International Banking: Coping with the Ups and Downs."

Looking Ahead: Challenge Questions

Describe the role of international trade organizations. Do you think they help or hinder world trade? Why?

Describe some efforts to stabilize world monetary markets.

What do you think will happen in the future concerning international money systems?

Riding the Dragon

Around the Pacific Rim, a new kind of power is emerging. APEC, the region's biggest trade network, can now influence more than half the world's economic production. The question is—will APEC make that production sustainable?

by Molly O'Meara

From *World Watch*, March/April 1997, pp. 8-18. © 1997 by the Worldwatch Institute. Reprinted by permission.

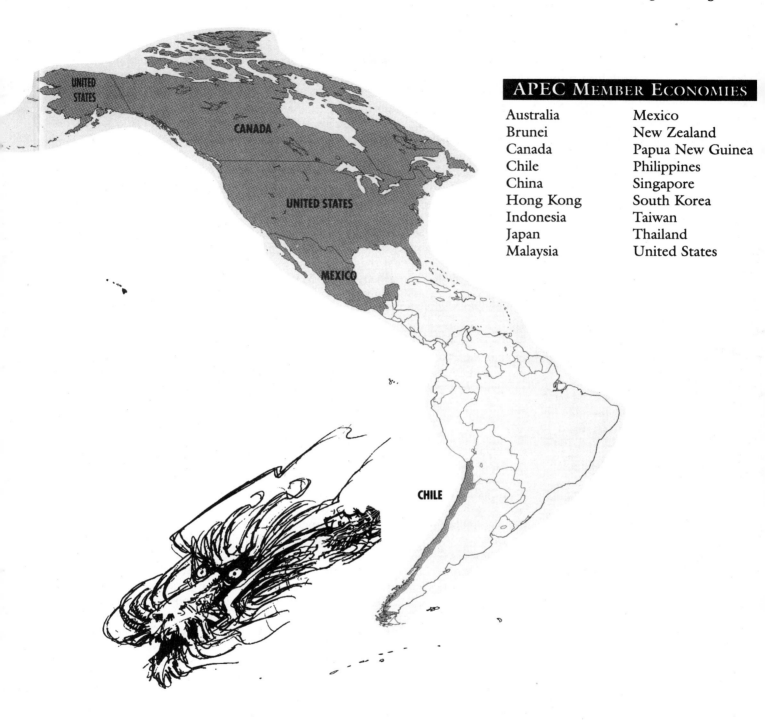

APEC MEMBER ECONOMIES

Australia	Mexico
Brunei	New Zealand
Canada	Papua New Guinea
Chile	Philippines
China	Singapore
Hong Kong	South Korea
Indonesia	Taiwan
Japan	Thailand
Malaysia	United States

"APEC Means Business!" Every few feet, it seemed, that slogan jumped from banners that lined the streets of Manila. The Philippines was hosting the 1996 meeting of the Asia Pacific Economic Cooperation forum, a loose conclave of 18 Pacific rim states—among them such economic giants as the United States, Japan, and China. To APEC's boosters, that slogan was a way of commending these annual meetings as a new paradigm in international negotiations—one that harnesses the private sector to achieve practical results. But in the mouths of critics, the slogan meant something very different. Many environmentalists, human rights advocates, and other activists see APEC as a dangerous new variation on an old theme: a collusion of big business and government that shuts social and environmental concerns out of the loop. In the debate surrounding the Manila meeting, from November 20 to 25, perhaps the only point of agreement was that APEC could be changing the nature of the trading game.

The Philippine government intended the APEC

meeting as a national "coming out" party. While many of its Southeast Asian neighbors had prospered during the 1980s, the Philippines had been mired in stagnant growth and burdened by runaway inflation. Frequent brown-outs plagued business and private life. But four years of economic reform under President Fidel Ramos had revived the economy, which grew by 7 percent in 1996. Foreign direct investment rose by 40 percent in the first half of that year; inflation had slowed to under 5 percent; and the lights were back on.

But the festivity in the streets was mingled with frustration. On Roxas Boulevard, the main route to the ministerial conference site, half the lanes had been reserved for the conference. On one side of the median, local traffic inched along in congestion even worse than usual; on the other side, in the nearly deserted "friendship lanes," a few shiny vehicles sped APEC visitors to their destinations. The highway between Manila and Subic Bay, where the heads of state were meeting, was lit by garlands of holiday lights—and by protestors who were burning Ramos and U.S. President Bill Clinton in effigy. The protestors' ire is not hard to understand: according to the government's own estimates, over a third of the population lives in poverty. Yet the country had just spent $15 million on cosmetic alterations for foreign visitors—a make-over that included the bulldozing of squatter settlements near the conference sites.

On the road to the summit, Ramos and Clinton burned in effigy.

My own excursions in and around Manila showed me a reality that seemed almost entirely divorced from APEC's rhetoric. An estimated 1 million vehicles already clog Manila's streets and that number is expected to double by 2002. The current level of congestion is already costing at least $51 million a year in wasted fuel. Manila's trademark "jeepneys" (converted U.S. army jeeps used now for public transport) are powered by inefficient, second-hand diesel engines that belch exhaust with health-threatening levels of pollutants. My taxis often crossed over the fetid Pasig River, which snakes through Manila, carrying much of the city's sewage and industrial waste into Manila Bay. Fishery yields in the bay have declined by 39 percent from 1975 to 1988; some 30,000 tons of dead fish washed ashore there about a month before the conference began. Thousands of squatter families who lack access to safe water make

their homes on the banks of the Pasig. The population of metropolitan Manila has ballooned from 1.5 million in 1950 to 8.9 million in 1990, an increase fed in part by the continual influx of migrants from the country's impoverished and environmentally degraded outer provinces.

It was against this backdrop that government officials, business leaders, and activists alike were all trying to articulate the long-term significance of APEC. How could the forum best foster trade and economic development in the Asia-Pacific region? And what will it mean for the region's already advanced state of environmental decay?

Avoiding "Euro-Sclerosis"

Every year, now, it seems that the APEC forum produces group photos of beaming presidents and prime ministers in local costume. But that simple, outward token of success belies the complexity within. APEC is a difficult creature to understand. Its structure grows more unwieldy every year and its acronym-rich language seems impenetrable—the Philippine government tried to decode it last year in an 83-page dictionary.

The reason for this complexity lies in APEC's unique history. APEC grew out of a set of less glamorous meetings convened by groups like the Pacific Basin Economic Council (PBEC), which was formed in the late 1960s and which continues to be important for business networking in the region. A more direct precursor is perhaps the Pacific Economic Cooperation Council (PECC), a forum set up in 1980 by academic economists and government officials to discuss trade and investment. In 1989, Bob Hawke, then Prime Minister of Australia, organized APEC to give these conversations a kind of official status. Hawke's original group consisted of Australia, New Zealand, Japan, South Korea, the United States, Canada, and the members of ASEAN. (ASEAN, the Association of Southeast Asian Nations, then included Brunei, Indonesia, Malaysia, the Philippines, Singapore, and Thailand. Vietnam has since joined.)

From its inception, then, APEC encompassed a huge range in level of development and wealth. The per capita GNP of Indonesia, for instance, is just $880, while Japan's is about $35,000. This disparity is largely responsible for APEC's amorphous structure, since ASEAN members initially feared that APEC would become a tool for strong-arming them in trade negotiations with the heavyweights. To coax them on board, Australian and Japanese diplomats had to assure them that APEC would be a purely consultative body, and that it would operate according to the model of consensus pioneered by ASEAN itself. This distaste for binding rules, along with the

Guide to APEC's "Ad-Hocracy"

APEC's fluid structure makes it difficult for NGOs to get a firm grip on forum activities. But all of the bodies on this chart are potential recipients of NGO input. For contact possibilities and conference schedules, check the Web sites in the Resources box.

AD-HOC INFORMAL LEADERS' MEETING

Ad-hoc Eminent Persons Group
(advisory panel of independent
economists, 1993-'95)

Official Ministerial (Foreign and Trade Ministers)*

*PECC, the Pacific
Economic Cooperation
Council, is the only
NGO granted official
observer status. It
can attend meetings
at the ministerial
level or at any of
the levels below.

Ad-hoc Special Ministerials
(includes Energy, Finance, Environment,
Sustainable Development)

Senior Officials' Meeting

Ad-hoc Expert Groups

3 Official Committees:

Budget & Administrative
Trade & Investment
Economic

APEC Business
Advisory Council

Ad-hoc Task Forces

10 Official
Working Groups:**
Trade Promotion
Human Resources Development
Fisheries
Tourism
Regional Energy Cooperation
Industrial Science & Technology
Telecommunications
Transportation
Marine Resource Conservation
Trade & Investment Data Review

**This is the only
area where a for-
mal process now
exists to channel
participation by
NGOs.

Expert Task Forces

links to business and academia, became hallmarks of the forum. In his book on APEC, *Asia Pacific Fusion*, Japanese journalist Yoichi Funabashi calls this approach the "APEC way."

The "APEC way" grew even broader in 1991, when South Korea scored a diplomatic coup with an agreement in which China, Taiwan, and Hong Kong joined APEC simultaneously. China tries to bar Taiwan's entry into all clubs of nations in which China is itself a member, but was placated by the notion that APEC members would be called "economies" rather than nations, that no national flags would be flown, and that Taiwan would use the alias "Chinese Taipei." Mexico and Papua New Guinea were added in 1993, and Chile was accepted a year later. By the time of the Manila meeting, 11 other countries were petitioning for membership, including Russia, Vietnam, and India.

> *Some supporters see the future of the world trading system in APEC ...*

The present roster accounts for 40 percent of the world's population, 46 percent of its exports, and 56 percent of its production. APEC includes the world's largest economies—the United States and Japan—as well as many of its fastest growing ones. Korea, Taiwan, Hong Kong, and Singapore have seen per capita income rise at an average rate of almost 7 percent per year during the past three decades. Indonesia, Malaysia, and Thailand have grown at an average annual rate of 6 percent over the past decade. And China's economy grew at 10 percent in 1995, its fourth straight year of double-digit growth.

As APEC grows, it is continually redefining itself. What began as a set of meetings among foreign and trade ministers has mushroomed to include the 10 working groups shown in the diagram on page 11. APEC is sometimes called an "ad-hocracy." It has not created its own huge pool of in-house experts, because participants want to avoid what they regard as the deadening effects of a rule-bound bureaucracy. In this connection, APEC supporters sometimes point to the European Union (EU) and speak of "Euro-sclerosis." Instead, APEC seeks advice from ad-hoc task forces, as well as from groups of economists, business people, and government officials. At the APEC forum in 1993, U.S. President Clinton added substantial weight to this ad-hoc approach when he invited his fellow heads of state to a casual gathering on Blake Island off the coast of Seattle, Washington. Meeting in seclusion and studied infor-

mality, the leaders pledged themselves to deepening their "spirit of community." The spirit of this first APEC leaders' meeting was encouraging but perhaps unconvincing, given the region's multiplicity of cultures and political systems, its ubiquitous trading frictions, and its territorial conflicts.

Indonesia's President Suharto repeated the Blake Island formula in 1994, when he played genial host to the region's leaders at Bogor Castle. Suharto, an army general who came to power nearly 30 years ago in a coup that left hundreds of thousands massacred, is a good symbol of the challenges that confront APEC's "spirit of community." Even so, leaders emerged from their retreat with a sense of economic—if not political—common ground. That summit produced the most specific goal to date: to achieve free trade throughout the vast Asia-Pacific region by the year 2020, although industrialized countries are supposed to reach the goal by 2010. In Osaka, Japan, in 1995, leaders agreed on an "action agenda" with two parts: measures for easing restrictions on trade and investment, and a plan for building cooperation in international development. The first part of the agenda deals with a fairly conventional range of trade issues, such as lowering tariffs, reducing market barriers, standardizing customs procedures, and streamlining visa procedures for business travel. But the less-publicized second part ventures into deeper water, to attack problems that underlie regional inequities. It calls for such measures as an analysis of regional labor markets, the sharing of ideas on how to encourage private investment in infrastructure projects, and the transfer of new energy technologies.

Progress on the second—development—part of the agenda has thus far been largely a matter of "nuts and bolts" projects, which are put together by the working groups. By the time of the Manila meeting, 320 joint activities were underway, including regularly updated reports on telecommunications regulations in each economy, a Who's Who of fisheries inspectors, and a database on small business statistics. Increasingly, these projects are inspiring government-industry seminars, training sessions, and international exchanges.

For the first—free trade—part of its agenda, APEC's approach has been to seek progress not through painstaking negotiations, but through peer pressure. In Manila, for example, each country put forth its own non-binding plan of action. Delegates learned of China's pledge to allow foreign securities firms to establish branches on its territory by 2000. They heard Singapore vow to break up its telecommunications monopoly by 2000, and the Philippines promise to reduce import tariffs to 5 percent on everything but agricultural products by 2004. There was a set of collective agreements as well. All members agreed, for instance, to contribute to a customs and tariff database which is supposed to be available on the Internet sometime this year.

The aggregate effect of these plans should be to accelerate the push for free trade well beyond the schedule that member nations have already committed themselves to at the World Trade Organization (WTO), the 128-member body set up in Geneva by the General Agreement on Tariffs and Trade (GATT). And in fact, the Manila agreement that got the most media attention was a decision to press the WTO to accelerate its own schedule. APEC has asked the WTO to eliminate by 2000 most tariffs on information technologies, such as computer chips or software.

In pursuit of its vision, APEC has been courting industry at the highest levels. Hundreds of executives were lured to an APEC Business Forum last year in Manila, where President Ramos, exulting in what he called a "sea of happy CEO faces," exclaimed: "Before APEC, it was business that linked the region." Academic economists also haunt APEC. The forum's free trade blueprint was laid out by the ad-hoc Eminent Persons Group, an assembly of independent "wisemen," many of them PECC economists. Led by C. Fred Bergsten, Director of the Institute of International Economics, a Washington-based think tank, the group met from 1993 to 1995. Its vision of a diverse, competitive membership committed to "open regionalism" (an interest in lowering trade barriers for non-member states) was calculated to secure a global role for APEC. In a recent issue of *Foreign Affairs*, Bergsten argued that global free trade could make all countries richer by spurring competition, and could save regional trade organizations such as the EU and NAFTA (the North American Free Trade Agreement between Canada, the United States, and Mexico) from becoming hostile blocs. APEC's approach, in Bergsten's view, puts it "in a strong position to assume leadership of the global trading system."

Is APEC Accountable?

APEC's leadership potential is exactly what worries many of its critics. In the Philippines, for the first time in APEC's history, criticism from the "third sector"—nongovernmental organizations focused on environmental and social problems—reached a thunderous volume. NGOs had tried to make themselves heard at the 1994 APEC meeting in Indonesia, but were denied a permit to meet and had to relocate to Thailand. At the 1995 forum in Japan, NGOs drew closer to the process by gathering in Kyoto, one hour by car from the official meetings in Osaka. In Manila, four parallel forums confronted the official meetings with tactics ranging from pickets to a policy dialogue. The direct successor to the Kyoto conference, the Manila People's Forum, criticized APEC on several

fronts but made its biggest headlines when the government interfered with its plans to highlight regional human rights problems. Among the speakers invited to the Forum was the Indonesian activist José Ramos-Horta, who recently won the Nobel Peace Prize for his crusade against human rights violations in East Timor, which Indonesia invaded in 1975. When the Philippines refused him entry, it created a media furor. Two other NGO conferences condemned APEC in its entirety; one of these was organized by labor unions and held in an abandoned factory to symbolize the effects of economic globalization on workers. Finally, representatives of a huge network of Philippine NGOs managed to discuss their concerns directly with President Ramos.

As I watched events at the Manila People's Forum unfold, I was reminded of an observation made by U.S. scholars Robin Broad and John Cavanagh in their book on the Philippines, *Plundering Paradise*. They likened Filipino activists to a local dessert called *halo-halo*, an unlikely mélange of ice cream, ice, fruits, gelatin, and corn—ingredients that "take on a surprisingly enticing flavor when combined. Like *halo-halo*, in union these groups become something more than the sum of their parts." In Manila, Filipino NGOs combined with their foreign counterparts to create something of a deluxe halo-halo of public concern about APEC—about what they saw as the forum's lack of transparency and the consequences of APEC-led free trade for human rights, women's rights, the welfare of workers, cultural survival, and environmental health.

Among these skeptics was New Zealand law professor Jane Kelsey, who cited the lack of regular channels for citizen input as evidence that APEC is the most "anti-democratic, secret, invisible and inaccessible" trade regime yet devised—far more so than NAFTA or the EU. Walden Bello, a professor at the University of the Philippines, pointed out that the United States is supporting APEC as part of its campaign to open markets and reduce trade deficits with Asian countries. He and some of his colleagues fear that the U.S. brand of rapid, "cowboy-style" trade liberalization would benefit global corporations at the expense of local enterprises. Broad and her husband Cavanagh, who has written a book on multinationals, coauthored a speech in which they noted that of the 100 largest economic units in the world, only 49 are

... and so do some critics, who question APEC's accountability.

countries; 51 are corporations. Many APEC skeptics, echoing Kelsey's point, argued that the multinational corporations promoted by APEC are even less accountable than APEC itself.

Concerns about globalization were perhaps most vividly expressed by Ian Fry of Greenpeace Australia, who took off his shoe to make his point: "This is an example of globalization," he said. "Somewhere in Brazil or Australia, erosion is caused by grazing cows to produce the leather for my shoe. A river in maybe Thailand was polluted by the manufacturing of the rubber sole, and it was put together by cheap labor in China. You see why this shoe was cheap: I did not pay for the environmental and social damage that was caused by its production."

Given regional trends, these concerns are not just matters for academic debate. APEC countries contain 10 of the world's 15 largest cities: Tokyo, New York, Mexico City, Shanghai, Los Angeles, Beijing, Seoul, Jakarta, Osaka, and Tianjin. If India succeeds in its membership bid, Bombay and Calcutta will be added to that list. Increasingly, from Los Angeles to Tianjin, urban demand for water is competing with agricultural needs. Disease and social problems associated with urban crowding are likely to grow more acute in many of the region's cities, and urban pollution is generally worsening. The World Health Organization ranks Xian, Shanghai, Guangzhou, Bangkok, Kuala Lumpur, Seoul, and Manila among the worst cities in the world for air pollution. In the countryside, rapacious deforestation continues apace. Asia is losing forest area more rapidly than any other region in the world; one study has estimated that a continuation of present trends would eliminate all of the region's remaining tropical timber in less than 40 years.

The region also has a gargantuan appetite for fossil fuels. It is home to the top two greenhouse gas emitters, the United States and China, as well as Japan, which ranks as number four. APEC energy ministers have noted with alarm that by 2010, regional electricity demand is projected to increase by 50 to 80 percent. Present energy consumption is thought to be growing by around 2.2 percent per year, compared with only 1 percent for the industrialized nations of the Organisation for Economic Cooperation and Development (OECD).

One type of pollution—toxic waste—is actually being brought into the region as a form of trade. Recycling plants in Thailand and the Philippines, for instance, accept shipments of electronics scrap or lead-acid batteries from the United States, the world's largest producer of hazardous waste. Studies done by Greenpeace have shown that many of these facilities are not equipped to deal with the material safely. A United Nations report has documented instances of "South-South" trade in toxic trash as well: Singapore, for example, has shipped hazardous waste to Thailand. And while there is growing international trend toward banning "North-South" trade in toxics, no such effort is underway for "South-South" trade. Given the rates of development in the Asia-Pacific, that could be a loophole with enormous potential.

Building an Environmental Agenda

There are signs that APEC is preparing to address at least some of the concerns raised by its critics. The environment is especially likely to get attention, since there seems to be an emerging consensus that environmental degradation is a drag on the region's economic development. Among the most visible signs of hope in this connection have been the announcements of the leaders themselves. Unlike more formal summits, where communiqués are usually hammered out well ahead of time, APEC leaders' statements can still surprise. Their initiatives on free trade, for example, are the stuff of diplomatic legend: in 1993, APEC leaders spurred the closure of the contentious "Uruguay Round" of negotiations on the GATT, and in 1994 they made headlines with their vow to achieve free trade in the Asia-Pacific.

On the environmental front, several leaders, including Canada's Prime Minister Jean Chrétien, the Philippines' President Ramos, and U.S. Vice President Al Gore, have been promoting a vision of "sustainable development" since that first leaders' meeting at Blake Island. Following the 1996 conference, a Philippine newspaper noted that the leaders' declaration—sprinkled with phrases like "giving a human face to development"—read "more like a United Nations document than a statement by the world's most powerful and promising economies committed to free trade."

And there's growing evidence that the leadership pronouncements on sustainable development are not merely some sort of "greenwash." Environmental awareness appears to be seeping into a broad range of APEC activities, although it's still too early to look for much in the way of concrete achievement. In 1994, for the first time, environment officials were pulled into the orbit of APEC conferences. But rather than delegate environmental concerns to a single body, leaders have asked all of APEC's organs to report on their work towards the "overarching goal" of sustainable development. That requirement has had a practical effect on a wide range of working group activities. The transportation working group, for instance, is now producing an inventory of the region's oil spill preparedness. The fisheries working group is training local farmers in sustainable shrimp culture, and the economics committee is attempting to analyze how population and economic growth will increase the demand for food and energy, as well as the pressures on the environment.

APEC held its first major "sustainable development" conference in Manila this past July, as a lead-up to the November summit. Delegates managed to agree on three general goals for top priority: sustainable cities, cleaner industries, and a sustainably managed marine environment. There was no agreement to give a similarly high profile to many other critical areas. For example, agriculture and forestry failed to make it onto the list. Logging, subsidies for domestic crop production, and other politically sensitive issues are making these areas stumbling blocks in APEC's trade discussions too. They have not even been given their own working groups (see the diagram on page 51). But participants hope that a partial and pragmatic environmental agenda will still allow for progress. Current efforts are focused on how these goals can be used to "add value" to existing environmental accords.

The potential of the cleaner industries initiative has been championed by Greg Mertz, Senior Counsel for Trade and Environment at the U.S. Environmental Protection Agency. According to the EPA, the widespread adoption of already existing cleaner technologies could yield major progress in a wide range of industries, including textiles, pulp and paper, electronics, and petroleum refining. For example, in electronics manufacturing—a rapidly expanding sector that is already a focus for APEC—toxic solvents can threaten factory workers, and communities in general if the ground water becomes contaminated. In the United States, the industry has responded to these problems with a set of innovations, such as better air filters in factories, and redesigned production processes to eliminate the need for certain chemicals. If these technologies were in global use, they could greatly advance international efforts to counter persistent organic pollutants.

Bergsten's group of economists had used the "value added" approach on a much more basic level as early as 1994. The group recommended the sharing of environmentally friendly technologies, advancing the principle of internalizing environmental costs (as Greenpeace's Fry was suggesting), promoting environmentally sound development projects, and harmonizing environmental standards which could affect such areas as air and water quality.

The standards issue has captured the imagination of Lyuba Zarsky, who directs the Berkeley-based Nautilus Institute for Security and Sustainable Development, a think tank that has taken the lead in researching APEC's environmental agenda. Zarsky argues that in any given industry, businesses competing for the largest markets tend to work with roughly similar environmental standards—usually the lowest standards that will meet the demands of those markets. And policy makers, generally focused on the short-term needs of their national industries, are often reluctant to upgrade standards unilaterally. Such a move, they fear, could divert scarce investment dollars or increase costs of production. APEC, Zarsky thinks, could break this impasse. She believes that APEC's primary goal should be to set high environmental benchmarks, which could be continually revised upwards. She sees such an opportunity, for instance, in the sustainable cities goal set in Manila. APEC could ensure that a host of standards affecting cities—including auto emissions, energy efficiency, and water treatment—are harmonized in ways that promote not only commercial but also ecological objectives. The same approach might allow for progress in the marine initiative as well. Zarsky thinks that APEC might be able to set standards for coastal management—a move that might help save rapidly disappearing mangrove stands and reduce land-based marine pollution.

Given the dismal environmental trends that afflict the region—and the power that many of the biggest and dirtiest industries have over national governments—APEC's future as an environmental boon is hardly assured. But many analysts regard "the APEC way" as the best available strategy. It is clear, in any case, that heavy reliance on the enormous WTO is probably not a prescription for success. In December 1996, the WTO's Committee on Trade and Environment, which had been locked for two years in disagreements between richer and poorer countries, finally delivered a weak report that did little to put international trade on a more sustainable footing. And the WTO's general effectiveness in Asia is still uncertain, because China's application for membership has not yet been accepted.

Regional trade agreements seem to offer more immediate opportunities for progress. The obvious precedent is NAFTA, which was the first trade agreement among countries of widely varying income levels to include environmental provisions. All three of the nations involved pledged not to lower their environmental standards to attract investment, and to enforce their own environmental laws while still adhering to free trade rules. During the NAFTA negotiations, critics of the agreement argued that NAFTA would tend to shift production from Canada and the United States to Mexico, where environmental and labor standards are easier to flout, and in some respects, those predictions have proved accurate. But much of this movement might have occurred even without NAFTA, and the agreement's supporters argue that the treaty's environmental and labor side agreements succeeded in wringing some benefit from the inevitable. Even if NAFTA were an unqualified success, however, its rule-bound approach would probably prove impractical in the immense Asia-Pacific region, where economic and cultural disparities are even greater than in North America. The APEC way, with its focus on cooperation, attempts in effect to make a virtue of necessity.

NGO Apathy

Over the next 15 years, growing energy demand in the Asia-Pacific region will probably require an investment of some $1.6 trillion in energy infrastructure. Much of this money is expected to come from the private sector through "build-operate-transfer" agreements, in which private companies build and operate powerplants; governments guarantee them a return on their investments; and the facilities are eventually incorporated into local electric utilities. The APEC energy working group is already attempting to educate officials in several countries on the potential of solar technologies. But at present, it's the big, wealthy fossil-fuel and nuclear industries that are winning the infrastructure bids. It would be possible to identify a similar predicament on almost any environmental front in the region. And APEC's growing ability to increase trade and investment is almost certainly going to make those predicaments worse, unless APEC's environmental agenda begins to gather force quickly.

Probably the only way to build an effective social and environmental agenda for APEC is to engage "third sector" NGOs. That's why the Manila NGO conferences were such an encouraging development. The conferences may serve as a useful precedent for NGOs elsewhere in Asia—even NGOs from countries that discourage such activities may be able to participate in international forums. Efforts at Manila began at a fairly advanced level because some Philippine NGOs had already forged a working relationship with the Ramos administration on sustainable development policies. At the helm of this movement is Nicky Perlas, director of the Philippine Center for Alternative Development Initiatives. Perlas says the biggest political achievement that he has seen during his 25 years in the environmental movement came last September, when Ramos authorized a plan known as "Philippines Agenda 21." Named after the famous plan of action produced at the Rio "Earth Summit" in 1992, the document was created with NGO guidance, and it attempts to reconcile economic development with the need to stabilize the country's various ecosystems. It takes precedence over the country's more conventional economic plan, "Philippines 2000," which has been circulating in one form or another since Ramos came to power in 1992. (Currently, at least 17 countries have their own Agenda 21s.)

It was clear during the Manila forum that Ramos was taking his commitment seriously. At one point, in the midst of his duties as host to the heads of state

assembled at Subic Bay, Ramos helicoptered back into the city to meet with some 150 NGO representatives at the presidential palace. The meeting, which had been arranged by Perlas and his colleagues, was intended to be a half-hour discussion of sustainable development. But it lasted over two hours. Ramos, who has announced a slew of initiatives to transform the Philippines into a "green tiger," seemed to be listening to the NGOs with real interest. (Presumably, since the Philippines has a single-term presidency, he is not seeking future votes.) Afterwards, he marked up the NGO declaration with instructions to his cabinet ministers and assured the group that their concerns would be conveyed to the prime ministers and presidents awaiting him in Subic. And indeed, much of the sustainable development language in last year's APEC documents apparently came from Ramos' meeting with the NGOs.

Despite the successes at Manila, most of APEC's "nuts and bolts" work is done between summits—not during them. Even among those NGOs following the summits, few pay attention to the forum the rest of the time, and that limits their influence. Another impediment is the novel structure of APEC itself. The Nautilus Institute's Zarsky says that both NGO and government officials often "simply don't know where or what to grab on to." Zarsky has encountered the problem first-hand, while traveling around the region engaging her counterparts in APEC-related dialogue. Her efforts landed her—quite by chance, as she tells the story—on the official U.S. delegation to that first ministerial meeting on sustainable development last July. "When I asked if they had made any arrangements for NGO participation, they invited me on the spot!" At the November summit, Zarsky's director of environmental programs, Jason Hunter, summed up the confusion when he said with undisguised puzzlement, "the government people are looking to us for help."

Another major obstacle to building a "third sector" in APEC is the curious apathy of most potential U.S. participants. Even though the United States is teeming with environmental NGOs, few have taken an interest in APEC. Rodrigo Prudencio, who coordinates the trade and environment program at the National Wildlife Federation, laments the common U.S. tendency to see APEC in terms of NAFTA—to assume that since APEC isn't getting the same kind of continual high-level political attention that NAFTA got, it isn't going anywhere. But of course, NAFTA is a treaty. APEC is not, and making it work requires a very different sort of effort. Prudencio fears that the failure to make this distinction is keeping U.S. NGOs offstage, waiting for a kind of political moment that may be many years off.

Danny Kennedy, a former adviser to Greenpeace Australia, calls the lack of interest among powerful

U.S. environmental groups "pitiful," given the urgent need for watchdog activity. A good example, says Kennedy, involves APEC energy ministers and the forum's Regional Energy Cooperation working group, all of whom are being watched by an NGO coalition organized by Australia's Climate Action Network. The working group is attempting to encourage heavier investment in renewable energy. But Australia is trying to use its influence as the current "shepherd" of this working group to promote its low-sulfur coal exports—a fact publicized by the NGO coalition.

Outside the NGO community, APEC continues to gather strength. Maurice Strong, the Canadian businessman who chaired the Earth Summit, recently pointed out a fact that is obvious but easy to forget: the key environmental stewards are not environmentalists, but the government and business leaders who manage the world's economies. These elites are already well represented in APEC, where they are influencing various unpublicized "technical" decisions—decisions that will eventually exert a profound influence on the region. This year, for instance, the energy working group will begin to discuss harmonizing energy efficiency standards for appliances; those standards will help determine the region's energy demand. Also this year, the transportation working group hopes to reach a consensus on automobile manufacturing standards. According to Kennedy, the working group is considering whether to make U.S. auto emissions standards the regional norm. But in the United States, car exhaust remains a major source of air pollution; "freezing" standards at current U.S. levels might actually increase the regulatory obstacles to further improvement.

Vancouver, Canada will be the venue of the leaders' summit this November, and Canada has already begun to host a formidable series of preliminary meetings. The schedule includes, for example, high-level conferences on energy and the environment. Another conference will explore the relationships among a set of basic trends: food demand, economic growth, energy needs, environmental problems, and population growth. (For more information, see the Web sites below.) Last year, Canadian officials pledged to look more closely into the environmental consequences of the region's growing economic integration. These meetings present an important opportunity to hold them to that promise, and to strengthen APEC's environmental agenda. That opportunity is not likely to repeat itself in the following year, since Malaysia, APEC's 1998 host, does not have a strong NGO tradition.

Perhaps the most urgent problem humanity faces is the task of reconciling the global economy with the natural world that ultimately sustains it. It is not yet clear what role APEC will play in the search for a solution. But given the size and wealth of the Asia-Pacific region, there is little hope of succeeding without it.

Molly O'Meara is a staff researcher at the Worldwatch Institute.

Resources

APEC Secretariat, 438 Alexandria Road, #14-01/04, Alexandria Point, Singapore 119958, telephone: 011 65 2761880, fax: 65 2761775, Internet: http://www.apecsec.org.sg.

Nautilus Institute for Security and Sustainable Development, 1831 Second St., Berkeley, CA 94710, USA, telephone: (510) 204-9296, fax: (510) 204-9298, Asia Pacific Regional Environment Network on the Internet: http://www.nautilus.org/aprenet.

Yoichi Funabashi, *Asia Pacific Fusion: Japan's Role in APEC* (Washington, DC: Institute for International Economics, 1995).

Challenges in Managing Technology in Transnational Multipartner Networks

John W. Medcof

T he high-profile establishment of research and development labs in the United States by leading high-tech Japanese companies signals a growing trend. Ever more R&D labs, such as NEC's lab at Princeton and Mitsubishi's at Cambridge, are being established by multinational corporations outside their home countries. The proportion of R&D conducted abroad varies with the home country of the firm. Japanese firms do relatively little; American firms, an intermediate amount; firms from some European countries conduct more than 70 percent of their R&D outside the home country. Although the majority of companies still prefer to keep most of their R&D at home, the trend toward establishing labs abroad is expected to continue into the foreseeable future. By the end of the 1980s, a number of organizations had developed sophisticated systems for managing networks of wholly owned R&D facilities spread over a number of countries. Such wholly owned networks can be called internal technology networks because, although they are transnational, each is internal to a single firm.

At the same time, however, another trend in technology management was beginning to attract attention: the proliferation of inter-organization collaborations for technology development and related purposes. Such collaborations have taken a number of forms, including operating joint ventures, research contracts, collaborative R&D, technology licensing, and agreements with universities and government agencies. Often they are called alliances, but when they include a number of cooperating partners they may also be called networks. Here we will call them external technology networks to distinguish them from wholly owned, internal networks.

Much has been written about managing collaborations. Most authors, though acknowledging that collaborations may involve multiple partners, couch their advice primarily in terms of dealing with a single partner. Michael Wolff (1994), editor of *Research-Technology Management*, points out that many writers who offer advice on collaboration management use the analogy of marriage, a two-partner proposition. However, collaborations involving multiple participants might more aptly be compared to communes, whose members are constantly changing.

Managing technology in external networks is a much more complex activity than that envisioned by those who think only in terms of internal technology networks or single-partner collaborations. Consider the following: At the simplest level, a firm can manage technology with one lab, wholly owned and located in the home country. A level of complexity is added if the firm creates an internal technology network consisting of a number of labs located in a number of countries. Collaboration with one other firm further complicates the picture. If the organization then joins one external network, the situation becomes yet more complex—and more complex again if it is involved in a number of them, simultaneously, and in succession (see **Figure 1**).

> *Organizations must meet technological challenges in ways that give maximum return from individual collaborations and help prepare them for the networked world of the future.*

From *Business Horizons*, January/February 1996, pp. 47-54. © 1996 by the Foundation for the School of Business at Indiana University. Reprinted by permission.

Figure 1
Levels of Complexity in Technology Collaboration and Networks

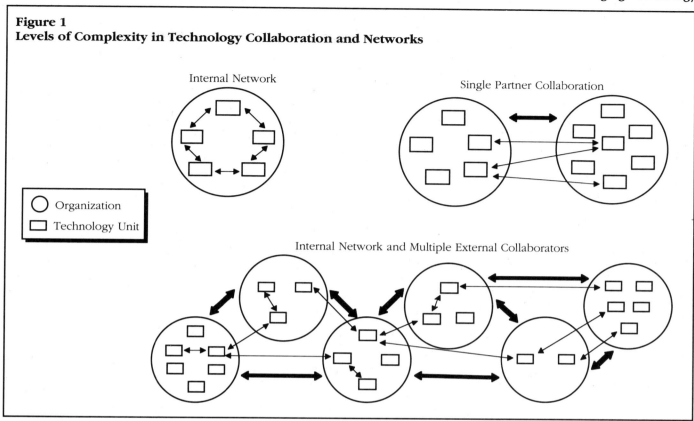

Because external networks will be with us for the foreseeable future, and will play an increasingly important role in the global management of technology, organizations should have long-term strategies for external network participation. Such strategies should envision what the networked world of the future will be like, and consequent planning and decision making should move companies toward a form that will be compatible with that vision. Unfortunately, much of what has been written about network management tends to see it primarily as a process of building out from, or adding on to, current management practice. This approach has its validity, for experience is a valuable teacher. However, it should not preclude a sense of working *toward* a vision of the future.

The management challenges presented by participation in a number of external networks, simultaneously and successively, are a quantum leap above those presented by internal technology networks and single-partner collaborations. In exploring those challenges, this article will attempt to envision how they can be met in a way that positions an organization most effectively for the networked future. The challenges will be presented under six headings: information technology infrastructure, organizational culture, disclosure policies, human resources, strategic networking, and harmonization with networks.

Information Technology Infrastructure

Advice about managing collaborations generally addresses the importance of good communication, but varies in the importance it gives to communication using information technology (IT). Advice on single-partner collaborations tends to emphasize face-to-face communication and the development of "chemistry" among people from the two organizations. It pays relatively little attention to communication using IT. Advice about internal technology networks generally recommends a substantial amount of face-to-face communication supplemented by an IT infrastructure. Such writers stress that IT is important but cannot substitute for face-to-face contact. Those who discuss external networks primarily stress the importance of IT communications, with little mention of face-to-face contact.

External technology networks are a particular variant of "virtual corporations," which many observers consider the management form of tomorrow. Byrne (1993) defines virtual corporations as temporary networks of independent companies linked by IT to share skills, costs, and access to one another's markets. They tend to evolve in form because they are created to exploit evolving opportunities. IT communication links—electronic mail, EDI, video-conferencing, networked CAD/CAM systems, virtual LAN services, groupware—make virtual corporations possible. But because they are constantly evolving, their IT networks need to be flexible.

External networks come into being when collaborating firms find they have common interests. In such cases, there may be significant incompatibilities among IT systems. Bridging those incompatibilities, and planning around the ones that cannot be bridged, can be a major headache. In the short to middle term, the challenge for the management of IT in external technology networks is to build a system that is able to link a number of partners, flexible enough to be adapted quickly and inexpensively to each of their IT systems, and yet capable of providing appropriate protection of proprietary information. Motorola, for example, is building what it calls X-LANS, external local area networks designed to handle data communications among company divisions as well as among alliance partners. Such corporations are preparing for the networked world of the future, in which a single IT network is permanently shared by all firms. With such a network, collaboration with a number of other firms would involve simple "hook-ups," rather than the introduction of hardware or software to bridge the various incompatibilities. Compatibility, in effect, will be a given.

Organizations that plan to participate fully in this future networked world need to think seriously about the likely form of the single, universal IT system. They need to think about how they can develop their own systems to be compatible with it and how they can influence its development. This influence will help align the universal system with the best interests of the firm.

Organizational Culture

Organizational culture is a crucial determinant of the success of any firm or partnership. But it is particularly so in external technology networks, which involve people from different countries, firms, and functional areas (such as marketing and R&D). Great potential exists for dysfunctions caused by differences in national, organizational, and functional cultures. In fact, note Forrest and Martin (1992), executives commonly blame cultural differences for network failures.

A select-and-bridge strategy is usually recommended for the management of culture in single-partner collaborations. This means making cultural compatibility a prime criterion for partner selection and then working to smooth over, or bridge, whatever cultural gap does occur. The more successful the selection, the less difficult the bridging job that follows. If a firm has only one collaboration partner, it is usually possible to hand pick a few people from its own ranks to work with the partner.

In the case of internal technology networks, the recommended strategy is to develop a single common culture across the whole network of labs. It should be consistent with (if not exactly the same as) the overall corporate culture, acting as a cohesive influence for network members dispersed around the globe and helping direct activity toward shared goals. Creating this common culture across globally dispersed and diverse units is a major undertaking, requiring both formal and informal activities and very strong support from top management. Maintenance of the culture also requires considerable time and resources. Nevertheless, building and maintaining a common culture is a worthwhile and achievable activity in internal technology networks. They consist of stable sets of people and units and endure for periods of time long enough to grow the culture and reap its benefits.

Building a common culture is much less feasible in external technology networks, however. This is true for a number of reasons. It is unlikely that the top managers of the organizations in a network will agree on a common culture. Usually they will be reluctant to give up their own cultures, which probably serve them quite well in a variety of business arenas. Such reluctance will be strengthened by the knowledge that their participation in a particular external network is not necessarily a long-term proposition. And even if a network culture could be agreed upon, it is unlikely that there would be time enough for the long process of disseminating it among all the people and organizations involved.

Selecting and bridging—the usual approach to the challenge of culture—is, of course, much more complex in multipartner networks than it is in dual collaborations. In bringing several firms together, the variety of strategic considerations is greater, making it more difficult to select partners on the basis of any one criterion, such as cultural compatibility. The cultural gaps to be bridged are often wider and more numerous. The amount of interaction with other firms requires the involvement of more people, so a firm cannot be as selective in assigning people to work with collaborators. This downgrades the quality of their participation in a number of ways, including sophistication in handling cultural differences. Further, given a variety of diverse partners, organizations have to adapt, simultaneously, to several different cultures.

Clearly, there is no elegant solution here. A company must select and bridge as best it can, given the constraints and resources available. Rather than trying to promote their own home cultures as "the best way," people working directly with network partners have to learn to work with cultural compromises. They have to acknowledge that cultures other than their own can be effective and that in networks, at least, respect must be given to them. Considerable cultural concessions may have to be made if the collaboration is to work. This cultural relativism puts strain on attempts to maintain the home cultures of firms.

On an optimistic note, it seems likely that a generic "network culture" will eventually develop. As more organizations become involved in external networks, more of their people will become adept at operating effectively in multicultural settings. Experienced individuals in the network arena will come to know each other and will trade experiences and advice. This interaction could lead to the development of an external network culture compatible with network activities and tolerant of the home cultures of collaborating organizations.

Arthur Chester (1994), a senior vice president of research and technology at Hughes, envisions the emergence of this kind of global business culture for technology management. He believes it will embody a global consensus about the preferred, and presumably most effective, way to manage technology. An organization that is truly working toward the future, as well as building out from current management practice, will work at developing its home organizational culture to be compatible with the emerging external network culture.

> *"Firms must contribute to the development of a network culture and begin to guide the evolution of the home culture toward adaptation with it."*

Thus, the challenge in managing culture in transnational external technology networks is twofold. First, companies must continue to use the select-and-bridge strategy, with all its complexities and shortcomings, for the near to medium future. Second, they must contribute to the development of a network culture and begin to guide the evolution of the home culture toward adaptation with it. This will require cultural shifts and clashes and may make the select-and-bridge strategy more difficult in the short run. But in the long term, it will help ensure inclusion in strategically important networks.

Disclosure Policies

Many managers with collaboration experience have reported that the inappropriate disclosure of proprietary information is their chief reservation about collaborations, even with a single partner. However, the need to guard proprietary information can conflict with the need for high levels of communication among partners. Because effective interaction is essential for successful collaboration, communication must be open to help prevent and deal with the misunderstandings that naturally arise when people from different cultures and organizations work together on complex problems under conditions of high uncertainty. Information, technical and otherwise, must

be able to flow freely to enable its optimal use in the venture. A key to ensuring such free flow of information is face-to-face contact and the establishment of trust. The disadvantage to this is that proprietary commercial or technical information may fall into the wrong hands—information that may have cost the original owner considerable money to develop or buy, and that may well be an important source of competitive advantage.

In internal networks, the issue of appropriate disclosure is not as thorny as it is in external collaborations. Most participants are employees of the networked firm, and disclosure to an outsider is not normally in their interest. Nor are close contacts with outsiders usually intrinsic to the ongoing business of the network. Normally, guidelines are provided for those contacts with outsiders that do occur. In short, in internal networks there is not much motivation or opportunity to disclose to outsiders, so the probability of inappropriate disclosure is quite low.

On the other hand, the motive and opportunity for disclosure do exist in external networks. The very *raison d'être* of a network is the sharing of technical and other information. People are expected to disclose certain information and are given plenty of opportunity to do so in the name of effective communication. Controlling disclosure in such circumstances can be extremely complex. One challenge lies in establishing and maintaining guidelines with the goal of allowing disclosures that facilitate the achievement of network goals but do no harm to the organization. As the firm participates in a succession of networks that overlap in time—each with multiple partners, each partner of which has a different kind of relationship to the firm—it may have to develop tailor-made disclosure guidelines for each partner. These may then be altered during the course of a relationship as the contingencies of the collaboration evolve.

In addition to developing and maintaining appropriate guidelines, there is the problem of communicating them effectively to the people involved. For example, a firm that encourages openness and trust among its employees as part of its attempts to make its internal network effective may pursue a policy of partial openness and trust for external network partners. Such a policy of selective disclosure may seem duplicitous, self-contradictory, and self-defeating to some organizational members. The likelihood of this is increased if they lack clear and full knowledge of the guidelines and their underlying rationale.

These difficulties are compounded by the impossibility and undesirability of providing detailed guidelines for all possible contingencies. Considerable judgment will have to be exercised by organizational members who will be too numerous to receive detailed, one-on-one explanations of the guidelines. Keeping those involved up-to-date with the guidelines and the subtleties of their implementation can be a daunting task.

Preventing inappropriate disclosure requires the cooperation of all the partners in a network. Cases of indirect disclosure show why this is so. Indirect disclosure might happen when information goes from one partner to another through an exchange of communication that is entirely consistent with the goals of the collaboration. From the receiving partner, however, the information can make its way (without any intention of harm, but perhaps through ignorance) to a competitor of the originator of the information. That competitor may use it for competitive advantage against the originating firm, and may or may not know where the information ultimately came from or that the originating firm considered it to be part of its competitive arsenal. To prevent this kind of indirect disclosure, a company must communicate its disclosure position to the other members of the network. Thus, all the difficulties described above for implementing guidelines with members of the home corporation will be present with members of other firms as well, but with less direct control.

It is important to see the disclosure challenge as a network issue rather than just an organizational issue. Although each firm will have unique concerns and will need guidelines of its own, disclosure can be dealt with effectively only in the context of the network as a whole. Part of the network-level approach is to include clear policies about disclosure in the network agreement. As with IT and culture, the solution over the long run is to work toward broadly shared methods of handling disclosure in external networks, and for each firm to develop its own approach to be compatible with the network system.

Human Resources

The success of a transnational external technology network hinges significantly on the ability of the people involved to cooperate effectively. Without the right people, the venture is doomed to fail. A strong project leader or champion is crucial to success. In addition, a "chemistry" must develop among at least some of the participants. And the people involved must not only know how to maintain confidentiality in protecting proprietary information but also how to discriminate between that which needs to be protected and that which can be openly communicated.

Negotiating skills and the ability to work with people from a number of countries, organizations, and functions are, of course, essential. People must be flexible yet remain true to the objectives of the collaborative venture and to the goals of their own organizations. Denis Tither (1994) has compiled the following list of requirements for the ideal networker:

- university graduation
- university research experience
- language training and experience
- industrial employment
- technology management experience
- sales/marketing training and experience
- team leadership training and experience
- proven problem-solving abilities
- honesty and integrity
- long-term strategy orientation
- communication and socializing skills
- diplomatic skills
- knowledge of politics and humanities.

This is a tall order, and one that few people can fill entirely. To complicate matters, such talents are needed in more than just a few key people. Collaborative ventures typically involve people from various levels and functional areas of each organization. These mixed groups must work relatively autonomously because key managers are not always directly available to monitor and intervene to ensure that activity remains on track. In short, collaborating organizations need a depth and breadth of such talent. Only if a firm has limited collaborations is it possible to hand pick the people to work on them. But a lack of the appropriate human resources could mean strategic opportunities missed or mismanaged. So a conscious, systematic approach to selecting and developing people is essential.

> *"Considerable judgment will have to be exercised by organizational members who will be too numerous to receive detailed, one-on-one explanations of the disclosure guidelines."*

Organizations may be able to install selection and development programs for external networks by building on the systems they already have in place. Some of what is already taught for internal networks will also be useful for external ones, such as negotiating skills. Other content may need considerable modification. For example, the emphasis on the home organizational culture will have to be replaced by a consideration of cultural relativism. Still other content will have to be entirely new, such as incorporating an understanding of strategic external networking. Job rotation placements for training purposes can be expanded to include placements in partner organizations. Human resource managers can begin to envision a time when working outside the home company is a normal training activity for most employees in a firm.

One change will be an increase in the number of people passing through the system. The first challenge, then, in the management of human resources for transnational, external technology networks is to select and develop people in sufficient numbers to staff all the organization's collaborative activities. In an ideal world, everyone in an organization would be capable of participating in networking activity.

The second challenge is to adapt the firm's human resource system to the "external" one. In other words, just as there will be a network IT system, culture, and disclosure guidelines in the future, there will be a network human resource system. Among other things, it could coordinate job rotation placements across firms; set up joint training programs to introduce the network culture and the shared IT network; and construct a common system for selecting people for network assignments. Other parties, such as universities, might be involved in providing these functions. These cooperative activities, if extensive, would constitute this external human resource system— a supra-organizational system, as it were. One can envision a time when large numbers of people routinely pass from the home company's human resource system, to the network's system, and back again.

The challenge in harmonizing the firm's own HRM system with the external system has two parts. One is to tune the home system into compatibility with the network system. The other is to influence the network system to evolve in directions of most benefit to the home organization.

Strategic Networking

Benjamin Gomes-Casseres of Harvard University has clearly articulated the difference between partnering (collaborating with one partner) and networking (collaborating with multiple partners). In his empirical study of external, transnational technology networks (1994), he found that networking is an activity with challenges that go far beyond those of partnering—supporting Wolff's observation that networks are more like communes than marriages. Gomes-Casseres has articulated five lessons of strategic networking, based on the experiences of pioneering networkers:

1. Remember that networks are only as strong as the two-partner relationships within them. An important part of networking is to be a good partner to each of the other members of a network.

2. Manage the group as a whole. A network should be more than just the sum of its parts. If that is to happen, the network must be managed as an entity.

3. Expand networks carefully, paying due attention to the value added by each new member. Bigger networks are not always better networks, and adjustment to new partners takes time and care.

4. Position your company strategically within and among networks. Being stuck in the wrong network can preclude your participation in others and even create enemies. Failing to participate in the right networks can cut you off from strategic

opportunities. Scanning the network environment is an essential activity that enables you to act strategically.

5. Be sure your firm can sustain network participation. Effective participation requires the commitment of resources, particularly time. Make sure you are able to commit them.

Gomes-Casseres, however, does not give full attention to one of the primary points about strategy being made here: that all networking activity should be planned and implemented with the "Network of the Future" in mind. As part of strategic networking, one should plan participations that enhance one's reputation as a network player, increase one's influence on the development of future networks (even those in which one is not a partner), and provide the best opportunities to develop one's own organization for the network realities to come.

Harmonization with Networks

The long-term goal of network management is to achieve a kind of unity, or harmony, with the networked world of the future. Such harmonization will come through two general thrusts. The first is to keep developing the firm toward compatibility with the evolving vision of the networked world. The second is to exert whatever influence is possible upon networks to help them evolve toward states that are compatible with the interests of the organization. The possibilities of substantial influence, of course, are higher in the first thrust than in the second.

Once again, a vision of the networked world of the future is essential for successful strategic networking. The vision we have developed is one in which external networks form a supra-organizational entity with their own IT, human resource, and disclosure control systems as well as their own cultures (see **Figure 2**). This supra-organizational entity evolves over time, taking on different hues from different industries and from different national origins of principal players. Individual firms will have to be in harmony with the supra-organizational entity and the networks it encompasses. Successful firms will be able to adapt to the variations over time, industry, and national influence. The most successful will progress beyond mere adaptability and achieve synergy with the supra-organizational entity.

If an organization is seriously committed to external networking as a way of doing business, planning and action should begin immediately. Individual decisions, made one at a time, should cumulatively lead to the integration of networking with other organizational activities. A variety of processes will have to be adjusted to the requirements of external networking. Firms will have to feel their way into the networked future because there are no good rules yet on how to proceed. The corporations that can propel themselves along this learning curve most quickly will find they have distinct competitive advantages.

Arnoud De Meyer (1993) of INSEAD contends that organizational learning is the essence of networking, and should take place primarily in two areas: (1) in learning the skills necessary for being a successful collaborator, and (2) in learning technical, marketing, and other information that will be of use to the firm in the current network and over the long term. The appropriate perspective to take in networking is that of a learning organization. Challenges and opportunities are settings for personal and organizational development, building toward the goal of an organization in harmony with its portfolio of evolving transnational, internal, and external technology networks. As part of that learning, organizations will have to develop mechanisms for keeping the vision of the networked world of the future immediately before them and up to date. This will require collecting and interpreting information about business practice, its environment, and its co-evolution.

A s companies develop their networking skills by feeling their way into the future, they will need feedback on the effectiveness of their activities. More must be learned about how to work with networks most effectively. To date, little has been published about proven methods for sustaining long-term

networking capabilities. So as managers develop approaches, their effectiveness needs to be evaluated. Of particular interest is the human element. Most of what has been written about people in networks has focused on the talents they need to function effectively. We need to learn more about how to develop those talents. We also need to learn more about the effects of stress in highly demanding networking roles, as well as how to support people in those roles.

Transnational external networking will be learned most effectively by firms that already have experience with single-partner collaborations and internal technology networks. Single-partner collaborations teach valuable lessons about working with outsiders in such areas as disclosure control. Internal transnational networks teach valuable lessons about cooperation among diverse groups operating at long distances from each other. Neither of these experiences alone, however, can completely prepare an organization for the unique demands of transnational, external networking.

A further challenge is to sway the evolution of the supra-organizational entity. To some extent this entity has a life of its own and is beyond the control of any single company. On the other hand, each company within the entity will have some influence upon its future direction. As an organization participates in its networks, it can try to turn them in directions favorable to its inter-

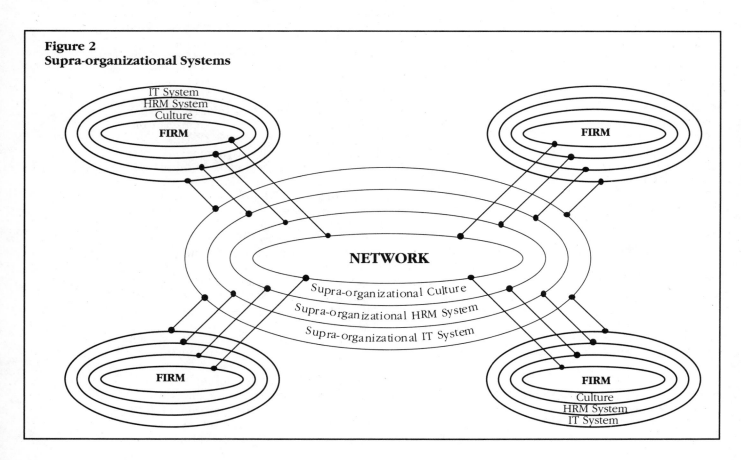

Figure 2
Supra-organizational Systems

ests. The long-term development of the supra-organizational entity should be of as much concern to a firm as are the affairs of the individual networks in which it is currently participating.

The initiative for these two thrusts—the development of the home organization and the influencing of the supra-organizational networked entity—must be expressed at the strategic level of the firm. They must be harmonized with technology and business strategy. Given the degree to which technological innovation now depends upon transnational external networks, firms that fail to take initiatives in these areas will forfeit their future prosperity.

It may be true that some firms may never become seriously involved in external networking. They may only occasionally, if ever, have even single-partner collaborations. If such activities are occasional, they can be treated as the exception rather than the rule. They can be handled by a few hand-picked people who will do what is necessary to make them work. However, if a business is to become seriously involved in external networking, measures must be taken to enable all its activities to be effectively integrated with networking.

References

F. Bidault and T. Cummings, "Innovating Through Alliances: Expectations and Limitations," *R&D Management*, 24, 1 (1994): 33-45.

J.A. Byrne, "The Virtual Corporation," *Business Week*, February 8, 1993, pp. 98-102.

A.N. Chester, "Aligning Technology with Business Strategy," *Research-Technology Management*, January-February 1994, pp. 25-32.

A. De Meyer, "Management of an International Network of Industrial R&D Laboratories," *R&D Management*, 23, 2 (1993): 109-120.

J.E. Forrest and M.J.C. Martin, "Strategic Alliances Between Large and Small Research-Intensive Organizations," *R&D Management*, 22, 1 (1992): 41-53.

B. Gomes-Casseres, "Group Versus Group: How Alliance Networks Compete," *Harvard Business Review*, July-August 1994, pp. 62-70.

O. Granstrand, L. Hakanson, and S. Sjolander, "Internationalization of R&D—A Survey of Some Recent Research," *Research Policy*, 22 (1993): 413-430.

O. Granstrand and S. Sjolander, "Managing Innovation in Multi-technology Corporations," *Research Policy*, 19 (1990): 35-60.

J. Hausler, H. Hohn, and S. Lutz, "Contingencies of Innovative Networks: A Case Study of Successful Interfirm R&D Collaboration," *Research Policy*, 23 (1994): 47-66.

R.M. Kanter, "Collaborative Advantage," *Harvard Business Review*, July-August 1994, pp. 96-108.

D. Littler, F. Leverick, and M. Bruce, "Factors Affecting the Process of Collaborative Product Development," *Journal of Product Innovation Management*, 12, 1 (1995): 16-32.

G.C. Nicholson, "How 3M Manages Its Global Laboratory Network," *Research-Technology Management*, July-August 1994, pp. 21-24.

D. Tither, "The People Factor in Collaboration and Technology Transfer," *Technovation*, 14, 5 (1994): 283-285.

M.F. Wolff, "Building Trust in Alliances," *Research-Technology Management*, May-June 1994, pp. 12-15.

John W. Medcof is an associate professor of organizational behavior at McMaster University in Hamilton, Ontario, Canada. The author developed this paper while a visiting professor at the Centre for Research on Organizational Management and Technical Change at the University of Manchester's Institute of Science and Technology in Manchester, U.K. He wishes to thank that institution for its partial support of this project.

The great escape

How do you say goodbye to a currency board? The more stable the economy, the easier the answer

JUST as slimmers sometimes have their jaws wired shut to stop them gorging, spendthrift countries find that abolishing their central banks can end the itch to print money. A currency board, which takes the place of a central bank as a country's monetary authority, operates on a simple principle: all currency in circulation and (usually) all of banks' reserves must be backed by foreign exchange. "Even if we have only eight kroons in circulation, we will have a D-mark in our vaults to back them," said Siim Kallas, the president of Estonia's central bank when it launched its currency board in 1992.

Estonia's currency board helped stabilise the Baltic country's economy. Hong Kong's, created in 1983, has kept the colony's currency steady despite the massive changes in China. Argentina's has put an end to decades of inflation. Their success has tempted others: Bosnia-Hercegovina and Bulgaria may introduce boards soon. But although the IMF's experts offer guidance about how to start up a currency board, economists have little experience of how to wind one down.

There are two easily distinguishable sets of reasons why countries may wish to abandon their currency boards—good ones, and bad ones. And the motive itself has much to do with whether a country can make the transition successfully.

For all its advantages, a currency board has inherent drawbacks. Precisely because the exchange rate cannot adjust, it reduces a country's ability to cope with shocks, such as a big change in commodity prices. A board can make a country vulnerable to inflation, because an inflow of foreign investment, which puts more foreign currency into the board's vaults, will automatically lead it to print more money. And in the event of a financial emergency a currency board has less freedom than a central bank to act as lender of last resort, because the board cannot boost the money supply to aid troubled banks. If a country on a sound financial footing wants to scrap its currency board for these reasons, it should be able to do so without difficulty.

How? One way is to stop covering the monetary base entirely with foreign currency, and gradually move to a mixture of foreign currency and domestic government bonds. The currency board will come to look like a central bank with a commitment to a fixed exchange rate. Eventually, as more and more domestic bonds back the currency, the board can engage in open-market operations, buying and selling the bonds to nudge interest rates, just as central banks do. Estonia is trying to move in this direction.

Another possibility is to announce that the currency will no longer be fixed at a specific rate. In 1973, for instance, Singa-

Two Baltic tales

Estonian success

Consumer prices
% increase on previous year

Sources: EIU; Deutsche Morgan Grenfell

Lithuanian doubts

Short-term interest rate %

pore and Malaysia abandoned their currency-board systems by allowing their currencies to float. Both countries had stable economic policies and strong capital inflows from abroad. Their currencies immediately appreciated instead of falling. In effect, they left the currency board from positions of strength.

But what about countries with more questionable motives? The subject is topical in another Baltic state, Lithuania, which introduced a currency board in 1994. In contrast to Estonia, the move did not have broad political backing. Lithuania's industry has been slower to restructure than Estonia's, and it has lost competitiveness as the real exchange rate has appreciated. Many businesses claim to be suffering.

These problems have been exacerbated by the fact that Lithuania pegged its currency, the lit, to the dollar. As the dollar has strengthened against the currencies of Lithuania's main trading partners in Europe, the country's trade deficit has ballooned to nearly 10% of GDP. Worse, the government reacted ineptly to a banking crisis, and in doing so weakened the credibility of its currency board. Despite the rules, it bailed out two big banks in 1995. Outsiders suspect that a chunk of the currency board's reserves are pledged to prop up the banking system.

Shedding the straitjacket

Given these problems, it is clear that many Lithuanians would like to wriggle out of the currency board's disciplines. The authorities say that they would like to keep the fixed exchange rate but not the board itself*. After this year, it plans to back only 80% of its lits with dollars. This, it argues, would provide the monetary flexibility to bail out dud banks (and so reduce some of the speculative pressure against the lit). Then, in 1999 or later, it plans to switch the currency's peg from the dollar to a basket of currencies.

But it is not clear that the government has the credibility to make these fundamental shifts in exchange-rate policy without scaring investors and risking a big devaluation. This is because Lithuania has failed to accompany its currency board with other essential economic measures. At 2.5% of GDP the budget deficit is showing no signs of shrinking. Privatisation has been haphazard and there has been relatively little foreign investment.

It is slow progress on these fronts, as much as the details of the monetary regime, that have made Lithuanians think their economy will do better without a currency board. And yet the very things that make the board uncomfortable could make it costly to leave behind. If the government's economic programme had truly succeeded in stabilising the economy, the move to a more flexible central bank might pass unnoticed by both currency markets and the public. But if investors think that Lithuania is acting from a position of economic weakness, they may not believe the government's promise to keep the currency stable. Abandoning a currency board because the discipline is too painful is not a prescription for economic health.

....

* "Monetary Policy Programme of the Bank of Lithuania for 1997-1999," Bank of Lithuania, 1997.

INTERNATIONAL BANKING

Coping with the ups and downs

" IF YOU see a banker jump out of the window, jump after him—there's sure to be profit in it," said Voltaire. In recent years, anybody rash enough to follow that piece of advice from the 18th-century French philosopher and satirist would probably have ended up in intensive care, along with the bankers. The list of financial institutions hospitalised after more or less spectacular defenestrations grows longer by the day. Big chunks of banking systems in some rich countries, as well as in many emerging markets, have had to be put on taxpayer-financed drip-feeds. This is not the first time that banks have proved to be remarkably accident-prone, nor is it likely to be the last.

Since the Bretton Woods system of fixed exchange rates was abandoned in the early 1970s, the banking industry seems to have jumped from one drama to another, including the Latin American debt crisis, the $150 billion American savings-and-loan (S&L) fiasco and, more recently, a property-related lending binge that forced several Scandinavian governments to bail out large chunks of their banking systems.

On top of this there have been some breathtaking individual problems, such as the collapse in February 1995 of Britain's Barings Bank after a rogue trader managed to blow an £860m ($1.4 billion) hole in its balance sheet, and Crédit Lyonnais, a state-owned French bank that earned itself a place in banking's house of horrors by running up losses amounting to some FFr21 billion ($4.2 billion) in 1992-94. The list grows longer by the day. In March the Italian government announced an emergency rescue plan for Banco di Napoli after the bank owned up to having lost over 3 trillion lire ($2 billion) last year.

Bubble trouble

Until 1990, Japan seemed to be immune from banking headaches, but now its system—which includes many of the world's biggest banks (see table 1 on the next page)—looks thoroughly sick too. At the end of March, the country's 21 largest banks announced ¥9.3 trillion ($86 billion) of provisions against their bad debts. Many of these are the legacy of the country's economic bubble, which burst in the early 1990s. In view of the important role bank finance plays in Japan's economy, the myriad links between its banks and its industrial companies, and Japanese banks' large investments abroad, the country's banking crisis is undoubtedly one of the most worrying in recent financial history.

Thanks to stories of reckless lending and, in some cases, corruption, bankers in Japan are now widely seen as sharp-suited gamblers rather than sober-suited financiers. This explains public opposition to a government plan to spend ¥685 billion of taxpayers' money on paying the creditors of Japan's troubled housing-loan companies, or *jusen*, whose bosses had lent vast sums for speculative property development in the days of the bubble economy.

Japan's taxpayers are not the only ones that face a huge bill for banks' financial follies. The French are still waiting to see whether they will have to pay even more for the rescue of Crédit Lyonnais, which last year spun off FFr135 billion-worth of its dud assets into a new company whose losses will be covered by the state. And in Scandinavia, bailing out troubled banks has cost anywhere between 2.8% and 4% of their home countries' GDP, according to the International Monetary Fund.

It is not just the bankers who made the bad loans that are under fire. Banking regulators, for their part, are being blamed for complacency. In Britain, one Bank of England official resigned after the Bank was criticised for failing to see the Barings disaster coming. In France, a parliamentary report on the Crédit Lyonnais affair scolded watchdogs for allowing the bank's problems to grow. And in Japan, the country's finance ministry, which oversees banks, has also been castigated for letting them get out of control. In December Kyosuke Shinozawa, Japan's top finance official, stepped down to atone for past mistakes. There has even been talk of stripping Japan's most powerful ministry of some of its regulatory responsibilities.

What caused so many banks to crash in such a relatively short space of time? Part of the answer is that in the mid- to late 1980s, interest rates in the economies that subsequently suffered banking crises stayed relatively low, while their economies grew strongly. At the same time, deregulation swept away many of the rules that had previously limited competition within the banking industry. The result was a breathtaking, credit-driven boom in property and share prices (see chart 2 on next page) that encouraged bankers to lend to all comers. When interest rates rose sharply in 1989, puncturing the bubble, borrowers began to default in droves and banks in many countries were quickly submerged by bad debts.

Fears about systemic risk in banking have led to calls for ever more rules and regulations. But, asks Martin Giles, would they be part of the solution or part of the problem?

Banking behemoths `1`

World's top ten banks, latest*

	Bank		Assets $bn
1	Tokyo Mitsubishi	Japan	819.0
2	Sanwa	Japan	582.2
3	Dai-Ichi Kangyo	Japan	581.6
4	Fuji	Japan	571.1
5	Sumitomo	Japan	566.0
6	Sakura	Japan	559.5
7	Deutsche	Germany	503.4
8	Industrial Bank of Japan	Japan	433.3
9	Norinchukin	Japan	429.3
10	Long-Term Credit Bank of Japan	Japan	371.6

*Japanese banks at March 31st 1995; Deutsche Bank at December 31st 1995
Sources: *The Banker*; Press reports

To make matters worse, bankers in Britain and America had lent enthusiastically to the property sector in the hope that the fat margins on such risky loans would offset declining profits in their more traditional corporate-lending business. These were being squeezed in two ways. On the one hand, mutual funds (unit trusts), which offer higher returns by investing people's cash directly in the money market, stocks and bonds, had broken the banks' monopoly over cheap deposits (or liabilities, in banking parlance). On the other hand, many banks' best corporate customers were deserting them, preferring to raise money directly from the capital markets by issuing bonds and shares.

Why banks are special

Banking is not the only industry that has been transformed by the dual forces of deregulation and stiffer competition. Many other kinds of firm are having to cope with the same trends. Inevitably, some companies go bust as a result. Usually, they promptly disappear—unless a government decides for some reason or other that a firm such as an airline or a car maker is "strategic", and bails it out. When it comes to banking, however, politicians everywhere seem especially reluctant to let the industry's flagships fail.

Why? One reason is that governments fear the political backlash that the failure of a big bank would cause. Most of these financial giants have thousands of small depositors, many of whom keep a substantial portion of their wealth in their accounts. Ensuring that Aunt Agatha, Anna and Akiko-san have somewhere safe to invest their savings is widely considered to be the government's responsibility. Hence the strong political will to keep large banks afloat.

But there is another, even more serious threat associated with bank failures that strikes fear into the hearts of politicians and central bankers everywhere. Dubbed "systemic risk", this is the danger that the sudden and unexpected demise of one or several banks could trigger a domino-like collapse throughout an entire banking system. The prospect of a financial meltdown is such a serious worry because its impact is likely to be felt on Main Street as well as Wall Street.

On the run

It is the side-effects (or externalities, in economists' jargon) associated with bank failures that make them such a special case. When, say, a steel producer collapses, its disappearance is unlikely to cause trouble for other steelmakers; indeed, they should benefit by picking up some of the failed firm's clients. But when a bank suddenly goes bust, its rivals may experience problems too.

To see why, consider a typical, profitable bank that takes in deposits and uses the money to make long-term loans. Just in case some depositors want their cash back quickly, it also keeps a small amount of liquid assets handy, a practice known as "fractional reserve banking". Now suppose that some unforeseen event—a sharp rise in interest rates, the collapse of an important borrower, a stockmarket crash—raises doubts about whether the value of a bank's assets (mainly loans) is enough to cover its liabilities (mainly deposits). Because loans are hard for outsiders to value, some depositors may assume the worst and withdraw their cash. As banks work on a "first come, first served" basis, others will follow suit, leading to a "run". This will force the bank into a fire-sale of its less liquid assets to raise cash, further weakening its finances and prolonging the run.

A systemic risk arises if the first bank's failure causes depositors who have doubts about other banks' financial solidity to run on them too. This can happen either because they think that their

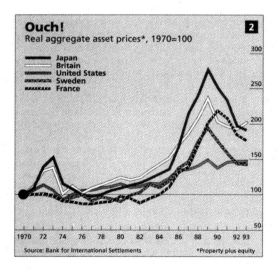

Ouch! `2`
Real aggregate asset prices*, 1970=100

— Japan
— Britain
— United States
—— Sweden
········ France

Source: Bank for International Settlements   *Property plus equity

banks have the same problems as the one that has just failed, or because the failed bank's fire-sale has depressed the market price of other banks' assets. Whatever the cause, once a system-wide panic has begun, it is devilishly difficult to stop.

It can also have a potentially devastating effect on the real economy. As banks struggle to stay afloat, they will call in their outstanding loans and refuse to make new ones, creating a credit crunch that can aggravate an economic downturn. This was precisely what happened in the 1930s. Between 1930 and 1933, some 9,000 American banks fell like ninepins; in Europe, the collapse in 1931 of Creditanstalt, Austria's biggest bank, also led to a series of other failures. These created the mother of all credit crunches, which made the Depression "Great". No wonder governments are anxious to ensure that history does not repeat itself.

Runs by small depositors still pose a threat to banks, as demonstrated by television pictures of people lining up to withdraw money from financial institutions in Japan, Taiwan and the Baltic states within the past year. An even bigger, though less televisual, threat comes from the wholesale markets. These include the interbank loan market, through which banks lend to one another, and payments systems, through which they make and receive payments on their own and customers' behalf. Such systems make problems more contagious among banks than among other types of firm. One example is Continental Illinois, a bad-debt-laden American bank that ran into trouble in 1984 after several Asian and European banks cut their lending to it. When rumours began to fly that other American banks might suffer the same fate, the Federal Reserve stepped in to rescue Continental.

To tackle systemic risk, governments have developed a three-legged approach. The first leg is to establish a lender of last resort, usually a country's central bank, which will provide liquidity during a financial crisis, either to individual banks or to the system as a whole. The second leg is to offer deposit insurance. Typically, this involves the government insuring small deposits, either in total or in part, so that a bank's customers are less likely to run if they suspect that it is in trouble. The snag with a safety net is that it tempts banks to take big risks in the knowledge that taxpayers will foot the bill if they fail. This danger, known as "moral hazard", creates a dilemma for governments. Without a net, bank failures could devastate an economy; with it, the number of banks that take excessive risks could rise.

To resolve the dilemma, governments rely on the third leg of their strategy: regulation and supervision. Yet in spite of volumes of rulebooks and armies of regulators, the cost of bank bail-outs continues to rise. In response, politicians, pundits and the public are apt to call for ever more regulation and more regulators. But a few central bankers are now beginning to admit what some academic experts have been telling them for some time: that this traditional approach to banking regulation is ineffective and needs to be rethought. . . .

Foreign Environment

- Financial Forces (Articles 13 and 14)
- Economic and Socioeconomic Forces (Articles 15 and 16)
- Sociocultural Forces (Articles 17 and 18)
- Political Forces (Articles 19 and 20)
- Legal Forces (Articles 21 and 22)
- Labor Forces (Articles 23 and 24)
- Competitive Forces (Articles 25 and 26)

For centuries most American businesses focused on the domestic markets. There were many reasons for this. The first was that during the 1800s the United States was probably the most rapidly developing country in the world, a huge continental market, limited only by the Atlantic and Pacific Oceans. This was true until the end of World War I, when the United States, for the first time, became the world's leading industrial nation. But distances between countries seemed greater than they do today, and communication was not as swift or sure. In addition, most Americans tended to have at least a partially isolationist outlook on the world. There were exceptions, notably in mining, agricultural commodities, and oil. The time between World Wars I and II was also marked by the worldwide Great Depression of 1929–1939, which was almost immediately followed by World War II. After World War II, the United States stood alone as the great industrial power. It was not really until the 1970s that the United States received notice, in the form of the first gasoline crisis, that its position in world economics had changed.

While many U.S. firms did extensive business outside the country, in the early 1970s these arrangements represented only about 6 percent of the total business in the United States. But, by the end of the 1980s, this figure was close to 33 percent. This means that nondomestic business activity matters greatly to U.S. companies. What goes on in Europe and the Pacific Rim has a direct impact on what happens on Wall Street as well as Main Street, U.S.A.

Doing business outside the United States is different from doing business within the country. First of all, there is the monetary problem. Every country has a different currency, banking system, and regulations affecting the financial system. Currency fluctuations can play havoc with the assets and profits of a firm.

Economic and socioeconomic forces also play a role. While the cold war is over and the United States and its allies won, it does not mean that doing business in Singa-

pore is just like doing business in Denver. True, with a few minor exceptions such as Cuba and North Korea, capitalism is rapidly becoming the preferred method of organizing an economy. However, that organization will not necessarily be a clone of the system in the United States. There will be Indonesian capitalism, Chilean capitalism, and Hungarian capitalism, just as there are American capitalism, British capitalism, and Japanese capitalism. Each system will be based on the same general principles, but each will be different, with its own unique twists.

One factor that is going to have tremendous impact on international trade is the need to develop infrastructure in the developing world, and to maintain appropriate infrastructure in the developed world. Highways, railroads, airports, telecommunication, and sewer systems are needed in all the developing countries, and they must be modernized and maintained in the developed world. Asia alone is expected to have over $1 trillion in infrastructure needs in the foreseeable future. Add to this the maintenance and modernization needs of the developed world, plus Latin America and Africa, and it is clear that there will surely be no shortage of work for contractors and engineers who are willing to go into these markets.

Among the fascinating aspects of the global environment are the differences in culture and ideas, as well as the many similarities. Human beings have a wide variety of answers to seemingly mundane, everyday questions. Customs and culture often play a role in how successful organizations will be when dealing in a foreign market. What may be rude and offensive in one society may be accepted or even expected behavior in another. Understanding these differences and why they are important can be the key to success in any market. This is especially true in China, as outlined in "Keeping Up on Chinese Culture."

The political environment also plays an important role in international trade. Some countries are more politically

stable than others. Nationalization of foreign assets is not unheard of, and corporations have little or no recourse when their assets are suddenly appropriated by the government. History teaches that this is a real risk. Learning to analyze and deal with this risk is something that multinationals have to do, as discussed by Frederick Stapenhurst in "Political Risk Analysis in North American Multinationals: An Empirical Review and Assessment."

The laws of many nations when dealing with world trade are in the process of developing. Industries are now international in scope. The world is a market for small, as well as large, businesses. Illegal business practices are

being identified because their cost is huge, as discussed in "The Scourge of Global Counterfeiting."

Labor is another important aspect of the trade environment. Different countries have different attitudes and rules concerning labor and its relationship to the economy, government, and corporations. Attitudes and practices differ significantly. For example, in the United States it is common for the relationship between labor and management to be adversarial, while in Germany, representatives from the labor unions often sit on the boards of their employers. The only thing that is certain about labor is that workers now compete in an international environment. No country has a corner on highly skilled labor, and if workers are going to be competitive in the future, they must have the skills necessary to succeed in the worldwide labor market. Some governments actually even support some of the less than ethical business practices of some organizations, as may be seen in "Wanted: Muscle."

Finally, the environment for international trade will be highly competitive. Global markets mean global competitors and global standards. Successful organizations are the ones that can change and adapt to meet the competition. Not being able to change will, by definition, spell disaster for any organization. Flexibility and adaptability, instead, will be the keys to effectiveness in the coming world business environment.

Looking Ahead: Challenge Questions

Doing business outside the United States is different from doing business inside. In what ways is the foreign environment different from the domestic environment?

Political risk has always been a part of international business. What approaches are North American multinationals using to deal with these risks?

One challenge in the coming century will be developing and maintaining the infrastructure. What opportunities do these needs provide for international firms?

INTERNATIONAL

Is There a Monetary Union in MONETARY

Asia's Future?

ARRANGEMENTS

BARRY EICHENGREEN

Barry Eichengreen is professor of economics and political science at the University of California, Berkeley. This article is adapted from the introduction to the Japanese translation of his International Monetary Arrangements for the 21st Century (published in English by Brookings in 1994).

During 1995–96 the yen-dollar exchange rate endured a cycle of violent fluctuation. From 100 yen at the beginning of 1995 the dollar fell to 80 yen in April. At that point worried central bankers in Japan, the United States, and Europe intervened and halted the dollar's decline. The U.S. currency then trended sharply upward, most recently breaching the 120-yen barrier in late January. Concern for the strength of the yen was replaced by worries about its weakness: alarm grew that an undervalued yen would fan conflict over the U.S.-Japan current account balance and make life difficult for Japanese firms that import components from East Asian suppliers.

 From *The Brookings Review*, Spring 1997, pp. 33-35.

There is no question that this cycle created problems for both the Japanese and U.S. economies. It discouraged international trade by forcing firms to hedge exchange risk by purchasing "cover" in the forward market. And it created special difficulties for a Japan seeking to restructure and streamline a depressed economy. An exchange rate of ¥80 intensified the pressure on Japanese exporters of manufactures. The problems experienced by the tradables sector deepened the distress of financial institutions holding claims on manufacturing firms. The economy's deflationary crisis was thus compounded by the yen's appreciation in 1995. And while depreciation in 1996 relieved the domestic profit sqeeze, the yen's volatility complicated investment planning. Japanese producers may be discouraged from developing sustainable outsourcing strategies and shifting production to other parts of East Asia. The sudden improvement in competitiveness may distract producers and policymakers from the search for a permanent solution to the structural problems of the Japanese economy.

Looking for a Quick Fix

The 1995–96 yen-dollar dustup elicited the predictable demands for international monetary reform. If the major industrialized countries that make up the Group of 7 could only agree to establish a new system of pegged-but-adjustable currencies or exchange rate target zones, observers argued, these painful exchange rate fluctuations could be avoided. And if the seven could not reach agreement as a group, then the countries whose currencies were being affected should establish a bilateral target zone. Thus, we have heard repeated calls for the establishment of a target zone for the yen-dollar rate or a common basket peg, surrounded by fluctuation bands of plus-and-minus 10 percent, for nine East Asian currencies (those of China, Hong Kong, Indonesia, Korea, Malaysia, the Philippines, Singapore, Taiwan, and Thailand).

The matter, unfortunately, is not so simple. Stabilizing exchange rates by establishing a new system of pegs, bands, or target zones would require significant compromises of domestic policy autonomy. Intervention by central banks is effective only if it sends credible signals of future shifts in monetary and fiscal policies—that is, when there is no

> Monetary unification banishes exchange rate volatility by abolishing the exchange rate. But it requires the participants to share responsibility for their common monetary policy.

conflict between domestic and international economic policies.

But in today's world, conflicts between domestic and international economic objectives are inevitable. The removal of controls on international capital movements and the development of modern information-processing technologies over the past several decades permit billions of dollars to be traded across borders at the stroke of a key. The domestic policy independence that capital controls once afforded national monetary and fiscal authorities has become a thing of the past. Currency traders, no longer limited by controls, are free to attack an exchange rate as soon as they begin to suspect that the government is less than totally committed to defending it—a practice that can greatly increase the cost of defending the currency peg. With the end of the Cold War and the disintegration of dominant political coalitions in countries like Italy and Japan, governments are necessarily fragile and hesitant to put the domestic economy through the wringer to defend the exchange rate at any cost. Weak governments find it infeasible to pursue the international economic policies needed to maintain a durable currency peg.

Thus schemes to peg the dollar, the yen, and the deutsche mark against one another, as had been the practice until the Bretton Woods international monetary system collapsed in the early 1970s, will prove unavailing. Exchange rates between these currencies will continue to float against each other.

Small Countries, Big Problem

For the United States and Japan, large countries that remain relatively closed to international transactions, this arrangement, while painful, is bearable. For small open economies, where a larger share of production is typically sold on international markets, the dislocations caused by exchange rate swings can be excruciating. Because the financial sector is small relative to global financial markets, a shift in market sentiment or in interest rates in the United States can elicit a flood of capital inflows that leads to a dramatic real appreciation or massive outflows that cause the exchange rate to depreciate alarmingly.

Whether these small open economies are in Europe, Latin America, or East Asia, they find it exceedingly difficult to live with exchange rate fluctuations. They are thus prepared to take drastic steps to limit exchange rate volatility. In some cases they have done so by replacing their central banks with currency boards. This approach has been used by countries with exceptional problems with inflation and financial stability, such as Argentina and Estonia. A parliamentary statute or constitutional amendment requires the board to tie the domestic currency to that of a major trading partner. Argentina's currency board can issue a dollar's worth of currency only when acquiring a dollar of reserves, effectively pegging the peso-dollar exchange rate at one to one. Currency traders do not question the monetary authorities' commitment to the currency peg, since the latter are required by law to defend it. But a currency board leaves the monetary authority little leeway to act as a lender of last resort in the event of problems in the banking system. And once the inflationary crisis has passed, countries find it hard to eliminate their currency board and reacquire monetary flexibility without exciting fears of a return to the bad old days. A person with an overeating disorder may be inclined to padlock the refrigerator and throw away the key, but he may regret the extremity of the step once starvation sets in.

Another solution to the problem of exchange rate instability is a monetary union, like that the members of the European Union are currently seeking to establish. Monetary unification banishes exchange rate volatility by abolishing the exchange rate. But it requires the participants to share responsibility for their common monetary policy. Conveniently for the small open economies of Europe, the larger partner they wish to join in monetary union, Germany, may be prepared to compromise its monetary autonomy in return for reacquiring a foreign policy role in the context of a European Union foreign policy.

A Single Asian Currency?

The question for the 21st century is whether analogous monetary blocs will form in East Asia (and, for that matter, in the Western Hemisphere). With the dollar, the yen, and the single European currency floating against one another, other small open economies will be tempted to link up to one of the three. But the linkage will be possible only if accompanied by radical changes in institutional arrangements like those contemplated by the European Union. The spread of capital mobility and political democratization will make it prohibitively difficult to peg exchange rates unilaterally. Pegging will require international cooperation, and effective cooperation will require measures akin to monetary unification.

The day when the countries of East Asia including Japan will be prepared to create a single Asian currency (or, for that matter, when the countries of the Western Hemisphere are prepared to join the United States in a monetary union) remains far away. The political preconditions for monetary unification are not in place. Operating a monetary union requires some pooling of political responsibility. History provides very different prospects for this in Western Europe and East Asia. Proponents of European integration can trace their antecedents back for hundreds of years. Jeremy Bentham advocated a European assembly, Jean-Jacques Rousseau a European federation, Henri Saint-Simon a European monarch and parliament. By the middle of the 19th century, intellectuals like Victor Hugo could speak of a United States of Europe. In the 1920s, the Pan-European Union lobbied for a European federation and attracted the support of Aristide Briand and Edouard Herriot, future premiers of France. Konrad Adenauer and Georges Pompidou, two leaders of the postwar process of European integration, were members of the Pan-European Union. The ideal of European integration is intimately connected with the liberal and democratic principles of the European Enlightenment and has roots in centuries of European history.

East Asia, in contrast, lacks a comparable tradition of political solidarity. It lacks a Jean Monet or Paul Henri Spaak to speak for regional integration. In part this reflects the ideological distance between China's communist government and market-oriented regimes elsewhere in East Asia. By contrast, in postwar Western Europe, variants of the social market economy were embraced by virtually all the members of the present-day European Union.

At a deeper level, East Asia lacks a Benthamite-Rousseauian-Saint Simonian heritage of collective democratic governance through integration. As Peter Katzenstein puts it, "the notion of unified sovereignty . . . central to the conception of continental European states, does not capture Asian political realities." Not only in China do the regions resist the attempts of the center to exercise its political will through the operation of political and legal institutions. The idea of a centralized state with a monopoly of force that regiments its citizens through the superimposition of a common set of institutions is a European conception, not an Asian one. Asian civil society is structured by ritual, ceremony, and economic networks as much as by force and law.

Consequently, integrationist initiatives in Asia have proceeded not through the creation of strong supranational institutions but by establishing loose networks of cooperation. It is revealing that the Asia Pacific Economic Cooperation forum, which is essentially just a consultative body, has succeeded where initiatives to create smaller, more cohesive Asian analogues to the European Economic Community or the European Free Trade Association have not.

Gazing far into the 21st century, one can imagine the development of a single Asian currency analogous to the Euro, the prospective single European currency. In a world of open international capital markets and politicized domestic policy settings, that will be the only alternative to floating exchange rates. As the economies of East Asia grow still more open and interdependent, pressure will build to work toward this goal. But as yet the political preconditions are not in place. An Asian monetary union is at best a very distant prospect.

Ignored Warnings

Long before the deluge, storm clouds were gathering over Asia's economy

By Keith B. Richburg and Steven Mufson

Washington Post Foreign Service

One year ago, as Asia finished another year of sky-high growth and its leaders boasted of a dawning Pacific Century, a little-noticed bank scandal in Thailand provided a hint of the shock the region was about to receive. The scandal, at the Bangkok Bank of Commerce, involved billions of dollars in questionable loans, including one to a convicted swindler known as the "Biscuit King." The bank's managers disguised their malfeasance using financial shell games, such as backing loans with vastly overvalued property.

The mess at the Bangkok bank exposed the weakness of Thailand's banks and the lack of government oversight in a deregulated financial system run amok. And though few guessed it at the time, that obscure and complex scandal was the portent for a larger economic meltdown that not only would send Thailand reeling into recession, but later would sweep through Indonesia, Malaysia, the Philippines and, eventually, South Korea, the world's 11th-largest economy.

By the end of 1997, the crisis had left behind bankrupt corporations and failed financial institutions across Asia, and a pile of regional currencies worth up to 40 percent less than before. It exposed a mountain of bad debt wrought by shoddy lending practices, and it underscored a generation of corrupt political and business practices long concealed by high growth figures. And perhaps most importantly, the crisis pierced the bubble of confidence that has allowed Asia to prosper for a decade on foreign investment.

Few can claim to have seen Asia's dramatic change in economic fortune coming. Indeed, at the start of 1997, most economists, regional analysts, and Asian academics and politicians were saying that the region's "miracle" growth was destined to continue well into the next millennium.

Looking back, however, the Thai bank scandal was the first—and perhaps the most glaring—of many warning signs that Asia's bubble of prosperity was about to burst. This story, reported with the benefit of hindsight, looks at how the gathering storm clouds in two key places—Thailand and South Korea—for more than a year signaled the eventual, region-wide economic crisis to come.

In many cases, the warnings were ignored by government officials anxious to conceal unfavorable news, by foreign investors anxious to keep the funds flowing and by an international community eager to keep the myth of the miracle alive.

"The relative complacency across the globe in the initial stages of the crisis was probably a contributing factor to the crisis," says Andy Tan, a Singapore-based analyst. After the Mexican currency crisis of 1994, Tan says, "there was a sense of complacency that this would be the same."

"If you look at all of these countries," says Bruce Gale, regional manager of the Political and Economic Risk Consultancy, "the problems were known, but there wasn't the political will to do anything about them."

Most analysts in the region say Asia is in a position to pick up the pieces from the shambles of 1997, as governments to varying degrees show a willingness to recognize the size of the crisis and make the necessary reforms, particularly in the banking and financial sector. As with the savings and loan scandal in the United States, which led to a shakeout of the American finance sector and greater regulation, so too might Asia retool by cleaning up its banking mess.

In most cases, the cleanup will involve shutting down banks and finance companies whose operations already have been suspended—16 banks in Indonesia, 14 merchant banks in South Korea, 56 finance companies in Thailand. Other banks will be forced to merge, and laws are being changed from Jakarta to Seoul to allow still other banks to merge with foreign partners.

But the process is likely to be longer than initially thought, and more painful, according to regional analysts, economists and investors. Asia is likely to face recession, more bankruptcies, higher unemployment and perhaps social unrest, they say. Where initially the turnaround seemed likely to come by the end of this year, most analysts now suspect Asia's troubles could last to the year 2000.

In addition, changes in global trade and investment patterns could slow recovery. Asia now is competing more with Latin America and Eastern Europe, and it may find it difficult to recapture its role as the favorite region for foreign capital. China, with its endless supply of low-wage labor, will challenge Southeast Asians increasingly in their traditional export fields. And perhaps most fundamentally, the crisis of 1997 has sapped investors confidence in the region.

THAILAND, WHERE THE ASIAN COLlapse began last summer, holds the first clues of its origin and shows how warning signs along the road to disaster either were missed entirely or deliberately ignored.

One year ago, Thailand was coming out of a decade of unparalleled economic growth, averaging 8 percent annually. For nine years in a row, the country reported a balanced budget. The technocrats in charge of financial and economic policy were considered among the most professional in the region; the history of political noninterference in economic management seemed well-entrenched; and the country boasted a relatively open, liberal investment policy.

"Every single person has been caught by surprise by the rapidity of the crisis and the depth of the crisis," a Western embassy economist in Bangkok says.

But Dominique Maire had his doubts. In 1996, Maire was a regional economist for UBS Securities based in Singapore. In September of that year, he and other UBS analysts spent two days in Bangkok talking with officials in charge of economic policy. "We asked what was going on," Maire recalls. "I told them exports were weakening, everyone was still concentrating on strong economic growth, investment plans were still high—but can you do something to prevent a slowdown?

"I remember in our case, after two days of meetings, I said, that's it—it's a major slowdown. That was the trigger point, after which I started cutting major forecasts."

Key to that 1996 reassessment were figures showing export performance for the last quarter of the year as sluggish at best. At the Beginning of 1996, the government had predicted an 18 percent growth in exports, but at midyear Thailand's export growth was in the single digits. Government officials insisted that the earlier growth projections

From *The Washington Post National Weekly Edition*, January 12, 1998, pp. 6, 7. (c) 1998 by The Washington Post. Reprinted by permission.

75

were on target and that Thailand simply was experiencing a brief cyclical downturn that had no long-term implications. And many foreign economists followed that line.

"Everyone was scurrying around trying to find cyclical explanations," says a hedge fund manager with long experience in Thailand. "But the drop in exports was crucial."

In fact, a long-term shift was underway, with profound implications for Thailand and the region. Thailand's traditional exports—footwear, garments, seafood—"got creamed," as one U.S. economist indelicately puts it. The main problem was increased competition from relative newcomers India, Burma and Vietnam, and from China, whose exports expanded as Thailand's contracted. In addition, higher labor costs and the relatively high value of Thailand's currency, the baht, compared with the U.S. dollar, meant Thais had "priced themselves out of the market," the U.S. economist says.

While exports were collapsing, trouble was brewing on an unrelated front: The country was embroiled in its biggest banking scandal. The issue received little outside attention; because some ministers in the government of then-Prime Minister Banharn Silpa-arfcha were touched by the scandal, the government tried to hide the depth of the problem.

The Bangkok Bank of Commerce, or BBC as it is widely known, was taken over by a government committee in summer 1996 after it was revealed in parliament that the bank was insolvent because of some $3 billion in outstanding loans, many of them with inadequate collateral. The beneficiaries included the late Rajan Pillai, a biscuit-maker and convicted swindler known as the "Biscuit King," who got 3 billion Thai baht (about $117 million at 1996 conversion rates), and members of Banharn's Chart Thai political party.

The bank's former president and treasury adviser have been accused of running the bank into the ground. The ex-president is fighting the charges in Thailand, while the ex-treasury adviser is fighting extradition from Canada.

The BBC mess led to the resignation of Vijit Supinit as governor of the Bank of Thailand, the country's central bank, eroding confidence in that institution. More importantly, it focused attention on a banking sector that was seriously out of control.

After Thailand allowed offshore banks in 1993–94 and began offering high interest rates on deposits, foreigners poured in money, attracted by the relatively stable exchange rates. Flush with foreign cash, the proliferating banks "went out and loaned shamelessly," one Western diplomat says. Facing liquidity problems, and with lax government oversight, the banks covered up their increasing volume of bad loans by making still more loans and, as the economist says, "that's where we were in mid-'96 when the rot started."

By early 1997, the bad news on exports and the worries over BBC combined to put

heavy foreign pressure on the baht. Analysts say they now believe the central bank was intervening in the futures currency markets even earlier than first revealed, in spring 1997. On Feb. 12, 1997, the Singapore-based Political and Economic Risk Consultancy group published its "Asian Intelligence" newsletter that for the first time warned of the extent of the impending crisis.

The pressure on the baht in January "betrayed worries not just about the gloomy run of Thailand's macroeconomic results, but also about the health of the country's financial institutions," the report said. "Serious surgery is needed to invigorate the country's financial institutions," it said, warning, "If panic takes hold of the market, reform may have to come to stave off, or respond to, a meltdown."

The meltdown did come in August, with the government suspending the operations of 58 ailing financial firms and going to the International Monetary Fund for a bailout.

JUST AS THE CRISIS IN THAILAND BEgan quietly with the mess at BBC, in South Korea the scandal had another name: Hanbo. In what should have been a warning sign of South Korea's coming financial crisis, the giant Hanbo Group went bankrupt in January 1997 with a debt of about $6 billion—the first of the big conglomerates to go under. The scandal caused South Korea's normally pliant banks to mutter publicly about the conglomerates' high debt levels.

The Hanbo Group's chairman and his son were convicted of siphoning $400 million from the group to bribe government officials and bankers in a futile attempt to keep the group afloat. To many analysts, the mess at Hanbo appeared unique. But others say Hanbo's crisis was indicative of the rot at the core of Korea's financial and industrial base.

In its February 1997 report, the Political and Economic Risk Consultancy group had rated Korea's banks among the region's most worrisome. "The recent Hanbo crisis has underlined just how much South Korea's banking system needs serious reform," the report said, adding that, among other things, the scandal exposed how Korean banks suffered under the "suffocating embrace from government" that made them "vulnerable to corrupt government officials."

As in Thailand, the banking scandal was the most visible and dramatic warning sign, but the roots of the economic problem were long in the making.

In Korea's case, double-digit growth in plant capacity since 1995 flooded markets with too many products, which then spurred a growth in inventories and price-slashing. This in turn caused a drop in profits for Korean firms, leaving them helpless in the face of crushing debts. With debts commonly equal to three to six times the cash invested in their firms, companies were having trouble finding

cash to make interest payments. The amount of corporate debt reached nearly twice the annual gross national product.

Even in fiscal year 1996, when Korea's economy grew at 7.1 percent (similar to Thailand's stunning growth that same year), 13 of the top 30 conglomerates were losing money, including four of the top 10. The loans mounted as investment slowed, indicating that from mid-1996, the firms were using borrowed money to cover operating costs.

BORROWING MONEY AND AMASSING debt seemed an attractive alternative to South Korea's corporate chiefs. It allowed them to navigate lean times while retaining control of their companies, rather than raising cash by issuing new stock and diluting their own stakes.

Merchant banks, relatively new in Korea, also played a role. They were, says Kim Kihwan, ambassador-at-large for economic affairs, "used literally as private coffers" by the conglomerates that owned them. The problems were compounded when companies went abroad for their borrowing, making them vulnerable to the collapse in the currency later in the year, after Thailand's currency troubles spread.

After the Hanbo mess was exposed, banks began taking a closer look at their loan portfolios, and started calling in loans to the most indebted firms. That created a domino effect of more companies failing.

The biggest blow to confidence came with the July collapse of Kia Motors, the country's eighth-largest conglomerate. Its debts were bigger than Hanbo's, and it brought down one of the country's premier banks, the Korea First Bank.

The crisis deepened as Southeast Asian currencies began collapsing in July and August. Many Korean merchant banks had borrowed U.S. dollars to buy high-risk bonds in Thailand. In addition, the loss of value of Southeast Asian currencies meant a loss of purchasing power for Korean goods.

Yet as late as September, many analysts, including the IMF, were making optimistic forecasts about Korea and its growth. And as late as November, with more big companies collapsing and the central bank spending half-a-billion dollars each day to prop up the sagging won, the government was still trying to cover up the extent of the crisis.

When on Nov. 12, Stephen Marvin, research chief for SsangYong Investment and Securities, issued a report to investors warning that "no beacon of light is visible" in Korea's financial mess, the finance ministry threatened to slap sanctions on SsangYong if it didn't halt distribution of the document.

Richburg reported from Bangkok and Hong Kong, Mufson from Seoul.

Africa's New Dawn

High risk and lack of credit make trade financing in sub-Saharan Africa difficult to obtain. But short-term loans through commercial banks and long-term investment funds are growing as its markets develop.

By G. Alisha Davis

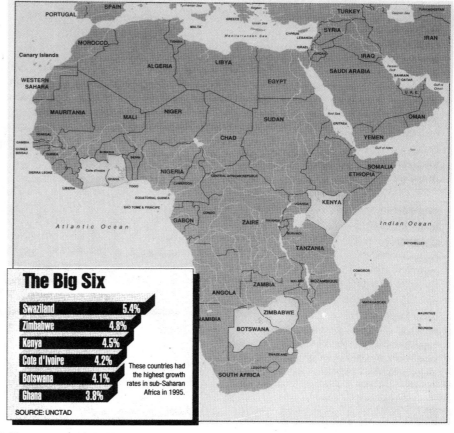

MAP/E. SHANE WEAVER

The Big Six

Swaziland	5.4%
Zimbabwe	4.8%
Kenya	4.5%
Cote d'Ivoire	4.2%
Botswana	4.1%
Ghana	3.8%

These countries had the highest growth rates in sub-Saharan Africa in 1995.

SOURCE: UNCTAD

When businesspeople think of Africa, they are likely to recall images of Rwandan refugees fleeing civil war, rather than the bold strides many governments are making in liberalizing their economies. Even when they do associate business with the continent, their perception tends to be an area with high risks and low — or at least unimpressive — rates of return.

Many foreign firms, particularly US companies, consider Africa their lowest-priority business region, or ignore it altogether. Even many multilateral banks, traditionally the most active financial institutions on the continent, are backing away. Africa, perhaps the area that needs it most, is the only place where lending by regional multilateral development banks is declining, falling from $5.2 billion in 1994 to $4.8 billion in 1995.

"When Americans look out across Asia and Latin America, they see potential trading partners. When they look out across sub-Saharan Africa, they see potential aid recipients," said the late Commerce Secretary Ronald H. Brown as he opened trading at the stock exchange in Abidjan, Cote d'Ivoire, during the five-country tour of the continent he conducted last year to promote US trade and investment. "That view has to change."

Although sub-Saharan Africa cannot match the booming "Asian tiger" economies of the Far East in attracting foreign investment, observers say it is not a market to be ignored. If businesspeople take a closer look, they will find that, in addition to South Africa, which attracts the lion's share of investment, lesser-known countries such as Zimbabwe, Kenya, Botswana and Cote d' Ivoire provide attractive investment opportunities.

"Investment in Africa is still incredibly risky," observes Jill Insley, a financial analyst at ABN-AMCO in San Francisco. "But, as with all new markets, the opportuni-

The Ten Largest Sub-Saharan African Stock Exchanges

Country	Exchange Established	Local Currency	# Of Listed Stocks	Established Stock Mkt. Capitalization
Botswana	1989	PULA	12	338
Cote d'Ivoire	1976	CFA Franc	26	520
Ghana	1990	CEDI	20	1,943
Kenya	1955	Kenyan Shilling	54	1,770
Mauritius	1989	Rupee	45	1,520
Nigeria	1960	Naira	180	1,300 (est.)
South Africa	1887	Rand	637	243,000
Swaziland	1990	Lilange ni	4	330
Zambia	1994	Zambia Kwacha	8	222
Zimbabwe	1946	Zim Dollar	76	3,900

SOURCE: FCA CORP.

Where We're Spending Our Money

US Foreign Direct Investment In Sub-Saharan Africa (in millions)

Country	1993	1994	1995
South Africa	$900	$1,013	$1,269
Nigeria	478	322	595
Cameroon	253	228	258
Liberia	181	197	229
Kenya	104	134	190
Ghana	117	143	170
Zimbabwe	127	144	150

SOURCE: BUREAU OF ECONOMIC ANALYSIS

ties are very good as well."

Many Asian firms are already finding that out; the continent is attracting increasing amounts of aid, trade and investment in transportation, telecommunications and energy from the Far East and Arab Middle East.

Banking On Success

Deciding you want to invest in or export to Africa is easy. Getting the money to finance your project is another matter. International lending has changed dramatically during the past decade due to many OECD governments and large companies migrating to bond markets. Bank facilities, however, still prevail for financing in Africa where, in many cases, bonds are not yet a viable option because of the high perceived risk in the region.

"Exploring financing opportunities within sub-Saharan Africa is something you don't take lightly," warns Ken Bruce, director of the trade underwriting desk at Pryor, McClendon, Counts & Co., a Philadelphia, PA, investment banking firm that has been active in trade finance to Africa since 1985, making it a veteran in a region that is only recently seeing investment activity. "There will be successes, and there *will* be failures."

One of the biggest problems US businesses face in initiating trade with Africa is financing — namely, a lack of credit and risk protection. Larger firms that invest in Africa, such as Coca-Cola, General Motors and AT&T, have the available cash required for equity financing, but small and midsize companies face the difficult task of raising the money.

"The first wall these companies run into is the Export-Import Bank of the United States," states Mr. Bruce. Due to government-wide policy decisions concerning the credit-worthiness of many African countries, legislative prohibitions and various repayment issues, the Ex-Im Bank is prohibited from providing trade financing for US exports to most African nations.

As for commercial banks, many are not active in sub-Saharan Africa, and those that are place significant restrictions on loans. "We have a big overhang of debt that many of the [African] governments owe us, so we are not increasing our per-country exposure on a long-term basis," notes Maurice Johnson, a vice president at Citicorp in New York. Last year, Mr. Johnson founded Citicorp's Africa Trade Finance Facility, which provides non-recourse financing for US exports to Af-

rica. "Our activity in the region is pretty much limited to short-term financing. Almost everything is done on confirmed letters of credit, and virtually everything is short-term unless you've got export credit agency support."

Types Of Financing

Although many banks are hesitant, it is possible to get financing in sub-Saharan Africa. For example, the Ghana Cocoa Board, a state-owned organization based in Accra that

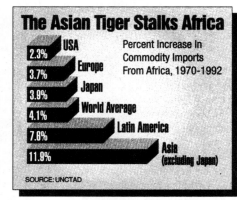

The Asian Tiger Stalks Africa

Percent Increase In Commodity Imports From Africa, 1970-1992

USA	2.3%
Europe	3.7%
Japan	3.9%
World Average	4.1%
Latin America	7.6%
Asia (excluding Japan)	11.9%

SOURCE: UNCTAD

oversees cocoa exports, secured improved terms in September from international commercial banks on its $275 million trade finance facility, making it one of the biggest African pre-export financing deals on the syndicated loan market. A total of 43 banks, including Citibank International,

Regional Lending By Development Banks
(percent change, 1989 to 1993)

Latin America	40%
Middle East/ North Africa	30%
Asia	15%
Sub-Saharan Africa	-20%

SOURCE: DEVELOPMENT BANK ASSOCIATION, INC.

Sumitomo Bank and Rabobank International, participated in the deal.

"It definitely shows that for deals where the financial structure is not weakened, banks are willing to see [profit] margins continue to fall," says Robert Halcrow,

head of syndications at Rabobank International in London.

Most banks like Citicorp require a trade letter of credit issued by the importer's bank on behalf of the importer and advised by the exporter's bank in favor of the exporter. Another option is a bill of exchange, essentially a promissory note or invoice signed by both parties involved in the trade and, usually, a bank. The exporter can obtain financing by discounting the bill with a bank for an amount equal to the face value of the bill less interest costs and fees.

Bills of exchange that are guaranteed by a bank can also be negotiated in the forfeiting markets. In Africa, forfeit receivables almost always consist of deferred payments under letters of credit. According to ABN-AMCO's Ms. Insley, amounts typically range from $1 million to $50 million, and maturities range from one year or less (short-term) for most of sub-Saharan Africa, to two years in Ghana, Kenya and Zimbabwe, three to five years in North Africa and up to eight years in South Africa.

Factoring is similar to forfeiting because it involves assignment by an exporter of receivables on a non-recourse basis against an advance payment. Mr. Johnson explains that the process at Citicorp can involve reassigning receivables to a correspondent factor agency in the importer's country, which pays the exporter and then collects payment from the importer.

If, for example, a US company wanted to export goods to Africa, it would ship the goods and then sell the invoice to a third-party factoring agency for less than the full value. Thus, the exporter would be assured of immediate payment, and the factoring agency would assume the risk, much as in forfeit-

Sub-Saharan African countries in which Ex-Im Bank support is not available:

Angola, Burkina Faso, Burundi, Cameroon, Central African Republic, Chad, Congo, Djibouti, Equatorial Guinea, Gambia, Guinea-Bissau, Liberia, Madagascar, Malawi, Mali, Mozambique, Niger, Nigeria, Rwanda, Sao Tome & Principe, Senegal, Sierra Leone, Somalia, Sudan, Tanzania, Togo, Zaire and Zambia
SOURCE: EXPORT-IMPORT BANK OF THE US

ing. Unlike forfeiting, however, factoring does not require a bank guarantee, can be used by small exporters and covers small amounts and maturities.

Although Africa has not yet been active in the $20 billion international factoring market, Andre Ryba, a senior banking official with the World Bank in Washington, DC, predicts the region will become far more important in the next century as an arena for trade and investment. When this happens, the foreign firms that have patiently expanded their roles and developed regional knowledge bases and marketing networks from years of trial and error will be in the best position to exploit Africa's economic opportunities.

Funding Through Funds

Many international fund managers are beginning to see just that. In the past few years, Africa has been home to some of the world's top performing stock markets. A number of investment houses have responded by launching Africa-specific funds. They include Morgan Stanley's Africa Investment Fund, Baring Asset Management's Simba Fund and Regent's Undervalued Assets Fund. In December 1995, the Simba Fund raised $30 million, which, although short of the $50 million hoped for, indicates the new interest in African stocks.

"The fund is looking for long-term growth for stocks in Africa and is aimed at export-oriented companies," explains Iban Ortuzar, investment analyst at London-based Baring Asset Management. "This is an attempt to avoid any possibility of losses due to exchange controls through currency devaluations."

The spread of the Simba Fund illustrates how uneven private investment in Africa is as a whole. South Africa receives the majority of investment, with 40 percent of the portfolio; Central, West and North Africa receive 10 percent each and East Africa gets only 5 percent.

"When people talk about investing in Africa, I think 80 percent of them really mean South Africa," says Tew Jones, research director at Fund Research, a consulting firm in London. "But there are 25 other African stock markets, too."

Mr. Tew argues that because of the economic changes many African governments have made in the past decade, Africa is now ripe for private and foreign investment. "In the past, [there were] essentially socialist governments, [which instituted] high protective tariffs that were not conducive to investment and economic growth. That is changing," he explains. "Today, you are looking at governments that have grasped the nettle of capital investment as a means of driving their economies forward and making them grow."

But not everyone predicts as bright a future for African economies as the analysts selling funds to investors. Most banks still offer only short-term financing; long-term funds for private investment, although gaining steam, have yet to explode. The fact is, Africa continues to become more marginalized in the global economy. With varying degrees of enthusiasm, many African governments have readied themselves for foreign investment, but little change will take place until the rest of the world catches on. Many Middle Eastern and Asian countries are waking up to the opportunities in Africa. European and US companies would do well to remember the early bird gets the worm.

Global Transfer Of Critical Capabilities

Henry P. Conn and George S. Yip

Effective human resource processes and other means, coupled with hard work, help transfer the capabilities so crucial to the success of foreign operations.

In the last decade or so, multinational companies from around the world have eagerly embraced globalization and have striven to develop and implement worldwide strategy. By now we all know how difficult this process is. Numerous barriers stand in the way of successful globalization. Some companies, however, have been spectacularly successful in taking their proven approach and replicating it across a range of markets. Examples include Toyota and Motorola worldwide, Disney in Japan, and, more recently, IKEA in Europe and the United States. Some companies have kept certain core aspects of their approach and significantly modified other aspects to suit local positioning; McDonald's in Asia Pacific (with common business systems but cuisine adjusted to local tastes) and Sears, Roebuck & Co. in Mexico (upscale image relative to mass merchant positioning in the U.S.) attest to this. Nevertheless, the business press is replete with examples of companies that have stumbled badly in transferring an approach proven in one market to other markets—Disney in Europe, Volkswagen in the U.S., and numerous companies in Japan, to name only a few.

Establishing, supporting, and leveraging foreign ventures is the essential building block in the globalization process. Yet failure can be more common than success, particularly in really tough markets such as Japan and China. In this article, we report that the effective international transfer of critical capabilities constitutes the single most important determinant of foreign venture success.

We draw this conclusion from a study of the experiences of 35 major multinational corporations (MNCs) in establishing 120 foreign operations. We also discuss the means for achieving successful transfer of critical capabilities, focusing mainly on the role of global human resource processes.

Much has been written about how to go about developing and compensating managers to compete globally. Our study is, however, one of the first to make the statistical link between effective global human resource processes and superior corporate performance.

Variations In The Performance Of Foreign Operations

What causes some companies to succeed in globalization and others to fail, particularly at the level of foreign operations and subsidiaries? To investigate this and other questions, we structured our research using the framework in **Figure 1**. Industry globalization drivers, such as internationally common customer needs, global scale economies, barriers to trade, and global competitive threats, influence the worldwide strategy companies try to implement, as well as the organizational structures they adopt to enable that strategy. The automobile and computer industries, for example, face much stronger globalization drivers than most segments of the food or apparel industries. And strategy and organization reinforce each other in their effects. Witness Asea Brown Boveri, whose acclaimed use of global strategy depends on its careful structuring of head office and subsidiary roles.

But however good the strategy and organizational structure, other key factors—particularly critical capabilities, people, management processes, and culture—intervene to affect implementation. The path to superior performance lies through these gatekeepers, which can accelerate, slow, or even derail the journey.

From *Business Horizons*, January/February 1997, pp. 22-31. © 1997 by the Foundation for the School of Business at Indiana University. Reprinted by permission.

The Role Of Critical Capabilities

We suspected that the effective transfer of critical capabilities would be a major contributor to success. These capabilities (sometimes called core competencies) are now widely recognized as essential to competitive advantage. In globalizing, therefore, MNCs need to be able to transfer the most critical capabilities within and between their networks of international operations.

McDonalds' tremendous overseas success has been built on the corporation's ability to rapidly transfer to foreign entrepreneurs the capability of operating the entire, complex McDonald's business system. Hong Kong's luxury hotel chains—The Peninsula Group, The Regent, and Mandarin Oriental—are in the process of a similar transfer as they expand globally. Although the hotels have attained success in the rest of Asia rather quickly, winning over the United States has been tougher. But at least one transfer has succeeded: In fewer than four years since start-up, the Peninsula in Beverly Hills, California has established itself as perhaps the premier hotel in all the Los Angeles area. This success springs in great part from the Peninsula's ability to transfer the right critical capabilities, especially its immaculate service, while adding other local requirements, such as a "stare-and-be-stared-at" swimming pool setup complete with cabanas for Hollywood negotiations.

In the automotive sector, exchange rate volatility and local content considerations have driven many Japanese manufacturers to push once "sacred" value-added design/development activities into their foreign market subsidiaries. Nissan, Toyota, and Honda have all pursued strategies whereby major elements of vehicle development are performed by in-country design teams. For those procedures that remain centralized, such as body engineering, there is heavy cross-fertilization of ideas resulting from temporary staff transfers as well as shared computer databases and telecommunications linkages.

In much the same way, aerospace manufacturers Boeing and McDonnell-Douglas have increasingly shifted value-added design and manufacturing work to "alliance" partners. This process, known as "offset" (in which partner design/manufacturing resource expenditures are offset, or used as payment for project equity commitments), is largely the result of efforts by the airframe manufacturers to defray the enormous expense of developing new aircraft and to favorably influence potential foreign customers (hoping, for instance, that JAL, ANA, and JAS will be more inclined to purchase from them if Kawasaki Heavy Industries has a significant level of design

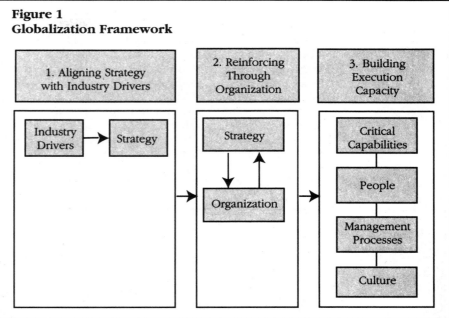

Figure 1
Globalization Framework

1. Aligning Strategy with Industry Drivers
   Industry Drivers → Strategy

2. Reinforcing Through Organization
   Strategy ⇄ Organization

3. Building Execution Capacity
   Critical Capabilities
   People
   Management Processes
   Culture

and manufacturing effort in the project). Typically, the foreign venture partner is most interested in receiving exactly the critical process/technology skills that a company such as Boeing designates as proprietary. However this issue is resolved, the success of the project rests on Boeing transferring the required skills and process knowledge to the foreign partner.

Defining Critical Capabilities

In our experience with clients and research participants, we have found the concept of "core competencies" to be ill-understood in practice—despite extensive academic discussion on the topic in recent years. Are core competencies "things we do well"? Activities that are unique to the company? Sources of competitive advantage? Some examples can illustrate the difficulties faced by companies trying to align their organizations on solid definitional ground.

General Motors, Toyota, and Volvo all know how to set up distributorships in markets outside their home base of operations, so none can claim a core competency in this regard. However, the lack of an effective distribution network could well be a significant source of competitive disadvantage. Accordingly, as a "thing we do well," the ability to define, structure, and manage distribution networks effectively across multiple country markets in the automotive industry is a "cost of doing business" activity, albeit a highly important one.

Likewise, the mere "uniqueness" of an activity clearly provides insufficient grounds for supporting a designation as a core competency.

Companies and entire industries—food service, data management outsourcing, contract inventory replenishment—have been founded with the intent to off-load "non-core" activities that, although potentially "unique," do not pass a value threshold of an activity in which the company must invest its own resources.

Finally, a source of "competitive advantage," though important to maintain and develop, may have little actionable value for the thousands of employees comprising the global organization. Coca-Cola's manufacturing infrastructure in Southeast Asia, funded by the U.S. government and later turned over to the company, provided Coca-Cola with a significant cost advantage in the region. However, this asset is region-specific and therefore of limited relevance to other country operations. It is also lacking in "animation," or the intrinsic ability of a process/knowledge "asset" to be nurtured, redefined, extended, transferred, and so on.

By definition, the term "critical capability" conveys that we are dealing with capabilities (discrete, meaningful, actionable, animate) that are critical (providing sustainable advantage, highly leverageable) to the corporation. Throughout our research, we have spoken to companies about critical capabilities as defined by their business and organizational competencies as well as various forms of intellectual property, such as patents, trademarks, software technology, and other non-patented but exclusive technological products and processes. Superior value is created when the business, organizational, and technological skills of a company are enhanced by or interwoven with key asset "nuggets" (such as brands, patents, and the like). In this regard, some examples of critical capabilities might include:

- Image branding/high-end merchandising
- Rapid commercialization of new technology
- System-wide franchise quality management
- Design for low-cost manufacturing

Collecting And Analyzing The Data

To investigate our framework, we developed a questionnaire structured to collect data from three levels of a company—the corporate CEO, the head of a line of business, and the heads of foreign operations or subsidiaries. **Figure 2** summarizes the topics we addressed at each level. We then recruited 35 major MNCs from North America, Europe, and Asia Pacific (listed in **Figure 3**), and asked each company to select two lines of business and identify three diverse countries it had entered within the last 5 to 15 years for each line of business. The country operations also had to vary in performance and be continentally or regionally dispersed.

The companies responded by identifying 120 foreign operations. About 70 percent of these operations were in developing markets in Asia, Latin America, and Eastern Europe, and the rest were in the United States, Canada, and Western Europe. On average, the companies had nine years of experience in these overseas ventures, and in total we collected more than 600,000 data points.

We measured the transfer of critical capabilities and most other variables, such as the effectiveness of the global processes for human resources, by asking respondents to rate these variables on a scale from 0 (not at all effective) to 10

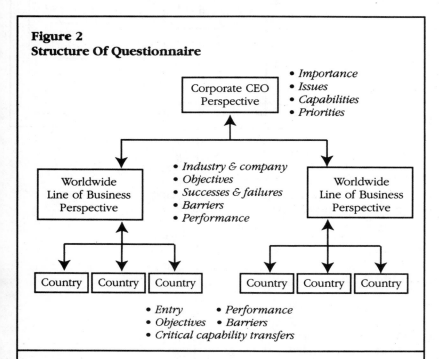

Figure 2
Structure Of Questionnaire

Corporate CEO Perspective
- *Importance*
- *Issues*
- *Capabilities*
- *Priorities*

- *Industry & company*
- *Objectives*
- *Successes & failures*
- *Barriers*
- *Performance*

Worldwide Line of Business Perspective

Worldwide Line of Business Perspective

Country   Country   Country   Country   Country   Country

- *Entry*   - *Performance*
- *Objectives*   - *Barriers*
- *Critical capability transfers*

Figure 3
Companies In The Study

North America HQ
Amoco
Amway
AMP
Baxter International
Dow Chemical
Du Pont
Eaton
Federal Express
FMC
General Motors
Molex
Pittston
PPG
Rockwell
Tektronix
Tenneco
Xerox

Europe HQ
Altana
Ansaldo
Barilla
Danfoss
Fiat
Finmeccanica
Jotun
Kværner
Lafarge Coppée
Montedison
Olivetti
Pirelli
Volvo

Asia-Pacific HQ
BHP
Canon
National Australia Bank
Telstra
TNT

(completely effective). To supplement the data collected from the questionnaires, we conducted personal interviews with 16 CEOs and 22 senior executives at the line of business head offices and country operations. We used correlation coefficients and multiple regression to estimate the relationships between variables. We also compared the characteristics of foreign operations that were "winners" with those of the "losers."

How The Foreign Operations Performed

One primary measure, Expected versus Actual Performance, was obtained by asking each Line of Business (LOB) head to rate the company's performance in each country relative to the firm's expectations at the time of entry. A rating of 100 meant that expected performance was equal to actual performance. This measure allowed direct comparison of performance across industries and countries, and correlated highly with such traditional measures of performance as sales growth and market share.

The foreign operations varied greatly. Fewer than half had performed satisfactorily relative to expectations at the time of entry. Moreover—and not surprisingly—the spread in performance decreased with the years since entry. This was because the poorest performers were closed down and the companies had time to fix other poor performers.

Successful Transfer Has The Strongest Effect On International Performance

We examined a wide range of factors that might affect the success of foreign ventures. These included the extent of globalization strategy, the fit of this strategy with globalization drivers, organization structure, barriers to entry, entry objectives and strategy, use of performance measures, human resource practices, and localization of strategy and management. But the effectiveness in transferring critical capabilities was far and away the most important in affecting performance. On average, a 20 percent improvement in transfer effectiveness was associated with a better than 7 percent improvement in performance.

In addition, high performers (the upper third of our sample) scored 22 percent better than low performers (the lower third of our sample) in transfer effectiveness. If the average performer were able to improve its capacity to transfer critical capabilities to the level of the highest performer in our study, the performance improvement would exceed 15 percent. Average transfer capability among all participants was 6.8 on a scale of 0 to 10.

Several of the comments made in the interviews were:

- "If only we knew what the company knows" (a country manager).
- "What parts of the past do we want to use as pivots of the future?"
- "The firm does practice the shared services concept in North America, but not in Europe, though we are looking at this now."

CEOs Want To Improve Critical Capabilities

As could be expected, the CEOs repeatedly identified critical capabilities as being among the issues for which their companies most needed improvement. These are shown in **Figure 4**. As one CEO put it, "It is still a matter of debate, inside and outside our group, as to whether a large company can be effective in leveraging its critical capabilities when entering a market like, say, China." Another CEO saw no easy solution:

> In terms of leveraging our knowledge across and around the Group, we do not have any simple solutions. We try and get our people around the world to work on common problems. . . . [T]hese may be common issues or ones common to a business across countries.

A third said, "We are mediocre, though improving in the exchange of know-how and best practices in manufacturing processes." The CEOs also recognized the competitive imperative to strengthen critical capability transfer. As one stated, "Early on, [our competitor] globalized their R&D capability, giving them a serious advantage."

But some CEOs are beginning to find solutions. Said one of our respondents, "(We are) establishing a more comprehensive and practical 'Corpus of Doctrine' reflecting the Group's experience in, and approaches to, strategy, marketing, operations, analysis, and reporting . . . to facilitate know-how transfer."

Figure 4
Identified Areas Most In Need Of Improvement

Strategic capabilities
- Fully exploiting worldwide capabilities
- Acting on changing globalization drivers
- Making moves against competitors around the world

Organizational capabilities
- Developing talent and leadership for innovation and renewal
- Leveraging global capabilities effectively
- Structuring for optimal global performance

Management process capabilities
- Nurturing global management talent
- Transferring best practices
- Stimulating transfer of critical capabilities

Figure 5
Types Of Critical Capabilities Identified and Percentage Of Respondents Listing Each

CEO	Line of Business	Country
		Sales management - 41%
Product development - 67%	Product development - 53%	Product development - 39%
	Low-cost manufacturing - 53%	Low-cost manufacturing - 32%
Brands and products - 33%	Marketing - 29%	Marketing - 20%
Partnering skills - 30%		Brands - 20%
Low-cost manufacturing - 29%		Channel - 20%
Customer service - 22%	Customer service - 29%	Customer service - 9%
Sales management - 13%	Sales management - 26%	

Many Critical Capabilities Identified

Figure 5 summarizes the critical capabilities identified by each level of management. CEOs in particular identified the general categories of new product development and technology as their companies' most critical capabilities. Aspects of these included design for manufacturing, time to market, patents and intellectual property, and technology in general. Other critical capabilities, in order of frequency, included partnering and alliance skills, low-cost manufacturing, customer service, product life cycle management, hiring and developing international managers, information technology, speed and flexibility, and quality management. Many of these capabilities were related to each other. One CEO said, "We have three interlinked capabilities: negotiating, developing contracts, and building relationships."

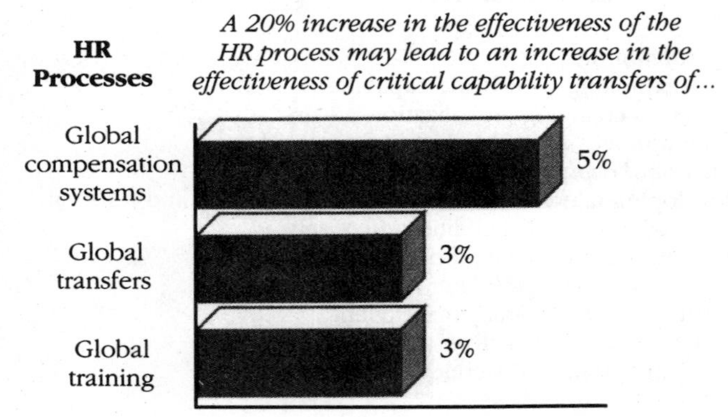

LOB heads were proportionately less concerned about new product development, but it still topped their list. Predictably, they saw operational issues as relatively more important, including capabilities in low-cost manufacturing, marketing, customer service, quality management, sales management, brands and products, channel management, product life cycle management, and hiring and developing global managers. The critical capabilities can also be very specific to individual industries. An LOB head of a mining company said, "Our critical capabilities are the ability to estimate the prospects for significant reserves and the ability to correctly assess political risks in the regions in which we operate."

The trend toward operational concerns was even more marked for country managers, although new product development was still a major concern. Other critical capabilities at country level were similar to those of the LOB heads.

The dispersion of activities in Figure 5 is noteworthy. Although differences in industries, product markets, and other factors clearly account for some of this spread, there still appears to be widespread confusion around what constitutes a critical capability. For example, "new product development" is defined at too high a level to be meaningful and actionable. Better definitions might be "rapid commercialization of new technologies" or "industry-leading styling."

Mismatch Between Management Levels

Within individual firms, the level of alignment was less than might be expected from the above picture. CEOs and LOB heads were each asked to identify six critical capabilities. On average, and even with a generous interpretation of similarity, only 2.1 of their selections matched. When coun-

Figure 6
Global Human Resource Processes Help Critical Capability Transfer

HR Processes	*A 20% increase in the effectiveness of the HR process may lead to an increase in the effectiveness of critical capability transfers of...*
Global compensation systems	5%
Global transfers	3%
Global training	3%

try heads were asked to name three critical capabilities, on average only 1.6 of these could also be found in the LOB list. Given this low degree of alignment, it is not surprising that these firms had difficulty determining exactly what critical capabilities to transfer.

Although the respondents did not agree on what comprised critical capabilities in their companies, we were able to establish that the transfer of those capabilities was the most important factor in the success of foreign operations through the statistical analyses relating such transfer to performance. In other words, we did not have to ask respondents directly whether they thought critical capabilities affected performance, but could deduce that from correlation and regression analysis.

Human Resource Practices As The Key Method For Enhancing Transfer

Certain human resource practices, we found, had a high correlation to the successful transfer of critical capabilities: global compensation systems, transferring managers from country to country, and having worldwide training systems. A 20 percent increase in the effectiveness of each of these processes may lead to an increase of 3 to 5 percent in the effectiveness of critical capability transfer (**Figure 6**).

At the same time, the use and effectiveness of these processes were all relatively low—in the 3 to 6 range out of a possible 10 (**Figure 7**). Companies faced many problems in this area. One CEO commented, "People from central 'X-state' [location of company HQ] are very loyal, but they do not like to move." Another CEO said, "I have worked in the international area for almost 40 years. There is no greater need than identifying and nurturing talent for local markets. All U.S. corporations have the same problem."

Some firms were beginning to force international experience. "To reach a certain management level," said one CEO, "it is mandatory to have 'out of country' experience." Other firms were working hard on the problem; one was putting together a skills matrix across its global operations and addressing how to take "a 25-year-old and develop him (or her) into a global manager [via, e.g.,] three functional careers, three geographic careers, and at least two business unit careers." Summarizing this issue, another CEO said, "My top globalization issue is people development and building a learning organization."

The low degree of global coordination of HR processes is not surprising, because country managers have the greatest autonomy in this area. The respondent country managers had more local autonomy in decisions about human resources (7.9 out of 10 overall) than about physical assets,

technology, or capital (**Figure 8**). Among different types of HR processes, country managers did indeed have the lowest autonomy in transferring personnel (6.5). But this relative lack of autonomy was more than offset by very high levels in training (9.0) and evaluating (8.9).

Consequently, head office managers can exert only limited influence on global strategy execution and capability transfer when most types of HR decisions are beyond their control. Again, MNCs face the dilemma of a need for local autonomy versus a need for global coordination.

Need For More Global Managers

The companies surveyed certainly recognize the need to change their HR processes. For instance, they all plan to increase the use of global manag-

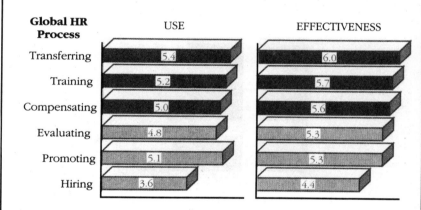

Figure 7
Average Ratings Of The Use And Effectiveness Of Global Human Resource Processes

Rated on a 0 to 10 scale, in which 0 = "Not used at all/Not at all effective" and 10 = "Always used/Completely effective"

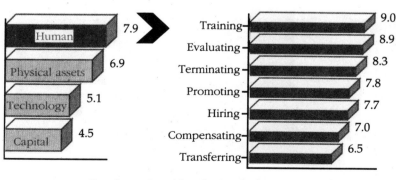

Figure 8
Degree Of Decision-Making Autonomy

Rated on a 0 to 10 scale, in which 0 = "No autonomy" and 10 = "Total autonomy"

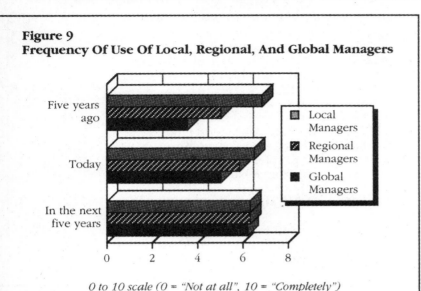

Figure 9
Frequency Of Use Of Local, Regional, And Global Managers

Legend:
- Local Managers
- Regional Managers
- Global Managers

0 to 10 scale (0 = "Not at all", 10 = "Completely")

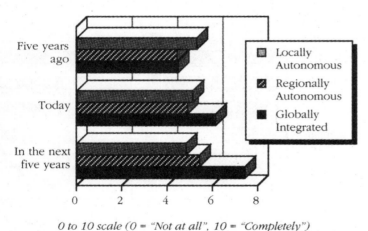

Figure 10
Frequency Of Use Of Management Processes

Legend:
- Locally Autonomous
- Regionally Autonomous
- Globally Integrated

0 to 10 scale (0 = "Not at all", 10 = "Completely")

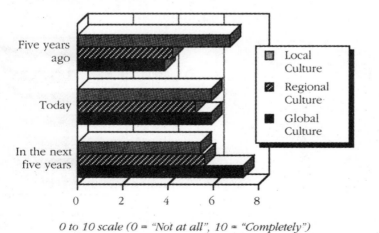

Figure 11
Gradual Shift To Global Culture

Legend:
- Local Culture
- Regional Culture
- Global Culture

0 to 10 scale (0 = "Not at all", 10 = "Completely")

ers relative to local managers (shown in **Figure 9**). The executives we interviewed made many telling comments:

• "We have to find a way of managing the free flow of talent and necessary skills around the world with the objective of building a competence-based organization."

• "The single most important issue is creating internationalists."

• "The limiting factor for our growth is human capital."

• "How do we seed the samurai, and how should we manage the development and transfer of excellence?"

• "[The company] now insists that its top 50 managers have both international and cross-functional experience."

Global Management Processes Also Help Make The Transfer

In addition to international human resource processes, global management processes in general helped the transfer of critical capabilities. Overall, a 20 percent increase in the use of global, as opposed to regional or local, management processes may lead to a 3 percent increase in the effectiveness of critical capability transfer. The use of global management processes is relatively low today. But companies plan to do much more in this regard and lessen their use of local management processes (**Figure 10**).

In commenting on the problem, one CEO said, "We fragment the understanding, focus, delivery, and leveraging of our critical capabilities through our information systems, patterns of communication, career paths, management reward systems, and processes of strategy development." Proposing a solution, another CEO said, "We need to weave our critical capabilities into the corporate strategic themes for, and across, each of our business's plans and budgets."

Global Culture Plays Key Role

Having a global company culture, rather than regional or local cultures, also plays a powerful role in the transfer of critical capabilities. We found that a 20 percent increase in the extent of having a global culture may lead to a 4 percent increase in the effectiveness of critical capability transfer. Several quotes highlight this effect:

• "A global culture is denationalizing operations and creating a system of values shared by managers around the globe."

• "Culture is the value-setter and lubricator."

• "We get what we measure. We need to change our performance measuring and compensation systems to encourage sharing and teaming."

• "Establishing a common culture across the division is also a key globalization factor."

• "We are more transnational or global than [our competitor] because we grew up as a result of many acquisitions, each with its own culture."

As with global human resources and other management processes, the companies were gradually shifting from a local orientation to more of a regional and international orientation. Within the next five years, and compared with five years ago, the companies planned to reverse the dominance of local culture relative to global culture (**Figure 11**).

Other Methods Of Transfer

We also asked country managers about three key methods for transferring critical capabilities: rotation of staff, dedicated global teams, and management meetings. As shown in **Figure 12**, these methods averaged a rating of only 5.2 (on a scale of 0 to 10) in use for transferring critical capabilities from headquarters or other units to a country operation. They rated an even lower average of 4.4 for transfer from country operations to headquarters or other units.

When asked about other methods of transfer, the country managers identified many different mechanisms. Some entailed the sharing of information: written communications, memos to share lessons, newsletters and magazines, release of information, data transfer, and information technology. One CEO said, "Designing and installing an effective global IT network is critical if we are to keep in touch, share, and deliver the best—internally and to our customers." But technology will not be the sole answer. Another CEO commented, "I do not see a cybernetic revolution ahead in addressing the issue of knowledge (including best practice) sharing."

Other transfer mechanisms related to training and education, and included training at home country operations, business academies, dedicated courses, and top-down training and implementation. Coordination mechanisms comprised cross-sector umbrella teams, a global executive committee that met monthly, application segment teams, and a global customer management process. As one CEO put it, "We have started the formation and use of 'Country Councils' whereby they bring the managers of the different businesses in a country together to share views but without getting tangled up in the details of each other's business."

Direct involvement by HQ also was cited. This took the form of strategy reviews, country visits, and central and regional control. Both technical support and head office support in general were also mentioned. Centers of excellence are also being used. One CEO mentioned, "We may

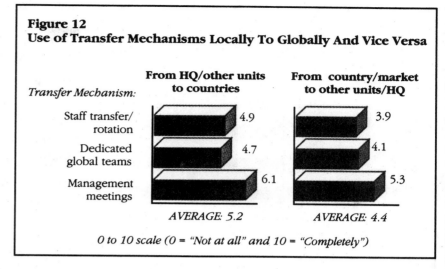

Figure 12
Use of Transfer Mechanisms Locally To Globally And Vice Versa

Transfer Mechanism:	From HQ/other units to countries	From country/market to other units/HQ
Staff transfer/rotation	4.9	3.9
Dedicated global teams	4.7	4.1
Management meetings	6.1	5.3
	AVERAGE: 5.2	AVERAGE: 4.4

0 to 10 scale (0 = "Not at all" and 10 = "Completely")

try and use a 'Centers of Excellence' approach for technology and best practice." Finally, simply having a customer focus or market focus could also be of help.

Incentives For Adapting Or Sharing Critical Capabilities

Some companies provided incentives for adapting or sharing critical capabilities. Rewards to local managers for adapting corporate critical capabilities to the local market included:

• management incentive programs and other financial rewards;

• recognition programs such as corporate quality awards; and

• praise and recognition in performance appraisals.

One company went so far as to have specific performance objectives defined for implementing capabilities worldwide. Similar, though fewer, rewards were given to local managers for sharing capabilities from their country with headquarters or other units. Being recognized for their local capabilities seemed to be particularly motivating.

Many firms, however, had no specific incentives. And many local managers recognized the operating and strategic benefits of adapting corporate critical capabilities without additional reward. In actuality, there may often be significant disincentives to transfer, such as when a disproportionate level of resource investment must be borne by the capability "source" unit vis-à-vis the "recipient," or in the midst of political concerns about helping a future rival for promotion.

Methods Of Gaining Cooperation

Many companies used direct mechanisms not only for the transfer of critical capabilities, but also for gaining the cooperation of country man-

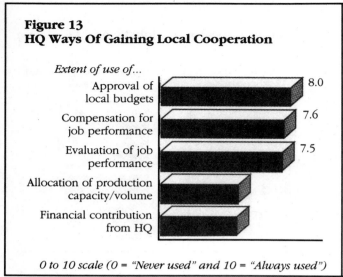

Figure 13
HQ Ways Of Gaining Local Cooperation

Extent of use of...

Approval of local budgets — 8.0
Compensation for job performance — 7.6
Evaluation of job performance — 7.5
Allocation of production capacity/volume
Financial contribution from HQ

0 to 10 scale (0 = "Never used" and 10 = "Always used")

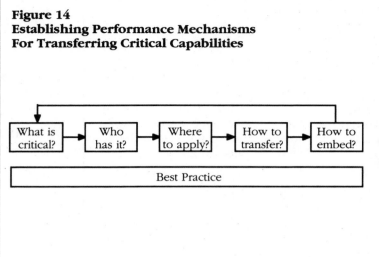

Figure 14
Establishing Performance Mechanisms
For Transferring Critical Capabilities

What is critical? → Who has it? → Where to apply? → How to transfer? → How to embed?

Best Practice

agers in global and regional strategies. Of the methods we asked about, approval of local budgets was at the top of the list—rating 8.0 in the extent of its use (**Figure 13**)—followed by compensation for job performance, evaluation of job performance, allocation of production capacity and volume, and financial contribution from headquarters. Executives also mentioned various other methods, some of which were formal (global policy directions, strategy integration systems, approval of strategic plans, capital authorization, global customer management, business management councils, international project organization, personnel selection) and some informal (training and follow-up, seeding personnel, esprit de corps, personal contact and relationships, and constant international networking).

These direct and indirect methods of headquarters control can be seen as counterweights to the autonomy enjoyed by country managers. Percy Barnevik, the CEO of Asea Brown Boveri (not a participant in this study), frequently proclaims the high degree of autonomy given to local managers in his company. Less publicized is the fact that ABB's head office managers use the allocation of production volume as a powerful weapon to gain compliance. Most of the industries, such as power generation systems, in which ABB's businesses participate suffer from excess capacity. Moreover, in a given line of business, ABB usually operates factories in more than one country. Getting a production order thus makes a huge difference in whether a local ABB manager will make his or her budget for the year. So ABB's head office may speak softly but it carries a very big stick! Most MNCs have similar secret weapons for influencing the hearts and minds of their local managers.

I f you truly want to be successful at globalizing your company, you need to establish permanent mechanisms for the transfer of critical capabilities. Start with understanding what is critical in your industries and lines of business. Then create and improve those capabilities, identify and recognize the sources and carriers, identify which types are needed in which countries, transfer and adapt them there, and embed them into your foreign operations.

Of course, a continuing feedback and learning loop is essential; **Figure 14** summarizes this process. Many of the executives in our study have pointed out what is needed:

• "We know our critical capabilities but have not done a good job in defining, communicating, and installing them."

• "We must be more explicit, exhaustive, and rigorous in communicating, educating, and practicing our critical capabilities."

• "Developing the understanding of how to transfer the lessons learned from one market to another [is crucial]."

• "View the company as a competence-based organization that delivers highest market impact through leveraging best practices worldwide."

You also need to recognize that HQ is no longer the owner of critical capabilities. Instead, it is increasingly a facilitator of their transfer. Critical capabilities may be created, adapted, and transferred by many different units: headquarters, line of business, country operation, business process, centers of excellence, teams, or a shared service center. Putting it all together can mean creating a multilevel spider web of transfer capabilities. As the CEOs put it:

• "We have now decided to change from informal networking to a formal comprehensive way of capturing, measuring, and installing best practices around our world. . . . In fact, it's not a choice, but a *must* if we are to be a leader."

• "In terms of leveraging our knowledge across and around the Group, we don't have any simple solutions. . . . [W]e try to get people from around the world to work on common problems. . . . [T]hese may be common issues or ones common to a business across countries."

• "Our focus is on the management and development of the intellect, information, and tools for tailoring, flexing, leading, and differentiating."

• "A virtual HQ is rapidly replacing a 'solid center HQ' as competence centers and responsibilities are spread across the network into the operating units."

Returning to the overall framework for this study, we can see that the global transfer of critical capabilities constitutes an essential step in moving from globalization potential to realized international competitive advantage. Even in light of the many ways to effect this transfer, in every case managers will have to work very hard to make it happen.

References

Christopher A. Bartlett and Sumantra Ghoshal, *Managing Across Borders: The Transnational Solution* (Boston: Harvard Business School Press, 1989).

Andrew Bartmess and Keith Cerny, "Building Competitive Advantage Through A Global Network Of Capabilities," *California Management Review*, Winter 1993, pp. 78-103.

Joseph H. Boyett and Henry P. Conn, *Maximum Performance Management: How To Manage And Compensate People To Meet World Competition*, 2nd ed. (Lakewood, CO: Glenbridge, 1993).

Joseph H. Boyett and Henry P. Conn, *Workplace 2000* (New York, Dutton, 1991; Plume 1992).

Gary Hamel and C.K. Prahalad, *Competing For The Future* (Boston: Harvard Business School Press, 1994).

J.K. Johansson and George S. Yip, "Exploiting Globalization Potential: U.S. And Japanese Strategies," *Strategic Management Journal*, October 1994, pp. 579-601.

Michael E. Porter, "Changing Patterns Of International Competition," *California Management Review*, Winter 1986, pp. 9-40.

C.K. Prahalad and Yves L. Doz, *The Multinational Mission: Balancing Local Demands And Global Vision* (New York: Free Press, 1987).

C.K. Prahalad and Gary Hamel, "The Core Competence Of The Corporation," *Harvard Business Review*, May-June 1990, pp. 79-91.

Joseph L. Raudabaugh, "Asian Investment: Lessons From The Japanese Experience," *Planning Review*, January-February 1995, pp. 38-40.

George Stalk, Philip Evans, and Lawrence E. Schulman, "Competing On Capabilities: The New Rules Of Corporate Strategy," *Harvard Business Review*, March-April 1992, pp. 57-69.

George S. Yip, *Total Global Strategy: Managing For Worldwide Competitive Advantage* (Englewood Cliffs, NJ: Prentice Hall, 1992).

Henry P. Conn is a vice president of A.T. Kearney, a global management consulting firm based in Chicago, Illinois. **George S. Yip** is Adjunct Professor at UCLA's Anderson Graduate School of Management. This article reports on a study conducted by A.T. Kearney. The authors thank the many companies who participated in the study, and the many A.T. Kearney staff members, as well as Professor Phil Smith of Michigan State University, who worked on it.

■ **Prepare To Walk a Moral Tightrope**

Put Your Ethics To A Global Test

What seems a cut-and-dried matter of ethics in the United States, may not translate to your operation overseas. As companies struggle to determine what's right and what's wrong, HR is helping them define global ethics and communicate this to workers across the globe.

Charlene Marmer Solomon

Charlene Marmer Solomon is a contributing editor at PERSONNEL JOURNAL.

Global scandals make headlines daily. There was the Daiwa Bank trading scandal, in which billions of dollars were lost from improper bond trading—and hidden by high banking officials. There was the 1995 U.S. Department of Labor report documenting child labor abuse in 56 countries where children are used to mine gold, among other things. Then there was the Ex-

xon Valdez disaster, the BCCI (Bank of Credit and Commerce International) debacle, and the Bhopal catastrophe. And there were other events that never made the newspapers: piracy of intellectual property, payments to third parties so companies could do business, nepotism and conflict of interest.

All these incidents have one thing in common: they're a matter of ethics—or a lack thereof. The issue of global business ethics is the ultimate dilemma for many U.S. businesses. As companies do more and more business around the globe, their assumptions about ethical codes of conduct are put to the test. Corporate executives may face simple questions regarding the appropriate amount of money to spend on a business gift, or the legitimacy of payments to liaisons to "expedite" business. Or they may encounter out-and-out bribery, child-labor disputes, environmental abuse and unscrupulous business practices. As organizations expand globally, HR managers must play a role in helping to define and achieve ethical behavior from employees throughout the world.

To accomplish this, many international businesses are creating codes of conduct, like the ones such companies as IBM, Xerox and Shell Oil have had for years. These three companies, and others, including Levi Strauss, Honeywell, Digital Equipment and H.B. Fuller, are taking their efforts even further—by incorporating their messages into everyday business practices and making them living documents.

What are global ethics and how do they impact business? Defining ethical behavior in a domestic setting is tricky enough. Not only do people respond differently to moral questions, but individuals—even in the same culture—interpret morality differently. When you add the cultural overlay, business ethics can become a quagmire of moral questions. Some even say the term "global ethics" is an oxymoron. Is it?

"One of the myths about global business ethics is that when you do business in other cultures, they will have a whole set of different ethical values and mores. That simply is blown out of proportion," says W. Michael Hoffman, executive director of the Center for Business Ethics at Bentley College in Waltham, Massachusetts, and co-author of "Emerging Global Business Ethics."

"When you dig deeply enough and scrape away all the trappings, the real ethical solid building blocks or principles of most cultures are the same."

For example, most people agree mistreating children is wrong, but they sometimes disagree about what constitutes mistreatment. For instance, most Americans consider child labor mistreatment. But in countries in which economic conditions warrant child labor, and laws and definitions of the family unit support it, it isn't regarded as cruel, but rather as a fact of life. "You have to understand the full context of the ethical decision-making of each culture. Once you un-

derstand it, you might say it's ethically incorrect without believing it's immoral," says Hoffman.

He says it's important for Americans—who sometimes get too moralistic—to walk a moral tightrope between the two extremes of ethical fanaticism and ethical relativism as we venture into other societies. "Ethical fanaticism is the position that says my ethical position is right, and I have the absolute answers. It doesn't recognize legitimate ethical disagreement and has no toler-

---

Contemplating Global Ethics: Where Do You Start?

1. **Think about your company's mission statement and values.**

2. **Clearly articulate those values. Define a code of ethical behavior.**

3. **Remember that cultural differences dictate flexibility and sensitivity.**

4. **Develop training in which employees learn—and apply—the company's values.**

5. **Create appraisal systems that reinforce the ethical behavior the company demands.**

6. **Communicate company ethics wherever and whenever possible.**
  —*CMS*

---

ance or appreciation of different perspectives, including cultural perspectives," Hoffman explains. "Ethical relativism is an equally bad extreme because it's saying there are no absolute values, which eventually leads to a state in which there's nothing right absolutely or wrong absolutely. It's a philosophical position that says I have no way of telling you you're morally wrong if you

go out and kill or eat people because there are no absolute values."

Walking the middle road isn't always easy, however. Some global actions clearly lack ethics, such as the actions of Nazi Germany, for example. But there are others that are gray, such as the use of DDT in countries where there are no substitutes and without which the crops would be consumed by insects. Even the use of bribes can be debated on moral grounds. Bribes of hundreds of thousands of dollars to line a military general's pocket, most would agree is wrong, but what about payments to people who take goods off the docks to expedite service? That isn't considered unethical under many circumstances.

Ethics are a matter of business. In response to these questions, some groups are taking a leadership role. The Caux Round Table is one such organization. Created in 1986 by Frederik Philips (former president of Philips Electronics) and Olivier Giscard d'Estaing (vice chairman of INSEAD), the Round Table brings together leaders from Europe, Japan and the United States. Their mission: To focus attention on global corporate responsibility, in the belief that the world business community plays a role in improving economic and social conditions.

Including such giants as Siemens AG, The Chase Manhattan Corp., ITT Corp., World Bank (France), Minnesota Mining & Manufacturing Co., Canon Inc. and Matsushita Electric Industrial Co. Ltd., the group has developed world standards to measure ethical behavior. The standards are based on two principles: the concept of human dignity, and the Japanese doctrine of *kyosei*—the idea of living and working together for the common good to enable mutual prosperity. The Round Table is proactive in its commitment to global responsibility. Founders believe business can be a powerful force for good because it's essential to provide employment and products and—more importantly—because it has the capacity to improve the lives of its customers and employees.

The Round Table lays out seven general principles that range from the general edict to protect (and where possible, improve) the environment, to more specific ideas, such as supporting the multilateral trade systems of the world. Underlying these ideals is the assumption that respect for cultural differences requires sensitivity and some flexibility. One of the most astounding aspects of the document is that it's values-driven but steeped in business acumen.

Indeed, Robert MacGregor, president of the Minnesota Center for Corporate Responsibility—the group largely responsible for the language of the *Caux Round Table's Principles for Business*— sees ethical behavior as a business imperative. "The world has shrunk and is so interconnected that behaviors everywhere affect behavior everywhere else."

For example, although a company can save money by laying off expensive American workers and hiring cheap child labor in Bangladesh, these types of actions will backfire financially for a company in the end. "We want companies to move their jobs and capital around the world while making money, [and still] following responsible standards."

H. B. Fuller Company, makers of adhesives and other specialty chemicals, agrees that honesty and trustworthiness—themselves important—translate into dollars and cents. Case in point: The St. Paul, Minnesota-based company pursued buying a subsidiary from a European adhesive manufacturer. It was the only American firm out of a dozen companies interested in the purchase. The European company was interested in H. B. Fuller's bid. but looked a little nervously at the U.S. company because the subsidiary wasn't making money and had too many people in the business. "Their perception of U.S. companies is that they don't think twice about having massive layoffs regardless of what it does to people," says Tony Andersen, chair of H. B. Fuller's board of directors. "We showed them through oral histories— examples within our company—that our corporate culture values people. That really counted to this large European company, which helped us finance the acquisition."

Clearly stating company values is the first step. H.B. Fuller's situation demonstrates how ethics stem from corporate values. "You've got to think through very clearly what your company's values are—what you stand for wherever you do

business," says John Buckley, ethics officer for Maynard, Massachusetts-based Digital Equipment Corp., which has more than 50% of its employees outside the United States. Digital's *Code of Business Conduct* clearly defines practices the company expects its employees to use in their daily activities. This substantial 27-page booklet, which addresses such ethical issues as managing company information and gift giving, provides the wisdom in a specific manner that requires employees to think about their behavior. For instance, in the section on gifts and entertainment, employees are given the following scenarios to think about: "You receive an unsolicited holiday gift from a supplier; you're invited to an annual trade show at a resort by a supplier who offers to pay your airfare and hotel bills; customers are visiting a Digital site for the day and you would like to take them to lunch. Do you know the proper business use of gifts and entertainment?" it asks.

The rest of the chapter details the company's position on gift giving and receiving, its implications and possible misinterpretations. It's straightforward and unambiguous, and offers the chance to question one's own actions.

"Wherever we do business, it's highly dependent on personal relationships between the people conducting the business. By basing our code of conduct on the company's core values, we believe it's more transferrable and adaptable internationally," says Buckley.

Step two: Communicate. Clear principles are one thing, but they're useless unless they're communicated to employees. Digital communicates its values through company newsletters, electronic transmissions and in training programs. Everyone receives a code of conduct booklet, and the company requires all managers to discuss the code with their employees at least once a year.

Honeywell Inc., based in Minneapolis, recently has translated its formal code of ethics into six foreign languages. Senior management regularly communicates the importance of ethics and compliance in newsletters, ethics presentations and other periodic communications. For example, a recent newsletter for the Asia Pacific region included a letter from the president talking about bribery. He reiterated that

bribery will not be tolerated at all, and that the company will walk away from business rather than engage in bribery.

Levi Strauss & Co., a recognized leader in corporate social responsibility, encapsulates its values in the company's mission statement, and reiterates them in an *Aspirations* statement and in a printed code of ethics. The San Francisco-based company clearly defines business ethics and commitment to employee respect and fair treatment. Its statements clarify what's important, and what's expected in behavior.

But Levi Strauss doesn't leave the translation of its statement to chance. Since 1988, the company's HR department has conducted global training on different aspects of the aspiration statement. Managers and employees from around the world participate in three- to five-day courses on various aspects of leadership—one of which is ethics. The three-day ethics course gives people the opportunity to understand the company's expectations and definitions, and also gives them the chance to identify their own moral principles to see where they overlap with the company's.

"When people are clear about their own values and can identify the principles that make up ethical behavior, they have the tools for looking at potential decisions and the possible impact on different stakeholders, and whether or not the decision is an ethical one based on these principles," says Richard Woo, currently senior manager for global communications and previously regional manager for community affairs for Asia-Pacific.

An important part of the ethics training is to help people learn a decision-making tool—a process for making ethical decisions—called the *Principled Reasoning Approach*. The Principled Reasoning Approach isn't simply a name; it relies on thoughtful evaluation and a rational process to figure out how ethical principles translate into behavior.

Here's an example: The company went through the process when it considered whether or not to enter the South African marketplace. Levi Strauss convened a cross-functional task force, called the South Africa Policy Group, made up of Levi Strauss' managers worldwide and included people from marketing, operations, finance and community affairs.

The group met over several months for one or two days at a time, and in between, members researched specific issues and reported back to the group. It researched the history of apartheid and the movement of businesses in the country—who decided to leave and who decided to stay. It identified the principle interests and who the different stakeholders were, including the anti-apartheid community that would be affected by Levi Strauss' decision. The task force sent several key members to South Africa to conduct site visits and interviewed the ANC, members of the current government and members of community organizations. Finally, it talked with other multinational corporations already doing business in the country.

All of this took place as South Africa was going through the changes that eventually led to its free elections. The task force was able to make a recommendation to the company: that when certain conditions changed—including free elections—it would be the appropriate time for Levi Strauss to enter South Africa.

Such an inclusive information-gathering process allowed the company to make an informed decision that was based on its principles. It was able to create milestones so the company could judge the most appropriate time.

Since free elections were held, Levi Strauss South Africa opened both marketing and production facilities, including a multiracial, multicultural management team. The business also maintains an active corporate social investment program, which includes charitable contributions to the community—so it can be part of helping the country grow through the transition.

Apprise your business partners of your standards.
Levi Strauss also has global sourcing and operating guidelines that address workplace issues. The company uses these guidelines to select business partners who will manufacture its products. Established in 1992, its guidelines were the first created by a multinational company for its business partners. The terms of engagement detail everything from environmental requirements to health and safety issues. Among them: wages, discrimination, child labor and forced- or prison-labor issues. To create these guidelines, the company used the Principled Reasoning

Approach. And to launch them, it conducted audits of contractors it was using worldwide.

Implementing the guidelines, Levi Strauss discovered that in Bangladesh, it had two contractors using workers in the factories who appeared to be underage. International standards have set a reasonable working age at 14. When the company brought it to the attention of the factory owners, the owners asked the company what it wanted the factory to do. There were no birth certificates so there was no way to know exactly how old these children were. Also, even if the children were younger than 14, they would very likely be a significant contributor to the family income and probably would be forced into other ways of making a living that would be more inhumane than working in a factory—such as prostitution or begging.

"So, we were faced on the one hand with a set of principles that were very clear, and on the other with the reality of underage workers and severely impacting their family incomes," says Woo. The solution? "The contractor agreed not to hire any more underage workers," he says. They also hired a physician to examine children who seemed to be less than 14 years old using growth charts identified by the World Health Organization. Although not hiring young workers may force them to find work elsewhere, Levi Strauss' position is to be ethically responsible for business issues it can control—such as responsible child labor conditions—as opposed to social conditions in a country that it has no control over.

Levi Strauss also negotiated for the contractors to remove the under-14 workers they already had from the production line and continue to pay them wages as if they were still working. In exchange, Levi Strauss covered the cost of the children's uniforms, tuition and books so they could go to school. When the underage workers reach the age of 14, they will be offered back their original factory jobs. The contractors complied with all this, "to maintain the contracts with us," says Woo.

As a result of the company's guidelines, the organization has made an impact on suppliers around the globe. It has brought about shorter work hours, seen infrastructures reinforced for better health and safety, seen fire extinguishers and fire exits put into workplaces, and seen

contractors install equipment to meet environmental guidelines.

Translate ethical behavior into performance.
Once guidelines such as Levi Strauss' are in place, it's crucial to reinforce principles and ethical actions. Honeywell encourages its business units to use its code as part of their performance evaluations. Levi Strauss includes ethical practices as part of its professional evaluation. In other words, it ties compensation to performance, which includes ethics. Employee's annual performance review includes questions about ethical dilemmas.

Accountability for the company's code of ethics counts at H.B. Fuller, also. The organization identifies people within the business who are in positions that could be subjected to difficult moral decisions. In addition to being sure these employees understand the code of conduct, they receive an "audit" in which they're asked about anyone who has done something that in their view might be questionable. "We communicate that it's really number one in importance," Andersen explains.

Despite its importance, ethics often fall by the wayside because companies aren't clear on what they consider right and wrong. "It's a difficult thing—to understand what's the bedrock that defines your company and the way you operate, while keeping an open mind and trying to learn business practices in other countries," says Buckley. "How do you make the trade off?"

You have to really think about it. Be open-minded. Learn. And be prepared to take the hard stand. "At some point you're going to come up with the decision of not pursuing a piece of business because it violates your values. It could be labor practices or environmental concerns or corrupt payments. It could be that you realize you can't do business while maintaining a diverse work force and that violates your principles."

Hoffman calls it the *child test*. "If the action gives you any pause—and you can't imagine explaining it to your child—then it's probably a good thing to stop, look and listen before crossing the track."

In any case, managers in multinational companies who are confronted with these situations have to think through their own ethics. It's more than a delicate balance; it's a critical balancing act.

CULTURE SHOCK

Keeping Up On Chinese Culture

Cross-cultural communication is tough. The solution? Learn about the customs of your global colleagues.

PHOTO: PHOTODISC

By

VALERIE

FRAZEE

[handwritten margin note: ※ major problem → we tend to think everyone is just like us ⇒ this article assumes U.S melting pot w/ Canadian mosaic*]*

Let's say you're in Shanghai on business. You're walking down the street and you pass a Chinese colleague. He asks, "Have you eaten yet?" Your answer, "No, not yet," sends him rushing off looking embarrassed and uncomfortable.

Would you have anticipated that reaction? Probably not. It becomes crystal clear when you understand that "Have you eaten yet?" is a common greeting—just like the expression, "Hi, how are you?" is in the United States. It's the Chinese way of saying "Is your belly full today?" or "Is life treating you well?" The usual response would be something like: "Oh yes, I've just had something. Thanks."

Clearly, not knowing this puts you at a disadvantage. And as American businesses are discovering that the world is their marketplace, they're also learning that these types of cultural misunderstandings are something they can't afford. This is true whether your employees are conducting negotiations abroad or your foreign colleagues are traveling to the States. It even applies when you're communicating internationally by phone, fax or e-mail.

Fortunately, this issue can be handled through training. Learning how things work in China—negotiating styles, the roles of men and women, dining customs and nonverbal behaviors—may not make us experts in Chinese culture, but it raises our awareness of our differences and prepares us for handling some of them.

China and it's neighbors. One of the things you have to be careful of is assuming if you know something about the culture of one country, that the same characteristics hold true for its neighbors. Often you'll find general similarities among the cultures of a region, and it's useful to note them. But recognizing the specific differences among the cultures is equally important. This is absolutely the case with China and surrounding Asian nations.

From a broad perspective, both Koreans and Chinese subscribe to a philosophy which dictates that one should be humble. "The issue of humility will affect how they greet you for the first time, how you exchange business cards, how you address each other very formally and how you bow with each other," Dean Foster,

director of the cross-cultural training division of Princeton, New Jersey-based Berlitz International Inc., explains. "They both share that—whereas Americans don't have any notion of humility."

On the other hand, Foster cites an example from his own experience of one key difference: "Very often [Chinese banquets] start with a little, sweet, dumpling kind of appetizer. And then you move through the meal and the final dish is a rich-tasting soup. We were having this and one of the Korean fellows sitting there was just struck by the Chinese banquet and how different it was from how they dined in Korea. And he said, 'Look at this: in China we start with dessert and we end with soup!' This, of course, would be the kind of observation you'd expect from an American."

Another interesting difference between China and some other Asian countries is that in China women are accepted in the higher levels of business. "[American women in management] are not a problem for China," Foster says, "because during the 40 years of communism, Chinese women did have access to fairly high levels of authority—not necessarily in the government only but even in the private sector. ... But I'm speaking only of China now. It would not be the same in Korea."

Chinese communication styles. Communication can be difficult between two Americans who've known each other for years—especially during high-pressure negotiations. So we shouldn't be surprised that when cultural differences are thrown in, the situation becomes quite a bit more complicated. But it should help to know a few things about how Chinese approach business discussions.

Keep in mind that Chinese often use an indirect form of communication, even in response to a direct question. This can be frustrating to Americans, who tend to prefer the opposite approach. Foster says: "They may or may not be attempting to be evasive. They may be unsure about what they want to say. They may be stalling for time. Or the person you're talking with may not have authority and doesn't want to venture an answer."

Also, don't let it throw you if the people you talked with in the first meeting aren't there for the second meeting—or if the people from the second meeting aren't there for the third. What may look to you like a problem is actually a positive sign. It probably means you're advancing through the hierarchy. The trouble is you may not know how high up the decision maker is. So the trick is to start as high as you can—but to do this requires a contact to arrange the first meeting.

Although there are more than 30 languages spoken in mainland China, two of them function as the primary languages of business: Mandarin and Cantonese. And while it's always helpful to speak the language of the country you're doing business with, these are difficult languages for westerners to master. So as a show of respect, it's certainly advisable that your

Culture Quiz

What Do You Do When ... ?

1. The Chinese have stalled and stalled and stalled. Now, you have only one more day in Beijing before your flight home. Suddenly, during the final day of the negotiations, they appear to soften some of their demands—but of course, they expect you to give up some of yours as well. How could you have handled this better from the start?

2. You are introduced to Mr. Zhang Minwen at a banquet. You address him as Mr. Minwen, and become aware of his unfavorable reaction. You guess that you've said something wrong. But what?
→Chinese→last name first

3. You admire a beautiful Ming vase at your Chinese associate's home. Suddenly, before you leave, he thrusts a paper bag into your hands. You peek inside and see the vase. What do you do?
→take it

4. You've finally closed the deal, after exhausting both your patience and your company's travel budget. Now, two weeks later, the Chinese are asking for special considerations that change the terms of the agreement. How can they do this? Why are they doing it? And most important, what do you do?

5. On a business trip to Shanghai, you are invited to a banquet. Should you ask if your spouse may accompany you?

Culturally Sensitive Behavior Would Be ...

1. This is a typical Chinese negotiating tactic. One way around this is to tell them you're leaving Friday—and actually leave the following Wednesday.

2. His name is Mr. Zhang. Chinese put their family name first.

3. You take it—because you admired it. You also reciprocate as soon as possible with an equally valuable gift.

4. The contract, for most Americans, represents the end of the negotiation. For the Chinese, however, it's just the beginning. Once a deal is made, the Chinese view their counterparts as trustworthy partners who can be relied upon for special favors ... such as new terms in the contract.

5. Spouses (wives or husbands) aren't welcome at business social functions.

Source: Dean Foster, director of the cross-cultural training division of Princeton, New Jersey-based Berlitz International Inc.

employees learn enough to be social on a basic level, but you shouldn't worry about their fluency unless they'll be making a long-term commitment to China.

If your employees don't speak Mandarin or Cantonese well enough to conduct business discussions, then you should provide them with a translator—since outside a few areas like Hong Kong, Chinese are unlikely to be fluent in English. And Foster advises: "If you're working with

translators, it's important in China to bring your own. If you rely on theirs, you'll only get half the story. You'll get the story they want you to hear."

From the U.S. point of view. No matter how you look at it, China's culture is extremely different from the States'. "China is geographically, metaphorically, historically and in every possible way, half-way around the world," Foster says. "The Chinese talk

from a very different point of view in terms of how they see the world and their expectations of human relationships. And these expectations are reflected in management styles and in the way we work with each other. One of the key problems that Americans and Chinese have had has been the Chinese expectation that any relationship is a personal relationship. And the American expectation is that it's nothing personal, just business."

Another fundamental difference lies in how Americans and Chinese respond to the concept of proprietary rights. Foster explains: "The Chinese really don't understand how an individual can own the rights to an idea—it's just culturally not part of their history. In China, you have to share ideas—they can't be owned. The entire group has to benefit from the idea." This, of course, is a difficult concept for Americans to grasp. Asking Chinese to pay someone for an idea is like asking Americans to pay for air.

So once you've organized some cross-cultural training, should you ask your employees to act Chinese when in China—and expect your Chinese colleagues to act American when in the States? It's not likely that would work very well. "Cross-cultural training programs aren't designed to make you Brazilian or Chinese—but they are designed to get you to see that the Brazilians and the Chinese may view business and the world a little bit differently," Foster says.

What you can do is encourage your employees to be Americans with a sensitivity for how their behavior will be interpreted by others. And if they can modify a few of the things they might have wanted to do without thinking, then they're sure to have a more successful experience in working with their global peers.

Valerie Frazee is special projects editor. E-mail frazeev@pjmag. com to comment.

American Involvement in Vietnam, Part II: Prospects for U.S. Business in a New Era

Clifford J. Shultz II, William J. Ardrey IV, and Anthony Pecotich

Clifford J. Shultz II is an assistant professor at the School of Management, Arizona State University, Phoenix, and an associate at the Columbia University Center for International Business Cycle Research. **William J. Ardrey IV** is a vice president of Fiduciary Communication Co., New York. **Anthony Pecotich** is a senior lecturer at the University of Western Australia, Perth. The authors give special thanks to Standard Chartered Bank, Tilleke & Gibbins, the Vietnamese Foreign Ministry in Hanoi, Ho Chi Minh City University, the Ho Chi Minh City College of Marketing, the Hanoi Institute for Research on Market and Price, and the numerous interviewees who graciously consented to give their valuable time.

W ith the stroke of President Clinton's pen last February, the Vietnamese trade embargo ended and U.S. business horizons expanded considerably. Many American firms, having already evaluated the risks and rewards of the Vietnamese market, have moved swiftly to penetrate it; others are only now evaluating the country and are moving more cautiously.

Over the course of the last two decades of the embargo, U.S. corporations were forced to watch and wait as businesses and governments from Australia, Japan, Singapore, Taiwan, Hong Kong, Indonesia, Malaysia, and the former Soviet Union—to name just a few of the major players—invested billions of U.S. dollars in one of the few world economies presently experiencing real GNP growth greater than 5 percent. Now U.S. firms have the unrestricted opportunity to compete in one of the world's most promising markets. But given the present mix of players and current business conditions, what are the prospects for U.S. business in Vietnam?

The purpose of this article is to address that question while providing more general insights into the considerations for market entry in authoritarian East Asian economies. The information we share here is based on data we have collected on site and via secondary sources during the last three years. Our methods included a combination of ethnographic techniques, personal interviews, and analyses of secondary data provided by the United Nations, ASEAN, institutions within the Vietnamese, American, and Australian governments, and various universities in the United States, Vietnam, and Australia.

Vietnam's unique history, its pervasive grip on the American psyche, and its extraordinary—if somewhat perilous—business opportunities make it a compelling study. Thus, this article is an assessment of the investment environment in Vietnam at the start of a new era in U.S. and Vietnamese relations.

WAITING FOR THE U.S. INVESTMENT FLOOD

T here has long been the perception in Vietnam that once the trade embargo was lifted, money would magically pour into this country of more than 70 million people and wash away the many problems that have inhibited development. Part of this optimism is well justified; the market potential of Vietnam *is* enormous and American firms are understandably eager to penetrate it. But even though the embargo may have deprived many U.S. companies of some potential profits, American trade sanctions and pressure within the international community combined to hurt Vietnam far more.

For years, the United States constricted the total flow of aid and investment into Vietnam, making it difficult for the country to rebuild after decades of war. More specifically, since 1965 the U.S. government has invoked the 1917 Trading with the Enemy Act to prohibit doing business with what was then North Vietnam. After the U.S. withdrawal in 1975, prohibitions against trading or investing in Vietnam continued and were ex-

> *With the lifting of the trade embargo, Vietnam is poised to grow and prosper. American firms looking to invest had better take note.*

From *Business Horizons*, March/April 1995, pp. 21-27. © 1995 by the Foundation for the School of Business at Indiana University. Reprinted by permission.

tended to include restrictions on economic and financial assistance from the IMF, the ADB, the World Bank, and other multilateral agencies. This U.S. pressure kept most other countries from supplying needed investment as well. And until Vietnam's withdrawal from Cambodia in 1989, most industrialized nations supported the American-led embargo. Add to these conditions the Vietnamese government's disastrous economic policies and expensive military activities of the 1970s and early 1980s, and one can understand just how close Vietnam came to the brink of economic collapse and social upheaval.

The only real aid flowing into Vietnam in the 1980s—mostly in the form of technical assistance and capital goods, and provided in rubles—came from the Council for Mutual Economic Assistance, controlled by the former USSR. But even that aid fell off in 1991 and, with the disintegration of the USSR, stopped altogether in 1992. Other countries have begun economic assistance in recent years—more than $200 million in 1991 and $600 million in 1992—but aid at this level is not nearly adequate for the task of rebuilding a developing country that has been cut off from capital and technology for decades. Direct foreign investment has flowed at significant levels only since 1991. The Vietnamese hope that the accelerating rate of investment aid from multilateral agencies, and the return of U.S. companies—with cash in hand—will be the catalyst that enables the country to claw its way to the oft-cited objective of "Asian Tiger" status. Indeed, Vietnam has paid a high price for independence, and in many respects the world passed it by. Now, however, with the advent of peace and political stability, most Vietnamese wish to make up for lost time and are urgent to prosper and become part of the world community.

So Vietnam is faced with the formidable task of building an economy that can support a population expected to exceed 81 million by the year 2000. By approving a renewal of IMF lending to Vietnam in July 1993 and lifting the embargo on February 3, 1994, the U.S. government has given heart to businesspeople who have long been optimistic about the prospects for Vietnam's economy. Private American businesses have given an additional vote of confidence to the Vietnamese; IBM, GE, Caterpillar, BankAmerica, Philip Morris, Citibank, IBM, and a host of other

> "For all Vietnam's progress and promise, the nation continues its three-steps-forward, two-steps-backward transformation called market socialism."

U.S. companies were setting up offices even before the embargo was lifted, and many more continue to follow.

ECONOMIC TRANSFORMATION

Vietnam would not be such a promising market, of course, had not the Vietnamese government restructured the political and economic foundation of the country. The most fundamental changes occurred in 1986, when the Seventh Party Congress implemented a policy referred to simply as *doi moi*, which loosely translates into "economic renovation" or "change for the new." This policy change included market-determined pricing and a tolerance for free enterprise. Results were striking and immediate as a private sector blossomed and foreign investors flocked to Hanoi and Ho Chi Minh City (HCMC, formerly Saigon). Yet for all Vietnam's progress and promise, the nation continues its three-steps-forward, two-steps-backward transformation called market socialism—a free market economy under the aegis of communist party leadership.

Any discussion about buying, selling, and doing business in Vietnam must bear in mind that Vietnam has been, and will continue to be, an authoritarian, single-party state. Although the economy continues to evolve as the country borrows administrative practices from Singapore, China, and other Asian economic models, support for economic reforms is not universal within the government. The present government continues to be led by the Communist Party of Vietnam (CPV), which intends to stay in power by ensuring that senior positions in government are held by party members.

In a sense, reform was forced upon the communists. Unlike neighboring China, where economic liberalization has enjoyed the unqualified support of both the senior leadership, headed by Deng Xiaoping, and a reformist faction that has kept the new economy marching forward since 1978, reform in Vietnam is supported by ambivalent factions within the CPV. Conservatives know that macroeconomic prosperity is by no means the only outcome of reform policies. These policies have also changed the face of Vietnamese society, and threaten to bring even greater social change, corruption, a widening gap between rich and poor, Western ideas on individual rights, and cries for political freedom that are imported along with investment capital and technology.

Despite the potential threats of "social depravity" and "cultural imperialism," *doi moi* was seen by the CPV as the only answer to Vietnam's desperate economic situation. To stay in power after years of deprivation, the Vietnamese government had to deliver greater prosperity. But the

CPV continues to pepper progressive laws with party rhetoric, so the central leadership in Hanoi remains divided to this day between hard-liners and reformers. Such division could permit the CPV to impede reforms despite the accelerating momentum of the reform movement.

By maintaining many inefficient socialist principles, the central government actually empowers local governments with deciding which line to pursue, conservative or reformist. In the absence of clear guidelines from the central government and the ruling party, local officials will be inclined to exert greater control over the economic development of their regions. American businesses hoping to initiate enterprises may find they will have to receive approval first from Hanoi, then from local governments whose officials will need to be convinced of the benefits of having a new American business in town. All this is despite recent efforts by the Vietnamese government to streamline the approval process for startup operations. In one of the poorest countries in Asia, this opens the system to more corruption and the danger of "foot-dragging" by conservatives in Hanoi at a time when a detailed law on foreign investment, a blueprint for a modern banking system, and rational codified tax policies are long overdue.

Still, the reform movement *is* accelerating, even though the government still holds 75 percent of Vietnam's assets, uses most of the bank credit, and employs a third of the work force, yet only contributes a third of the country's GDP. In the face of extraordinary challenges, the private sector contributes more than 40 percent of industrial output and employs the other two-thirds of the working population. Private sector output is growing exponentially, and statistics on the private sector are indicators of the tenacity, industriousness, and entrepreneurship of the Vietnamese and, more generally, Vietnam's investment potential.

A Foundation for Growth

Vietnamese economic planners are encouraged by the examples of Korea, Indonesia, Thailand, and China. These countries have all turned their economies around in less than two decades. The politically astute Vietnamese leaders can see that citizens of these countries have forgiven many of the sins of their respective governments. Political freedoms may inch along, the gap between rich and poor can widen, corruption can be ignored, the environment can be exploited; in the end, many transgressions will be tolerated as long as the people have a solid belief that greater wealth will be delivered and the quality of life will improve. American firms setting up in Vietnam can gain confidence from the country's economic

performance under *doi moi*, even if government-imposed business policies often seem to be at conflict or, worse, wildly out of sync with Western logic and standard international business practices. And for a transforming economy moving from Marx to market, only serious economic reversals will cause the political instability that authoritarian governments fear—such as the former Soviet Union's inability to deliver basic goods to its citizens, which facilitated the disintegration of the USSR, or the rampant inflation and sociopolitical uncertainties that fueled the Tiananmen demonstrations in China. If Vietnam is progressive but cautious, the government can truly lead the country to an era of rapid growth and rising standards of living for its citizens.

> "By selling rice, oil, and other products, Vietnam has begun to develop links with the more industrially advanced world."

To date, economic reforms have had the most success in the agricultural sector, permitting Vietnam to transform itself from a net importer to a major exporter in less than a decade. In contrast to other transforming economies—such as China, where rural policy is constantly changing, causing farmers to be skeptical of investing heavily for fear of another "great leap forward"— there is a high level of confidence that rural reforms will remain in effect. According to one property developer from Singapore, the Vietnamese people truly believe they will be able to pass their land to the next generation through transferable leases (a significant individual incentive), despite state ownership laws for all land (Ong Beng Kheong 1994).

At the same time, Vietnam has beaten down inflation to about 6 percent, which is superb compared to the 400 percent rate the country experienced in 1988. By selling rice, oil, and other products, Vietnam has begun to develop links with the more industrially advanced world. Its top five export markets in 1992 were Japan, Singapore, Hong Kong, China, and France, and the country recently signed export agreements with the EEC, expanded markets in the Middle East, and resumed trading with other former Soviet bloc nations. Vietnam may now have gained the experience necessary to profit from the opportunity to sell to the United States and gain access to Western technology with fewer restrictions.

At bottom, Vietnam is clearly committed to development. According to Pham Chi Lan (1992), Deputy Secretary General of the Vietnamese Chamber of Commerce and Industry, "Market forces are now the driving force in Vietnam's economic development." And as chairman of the Ho Chi Minh City Foreign Trade and Investment Development Center, which works to promote international trade in HCMC as Vietnam liberalizes its markets, restructures its industries, and becomes active in international trade, Pham Chi Lan stated, "The key will be to bring the right people together and to take full advantage of the opportunities" (1994).

Cautious Optimism

Fundamental statistics seem to support cautious optimism. Vietnamese exports, for example, increased from $2 billion in 1991 to $3 billion in 1993; the imports of consumer goods and other predictor variables of consumer wealth and consumption patterns continue to increase exponentially. Development also continues at a dizzying pace, as 73 projects worth more than $1.5 billion await approval in HCMC alone. Some of these are in property, such as the Saigon Tower joint venture to build commercial office space ($10 million) and a Ba Son shipyard development project ($6.6 million). Moreover, Vietnam supplies 58 percent of its consumer goods domestically, including more than 60 percent of the food, liquor, cigarettes, and even home appliances bought by its citizens, and sells abroad about as much as the nation buys from foreigners, although a troubling trend toward deficit trading is emerging. The most recent statistics from the General Statistical Office (1994) indicated Vietnam's exports for the first half of 1994 totaled $1.6 billion dollars, a 26 percent increase over the same period last year, while imports totaled $1.8 billion dollars, a 30.6 percent increase over that same period.

> "Some consumers in Vietnam will move slowly toward embracing a purely consumer culture; others are already completely smitten by it."

Particularly noteworthy is a growing concern among Vietnamese about sustainable development. During one of our meetings in January 1994, a senior official in HCMC discussed new forest regulations to prevent exploitation. After learning environmental lessons from their comrades in Eastern Europe and China, and after suffering the effects of defoliants, napalm, and other toxic chemicals used during the war, the Vietnamese seem keenly interested in avoiding any new environmental catastrophes. But here, too, there are conflicts. Many projects and policies, some of which have already begun and some of which are planned, are clearly detrimental to the environment. So we wonder whether "politically correct" conversation is also creeping into Vietnamese policy discussions.

The Vietnamese government also responded positively to a complaint frequently lodged by U.S. companies in Asia—namely, trademark infringement. The Vietnam Union of Cigarette Producers shut down a Marlboro cigarette counterfeiting operation in response to a December 1, 1993, protest by the Philip Morris group. Though this decision was partly a gesture to influence U.S. congressional delegations and other officials to lift the trade embargo, it also suggests that the government is serious about involving U.S. companies in Vietnamese development.

SO, WHERE EXACTLY IS THE OPPORTUNITY?

Vietnam is still a poor country, with an official per capita GDP of about $250 and more than 80 percent of its population living in rural areas, engaged in agriculture. The country has, however, a rural population that continues to benefit from economic reforms, as well as a growing urban population and developing Western-style markets for goods and services.

Partly because of the various wars over the past 50 years, which took a portion of the population off the land, and partly because of the burgeoning economies in the cities, urban areas are growing in wealth and population density. This urban population, which has readily embraced free enterprise, is an emerging force that will help drive much of the economy. Middle classes and even upper classes are forming. These trends suggest that domestic economic successes can now be combined with foreign investment to facilitate more rapid growth. For example, Ho Chi Minh City is expected to grow at about 11 percent and attract more than $1 billion in investment capital. Within a few years, this will be a market with considerable wealth and buying power.

Emerging Consumer Markets

As a traditional Asian culture and an authoritarian socialist political environment, Vietnam is an interesting case study of the diffusion of consumer culture. Some consumers in Vietnam will move slowly toward embracing a purely consumer culture; others are already completely smitten by it. Like many countries with growing economies, the young urbanites are proving to be opinion leaders who prefer imported motorbikes to bicycles, Western-style sneakers to domestic designs, and Western music and popular culture. The pent-up consumer frustration felt by many Vietnamese has been expressed well by Hoang Ngoc Nguyen (1992):

After two or three decades of living in a penurious economy and self-imposed austerity, a consumer boom is evident. Japanese scooters, color TV sets, VCRs, refrigerators, and other electronic appliances are common, even in remote areas.

The rate at which this consumer boom is diffusing into Vietnamese society is accelerating and a discernible market segmentation pattern is emerging with the diffusion process. That pattern roughly differentiates consumers along North-South, urban-rural, and old-young lines, though recent observations suggest to us that the North-South differences are dissipating somewhat, at least in terms of consumer needs and wants, whereas others are becoming more apparent. Young consumers, for whom the war with America is a history lesson, have ambitions and consumer desires hardly distinguishable from many youths around the globe.

The university students we recently interviewed were almost unanimous in their career plans: to work for a foreign-owned company or joint venture and enjoy all the material benefits such employment offers. The idea that an entrepreneurial spirit is healthy, not subversive, is slowly becoming accepted by both the government and Vietnamese society. As Vietnam grows in wealth and expands contact with the outside world, demand for American consumer goods ranging from soft drinks to cosmetics is bound to increase.

The desire for Western products and the affinity for Western images indicates that some U.S. firms have product lines perfectly positioned to exploit current Vietnamese market conditions. Not surprisingly, many firms have moved swiftly to leverage such competitive advantages. Pepsi-Cola, for example, began production within hours of the announcement of the ending of the embargo. More than 40 million cases of soft drinks are already sold annually in Vietnam, a figure that is expected to increase fivefold within the next decade; such packaged consumer goods, the easiest Western goods to purchase, are relatively inexpensive.

An increased interest in marketing and consumer behavior has led the government to compile databases to track consumer spending and foreign companies to employ market research firms to measure purchase patterns. The segmentation schema mentioned earlier will segment even further. Consumer behavior will continue to be influenced by returning Viet Kieu (overseas Vietnamese), interaction with tourists and expatriates, and general information diffusion from television and periodicals. If Vietnam's economy manages to grow faster than its population, prospects for a modern consumer market are good.

Export Market

Like many Asian economies, Vietnam's governmental policy and tax code favor foreign businesses that set up to export. Imports of equipment, for example, are free of tariff and tax, and the seafood industry is an excellent illustration of the country's ability to build a healthy, value-added export industry. Petroleum, agricultural products, and minerals are good illustrations as well. Basic low-tech and labor-intensive manufactured goods, such as shoes and textiles, soon will be.

An important benefit of lifting the embargo has been Vietnam's integration into the world economy. Exports for all of 1993 saw Vietnam increasing coffee exports by 25 percent, tea by 30 percent, sea products by 22 percent, and garments by 22 percent. As one of the world's poorest economies, the newly embargo-free Vietnam will be entitled to favorable quotas on its exports to the developed world.

The Multilateral Aid Market

Every businessperson and government official seems quick to point out Vietnam's inadequate infrastructure. Although the Australians are busy upgrading the international telephone system, Vietnam badly needs new roads, power plants, ports, transmission lines, and other investments in infrastructure. More than $2 billion is slated for investment in one project alone to build a major North-South highway. Ten American companies have already registered intentions to bid for two sections of this contract, and American companies that have established some sort of operation in Vietnam clearly have an op-

> "The idea that an entrepreneurial spirit is healthy, not subversive, is slowly becoming accepted by both the government and Vietnamese society."

portunity to capitalize on the good will fostered by the recent warming of relations between the U.S. and Vietnamese governments. General contracting and heavy equipment companies, for example, are natural suppliers.

Some observers have suggested that many East and Southeast Asian brands have become so firmly entrenched in the market that it will be difficult to acquire significant market share in many industries. Ironically, says Nick J. Freeman (1993), U.S. business now needs Vietnam more than Vietnam needs U.S. business. Despite the absence of Americans from the Vietnamese market and the resultant successful efforts by other nations to fill the vacuum created by that absence, American companies still enjoy very good brand image in Vietnam. Coca-Cola, for example, has been smuggled into Vietnam for years and never really left the country. Its advertising slogan in Vietnamese is *Vui Mung Gap Lai Cac Ban*, ("Good to See You Again"), in contrast to the newer Pepsi publicity blitz that declares Pepsi-Cola *Su Lua Chon Cua The He Moi* ("the Choice of a New Generation"). Furthermore, a can of soda, for which a Vietnamese would pay anywhere from 30 cents to a dollar, is equivalent to an American spending about $15 per can—a pretty strong indicator of brand image and customer loyalty.

Nevertheless, American corporations will have difficulty converting existing brand loyalties in the electronics industry, for example, or perhaps even in the personal computer industry. Still, American firms have (at least) two advantages over other players. First, many American products are simply perceived to be superior to many other non-American products. Second, the Vietnamese government is keen to establish mutually beneficial commercial ties—and therefore implicit political ties—that will enable the United States to serve as an important counterbalance to the emerging political clout of historical regional nemeses China and Japan.

This tendency for the communist Vietnamese government to see America as a potential political ally may seem extraordinary (and more than a little ironic) to most Americans. Yet to the Vietnamese, the *realpolitik* of a new era requires good relations with the United States. Twenty years after the fall of Saigon, such vision is both economically and politically expedient. Consequently, some projects have been earmarked specifically for American concerns. For example, Vietnam has long favored U.S. investment in its oil fields; it keeps an eye on China's claims to some choice fields and again welcomes U.S. investment, as much for strategic political reasons as immediate economic value.

Other Opportunities

Finally, the authors have observed a rapid growth of import-export businesses and cash businesses such as hotels, restaurants, and car rentals, many of them managed by Viet Kieu. These companies are reshaping the commercial and physical landscape of urban Vietnam because they often provide services to other investors and deep-pocketed expatriates, and because the return on investment is relatively quick. Generally, however, companies would be well advised to think in terms of long-run returns on investment rather than aiming for the "quick hit."

One of the most striking outcomes of Vietnam's renovation is a feeling of rebirth shared by almost every Vietnamese we have encountered. Indeed, the eagerness of the people to improve their country, their enthusiasm to learn how to accomplish that goal, and the role they expect American business to play in the process are remarkable. With the mutually beneficial support of foreign partners, the nation's prospects are promising, and most Vietnamese consider American businesses to be among the most desirable partners. Many sources say American investment is welcomed for its own sake as well as to balance Chinese and Japanese investments in the region, but investors should also note that most Vietnamese genuinely like Americans as well as American products.

Before the embargo was lifted, a steady flow of businesspeople, U.S. lawmakers, diplomats, and academics visited the major cities and assured themselves that (a) Vietnam was committed to reforms and (b) the benefits to U.S. firms outweighed any ideological differences with the Vietnamese government. Nevertheless, business managers with high expectations may be disappointed if they expect quick returns from their investments. Prudent investors have learned that respect for the following factors is required for any successful operation.

First, Vietnamese workers are dedicated and literate, but their basic accounting and managerial skills are sadly lacking. Even though Vietnamese generally possess a great desire to learn these skills, especially the younger people, U.S. companies can expect to invest heavily in training their employees. This investment in basic human resource development does not include the substantial investments in modern manufacturing facilities and equipment that are necessary for most enterprises.

Second, political forces continue to shape policy and therefore affect business operations; so does individual profiteering. Although the investment climate is very favorable, the Vietnamese governmental authorities, especially at the local levels, have the power to make or break a project. Almost 75 percent of foreign-sponsored projects are joint ventures, which require substantial interaction with local partners, whether provincial governments or individual Vietnamese citizens. Consequently, patience and circumspection will be required in the formative stages of any operation.

To be sure, Vietnam is a resource-rich nation with dynamic and industrious citizens who crave the goods and services consumed by many of their more prosperous Southeast Asian neighbors. At this juncture, however, because of poor infrastructure, the necessary evolution and accompanying confusion of its legal code, and limited managerial acumen, Vietnam still functions much more like a teetering "tiger on a bicycle" (Fforde 1993) rather than a bona fide Asian Tiger. But if U.S. business leaders understand that Vietnam's promise outweighs its peril, there are virtually countless opportunities to sell goods and services to the Vietnamese and set up facilities to produce for the local market and for export. As we embark on a new era, Vietnam is going to grow and prosper. As it does, astute investors stand to prosper as well.

References

Thomas A. Bernstein, "Ideology and Rural Reform: The Paradox of Contingent Stability," in Arthur L. Rosenbaum, ed., *State and Society in China* (San Francisco: Westview Press, 1993).

Laurence J. Brahm, *Foreign Investment and Trade Law in Vietnam* (Hong Kong: Asia 2000, 1993).

Adam Fforde, "Vietnamese Commerce: The 'Tiger on a Bicycle' Syndrome," *Columbia Journal of World Business*, Winter 1993, pp. 48-55.

Nick J. Freeman, "United States' Economic Sanctions Against Vietnam," *Columbia Journal of World Business*, Summer 1993, pp. 12-22.

General Statistical Office, Hanoi, 1993; 1994.

Hoang Ngoc Nguyen, "The Scope and Prospects of Foreign Direct Investment in Vietnam," *Contemporary Southeast Asia*, December 1992, pp. 244-256.

Stanley Karnow, *Vietnam: A History* (New York: Penguin, 1991).

Le Van Minh, Tilleke & Gibbins-HCMC, interview with authors, January 4, 1994, Ho Chi Minh City.

Lee Kuan Yew, "Asia Won't Be a Repeat of Europe's Wartorn Past," interview with Fareed Zakaria, *Singapore Straits Times*, March 12, 1994, p. 34.

Nguyen Xuan Oanh, NXO Associates, interview with authors, January 5, 1994, Ho Chi Minh City.

Ong Beng Kheong, EVP Colliers Jardine HCMC, interview with authors, January 5, 1994, Ho Chi Minh City.

Pham Chi Lan, in the foreword to Laurence J. Brahm, *Foreign Investment and Trade Law in Vietnam* (Hong Kong: Asia 2000, 1992), pp. v-vi.

Pham Chi Lan, Ho Chi Minh City Foreign Trade and Investment Development Center, interview with authors, January 4, 1994, Ho Chi Minh City.

Philip Shenon, "New Vietnam Combat: Coke vs. Pepsi," *New York Times*, February 7, 1994, pp. D1-D2.

Clifford J. Shultz II and Khai Le, "Vietnam's Inconsistencies Between Political Structure and Socio-economic Practice: Implications for the Nation's Future," *Contemporary Southeast Asia*, September 1993, pp. 179-194.

Clifford J. Shultz II and Anthony Pecotich, "Vietnam: New Assessments of Consumption Patterns in a (Re)Emergent Capitalist Society," paper presented at the Association for Consumer Research Conference, Singapore, June 14, 1994.

Clifford J. Shultz II, Anthony Pecotich, and Khai Le, "Marketing and Consumption Activity in the Socialist Republic of Vietnam," in Clifford J. Shultz II, Russell W. Belk, and Güliz Ger, eds.. *Consumption in Marketizing Economies* (Greenwich, CT: JAI Press, 1994), pp. 225-257.

Ton Si Kinh and Pham Vyen Nguyen, *Development Trends of Foreign Direct Investment in Vietnam* (Ho Chi Minh City: Institute for Economic Research, 1993).

Vietnam: A Guide for the Foreign Investor (Washington, DC: Price Waterhouse, May 1993).

Vietnam Investment Evaluation (Ho Chi Minh City: Banque IndoSuez Regional Research, 1993).

Vietnam Investment Review, January 9, 1994, p. 9.

Political Risk Analysis in North American Multinationals: An Empirical Review and Assessment

Frederick Stapenhurst

The author is with the Canadian International Development Agency, Ottawa, Canada.

Political risk analysis (PRA) emerged during the late 1970s as an important component of environmental assessment. This article replicates a 1987 study that examined the approach to PRA in North American corporations, and assesses the changes that have occurred. The principal finding is that while there has been relatively little change within the "continuing practitioners" regarding organizational approach to, and use of, PRA, there are a number of significant differences between these corporations and "late adopters" of PRA.

INTRODUCTION

It is generally recognized that corporations must first assess, and then adapt to their external market and environment if they are to survive and prosper (Stoffels, 1983). In order to do so, corporations must comprehensively scan the business environment for both opportunities and risks (Thomas, 1974; Fahey & King, 1977; Porter, 1980, 1986; Hax and Majluf, 1984).

There was an early emphasis on the assessment of techno-logical and economic factors within the environment but during the 1970s, with such factors as the Iranian Revolution, the social and political upheavals in Latin America, and increased terrorism, political analysis came to the fore and was undertaken by an increasing number of multinational corporations (MNCs) and international banks. The emergence of political risk analysis (PRA) as a "new corporate function" was widely reported (Kobrin et al., 1980; Grosse and Stack, 1984; Stapenhurst, 1990; Preble et al, 1988).

Over the past half decade, the political environment within which corporations operate has become increasingly complex. The integration of the former centrally planned economies of the (former) Soviet Union, Eastern Europe, and China into the world economy and the emergences of a single European market are political developments that have presented oppor-tunities to international corporations. At the same time, the Iraqi invasion of Kuwait, the disintegration of Yugoslavia, and the collapse of various governments in Africa are examples of some of the recent political events that have resulted in heightened political risk.

It could be expected, therefore, that the corporate use of PRA would have become more widespread and more sophisti-cated and that it would be better integrated into corporate decision making. Despite some largely descriptive reports (Rogers, 1992; Stapenhurst, 1992a), little is known regarding the evolution of the PRA function. The research in this article replicates an earlier study carried out in 1987 (Stapenhurst, 1988, 1990); it seeks to determine how PRA, as a corporate function, has evolved over the past 6 years. In particular, it compares PRA in those corporations that have only recently adopted a formal approach to such assessments with corpora-tions that have been long-time practitioners.

LITERATURE REVIEW

Academic research on PRA has unfolded along three separate lines: studies of individual perceptions of the political environ-ment; conceptual approaches to PRA methodology and pro-cesses; and empirical surveys.

Individual Perceptions

First, originating at the microlevel, there were studies of *individual perceptions* of the political environment, which asked the question: "How do individual managers get informa-tion about their environment?" Examples include Kobrin et al. (1980), Grosse and Stack (1984), and Low et al. (1989), which built on the earlier research on scanning by Kefalas and Schoderbeck (1973) and Keegan (1974).

Conceptual Approaches

Second, research was conducted on the *methodology and process* involved in environmental scanning and assessment, including PRA. Ansoff (1975) developed a model for detecting

From *The International Executive,* March/April 1995, pp. 127-145. © 1995 by John Wiley & Sons, Inc. Reprinted by permission.

and responding to what he called "weak signals" in the environment and thus managing strategic surprise; systems theory foundations of environmental scanning were articulated by Kahalas (1971) and Neubauer and Solomon (1977) developed a scheme for assessing external strategic pressures. Segev (1977) modeled the process of interaction between strategy making teams and environmental analysis units; Rodriguez and King (1977) wrote on the development of data bases of various kinds of external information required for planning.

Extending this early research on environmental scanning, Kobrin (1981) undertook a major review of the conceptual state of the art of PRA and Brewer (1981, 1983) initially extended the analysis to consider more specifically the links between PRA and capital budgeting decisions and then examined the relationship between political instability, political risk, and the foreign investment decision.

Empirical Surveys

Third, in parallel to this conceptual analysis of the role of scanning and PRA in strategic decision making, several studies examined the *empirical state of the art.* Following reports of a slow adoption of formalized scanning and assessment techniques (Fahey and King, 1977; Stubbart, 1982), Thomas (1980) found that scanning was a permanent, persuasive, and multilevel activity that surveyed social, political, economic, and technological conditions. Similarly, Diffenbach (1983) noted an evolution of corporate environmental analysis from an *appreciation* of the need for such analysis by corporations in the mid to late 1960s, although a focus on *analytical methodology* in the early 1970s to an *application* phase in the late 1970s and early 1980s. Lenz and Engledow (1985) conducted a field study of 10 "leading edge" corporations and determined that the most effective environmental analysis units were those whose activities were integrated into strategic planning processes and who were thus able to influence directly the formulation of strategy.

Surveys have shown that PRA emerged as a *distinct corporate function* in the 1970s (Blask, 1976; Kobrin et al., 1980; Korth, 1981; Burton and Inoue, 1983; Grosse and Stack, 1984; Mascarenhas and Sand, 1985; Hefernan, 1986; Low et al., 1989; Stapenhurst, 1990).

Kennedy's (1984) findings showed that, while prior to 1979 analysts in American corporations spent most of their time on other responsibilities besides PRA, after 1979 more than half of them were employed almost solely for PRA. By contrast, Stapenhurst (1990) showed that most PRA units comprised less than five, and often less than three analysts, all of whom had other responsibilities besides PRA; he also showed that the mean amount of time spent on PRA by North American analysts was 39% (Stapenhurst, 1990).

Regarding the *methodological approach,* in the mid 1970s Blask (1976) found that 5 percent of US banks had NO formal system of country evaluation, and an additional 8 percent had unsophisticated checklists or qualitative systems. Several years later, Burton and Inoue (1983) noted a trend toward greater elaboration by a progression from nonsystematic to systematic,

subjective to objective, and qualitative checklist to other quantitative methods. However, Grosse and Stack (1984) noted a falling back among US MNCs, with 64 percent using a checklist format. More recently, Stapenhurst (1990) indicated a swing back to the use of more sophisticated methodologies, with only 25 percent of corporations using simple checklists, 50 percent using more complex structured/qualitative formats, and nearly 25 percent using scenario development.

Fahey and King (1977) and Stubbart (1982) reported that the most common process for undertaking PRA among American corporations was "irregular" scanning, followed by "regular" scanning. While Fahey and King found that 17 percent of the corporations surveyed undertook "continuous data collection and processing," Stubbart (updating his study 5 years later) found that these "continuous scanners" had slipped back to become "regular scanners." Interestingly, Lenz and Engledow (1985) declared in their study of 10 leading edge corporations, that each firm was using a continuous process of intelligence gathering. Stapenhurst (1990) showed that approximately one-half of corporations used the "non-regular (ad hoc)" approach to PRA, and 30 percent used "regular report periodically updated."

With regard to *integration,* Stapenhurst (1990) confirmed the findings of Kobrin et al. (1980) that PRA tended to serve as an input into decision-makers' subjective impressions on non-economic factors and their likely impact on operations, which in turn serve as a background against which decisions are taken. Indeed, one of the continuing failings of political analysts is the integration of their analyses into corporate decision making; and there appears to be substantial scope to improve the integration of PRA into corporate decision making.

Kobrin et al. (1980) also reported that the PRA assessment responsibilities in American (nonbank) MNCs were most commonly located in the international division, followed by finance/treasury, planning, and legal departments. Kennedy (1984) noted a locational shift, finding that the most usual location was the strategic planning department. In the same year, Grosse and Stack (1984) reported that, for US banks, the PRA was located in the international division (55% of cases) or in economics (36%). Stapenhurst (1990) also noted a locational shift away from finance/treasury and legal to strategic planning and economics.

Kennedy (1994) found that 84 percent of PRA units in (nonbank) US corporations reported directly to a member of the corporation's Board of Directors. Stapenhurst (1990) suggested a trend away from such high level reporting, with most PRA units reporting to a staff or line manager.

Stapenhurst (1990) also found that the principal end uses of PRA was to assist in specific loan/investment decisions and in strategic planning, which confirmed the earlier findings of Kobrin et al. (1980).

Regarding *general corporate characteristics,* Stapenhurst (1990) found that among firms practicing PRA, while a significant minority of corporations were highly international (i.e., with over 80% of total loans/sales to foreign countries), most reported that foreign loans/sales account for less than 40 percent of the total. They were typically active in more than 20 countries and their foreign operations dated from before World War II. With regard to regional breakdown of foreign operations, he noted a heavy concentration in the developed counties of Europe and in Latin America and Australia.

RESEARCH DESIGN AND METHODOLOGY

Using the same corporate data base and survey instrument as reported earlier (Stapenhurst, 1988, 1990), survey research was conducted using a questionnaire mailed to, and subsequent interviews with, corporate political risk analysts, to determine the evolution of PRA over the past 5 years.

The questionnaire was mailed in January 1993 to 40 of the 48 respondents to the Stapenhurst survey (three of the original respondents had not put the name of their company on the completed questionnaire, and thus were not traceable; five other companies had either ceased business or had merged with other corporations). A subsequent mailing to all nonrespondents was undertaken 6 weeks after the initial mailing. Twenty-seven responses were received (67.5% response rate); of these, eight reported that either the PRA function had been discontinued or that international business activities had ceased, and one corporation reported that all information regarding its PRA activities as confidential. There were thus 18 usable responses; for the purpose of this study, these corporations are referred to as the "continuing practitioners." (Occasional reference will be made to the original 1987 population of 48 respondents, which included the continuing practitioners at that time; this group will be referred to as the "original practitioners".)

In addition, the questionnaire was also sent to 17 corporations that had not been part of the earlier survey but were known to have more recently established a formalized PRA system. Ten responses were received (58.8% response rate); these are referred to as the "late adopters."

Comparisons were then made between the initial (1987) responses of the continuing practitioners and their subsequent 1993 responses to determine what change, if any, had occurred in the organizational approach to, and role of, PRA over the past 6-year period. In addition, comparisons were made between the 18 continuing practitioners and the 10 late adopters responding in 1993 to determine if there were any differences within the two groups of companies. Given the broad coverage of corporations, the conclusions drawn are believed to represent a valid overview of the evolution and current practice of PRA in North American corporations.

SURVEY RESULTS

Table 1 indicates that there *were a few significant differences regarding the role of, and approach to, PRA between the continuing practitioners of PRA reporting in 1987 and their reporting today.* The principal differences concern the organizational approach to PRA, and in particular, the relative emphasis on the use of outside consultants, as opposed to in-

house analyses, and the extent to which political analysts have additional responsibilities.

By contrast, as Table 2 indicates, there *were a greater number of significant differences regarding the role of, and approach to, PRA in 1993 between the continuing practitioners and the late adopters.* These differences were in the areas of the methodology, the use of outside consultants, relative to in-house analysis and methodological approach; integration of PRA, the extent to which senior management receives PRA reports and the location of the PRA unit; and the percentage of investments made overseas.

Organizational Approach
Regarding organizational approach, the continuing practitioners in 1993 reported *the establishment date of a formalized PRA unit* in the late 1970s or early 1980s (median date: 1977, compared with reported 1978 for the original practitioners). By contrast, most late adopters established their PRA unit in the early to mid 1980s (median date: 1983; see Table 2).

Although not statistically significant (at $\alpha = 0.10$), there was some decline in the *number of analysts* undertaking PRA. The mean number of professionals working in PRA units in the continuing practitioners was 1.4 in 1993, down from 2.2 reported by them in 1987 (and 2.3 reported by all respondents in 1987; see Table 1). Similarly, there was little difference between the continuing practitioners (mean of 1.4 political analysts in 1993) and the late adopters, who reported a mean of 1.7 analysts (Table 2).

Coupled with this downsizing of PRA units was a move toward the greater *use of external consultants.* In 1987, among the continuing practitioners, the mean reported reliance on outside consultants, relative to in-house analyses, was 35 percent (the reported mean for original practitioners was 29%). By 1993, the proportion of political analyses undertaken by external consultants had risen to 47.8 percent for continuing practitioners (see Table 1). However, although for the original practitioners the dispersion around 35 percent was narrow, with only four corporations relying on consultants for 80–100 percent of the analyses, in 1993 there was a concentration of companies at both lower ends, that is using outside consultants for less than 20 percent of the analyses (five corporations), and at the higher end, that is using consultants for at least 80 percent of the analyses (four corporations).

Similarly, as Table 2 shows, there is a clear dichotomy in 1993 between the continuing practitioners and the late adopters: whereas the reported mean reliance on outside consultants for continuing practitioners was 47.8 percent, for late adopters it was only 35 percent. This difference is significant at $\alpha = 0.05$.

According to Rogers (1992), in the late 1980s there was a wholesale downsizing of staff functions, including PRA, in US corporations in response to intense pressure to reduce costs. This led to an increased need for external consultants; at the same time, however, the quality and relevance of external analyses had been brought into question. Ernest Brown, Vice President at Salomon Brothers, states: "We don't consume

Table 1. Difference Between Original and Continuing Practioners

| | Mean/Freq. | | | |
| | 1987 | | 1993 | |
	$(n = 48)$[a]	$(n = 18)$[b]	$(n = 18)$[b]	t-Stat
Organizational approach				
Date established	1978	1977	1977	
No. of analysts	2.3	2.2	1.4	0.46
External consultants	29	35	47.8	− 1.7[c]
Other responsib, Y/N	47/1	18/0	18/0	
% Time on PRA	40.6	46.9	20.7	2.19[d]
Methodology				
Checklisting	12	5	6	
Structured reports	25	10	7	
Scenario building	9	5	5	−1.29
Investment modeling	0	0	1	
Other	0	1	2	
Process				
Ad hoc	21	4	7	
Regular studies	15	7	8	− 0.1
Continuous assessments	10	6	4	
Other	1	0	1	
Integration				
Reports received				
Board of Directors	28.8	33.3	29.3	0.54
President/CEO	52.0	52.0	48.8	1.37
Head/strategic planning	57.5	54.5	60.0	0.85
Reporting lines				
Board of directors	0	0	0	
President/CEO	10	4	2	
Other executive officer	13	7	10	0.28
Line manager	4	1	1	
Staff manager	20	6	5	
Location				
Separate unit	3	1	2	
Finance	5	0	1	
Strategic planning	10	4	2	0.85
Economics	13	4	6	
Other	16	9	7	
Purposes[e]				
Inv./loan decisions	32	11	10	
Strategic planning	8	11	13	
FX operations	1	5	2	1.47
Day-to-day operations	3	4	2	
Other	2	4	0	
Corp. characteristics				
% Sales/loans overseas	40.6	41.1	47.6	− 0.9
% DFI/total investment	25.0	37.1	42.9	1.3
No. of Countries	16.8	19.6	18.2	0

[a]Original practitioners.
[b]Continuing practitioners.
[c]Significant at α 0.10; tcv (40, 0.10) = 1.684.
[d]Significant at α 0.05; tcv (40, 0.05) = 2.02.
[e]Multiple citations.

external stuff much. We find it either too general or so consistently alarmist as to be useless." Another criticism often mentioned regarding external consultants is that they often come from academia, with little corporate experience; as a result, their analyses may be less suited for corporate purposes. According to Paul Sachs, President of Multi-National Strategies, a PRA consulting firm, such academic PRA "Tends to be written by young people . . . [who] tend not to have had responsibility for managing money," (*Euromoney,* 1992). Nonetheless, the use of external consultants is often considered useful for those countries where in-house expertise is limited.

With regard to continuing practitioners, the trend has been toward the downsizing of PRA units, a greater use of outside consultants, and somewhat less time spent by each analyst on PRA. This finding is generally consistent with Rogers (1992: 4), who noted that "the global economic threat on U.S. companies found the slashing away at perceived "fat" in the organization. Layers of middle management were pared away, including in-staff functions such as [political risk analysis]." He also noted that, quoting Bill Kelly of Ford Motor Company, "There is a growing need for consultants in specialized, niche areas which are beyond the capabilities of the firm. . . . There will be more contracting out of this type of work" (p. 6). However, it does not explain the trend of the late adopters that have established somewhat larger PRA units, which function with limited reliance on outside consultants. Could it be that these corporations: have viewed "the rise and fall of PRA" in the earlier adopters of PRA; have seen the competitive advantages of undertaking PRA; and have aggressively built up an in-house capability? Or are they simply destined to follow the trend of the earlier practitioners: will we see a retrenching of the PRA function in them as well?

Methodologies Used

Several differences can be seen in Table 2 regarding *methodology used in 1993* by the continuing practitioners and the late adopters. Two-thirds of the continuing practitioners still used unstructured check-listing (six corporations) or the structured qualitative approach (seven corporations) and there was little use of statistical analyses (used by only one corporation), but greater use of scenario building (five corporations) and other, custom-tailored methodologies (two corporations).

Interestingly, none of the late adopters were using the unstructured checklist approach: structured qualitative reports and scenario building were their favored methodologies (used by five and three corporations, respectively). The differences between continuing practitioners and these late adopters is significant at $\alpha = 0.10$.

Regarding the *predominant process* followed in undertaking PRA, there were no significant differences (at $\alpha = 0.10$) between continuing practitioners and the late adopters. Seven continuing practitioners and five late adopters in 1993 used the "nonregular (ad hoc) studies" approach; the second most popular approach was "regular studies, periodically updated" (used by eight continuing practitioners and four late adopters). The "continuous (organized data collection and processing)"

was reportedly used by four continuing practitioners and three late adopters in 1993 (see Table 2).

The late adopters have, on average, adopted relatively more sophisticated methodologies, perhaps drawing on the literature highlighting "best practices" (Kobrin, 1981; Lenz and Engledow, 1985; Mascarenhas and Sand, 1985, among others). By contrast, it seems apparent that the continuing practitioners are generally satisfied with the methodologies and processes they have been following for PRA; there was little change in methodologies used since the mid 1980s. Alternatively, there it could be that a degree of organizational inertia hinders them from adopting new, more sophisticated approaches.

In contrast, there has been relatively little change regarding the predominant process involved in PRA: among continuing practitioners there seems to general satisfaction with the process originally adopted. Among the late adopters there is a wide dispersion of processes adopted, with five corporations opting for the relatively unsophisticated nonregular (ad hoc) studies approach. Perhaps it is misleading to think of a "hierarchy" of approaches, where the nonregular (ad hoc) approach is considered somehow inferior to "regular studies (periodically updated)" that in turn are inferior to the "continuous (data collection and processing)" methodology, as postulated by several authors (Fahey and King, 1977; Stubbart, 1982; Lenz and Engledow, 1985; Preble et al., 1988). Rather, it may be that there is an optimal approach or process for each corporation, which is a function of the needs of that particular organization for PRA. Once this particular approach is in place, there is little incentive to change, unless corporate needs change.

Integration of PRA into Decision Making

With regard to the integration of PRA into decision making, significant differences were noted between the continuing practitioners and late adopters with regard to *the frequency with which senior decision-makers receive PRA reports* as well as with regards to the location of the PRA unit.

In 1987, the continuing practitioners reported that in their corporations, the Board of Directors received PRA reports 33.3 percent of the time (roughly comparable with the 28.8 percent reported by the original practitioners). In 1993, among continuing practitioners the frequency was essentially unchanged, with the Board of Directors receiving the reports 29.4 percent of the time (Table 1). By contrast, among new adopters the frequency was much less, with Directors receiving PRA reports only 11 percent of the time; the difference between continuing practitioners and late adopters is significant at $\alpha = 0.10$ (Table 2).

As Table 1 shows, the frequency with which the Chairman/President received PRA reports fell slightly from 52.0 percent of the time among original practitioners in 1987 to 48.8 percent of the time for continuing practitioners; Table 2 indicates that it was 52 percent for the late adopters. These differences were not significant at $\alpha = 0.10$.

Similarly, with regard to the frequency with which the Head of Strategic Planning receives the PRA reports, there was again no reported significant difference at $\alpha = 0.10$ (57.5% of the

Table 2. Difference Between Continuing Practioners and New Adopters

	1993 Mean/Freq.		
	Late (n = 10)	Continuing (n = 18)	t-stat
Organizational approach			
Date established	1983	1977	
No. of analysts	1.7	1.4	− 0.59
External consultants	35.0	47.8	2.36[a]
Other responsib., Y/N	8/2	18/0	
% Time on PRA	32.2	20.7	0.6
Methodology[b]			
Checklisting	0	6	
Structured reports	5	7	
Scenario building	3	5	− 1.77[c]
Investment modeling	0	1	
Other	3	2	
Process			
Ad hoc	5	7	
Regular studies	4	8	
Continuous assessment	3	4	0.78
Other	1	1	
Integration			
Reports received			
Board of directors	11.0	29.3	2.03[c]
President/CEO	48.0		− 0.5
Head/strategic planning	2.0	60.0	− 0.3
Reporting lines			
Board of directors	0	0	
President/CEO	3	2	
Other executive officer	3	10	0.71
Line manager	1	1	
Staff manager	3	5	
Location			
Separate unit	3	2	
Finance	2	1	
Strategic planning	2	2	− 3.1[a]
Economics	1	6	
Other	2	7	
Purposes			
Invest./loan decisions	7	10	
Strategic planning	5	13	
FX operations	2	2	− 0.4
Day-to-day operations	4	2	
Other	2	0	
Corp. characteristics			
% Sales/loans overseas	36.7	47.6	1.32
% FDI/total investment	30.0	42.9	1.82[c]
No. of countries	20.0	18.2	− 1.6

[a]Significant at $\alpha = 0.05$, tcc (28, 0.05) = 2.024.
[b]Multiple citations.
[c]Significant at $\alpha = 0.10$, tcv (28, 0.10) = 1.701.

time among original practitioners and 54.5% of the time for continuing practitioners in 1987, compared with 60.0 percent of the time for continuing practitioners in 1993 (Table 1), and 52.0 percent of the time for late adopters (Table 2).

There were no significant changes with regard *to whom the PRA unit reported*. In 1987, none of the continuing practitioners indicated that their PRA unit reported directly to the Board of Directors; in four corporations (21% of reporting corporations) the PRA unit reported directly to the President or Chief Executive Officer. In 1993, among the continuing practitioners, still no PRA units reported to the Board of Directors and in only two (11% of respondents) did the PRA unit report to the President or CEO (Table 1). In contrast, among late adopters the level to which the PRA unit reported was somewhat higher: none to the Board of Directors but in three corporations, or 30 percent, to the President or CEO (Table 2).

As Table 1 indicates, the proportion of units reporting to an Executive Officer other than the President or CEO rose from 38 percent (seven corporations) among the continuing practitioners (and 28% or 13 corporations among original practitioners) in 1987 to 55 percent (10 corporations) of continuing practitioners. Table 2 shows that 30 percent (three corporations) of late adopters reported at this level.

The proportion of units reporting to a staff or line manager declined somewhat from 38 percent of continuing practitioners in 1987 and 50 percent (24 corporations of original practitioners) to 33 percent, or six continuing practitioners in 1993 (Table 1). For late adopters it was 40 percent (four corporations) (Table 2). None of these differences were statistically significant.

Because of the need for *better* integration of PRA into corporate decision making has been well-documented in the literature (Levinson, 1986; Stapenhurst, 1988, 1990, 1992a, b; Rogers, 1992), this general lack of improvement is surprising. It is *possible* that PRA is better disseminated within the corporation and is being incorporated into decision making at a lower level of decision making; alternatively, this may again be an example of continuing organizational inertia, in which case the PRA function will continue to be criticized for its "lack of corporate relevance." An example of the former is the practice at Chase Manhattan Bank, where the country-limit setting now takes place in its three annual meetings, in New York, London, and Hong Kong. There is, according to Vice-President Dominique Clavel, " . . . a constant dialogue with the people in the field who clearly have more access to information on local developments but might also run the risk of being less independent." The outcomes of these conferences are subsequently reviewed by the bank's country risk committee (*Euromoney*, 1992).

Although no significant differences (at $\alpha = 0.10$) regarding the *location* of the PRA unit were noted between the continuing practitioners in 1987 and 1993, there was (at $\alpha = 0.05$) between the continuing practitioners and new adopters (see Tables 1, 2, respectively). In 1987, the most common location for the PRA unit were within economics and strategic planning departments (four corporations in each). By 1993, among continuing practitioners, economics remained the single most common location reported by six corporations, but only two corporations reported the location of the PRA unit within strategic planning (Table 1). Contrastingly among the late adopters, there was a tendency to establish a separate unit (three corporations); two corporations located the function with economics or strategic planning (see Table 2).

With regard to use, an interesting change has occurred: the greater *corporate use of PRA* for single, as opposed to multiple, purposes. Twelve continuing practitioners (66% of respondents) in 1987 stated that PRA was used for multiple purposes within their corporations; this had fallen to nine (50% of continuing practitioners) in 1993. Among the late adopters 60 percent (six corporations) reported multiple uses of PRA. However, these differences are not statistically significant.

PRA was used by continuing practitioners in 1987 primarily as input into specific investment/loan decisions in 1987 (11 citations), followed by strategic planning (26 citations) and day-to-day operations (five citations). By 1993, for continuing practitioners this had changed to 11 citations for specific investment/loan decisions, 13 citations for strategic planning, and two citations for day-to-day operations (Table 1). For late adopters the variation was more even with six citations for strategic planning, five for specific investment/loan decisions, and four for day-to-day operations (Table 2). However, none of these reported differences were statistically significant.

Perhaps the biggest problem facing analysts is ensuring that their analyses are relevant to the corporation. Indeed, they have been criticized for being too absorbed in conceptualization rather than implementation. This is attributable to three factors: an early emphasis on theoretical models, little prior experience by analysts in business issues, and in some cases, spurious results (Rogers, 1991). Currently, at Citibank assessments are used to distinguish between those countries in which the bank will take exposures of up to 1 year, those with 1–5 year exposures, and those where longer term exposures are deemed acceptable. By contrast, Chemical Bank also used its analyses to set country limits by product for each country and even intraday trading limits, in addition to setting more general cross-border financing limits.

Firm Characteristics

Can differences in firm characteristics explain the changes and differences in approach to PRA? There is some, albeit limited, evidence that the degree of globalization affecting a corporation is associated with the extent of adoption of PRA. In 1987, the mean *percentage* of sales or loans made to foreign countries as a proportion of total sales or loans was for the continuing practitioners, 41.1 percent; in 1993 it was 47.6 percent for continuing practitioners and 36.7 percent for late adopters (Tables 1, 2), respectively. Although none of these differences are statistically significant, at $\alpha = 0.10$, the reported differences regarding foreign investment were: the mean proportion of foreign direct investment to total investment had increased, from 37.1 percent for continuing practitioners in 1987 to 42.9 percent in 1993 (Table 1) but was only 30 percent for the late adopters (Table 2).

In 1987, the mean *number of countries* in which original practitioners were active was 19.6; in 1993 the mean number was 18.2 for continuing practitioners and 20 for late adopters.

There was not a great variation for the *regional breakdown of foreign operations* among the original practitioners, continuing practitioners, and new adopters. It was: North America (excluding home country), 16 percent for 1987 respondents, 28 percent for continuing practitioners, and 15 percent for late adopters; Latin America: 16, 4, and 20 percent, respectively; Europe: 27, 28, and 39 percent; Africa: 6, 8, and 3 percent; the ASEAN countries: 12, 7, and 10 percent; Australia/New Zealand/Japan: 13, 8, and 9 percent; other Asia (including the Middle East); 10, 17, and 5 percent, respectively. None of these differences are statistically significant.

In short, with the only exception of the degree to which investment in undertaken overseas, there is little difference in the nature of respondents' overseas operations. In other words, it seems unlikely that differences in firm characteristics can explain the changes and differences in corporate approaches to PRA.

INTERPRETATION

The results of this study only partially confirm earlier research that suggested that corporate PRA has gone through a "shakeout" phase (Levinson, 1986; Rogers, 1992; Stapenhurst, 1992a, b). Although there has been some shedding or scaling back of PRA in certain North American corporations, this has been offset, at least in part, by its adoption in other corporations. Indeed, among those corporations that were practicing PRA in the mid 1980s and are still practicing (the continuing practitioners), the only significant differences are in the areas of organizational approach to PRA, specifically regarding the use of outside consultants (which has increased) and the percentage of time analysts spend solely on PRA (which has declined).

Perhaps more interesting than the reported differences are the similarities. Judging by the relative lack of change in organizational approach to PRA, or the degree of its integration into corporate decision making, it appears that, at least among the continuing practitioners, management is satisfied with the results of PRA.

Also noteworthy are the differences between the continuing practitioners of PRA, which on average adopted a formal approach to PRA in the mid 1970s, and the late adopters, which established the function in the mid 1980s. The late adopters rely to a greater extent than the continuing practitioners on in-house analysis, as opposed to outside consultants; they use more sophisticated methodologies, but are integrating the results of their PRA less well into corporate decision making. What can explain these differences? Whereas it is possible that the late adopters have followed developments in the field, and thus have adopted more sophisticated, and proven, methodologies, why then have they not followed recommendations suggesting that *integration* is critical for PRA? Perhaps definitions and methods for measurement now current in the literature regarding integration need to be revised. Alternatively, perhaps these corporations quite simply have not learned from others' experience and are destined to suffer from the same mistakes. Regarding location, too, the late adopters have tended to shun establishing the PRA unit as part of the strategic planning department, favoring instead a separate independent unit.

It was thought that some of these differences could be explained by differences in corporate characteristics; however, there were few.

CONCLUSIONS

The major finding of this study is the lack of large-scale change regarding the role and importance of PRA in North American corporations over time and the lack of incorporation of "lessons learned" regarding the integration of PRA into corporate decision making.

The tentative conclusions to be drawn are twofold. First, that MNCs still practicing PRA (the continuing practitioners) are generally satisfied with the organizational approach that they have adopted and the degree to which PRA is integrated into decision making. Apart from small, statistically insignificant changes (at $\alpha = 0.10$), the only noticeable differences related to their reliance on outside consultants (which has increased) and the time devoted to in-house analyses (which has declined). The critical question is whether this lack of change represents general satisfaction with the results of PRA, or simply organizational inertia.

The second conclusion is that those corporations that have only more recently adopted PRA (the late adopters) seem to have adopted somewhat different organizational approaches, methodologies, and methods of integration, which are perhaps better suited to their own individual needs for PRA. This may indicate a willingness to adopt lessons learned from other practitioners that have been well-documented in the literature. However, it is surprising that, despite the need for close integration of the results of PRA into corporate decision making (also well-documented in the literature), these companies report a relatively low level of such integration. Perhaps the definitions and methods of measurement of such integration now current in the literature need to be revised. Alternatively, perhaps these corporations quite simply have not learned from the experience of others and are destined to suffer from the same mistakes.

RECOMMENDATIONS FOR FURTHER STUDY

Recommendations for further study are essentially threefold. First, more research is needed into why late adopters of PRA have tended to establish larger in-house capabilities, while continuing practitioners have scaled down on their PRA staff and rely more on outside consultants. What are the relative costs and benefits of each approach? Is the final outcome purely corporation-specific? Or are the late adopters simply destined to follow the trend of the earlier practitioners: will we see a retrenching of the PRA function in them as well?

Second, more research is required into how PRA is incorporated into corporate decision making. There is not discernible trend to better integrate PRA into decision making. Is it *possible* that PRA is better disseminated within the corporation and is being incorporated into decision making at a lower level?

And finally, further examination should be undertaken on the process followed in undertaking PRA. Earlier studies, suggesting a hierarchical approach, with firms moving along a spectrum from irregular, through regular to continuing analyses may be wrong. Perhaps there is an "ideal" process, relevant for each individual corporation, given its particular needs for PRA.

REFERENCES

Ansoff, H. I. (1975) "Managing Strategic Surprise Through Response to Weak Signals." *California Management Review,* 18, 21–35.

Blask, J. K. (1976) *A Survey of Country Evaluation Systems in Use,* Washington: The Export–Import Bank.

Brewer, T. L. (1981) "Political Risk Assessment for Foreign Direct Investment Decisions: Better Methods for Better Results," *Columbia Journal of World Business,* Spring, 5–12.

Brewer, T. L. (1983) "The Instability of Governments and the Instability of Controls on Funds Transferred by Multinational Enterprises: Implications for Political Risk Analysis," *Journal of International Business Studies,* Winter, 147–157.

Burton, F. N. and Inoue, H. (1983) "Country Risk Evaluation Methods: A Survey of Systems in Use," *The Banker,* January, 41–44.

Diffenbach, J. (1983) "Corporate Environmental Analysis in Large U.S. Corporations," *Long Range Planning,* 16, 107–116.

Euromoney, (1992) "How to Rate a State," September, 61–64.

Fahey, L. and King, W. R., "Environmental Scanning for Corporate Planning," *Business Horizons,* 20, 61–71.

Grosse, R. and Stack, J., (1984) "Noneconomic Risk Evaluation in Multinational Banks," *Management International Review,* 24, 41–59.

Hax, A. C. and Majluf, N. S., (1984) *Strategic Management: An Integrative Perspective,* Englewood Cliffs: Prentice Hall.

Hefernan, S. (1986) *Sovereign Risk Analysis,* London: Allen and Unwin.

Kahalas, H. (1971) "Long Range Planning—An Open Systems View," *Long Range Planning,* 10, 78–82.

Keegan, W. (1974) "Multinational Scanning: A Study of Information Sources Utilized by Headquarters Executives," *Administrative Science Quarterly,* September, 411–421.

Kefalas, A. and Schoderbeck, P., (1973) "Scanning the Business Environment—Some Empirical Results," *Decision Sciences,* 4, 63–74.

Kennedy, C. (1984) "The External Environment-Strategic Planning Interface: U.S. Multinational Corporate Practices in the 1980s" *Journal of International Business Studies,* Fall, 99–108.

Kobrin, S. J. (1981) "Political Assessments by International Firms: Models or Methodologies," *Journal of Policy Modelling,* 3, 251–270.

Kobrin, S. J., Basek, J., Blank, S., and Lapalombara, J. (1980) "The Assessment and Evaluation of Non-Economic Environments by American Firms: A Preliminary Report," *Journal of International Business Studies,* 11, 32–47.

Korth, C. M. (1981) "The Seat-of-the-Pants Analyst Needs Professional Help," *Euromoney,* May, 124–127.

Lenz, R. T. and Englelow, J. L. (1985) "Environmental Analysis Units and Strategic Decision-Making: A Field Study of Selected 'Leading Edge' Corporations," *Journal of Business Strategy,* Fall, 61–89.

Levinson, M. (1986) "Where's the Next Revolution?" *Across the Board,* January, 40–46.

Low, P. S., Stening, B. W., and Stening, K. (1989) "The International Political Risk Assessment Activities of Australian Corporations: A Pilot Study," *International Journal of Management,* 6, 341–349.

Mascarenhas, B. and Sand, O. (1985) "Country Risk Assessment Systems in Banks: Patterns and Performance," *Journal of International Business Studies,* Spring 19–35.

Neubauer, F. F. and Solomon, N. (1977) "A Managerial Approach to Environmental Assessment," *Long Range Planning,* 10, 13–20.

Porter, M. E. (1980) *Competitive Strategy.* New York: The Free Press.

Porter, M. E. (1986) *Competition in Global Industries,* Boston: Harvard Business School Press.

Preble, J. F., Rau, P. A., and Reichel, A. (1988) "The Environmental Scanning Practices of Multinational Firms—An Assessment," *International Journal of Management,* 6, 18–28.

Rodriguez, L. J. and King, W. K. (1977) "Competitive Information Systems," *Long Range Planning,* 10, 45–50.

Rogers, J. (1992) "Political Risk Analysis: State of the Art 1989," *Risk Management Review,* Spring, 4–7.

Segev, E. (1977) "How to Use Environmental Analysis in Strategy Making," *Management Review,* 66, 4–13.

Stapenhurst, F. (1988) *Political Risk Analysis in Canadian and U.S. Based Multinational Corporations,* unpublished dissertation, International Graduate School, St. Louis.

Stapenhurst, F. (1990) *Corporate Political Risk Analysis: A Comparison of U.S. and Canadian Approaches,* ASAC Conference, Whistler, British Columbia.

Stapenhurst, F. (1991) "Corporate Political Risk Analysis: A Comparison of U.S. and European Approaches," International Trade and Finance Conference, Marseille, 1507–1518.

Stapenhurst, F. (1992a) "The Rise and Fall of Political Risk Analysis?" *Management Decision,* 30, 54–57.

Stapenhurst, F. (1992b) *Political Risk Analysis Around the North Atlantic,* New York: St. Martin's Press.

Stoffels, J. (1983) "Environmental Scanning for Future Success," *Managerial Planning,* November/December, 4–12.

Stubbart, C. (1992) "Are Environmental Scanning Units Effective?" *Long Range Planning,* 15, 139–145.

Thomas, P. S. (1974) "Environmental Analysis for Corporate Planning," *Business Horizons,* 17, 27–38.

Thomas, P. S. (1980) "Environmental Scanning—The State of the Art," *Long Range Planning,* 13, 20–25.

The Scourge Of Global Counterfeiting

Alexander Nill and Clifford J. Shultz II

The violation of Intellectual Property Rights (IPR) in the form of counterfeiting is emerging as one of the most troublesome problems for companies as we enter the coming millennium. Indeed, despite efforts by countries to improve mechanisms of international enforcement, losses attributed to IPR theft are increasing exponentially. Consider that the value of counterfeit goods on the world market has grown by 1,100 percent since 1984. The International Anti-Counterfeiting Coalition (IACC) estimates that 5 to 8 percent of all products and services worldwide are counterfeit.

American companies lost $61 billion to foreign piracy of intellectual property in 1986. A conservative estimate indicates that those losses had ballooned to $200 billion by 1994. And the losses are not just monetary. In 1993, an estimated 750,000 jobs were lost due to foreign counterfeiting of U.S. products. Watches, toys, and textiles, which carry a high brand image and require a relatively simple production technology, top the list of goods seized by the U.S. Customs Service, which typically impounds more than $30 million worth of counterfeit merchandise each year.

The explosive growth of many forms of counterfeiting is attributed primarily to strong brand affinity, huge financial incentives, and the global diffusion of technologies for mass production. Producing counterfeit goods, which often nearly replicate authentic merchandise, offers tremendous cost advantages because almost no investments in product research and development or brand name advertising are required. Companies in newly industrialized and emerging economies are often lured by the tremendous profit margins and the low risk of counterfeiting. Many businesses in these countries have attained the capability of mass production and distribution, but they lack the name and brand recognition and thus find it difficult to compete with established products. So they often resort to re-producing products already well known in the world marketplace. Unfortunately, these profits come at the expense of legitimate marketers, laborers, and consumers.

How can legitimate companies protect their brands and ultimately their entire organizations from counterfeiters? Several strategies are often invoked, most of which attempt to deter producers or suppliers of counterfeit products. But given that the counterfeit business is booming, and that a large portion of the losses can be attributed to consumers who willfully purchase counterfeit goods, we believe that companies should also focus on consumer demand. Here we discuss demand-side issues, with an emphasis on ethical consumer decision making, and suggest questions to consider should companies choose to implement marketing campaigns to reduce consumer demand for counterfeit goods.

> Campaigning for ethical consumer decision making plays a prominent part in a demand-side solution to a worldwide problem.

Conventional Remedies: Eliminate The Supply Of Counterfeit Goods

Most conventional, supply-side remedies include everything from diplomatic and legislative pressure to high-tech product labeling. These tactics are designed to coerce compliance from perpetrating firms and governments and to aid in detecting bogus products. Some of these efforts are effective, some are not. Meanwhile, pirates brazenly continue to flout anti-counterfeiting laws and international trade agreements.

It is beyond the scope of this article to discuss the massive and often Byzantine domestic and foreign anti-piracy legislation. Suffice it to

From *Business Horizons*, November/December 1996, pp. 37-42. © 1996 by the Foundation for the School of Business at Indiana University. Reprinted by permission.

say that in many cases a company that tries to sue a pirate finds itself in costly and ongoing litigation with uncertain outcomes. Lawsuits against IPR infringement and pirating are fraught with difficulties and, quite simply, cannot solve the problem. Moreover, some countries, such as the People's Republic of China, did not ratify the multilateral agreement of Trade-Related Intellectual Property Rights (TRIPS) of the World Trade Organization (WTO). Often in emerging economies, there is the prevailing belief that the infringement of IPR constitutes no wrongdoing. According to the U.S. General Accounting Office, it is assumed that "intellectual property should be considered the common property of mankind and relevant laws should facilitate access to intellectual property as a development tool rather than place restrictions on its use."

Even when there are lucid laws against counterfeiting, as is the case in most countries that pledge allegiance to the TRIPS agreement, and even if the violated company wins its suit, enforcement remains a fundamental problem. To complicate matters, organized crime has been lured by the tremendous profits and the low risks counterfeiting entails. FBI officials believe that IPR theft will continue to be a major crime in the twenty-first century because of impunity. In the end, many foreign governments are unable or unwilling to enforce anti-counterfeiting laws because of a lack of financial means or because of expected economic and political repercussions.

CONSUMER DEMAND FOR COUNTERFEIT GOODS

All the statistics cited above suggest that an enormous demand exists for counterfeit merchandise—demand which, of course, initiates the supply. Ironically, American firms that control rights to intellectual property are often plagued by counterfeit goods sold in their own home market. The United States has proven to be not only a major victim of IPR infringements, but also a major target market for counterfeit merchandise.

Consequently, companies need to design, implement, and sponsor marketing and advertising campaigns that can reduce the demand for counterfeit goods. The effectiveness of such campaigns would depend on several factors, including product category, strength of brand image, individual characteristics of consumers, marketing communication methods, and routes of persuasion.

Note also that message or ad copy content depends on whether a consumer is actually aware the product is fake. In some cases a counterfeit product is sold to consumers and businesses without their knowledge. This strategy is

often used by pirates that target pharmaceuticals, industrial parts, and consumer goods. For example, the cognac producer Hennessy suffered considerably from counterfeiting in East Asia, where the brand holds a very high image and a businessman's choice of a specific cognac brand is seen as a reflection of his social standing and appreciation for his guests. Local bars that sold the cognac by the bottle used empty Hennessy bottles and refilled them with a cheaper brand, without informing customers. If consumers are oblivious, as in the Hennessy case, a marketing campaign does not have to address consumers' attitudes toward counterfeiting. It is enough to inform them about the possibility of being duped by a brand pirate and enable them to distinguish between the counterfeit and the genuine product. This was, in fact, the essence of a successful Hennessy campaign against the counterfeiting of its product.

In other cases, consumers voluntarily and deliberately buy a counterfeit good. Sometimes people are aware a product is bogus but do not realize or appreciate the differences in quality between the authentic versus the counterfeit good. An ad campaign that focuses on informing the consumer about these differences might be a successful strategy. This is especially true if the counterfeit good imposes potential risks and threats to the consumer, as is the case for many pirated pharmaceutical products.

Often, however, despite being well informed about the specific qualities of the authentic versus the fake product, consumers still buy the "knock-offs." This is called non-deceptive counterfeiting and usually involves goods that offer low physical, financial, and performance risks to the consumer. Such goods tend to be of low or moderate technical complexity and carry a high image and the prestige connected to a well-known brand name, such as Polo, Ray Ban, Gucci, Rolex, or Chanel. It is not in the consumer's immediate self-interest to pay a considerably higher price for the authentic good if the counterfeit item offers similar qualities. Consumers who purchase these goods subject themselves to social risk because the goods are of high symbolic value and social visibility. However, as long as the counterfeit good is not readily discernible as fake, it fulfills its function as well as the authentic item.

A "Robin Hood mentality" also frequently influences consumers who willfully purchase counterfeit goods. These consumers feel little sympathy for gigantic multinational corporations that complain about lost profits. They don't perceive buying a fake Polo shirt or counterfeit Ray Ban sunglasses from a street vendor as misbehavior—even though such behavior is, indeed, willful theft.

ETHICAL DECISION MAKING, MORAL REASONING, AND THE PURCHASE OF COUNTERFEIT PRODUCTS

Non-deceptive counterfeiting has far-reaching implications for ethical decision making and, in turn, for strategies to deter it. Whereas buying a counterfeit good might be advantageous to the immediate self-interest of the individual purchasing manager or consumer, it is harmful to the holders of brand copyrights and workers in legitimate operations. Moreover, counterfeiting is detrimental to society in the long run because it has a chilling effect on technology developments. A society that tolerates piracy creates disincentives for technological innovation and product development. This situation represents a typical ethical dilemma: The immediate short-term self-interest of individuals is in conflict with the interests of society.

An important part of the design for an anti-counterfeiting ad campaign should be seen as a logical extension of the theory of, and empirical research into, ethical decision making. People are made aware of the ethical issues involved; awareness is a prerequisite for ethical reasoning. Thus, some consumers likely will refrain from purchasing counterfeit goods when they become aware of the ramifications of buying fake merchandise. The quality of the design of the campaign depends on determinant factors of the ethical decision-making process. And among the most important of these are individual differences.

Individual characteristics, such as gender, age, and education, have varying effects on the way a person approaches ethical decision making. Social environment and cultural background also play a role in the process. So it is advisable for firms to consider the individual and cultural differences of prospective buyers of counterfeit goods when designing anti-counterfeiting campaigns. A young, "Generation X," English-speaking, American purchaser of counterfeit fashion products or software would require a vastly different message, ad content, and medium than would an older, Mandarin-speaking, Chinese businessman in Shanghai. In other words, segments of buyers of counterfeit products can be defined and measured. And just as firms alter their marketing campaigns to coincide with the wants and interests of consumers who buy legitimate goods, they should alter their anti-counterfeiting campaigns to coincide with the interests, values, language, and information-processing capabilities of the "segments" that buy fake goods.

Ultimately, moral reasoning influences behavior when one is exposed to an ethical dilemma. The decision to willfully purchase a counterfeit good is no exception. Most actions with moral overtones, including purchase decisions, can be categorized in three levels of moral development, each of which encompasses two stages (outlined in the **Figure**). At the preconventional level (stages 1 and 2), a person's moral reasoning is based on the expected personal consequences, especially when expressed in terms of physical punishment, reward, or exchange of favors. Mainly children reside at this level of moral development. At the conventional level (stages 3 and 4), moral reasoning focuses on maintaining the expectations of one's reference group and on adhering to the conventional order of society. At the post-conventional level (stages 5 and 6), there is a clear effort to define moral principles and values apart from referent groups or authorities. The individual defines self-chosen ethical principles that are consistent and often universal.

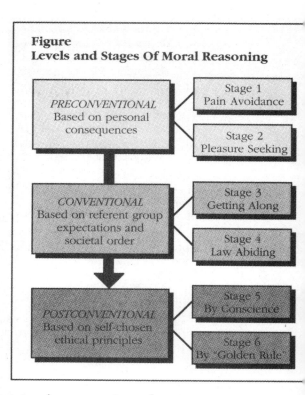

Figure
Levels and Stages Of Moral Reasoning

- *PRECONVENTIONAL* Based on personal consequences
  - Stage 1 Pain Avoidance
  - Stage 2 Pleasure Seeking
- *CONVENTIONAL* Based on referent group expectations and societal order
  - Stage 3 Getting Along
  - Stage 4 Law Abiding
- *POSTCONVENTIONAL* Based on self-chosen ethical principles
  - Stage 5 By Conscience
  - Stage 6 By "Golden Rule"

When designing an anti-counterfeit campaign that alludes to the ethical decision-making process of prospective customers, it is important to note that most adults in Western urban societies typically reason at stages 3 to 4. In addition, their moral development tends to occur one stage at a time in a sequential order. Even though the progression to higher stages of reasoning usually depends on exposure to an environment that stimulates reasoning at a higher level, a person is not able to comprehend the reasoning embodied two stages higher. "Hence," state Weber and Green (1991), "a stage 2 person should not be expected to leap to stage 4 or stage 5 simply by being exposed to reasoning at these levels."

It seems advisable, then, to adapt the basic content of an anti-counterfeit ad campaign to conventional moral reasoning (stages 3 and 4) to try to persuade the majority of the population. Individuals at stage 3 value approval from others and try to conform to what is perceived as normal and acceptable social behavior. Their behavior, as Weber and Green put it, could be characterized as a "getting along" decision. People at stage 4 are mainly concerned with society's norms and laws, which are perceived as prerequisites for a stable social order. They try to be good citizens who heed and foster the commonly accepted codes of the social system. Thus, an effective ad might demonstrate or argue that the purchase of counterfeit goods is detrimental to the local or domestic work force and is not approved by the members of society. The message: *A good citizen does not buy counterfeit merchandise.* It could also be emphasized that counterfeiting is unlawful and constitutes an assault on the conventional order of society.

Paths Of Ethical Decision Making

Beyond the level of moral development, the way ethical problems are evaluated by prospective willful buyers of counterfeit goods is also crucial to the design of a successful anti-counterfeit campaign. When making ethical judgments, people tend to follow one of two paths, as described by Hunt and Vitell (1986):

1. They consistently apply the same standard of ethics regardless of the situation (deontological evaluation). Evaluations of ethical dilemmas are based on duties and the inherent rightness of an action without considering the consequences.

2. They vary the standard relative to the sum total of goodness versus badness likely to be produced in the situation (teleological evaluation).

An anti-counterfeit campaign based on the "first path" would take a "Thou shalt not steal" approach, focusing on the inherent wrongness of the action. The primary message could be that counterfeiting is stealing and stealing is inherently wrong. A second message might suggest that counterfeiting is unlawful and it is the duty of every good citizen to respect the laws and norms of society.

By following the "second path," consumers would assess the consequences of their purchases. To dissuade these consumers, a campaign should emphasize the pernicious consequences of counterfeiting, such as the loss of American jobs, damage to the American economy, or contributions to organized crime.

Perceived Product Value

As hinted earlier, the extent to which consumers believe the counterfeit item replicates the authentic item and thus provides good value will affect the likelihood of a willful purchase. Bloch (1993) argues that, at bottom, people purchase counterfeit goods because they "are getting prestige without paying for it." So the perceived value of the counterfeit good becomes crucial to consumers who follow the second path of ethical decision making. For these consumers, buying a fake product for a good price constitutes a positive consequence that has to be evaluated against the negative consequences portrayed in the campaign. On the other hand, perceived value is irrelevant to consumers on the first path because they will appreciate appeals to the inherent wrongness of buying counterfeit goods.

Communication And Persuasion

In addition to the two paths of ethical decision making and cultural forces, the form of communication and routes of persuasion are also important. Depending on involvement and motivation, consumers can be persuaded by *central* or *peripheral* routes. In the central route, attitudes are formed and changed upon deliberate and careful consideration of all available facts. The consumer becomes highly motivated, actively searches for information, and processes that information meticulously. Logical arguments about product or brand attributes are emphasized.

In the peripheral route, a brand's attributes are not actively assessed. Rather, attitudes are formed upon associating the brand with executional cues in the ad. For example, ads for many fashionable brands typically connote a desirable lifestyle—fun, excitement, health, wealth, pleasure, sex appeal—thus creating positive associations with the brand and the lifestyle depicted in the ad. Coke, Polo, Levi's, and Marlboro ads all focus more on lifestyle than on product attributes and are illustrative of marketers' attempts to reach consumers via the peripheral route.

With respect to the two paths of ethical decision making discussed previously, people who primarily follow the second path when facing dilemmas will be more inclined to assess logical, fact-oriented information; they will change attitudes upon careful assessment of the costs and benefits of product/brand attributes. This is essential for the central route of persuasion.

In contrast, people following the first path will be less inclined to weigh the pros and cons of an alternative. Instead, they will tend to rely on their conscience. Emotional cues are more likely to evoke a reaction from a person's conscience, so an anti-counterfeiting campaign that focuses on, for example, the suffering of people who lost their jobs to counterfeiters might elicit a stronger effect than one focusing on pure information and numbers. The peripheral route of persuasion is preferable for an anti-counterfeiting advertising campaign when prospective buyers are on the first path of ethical decision making.

Counterfeiting, ethical decision making, and the collective forces that affect consumers' willful purchases of counterfeit products are multifaceted and complex issues. Eradicating counterfeit goods is clearly in the best interests of legitimate companies and arguably in the best interests of entire societies. Although considerable attention has been focused on mechanisms to eliminate the supply of counterfeit goods, companies must also address consumer demand for these goods.

The ethics and communication literature provides foundations from which sound marketing and advertising campaigns can be created to deter consumer purchases of counterfeit products. A well-conceived and well-administered campaign that applies fundamental tenets from this literature could be instrumental in eradicating markets that drive the supply of counterfeit goods and, in turn, cost American companies, labor, and society at large dearly.

Before administering any anti-counterfeiting campaign, managers should appreciate the fact that the campaign will not only decrease the demand for counterfeit goods, it will also have a positive impact on the image of the company and its brands. To optimize the probability of this "double value" outcome, the anti-counterfeit campaign must be viewed as an integral part of the larger promotional strategy of the firm.

References

D. Aaker, R. Batra, and J. Myers, *Advertising Management* (Englewood Cliffs, NJ: Prentice Hall, 1992).

I. Ajzen and M. Fishbein, *Understanding Attitudes And Predicting Social Behavior* (Englewood Cliffs, NJ: Prentice-Hall, 1980).

H. Becker and D. Fritzsche, "Business Ethics: A Cross Cultural Comparison Of Managers' Attitudes," *Journal Of Business Ethics,* May 1987, pp. 289-295.

J. Blatt, "Battling Counterfeit Products On The U.S. Side Of The Pacific Rim," *The International Computer Lawyer,* December 1993, pp. 2-16.

P. Bloch, "Consumer Accomplices In Product Counterfeiting: A Demand Side Investigation," *Journal Of Consumer Marketing, 10,* 4 (1993): 27-36.

N. Bowie and R. Dushka, *Business Ethics* (Englewood Cliffs, NJ: Prentice Hall, 1990).

V. Callan, "Predicting Ethical Values And Training Needs In Ethics," *Journal Of Business Ethics,* October 1992, pp. 761-769.

S. Chang, "Cracking Down On Pirates," *Business Korea,* May 1993, pp. 24-26.

L. Chonko and S. Hunt, "Ethics And Marketing Management: An Empirical Examination," *Journal Of Business Research,* August 1985, pp. 339-359.

M. Conlan, "Rx Drugs Bought In Mexico Pose New Threat In U.S.," *Drug Topics,* April 20, 1992, pp. 76-79.

R. Feinberg and D. Rousslang, "The Economic Effects On Intellectual Property Right Infringements," *Journal Of Business*, January 1990, pp. 75-90.

O. Ferrell and S. Skinner, "Ethical Behavior And Bureaucratic Structure In Marketing Research Organizations," *Journal Of Marketing Research*, February 1988, pp. 103-109.

R. Ford and W. Richardson, "Ethical Decision Making: A Review Of The Empirical Literature," *Journal Of Business Ethics,* March 1994, pp. 205-221.

W. Frankena, *Ethics* (Englewood Cliffs, NJ: Prentice Hall, 1963).

G. Grossman and C. Shapiro, "Foreign Counterfeiting Of Status Goods," *Quarterly Journal Of Economics,* February 1987, pp. 79-100.

M. Harvey and I. Ronkainen, "International Counterfeiters: Marketing Success Without The Cost And The Risk," *Columbia Journal Of World Business,* Fall 1985, pp. 37-45.

M. Harvey, "Industrial Product Counterfeiting: Problems And Proposed Solutions," *Journal Of Business And Industrial Marketing*, Fall 1987, pp. 5-13.

H. Hinterhuber and A. Nill, "Unternehmensethik im Kontext interkultureller Geschäftsbeziehungen" ["Business Ethics In The Context Of Intercultural Business Relationships"], *Journal Für Betriebswirtschaft* (Wien), 6 (1993): 258-277.

S. Hunt and S. Vitell, "A General Theory Of Marketing Ethics," *Journal Of Macromarketing,* Spring 1986, pp. 5-15.

I. Kant, *Grundlegung zur Metaphysik der Sitten [Laying The Foundation For The Metaphysics Of Morals]* (Hamburg: Felix Meiner Verlag, 1965).

A.M. Keats and J. Joyner, "Counterfeiting Reaches New Levels," *National Law Journal,* May 8, 1995, pp. 19-22.

G. Laczniak and E. Inderrieden, "The Influence Of Stated Organizational Concern Upon Ethical Decision Making," *Journal Of Business Ethics,* May 1987, pp. 297-307.

S. Lysonski and W. Gaidis, "A Cross Cultural Comparison Of The Ethics Of Business Students," *Journal Of Business Ethics,* February 1991, pp. 141-150.

C. McNichols and W. Zimmerer, "Situational Ethics: An Empirical Study Of Differentiators Of Student Attitudes," *Journal Of Business Ethics,* June 1985, pp. 175-180.

"Deadly Medicine," *Newsline,* August 1, 1991, pp. 22-38.

A. Nill and C. Shultz, "Marketing Ethics In The United States And Europe: Discussion, Comparison, And Integration," in S. Grossbart and D. Lascu (eds.), *Proceedings: The Twentieth Annual Macromarketing Conference: Understanding Change From A Macromarketing*

Perspective (Richmond, VA: University of Richmond, 1995), pp. 15-25.

A. Nill, *Strategische Unternehmensführung aus ethischer Perspektive [Business Management From An Ethical Perspective]* (Münster: LIT Verlag, 1994).

M. Nyaw and I. Ng, "A Comparative Analysis Of Ethical Beliefs: A Four Country Study," *Journal Of Business Ethics*, July 1994, pp. 543-555.

C. Orpen, "The Attitudes Of United States And South African Managers To Corporate Social Responsibility," *Journal Of Business Ethics*, February 1987, pp. 86-96.

R. Petty, J. Cacioppo, and D. Schumann, "Central And Peripheral Routes To Advertising Effectiveness: The Moderating Role Of Involvement," *Journal Of Consumer Research,* February 1983, pp. 135-146.

R. Petty, E.D. Wegener, L. Fabrigar, J. Priester, and J. Cacioppo, "Conceptual And Methodological Issues In The Elaboration Likelihood Model Of Persuasion: A Reply To The Michigan State Critics," *Communication Theory*, November 1, 1993, pp. 336-362.

D. Randall and A. Gibson, "Methodology In Business Ethics Research: A Review And Critical Assessment," *Journal Of Business Ethics,* June 1990, pp. 457-471.

D. Ruegger and E. King, "A Study Of The Effect Of Age And Gender Upon Student Business Ethics," *Journal Of Business Ethics*, March 1992, pp. 179-186.

J. Sasser, "Stop, Thief," *International Management,* September 1, 1990, pp. 48-51.

A. Schopenhauer, *Preisschrift über das Fundament der Moral [Prize Essay On The Basis Of Morality]* (Stuttgart: Suhrkamp Verlag, 1979).

C. Shultz and B. Saporito, "Protecting Intellectual Property: Strategies And Recommendations To Deter Counterfeiting And Brand Piracy In Global Markets," *Columbia Journal Of World Business*, Spring 1996, pp. 18-28.

V. Smith, "A License To Sell Counterfeit Goods?" *The Solicitors' Journal*, August 20, 1993, pp. 822-824.

J. Sweeney, S. Greenberg, and M. Bitler, "Heading Them Off At The Pass—Can Counterfeit Goods Of Foreign Origin Be Stopped At The Counterfeiter's Border?" *The Trademark Reporter*, September 1, 1994, pp. 477-494.

United States International Trade Commission, *Foreign Protection Of Intellectual Property Rights And The Effect On U.S. Industry And Trade* (Washington, DC: USITC Pub. 2065, at Appendix H, H-4, February 1988).

United States General Accounting Office, *International Trade: Strengthening Worldwide Protection of Intellectual Property Rights* (Washington, DC: GAO/NSIAD-87-65, at 8, 1987).

J. Weber and S. Green, "Principled Moral Reasoning: Is It A Viable Approach To Promote Ethical Integrity?" *Journal Of Business Ethics,* May 1991, pp. 325-333.

J. Weber, "Exploring The Relationship Between Personal Values And Moral Reasoning," *Human Relations,* April 1, 1993, pp. 435-463.

J. Weber, "Managers' Moral Reasoning: Assessing The Responses To Three Moral Dilemmas," *Human Relations,* July 1, 1990, pp. 687-702.

B. Weinstein, "Cheat On The Street: Sidewalk Sales Beware The Bogus Bargain," *Washington Post,* September 22, 1994, p. D5.

Alexander Nill is an assistant professor of management at Innsbruck University in Austria and is currently a visiting assistant professor at the American Graduate School of International Management. **Clifford J. Shultz II** is an assistant professor of marketing at the School of Management, Arizona State University West, Phoenix, Arizona. The authors wish to thank the ASU, FGIA, SRCA, and IIM programs for their support of this project, as well as the anonymous reviewers for their helpful comments on earlier drafts of the manuscript.

CHINA

Rule by Law

As parliamentary chairman Qiao Shi pushes for legal reform, delegates to the National People's Congress will be watching for signs of a split between him and party chief Jiang Zemin.

By Matt Forney in Beijing

In the same Great Hall of the People where the Communist Party held its funeral for patriarch Deng Xiaoping four days earlier, China's rump parliament opened on March 1 with the promise of two weeks of muted debate. The country's new "collective leadership" is enjoying its honeymoon period, and nobody, including the parliament's prickly chairman, Qiao Shi, is expected to pick a spat.

That doesn't peg this annual National People's Congress session as insignificant. Qiao has structured the meeting around legislation which could have an impact on everyone from political dissidents to the People's Liberation Army to residents of China's most populous city.

For the past five years Qiao has staked his career on legal reform—albeit without threatening party authority. And he is expected to push his reform ideas in his closing remarks scheduled for March 14. That in itself could pressure President Jiang Zemin, who as the designated "core" of the Communist Party is considered by many to be above the law. Although critical eloquence is quickly swept from the floor of the Great Hall, Qiao has striven to shed the congress's image of a rubber-stamp.

Observers will scrutinize Qiao's every word for evidence of a split with Jiang.

Back in 1989, Qiao turned down the position of party secretary-general that Deng eventually awarded to Jiang. Since then, few leaders other than Jiang's associates from his power base of Shanghai have lent him their unambiguous support.

"Premier Li Peng doesn't go out of his way to give Jiang face, but he gives it when it's necessary," says a Western diplomat and veteran NPC-watcher in Beijing. "Qiao doesn't give it even when it's necessary." This year, however, Qiao's opening comments included what was for him a rare reference to Jiang as the "core." Last year he avoided that obligatory fillip until his closing words.

The most progressive legislation on the docket would eliminate, at a stroke, an entire category of political dissent. Barring the unexpected, delegates will vote on March 14 to delete a 17-year-old list of "counter-revolutionary" statutes from the nation's criminal law.

This is not a human-rights breakthrough, however, and it won't lower the prison population. State prosecutors already prefer charging dissidents with criminal offences, such as leaking state secrets. And most of the doomed counter-revolutionary statutes have already been rewritten to find a new home in the State Security Law of 1993, which covers:

● "Plotting or carrying out activities for endangering state security together with organizations, institutions or individuals outside the country."

● "Establishing social organizations or enterprises or business institutions" which endanger state security.

● "Publishing or disseminating written or verbal comments" that threaten the state—a statute clearly aimed at curtailing dissidents' contact with foreign journalists.

One of the most prescient critics of transferring counter-revolutionary clauses to the State Security Law was Wang Dan, who served three-and-a-half years in prison for his role as a student leader during the 1989 Tiananmen uprising. In 1994, Wang noted that the law was self-defining: the kind of action that harms state security is "an action harmful to state security"—a tautology that covers almost any critical utterance. Wang predicted that Beijing would stop charging dissidents with counter-revolutionary crimes, and instead charge them with endangering state security.

Wang predicted his own fate. Last October, a three-judge panel sentenced him to 11 years in prison for "conspiring to subvert the government" by publishing overseas and writing to foreign groups. He was sentenced according to both the counter-revolutionary statutes *and* the state security law.

From *Far Eastern Economic Review*, March 13, 1997, pp. 14-15. © 1997 by Review Publishing Company Limited. Reprinted by permission.

"Wang's was a bridge verdict spanning the transition from laws on counter-revolution to those on state security," says Robin Munro of Human Rights Watch/Asia.

One thing to watch: the Tiananmen uprising of 1989 is still officially "counter-revolutionary turmoil." But the phrase loses its foundation if a crime by that name no longer exists—which could facilitate a reassessment of the uprising. "The term for the turmoil is political, not legal," says Chen Guangzhong, former president of the Politics and Law University in Beijing who helped draft the new criminal law. "But," he admits, "it could add impetus for a reassessment."

Other significant legislation would give China a legal basis to invade Taiwan. The National Defence Law, drafted by the Central Military Commission, mandates army "crackdowns on any attempts to seek independence and separate the motherland," said Defence Minister Chi Haotian last year. Chi immediately added the need to "keep on the high alert against the activities of Taiwan independence elements." China, therefore, could insist on "rule of law" as it scrambles the jets to attack its "renegade province."

The law also directs the PLA to quell unrest in Tibet and largely Muslim Xinjiang province in the far west. Soldiers haven't opened fire on Tibetans since 1989, but did so in the Xinjiang hotspot of Yining only last month. China insists 10 people or fewer were killed; Muslim separatists put the figure at more than 100.

The defence law will also put the 3-million-strong People's Liberation Army under the explicit control of the Communist Party. That, of course, has been standard policy since the communists came to power and established their dictatorship of the proletariat in 1949. Less than three hours after Deng Xiaoping died on February 19, China's top generals swore "to obey the leadership of the Communist Party Central Committee." The problem is, China's constitution holds that the armed forces "belong to the people" and report to the State Military Commission, which in turn subordinates itself to the National People's Congress. The party garners no mention.

The debate may sound academic. It is not. Last year, literary critic Liu Xiaobo was sentenced without trial to three years in a labour camp for demanding party chief Jiang Zemin's impeachment. Jiang, he wrote, had violated the constitution by insisting that the party controls the military. Any first-year law student would observe that the accusation, although politically sensitive, was correct.

N either the changes to the criminal law nor the new defence law are expected to elicit much debate from delegates. On the year's most hotly contested issue, however, delegates are being handed a *fait accompli*.

The delegates will be asked to approve the State Council's elevation of China's most populous city, Chongqing in mountainous Sichuan province, to the status of a province. The move strengthens Beijing's control over Sichuan by wrenching a major industrial city away from the provincial capital, Chengdu. It also enables Beijing to more closely monitor resettlement of 800,000 people in greater Chongqing who must move to higher ground before the Three Gorges dam project is complete in 2009.

Chengdu officials are enraged by the decision, though silently. Bureaucrats in the city refused requests to be interviewed on Chongqing's status. In the unlikely event that delegates reject this decision, it would be the first time an NPC vote has changed state policy.

Last year, Chongqing for the first time received its resettlement funds directly from Beijing, instead of through Chengdu. Beijing has already promised more this year. Chongqing officials estimate that 20,000 bureaucrats in Cheng-du who used to administer Chongqing's affairs are now redundant. Beijing has already appointed Chongqing's de facto mayor, instead of approving Cheng-du's appointment, as was past practice. Chongqing has even designed new licence plates for its cars.

Still, no deep divisions within the NPC are expected over the new slate of laws. With memories of Deng's funeral still fresh, nobody wants to send the first ripples from a rocking boat. In all likelihood, serious legal reform will wait for future congresses.

LABOUR

Wanted: Muscle

ILO seeks more power to police workers' rights

By Shada Islam in Brussels

Just four months ago, Asian governments were claiming victory in their debate with the West over workers' rights. Many countries in the region have long viewed Western attempts to link trade and labour issues as nothing more than protectionism disguised under a moral cloak. So they were jubilant when the World Trade Organization decided at its December meeting in Singapore that it was best to let the International Labour Organization deal with the matter. Though the ILO monitors the application of global labour rules, it has no power to enforce them.

But those who thought the issue was safely buried are having to think again. United States President Bill Clinton has just unveiled a "code of conduct" for American companies that is designed to curb labour abuses in Asian and other developing countries. Firms that sign on—at the moment they include Nike, Reebok and Liz Claiborne—promise to stop employing young children, to pay the minimum wage established by local law and to recognize the right of workers to associate freely and bargain collectively.

More significantly, the ILO is demanding greater powers to police workers' rights worldwide. The organization's director-general, Michel Hansenne, wants governments to sign a new declaration next year giving it greater powers to promote "core" labour standards, such as freedom of association, collective bargaining and bans on forced or child labour and sexual or racial discrimination.

Hansenne wants to plug a key loophole in the present system, under which countries can escape ILO scrutiny in some sectors simply by not ratifying the related conventions. It's a tactic Asian—and Western governments too—have often used:

Bangladesh, Pakistan, Thailand and Indonesia haven't put their names to the ILO convention prohibiting gender discrimination. Pakistan, India and Bangladesh haven't ratified the convention setting a minimum age for workers, and Malaysia hasn't ratified the convention banning forced labour.

Hansenne's plan is to have a new declaration annexed to the ILO constitution that would make the core principles binding on all members, regardless of whether or not they have ratified specific conventions.

Asian trade officials in Geneva say they're ready to take a closer look at Hansenne's proposal—but under certain conditions. "The important thing," says Pakistan's ambassador in Geneva, Muneer Akram, "is that the declaration is implemented in a nondiscriminatory and universal manner. In no way must this be linked to trade." Another Asian trade official in Geneva, meanwhile, stresses that instead of trying to get a new declaration, the ILO should try to get more countries to ratify the existing core conventions.

Some analysts believe Hansenne's proposals don't go far enough. "The real problem is that the ILO has no power to take action against countries which flout its rules," says Willem van der Geest, research director at the Brussels-based European Institute for Asian Studies. On the other hand, he says, there's very little the agency can offer countries that do adopt good labour practices.

ILO officials argue that even though they don't have an army at their disposal, "moral pressure" is effective. In recent years, says Francis Maupain, the agency's legal adviser, complaints about curbs on freedom of association in the Philippines, Sri Lanka, India, Pakistan, Indonesia and

Malaysia have led to changes in local laws. "The publicity given to these cases was reasonably effective in ensuring compliance with ILO rules," says Maupain.

As for rewards, Hansenne is pressing for a ground-breaking new system under which the ILO would give its tag of approval to countries that can prove they're respecting fundamental labour rights and freedoms. Maupain says current voluntary codes and "no sweat" labels given by sectors and companies to allay concerns about workplace conditions are "chaotic and selective." For instance, he says, they may cover concerns about child workers, yet ignore gender discrimination.

Asians are likely to balk at the idea of "global social labels." Their main concern is that by making the proposal, the ILO is getting involved in trade issues. Says Akram: "We can't accept any connection between trade measures and labour standards. By talking about social labels, this proposal seems to be bringing the trade-labour link back on to the international agenda through the back door."

The ILO's experts, however, argue that a strengthened supervisory role for the agency is probably Asia's best guarantee against unilateral trade measures, consumer boycotts and the confusing proliferation of voluntary social codes and labels. "Asian countries stand to lose the most through the trials by accusation" conducted by Western consumers and trade-union groups, insists the ILO's director for information, Michel Barton. Once they've looked at the pros and cons of a global social label, he says, most Asians will realize that it makes good business sense.

 From *Far Eastern Economic Review*, May 1, 1997, p. 49. © 1997 by Review Publishing Company Limited. Reprinted by permission.

Global economy, local mayhem?

**Rioting strikers in South Korea, France, Argentina and elsewhere
are not a sign that "globalisation" is a disaster**

IT LOOKS like a delicious irony, and the enemies of global
capitalism are pouncing gleefully upon it. Having grown
rich on exports, South Korea, the erstwhile tiger, has suddenly
come to resemble famously arthritic countries such as Germany and France. Its economy is still growing at a healthy 6%
or so. But its president believes that its future prosperity depends on making its labour market more flexible, helping
(says he) its firms to compete better internationally. New laws
that would make workers easier to fire have provoked bitter
clashes and strikes over the past few weeks. Now that even the
tigers are being clawed, say globalisation's critics, is it not
plain that the ever-freer international flow of goods and capital, and the competition it unleashes, ends up by hurting
workers everywhere? "Why should workers bear the brunt of
globalisation pain?" huffs a columnist in the *International
Herald Tribune*.

The events in South Korea do contain a moral about globalisation, but it is not this one. If anything, the intellectual case
for believing that open economies and flexible labour markets
are net creators of wealth and jobs has been growing increasingly strong. Since 1993 even the European Union has paid
lip service—though little else—to the idea of labour flexibility.
What South Korea underlines is that most governments have
so far done an inept job of explaining the issues to their voters.

To many workers, especially those previously in secure
employment, the "flexible labour market" is a euphemism for
freeing employers to cut wages and abolish jobs at will. The
trade unionists who have taken to the streets all over the
world argue that the only beneficiaries of this sort of flexibility are the big companies that scour the world in search of
places where desperate people are willing to work for less
money, and in worse conditions. In this view the "Manic
Logic of Global Capitalism" (the subtitle of the latest populist
tome on the subject) is to make people beggar their neighbours by turning their own country into a sweatshop.

Yet to portray the impact of globalisation and the case for
flexible labour markets in this way is a travesty. The growing
integration of the world economy has in general been an engine of mutual enrichment. Indeed, there could be few better
illustrations of this than South Korea itself. Far from making
it into a sweatshop, globalisation—in the form of access to
overseas markets—has hoisted South Korea's wages by an average of 15% a year for ten years. Over the same period South
Korea has become not only a fast-growing market for the
products of the rich world but a big overseas investor and
employer in its own right.

Why, then, do the critics of globalisation continue to strike
such a responsive chord? It is human nature to fear change—
and the instinct of many trade unionists to oppose it. But part
of the answer stems from a misunderstanding. The point of a
flexible labour market is not to win some global ugliness contest for jobs (the bulk of foreign investment by multinationals

anyway flows between rich countries, in search of markets,
not to poor ones in search of cheap labour). It is to enable your
own country to react quickly to change—technological and
otherwise—by switching people and resources swiftly from
declining industries to growing ones.

Again, South Korea is an excellent illustration. Its new labour laws are not designed to staunch a flight of manufacturing jobs abroad; with virtually full employment, that is
hardly South Korea's problem. The changes are needed to release the *chaebol*, its big conglomerates, from a trap: unable
to sack people, they have been forced to diversify into businesses about which they know nothing, simply to find berths
for surplus workers. A freer labour market would help the
chaebol to focus their activities and boost productivity. Small
firms should benefit, too. Until now, the conglomerates have
grabbed all the brightest workers for themselves.

Claims about the virtue of flexible labour markets are not
just theory, to be taken from economists on trust. A huge
worked proof exists in the contrast between America's ability
to create a net 8m jobs since 1991 and the European Union's
loss of nearly 5m. Moreover, it turns out that much of America's new employment has consisted not of the deadbeat
"McJobs" some expected but of good jobs in new industries,
especially in services; the reward, in other words, for running
an economy capable of listening to the signals of the market
and adapting fast to new technology.

Perspective, please—and consent

How are governments to persuade nervous workers of these
truths? Certainly not by pretending that the vast changes under way in the world economy will claim no victims at all.
The jobs of many unskilled workers in the rich world may
indeed migrate. German companies expect to employ at least
300,000 more people abroad in the next three years—mainly
in the lower-wage countries of Central and Eastern Europe.
But these dislocations need to be put into perspective. Germans have gained far more than they have lost from the emergence of a great new market to their east; and they have lost
more than they have gained by allowing rigid and expensive
labour laws to stifle the creation of new jobs at home.

It will, naturally, always be hard for governments to persuade workers to trade their immediate job security for a
vague promise of future opportunity. Different societies will
strike the balance in different ways. But the other moral from
South Korea is the folly of trying to free up labour markets
without popular consent. You might expect South Koreans,
richer than ever and basking in full employment, to feel less
threatened than anxious Frenchmen and Germans by ideas
for changing employment law. But, quite rightly, they turn
out not to want controversial legislation thrust down their
throats in a manner reminiscent of their country's authoritarian past. Affluence, it seems, breeds democrats; just another
benefit, as it happens, of rampaging global capitalism.

GLOBAL DEREGULATION

IN THE NEW GLOBAL ECONOMY, FREEDOM FROM EXCESSIVE REGULATION IS A STRONG ASSET. JAPAN IS MOVING IN THE RIGHT DIRECTION. GERMANY AND FRANCE AREN'T, AND THEY ARE PAYING THE PRICE.

A CENTURY AND A HALF AGO millions of German peasants crossed the ocean to find new homes in the Americas. They were fleeing a rigid social and economic system and seeking opportunity for their children.

In the 1990s it is German industry that is emigrating, and for many of the same reasons that drove the ancestors of so many of today's Americans from their old homes.

German industry has lost none of its technological and managerial prowess, but products made in Germany are becoming increasingly uncompetitive in cost. The latest survey by the Institut der deutschen Wirtschaft shows that, on average, industrial labor now costs $31.76 an hour in western Germany and $20.82 in the eastern part, versus $20.26 in France, $14.63 in Britain and around $17.50 an hour in the U.S.

Since there is no way that German workers can be worth 55% more than U.S. workers, the consequences are predictable. National statistics are not available for the number of jobs that German companies have created abroad, but the picture is clear at the company level, as our table (*see next page*) shows. Nearly every day reports tell of expansion in the U.S. or abroad by a German company. The latest: Bayer Corp., the U.S. subsidiary of German Bayer Group, which announced last month it planned investing a further $6 billion in the U.S. by 2000.

It is not merely the level of wages that is driving these good Germans away from their homeland. The corporate restructuring that has made U.S. industry so much more competitive in the past decade and a half is almost impossible in Germany. Blame the unions in part. Blame the stuffy German business establishment, too.

The attempted $5 billion hostile takeover of Thyssen by Gerhard Cromme, chairman of Fried. Krupp-Hoesch, was immediately blocked by the powerful steel industry union, IG Metall, with the backing of the opposition Social Democratic Party. The proposed takeover made economic and operational sense.

But it wasn't just that the unions were against the deal. That it was hostile aroused the opposition of much of the German business establishment. The deal was right, but it wasn't polite. But this hostile takeover would have been a done deal in the U.S., or even the U.K. Not in Germany.

Instead of an outright merger, the two companies will combine their steel operations. Thyssen's threatened managers will run the merged steel operation. And to win a union okay the companies had to agree not to lay off more than a handful of people for at least three years. The combination will do little to reduce overcapacity in the German steel sector or to make the new operation world-competitive.

A few weeks earlier, in Germany's coal industry, union diehards and their political allies won an even more smashing victory. In an effort to reduce Germany's budget deficit, Chancellor Helmut Kohl's Christian Democrat-led coalition proposed to reduce the $5.24-billion-a-year subsidy for Germany's out-of-date coal industry. This subsidy is equal to $61,650 a year for every one of the 85,000 German mining jobs. It would be cheaper to retire most of the work force on full pay than to keep them digging.

The Kohl government didn't propose eliminating the subsidy. It merely proposed cutting it by reducing the 85,000 work force to 25,000 by 2003. Mass marches by egg-throwing union mobs, backed by local opposition politicians, forced the Kohl government into a humiliating cave-in. It will leave the work force at 39,000 miners, and the subsidy per job will increase to $87,000 a year. German coal today costs around $180 a ton, versus around a $65-a-ton world price.

Construction workers, too, took to the streets in Bonn, still the seat of national government, to protest job cuts. Once again protest worked: The Kohl government caved in here, too,

German industry is fleeing Germany. Why?

Deutsche hegira

By Howard Banks

Reprinted with permission from *Forbes* magazine, May 5, 1997, pp. 130-133. © 1997 by Forbes, Inc.

agreeing to pump another $7.5 billion into construction projects.

Much of the business establishment is hardly more progressive than the unions and politicians. Dieter Vogel, chairman of Thyssen, called Cromme's unwelcome bid for his company "Wild West tactics"—code for vulgar, American-style behavior.

In Germany it is still difficult and costly to fire anybody. The workweek is restricted, with overtime rates being paid after 37.5 hours, 35 hours in the metals industry. And long paid vacations, averaging six weeks, plus liberal sick leave (which leads to high absenteeism) means that Germans work much less of the year than American or British workers.

Germany is paying a terrible price for this refusal to change. German unemployment is now running at around a 12% unadjusted rate and seems to be on a rising trend. When labor is overpriced, employers will shop elsewhere.

Even this unpleasantly high number disguises the real level of joblessness in Germany. Government-funded training schemes are mostly little more than disguised unemployment insurance. This and early retirement probably add another 4% to 5% to Germany's real unemployed.

To keep the jobless quiet, the government supports them with high benefits. With at least one child, the unemployed can collect 57% of their former income indefinitely, tax free, with more for the first six months on the dole.

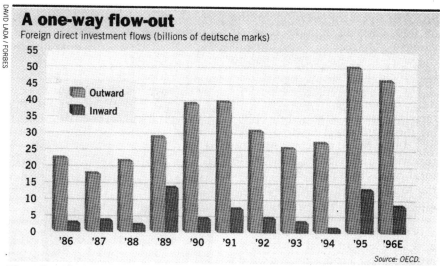

DAVID LADA / FORBES

A one-way flow-out
Foreign direct investment flows (billions of deutsche marks)

Since the mid-1980s German industry has been a major investor outside Germany. But foreign firms, turned off by Germany's high costs, have largely shunned the country as a place to invest.

Source: OECD.

Around 1988, when U.S. corporate restructuring was at its height, German companies began to invest abroad (*see chart, above*). Until then, German companies had done little direct investment abroad in comparison with companies in most large, industrialized countries, especially the U.S. and the U.K. Now the Germans are catching up.

While the U.S. was sending money and jobs overseas, foreigners were sending money and jobs to the U.S. as well. It was a two-way flow. In Germany's case the flow is all one way—out. Thomas Hatzichronoglou, a noted expert on global business trends with the Organization for Economic Cooperation and Development, says that foreign firms with operations in Germany are cutting back there. "In 1991 foreign affiliates in Germany employed 963,000 people. By 1994, the latest detailed survey we have, that was down to 799,600, and from what we know that number continues to fall," he says.

The resulting unemployment explains why Germany is having such trouble reducing its public sector budget deficit sufficiently to meet the 3% deficit target for European mon-

Is this any way to run an economy?

Company/business	1985 employment			1995 employment		
	German	foreign	% foreign	German	foreign	% foreign
BASF/chemicals, pharmaceuticals	87,292	42,881	32.9%	63,715	42,850	40.2%
Daimler-Benz/cars, trucks and aerospace	257,538[1]	62,427	19.5	242,086	68,907	22.2
Henkel kGaA/chemicals	16,006	15,015	48.4	14,684	27,044	64.8
Hoechst/chemicals, pharmaceuticals	61,642	118,919	65.8	39,108	122,510	75.8
Krupp/steel	59,978	7,424	11.0	49,112	17,240	26.0
MAN Group/capital equipment	52,264[2]	8,513	14.0	45,085	11,418	20.2
Mannesmann AG/machinery	77,174[1]	32,280	29.5	78,015	41,660	34.8
Metallgesellschaft/materials	21,384	3,458	13.9	18,571	4,870	20.8
SAP/software	749[3]	191	20.3	4,345	4,851	52.8
Siemens/electrical and electronic	240,000	108,000	31.0	211,000	162,000	43.4
Veba/energy and transport	68,689[1]	5,361	7.2	125,158	24,930	16.6

[1]Figures are for 1986. [2]Figures are for 1987. [3]Figures are for 1988.

Since 1985, with the exception of SAP and Veba, these big German companies have cut jobs at home—absolutely and relatively— while creating thousands of new jobs in other countries.

etary union in the Maastricht Treaty. The German Bundesbank has reported that the deficit in the first two months of this year was a third higher than the target rate. Germany's finance minister, Theodore Waigel, has appealed to the rest of Europe to be generous about (i.e., turn a blind eye to) his inability to meet the Maastricht targets.

There are other factors adding to the cost of Germany's job crisis.

During the U.S. restructuring period in the 1980s, the Reagan Administration slashed taxes and went for high growth. The resulting job creation, especially among small, fast-growing firms, helped cushion the loss of jobs from restructuring. Germany has no such crutch. Economic growth is slow—coming off a

In the end, the unions and politicians will have to bow to economic reality. Until then, German business will vote with its feet.

recession, it is just creeping at 2% to 2.5% this year, after 1.4% in 1996. And Germany is still only talking about cutting taxes.

Germany and other European Union countries are trying to create a common currency. An odd feature of the single-currency process is that if Germany doesn't make it into the European Monetary Union on time, the deutsche mark will rise as

investors holding other European currencies sell them and go back to the mark (and the dollar and yen) as safe havens. The last thing that German industrialists want is a stronger mark, which will make even more of their exported production uncompetitive.

Germany is by no means going down the drain. In the end the unions and the politicians will have to bow to economic reality and loosen the legal and customary straitjacket in which German industry operates. Until that happens, German business will continue to immigrate to more hospitable climes. "Change is coming to Germany," says Jürgen Dorman, chairman of the board of management of Hoechst AG. "But it will take longer than in America."

Investing in India: Strategies for Tackling Bureaucratic Hurdles

Sanjiv Kumar and Leena Thacker-Kumar

Burgeoning business opportunities in India for foreign investors are well worth the bit of careful strategic planning required to maneuver around the bureaucratic obstacle course.

Although free-market reforms have spurred foreign investment in India, bureaucratic hurdles continue to shackle foreign investors and impede the flow of investment. From July 1991—when the free-market reform policy started—to December 1994, almost 19,000 foreign investment proposals worth $130 billion were filed with the government. But only a few of these investment commitments have actually been implemented, while others languish at various pre-implementation stages.

Foreign companies generally have reacted positively, even excitedly, to the prospect of investing in India. Approximately 422 American firms have set up operations in India, ranging from such well-known multinational corporations (MNCs) as McDonald's, Coca-Cola, Motorola, AT&T, and IBM to small companies such as Liebert Corporation and Bry-Air. According to a recent Ernst & Young survey, U.S.-based MNCs cite India as one of their top priorities for foreign investment. But bureaucratic interference still continues to bog them down. As reported in Abdoolcarim (1994), an *Economist* survey of 16 major foreign corporations and joint ventures located in India indicated that inept and interfering bureaucracy has been the biggest obstacle for foreign investors. The labyrinth of bureaucratic obstacles causes project overruns and costly delays for businesses. "American executives," reports Burns (1995), "are finding that the Indian bureaucracy, though gradually releasing its tight grip on the economy, wields wide powers, compounding inefficiencies from decades of socialism."

So what can foreign investors do, if anything, to successfully negotiate the murky waters of Indian bureaucracy and still reap the benefits of investing in India? In this article, we attempt to provide insights on how foreign companies can leverage their decisions to alleviate bureaucratic woes and improve their chance of business success. Though some level of bureaucratic obstacles invariably will be encountered, an active effort to "deal with bureaucracy" will minimize the frustration and costs associated with bureaucratic hurdles. This would mean proceeding with planning and implementation decisions with one eye keenly focused on how each decision will affect the firm's ability to handle the red tape. For example, decisions about where to locate, who should be the Indian partner (most foreign investment in India is in the form of joint ventures), which managers to select and appoint as parent representatives, and the nature of expatriate training and support can all serve as potential tools in overcoming bureaucratic impediments.

BUREAUCRATIC HURDLES

Before delving into the strategic decisions of doing business with India, an up-front understanding of the nature of bureaucratic challenges will allow foreign investors to leverage their decision-making process more effectively. We begin, therefore, with a portrait of the bureaucratic hurdles likely to be encountered.

Levels of Bureaucracy: Central versus State

The Indian federation, or union, is organized into 25 states and seven centrally administered union territories. Although the systems of government at the central and state levels closely resemble each

From *Business Horizons*, January/February 1996, pp. 10-16. © 1996 by the Foundation for the School of Business at Indiana University. Reprinted by permission.

other, the Indian constitution provides three lists for demarcating areas of jurisdiction: the union list, the state list, and the concurrent list. The union list includes items on which the central government has exclusive authority to make and enforce laws, such as foreign affairs, customs duties, and taxation of income. Likewise, the state list contains areas (law enforcement, land policies) over which the state has exclusive authority to make and enforce laws. Both the central and individual state governments have control over items on the concurrent list, such as labor welfare and price controls.

Understanding whether a particular approval or license is within the jurisdiction of the union, state, or concurrent list will allow a foreign investor to target its efforts toward the appropriate government level(s). It is important to note that bureaucratic processes (getting licenses and approvals) related to items on the union list are fairly streamlined. However, the lower rungs of the government (state and municipal) are still struggling to streamline their processes. The need to reform bureaucratic processes has not permeated uniformly across all states and down to lower government levels. "At the lower levels, there is no sense of urgency, no sense that the world is not going to wait for you," said the president of AT&T India (Abdoolcarim 1994). As such, although negotiating bureaucracy at the central level may not be difficult, the going can be very arduous at the state level.

Take, for instance, the experience of the American agro-business company, the Cargill Corporation. It took Cargill just 30 days to receive the go-ahead from the central government for a wholly owned, $15 million salt-processing venture, which was expected to boost much-needed foreign reserves of India by exporting one million tons of salt. Despite these obvious advantages, however, Cargill could not obtain the land needed to set up the venture. The government of the northwestern state of Gujarat turned down the company's initial choice of land on the coast. Its second choice—also on Gujarat land, but under federal jurisdiction—was disputed by the organized Small Scale Salt Manufacturers of Gujarat. In the end, Cargill had to pull out of the salt venture. And this experience occurred in a state that has been a leader in drawing foreign investment.

State-Level Bureaucracy: Not All States Are Equal

What are some of the bureaucratic problems faced at the state level? Some of the key obstacles are:
- power connections;
- environmental clearances;
- labor laws;

- approvals for other requirements, such as land and water; and
- implementation of regulatory compliance.

Obtaining a power connection is within the domain of the state authorities. Depending on the state in which the unit is being set up, obtaining a power connection can take from six to 18 months. In some states, this may involve seeking approvals from nine different agencies and filling out 40 different forms. Even if a firm were to try to establish its own power generator, it would still require approvals by state government authorities. In addition, if excess power were generated, it could not be sold to adjoining plants.

Environmental clearances, regardless of the nature of the unit being set up, are required by most states and may entail filling multiple forms. Though some states, such as Punjab, have actively reduced the clearance requirements only for hazardous industries (dubbed the "red category"), others still require clearances for all units, regardless of industry.

Labor law in India is a morass. Labor laws are on the concurrent list; this means that while both central and state governments get to formulate policies, it is the state that implements them. Currently, as many as 51 different acts define labor, wages, and units. Though there is a need for uniform labor laws for all states, no action has yet been taken by the central government.

Other requirements, such as land, water, and natural resources, are under the jurisdiction of the state and may pose challenges for the foreign investor. For example, in some states, companies have to deal with nine different agencies and go through 29 steps to get approval for land acquisition. For water connection, a company may have to deal with 11 different agencies and fill out 21 forms.

Implementation of regulatory compliance, much of which is on the concurrent list, is not well coordinated at the state level. For example, if a company has to comply with six different laws enacted by the central government but implemented by the state, as many as six different inspectors may come to check compliance. Additionally, the firm may have to maintain six different books to exhibit compliance with each of the six different acts for each of the six inspectors. Naturally, this redundancy imposes additional costs on the firm. Although some states are trying to create a better system of consolidating redundancies, these procedures will take time to implement. Until then, foreign investors have to learn to comply with these many superfluous requirements.

The problem of working at the state level is further compounded when foreign investors have to seek approval from the very top state official even for a small decision. Although states are trying to decentralize decision making, their attempts have had little impact, having fallen victim to an ingrained culture in which lower-level officials are afraid to make decisions.

So a foreign investor has to be ready to deal with various agencies, forms, and obstacles at the state level. Although understanding the nature of such bureaucracy is a necessary first step, there are decisions that can help foreign investors deal with it. Based on our experience, a company can use its decisions about location, joint venture partners, selection of managerial personnel, and expatriate training and support to minimize costs of bureaucratic interference and improve business success.

LOCATION DECISIONS

Not all of India's states have the same number or type of bureaucratic hurdles. Some are more investor-friendly than others. The choice of the right state in which to locate is critical for a foreign investor. **Table 1** outlines the top ten states in terms of attracting foreign investment.

How does a company choose the right state for its location? We suggest that a firm should examine a combination of three factors in its choice: (a) infrastructure, (b) political leadership, and (c) incentives.

Infrastructure

This is probably the most vulnerable spot when it comes to a state trying to attract foreign investment. For example, even a state like Tamil Nadu, which has one of the best infrastructures in India, faces substantial power shortages every day (a deficit of two million kwh/day). **Table 2** lists the top ten states in terms of infrastructure development.

Most states are unable to undertake infrastructure development projects because they face severe budgetary constraints. This problem has been compounded because many states have bargained away their current source of income—the sales tax—as potential incentive to attract foreign investment. So the crucial question for the foreign investor is: Does the state have the requisite infrastructure to support its goals? The biggest infrastructure constraint a foreign investor should consider is power. Other important considerations are roads, bridges, airports, and telecommunications.

Political Leadership

With states becoming more competitive in drawing foreign investment, the political leadership of a state plays a critical role in helping iron out bureaucratic hurdles. In evaluating leadership, foreign investors should focus less on the political affiliation of the ruling party in the state and more on the leaders' attitudes toward foreign investment.

It is not necessary for the state government to have the same party affiliation as the central government for it to be investor-friendly. For example, Karnataka, where the ruling party is different from that of the union, has been very active in smoothing out bureaucratic approval processes. To facilitate foreign investment, its leaders have started an approval process much akin to that of the central government. These efforts are starting to pay off as more foreign investment is pouring into Karnataka.

A state's political leadership is the most important influence on the attitudes and activities of administrators toward business and foreign investment. Note Joglekar et al. (1994), "Only a pragmatic political leader, even if for reasons of expediency, can lay down a clear and attractive industrial policy. [Moreover], the bureaucrats, no

Table 1
India: Top Ten States in Attracting Foreign Investments: August 1991 to July 1994

Rank	State	% of Total Foreign Investment
1	Maharastra	20.44
2	Gujarat	16.76
3	Uttar Pradesh	11.79
4	Madhya Pradesh	10.40
5	Andhra Pradesh	7.35
6	Tamil Nadu	5.05
7	Rajasthan	4.53
8	Haryana	3.90
9	Karnataka	3.78
10	Punjab	3.66

Source: Nayar (1995)

Table 2
India: Top Ten States in the Development of Infrastructure

Rank	State
1	Punjab
2	Haryana
3	Kerala
4	Tamil Nadu
5	Gujarat
6	West Bengal
7	Maharastra
8	Uttar Pradesh
9	Andhra Pradesh
10	Karnataka

Source: Joglekar et al. (1994)

matter how intelligent, need to be motivated and given a direction."

A lack of clear political leadership, even in a relatively advanced state, may act as a major disincentive for foreign investors. Take, for example, Kerala, which is one of the top three states in infrastructure development and has one of the highest literacy rates in the country. Despite these advantages, it has been unable to attract investment because of the lack of political leadership in settling the conflict between the state government and trade unions. Sensing the importance of political leadership in attracting investment, some state governments—Gujarat, Uttar Pradesh, Madhya Pradesh—have actively embarked on administrative reforms, such as instituting training programs to help bureaucrats cope with their new roles as facilitators rather than regulators.

Incentives

Individual states usually compete for foreign investment by offering subsidies, sales tax exemptions, power concessions, and tax holidays. These incentive packages, however, very often cancel each other out. For example, the packages offered by Maharastra, Gujarat, and Karnataka were almost the same, so their relative ability to gain an advantage in drawing foreign investment fizzled out. Some states, such as Rajasthan, rely heavily on incentives to draw foreign investment. However, such large incentives may be offered to make up for the lack of a coastline, major financial centers, and a skilled work force. Thus, the attractiveness of a state's incentive package should be counterweighed by factors that can make it difficult to do business in that state. Incentives should serve as a necessary—but not the only—condition for evaluating location decisions.

PARTNERSHIP DECISIONS

One of the best ways to circumvent the costs of dealing with bureaucracy is to have the right partner in starting a joint venture. How does a company choose the right partner? We suggest that the foreign investor focus on two questions before forming a partnership: (a) Does the would-be partner know the ropes? (b) Has due diligence been exercised in investigating the potential partner?

Does the Partner Know the Ropes?

Besides some common business criteria used to evaluate a good partner—compatibility, commitment, combined strength—the ability of the partner to work the bureaucratic processes should be considered as an important criterion. Big indus-

trial groups are good candidates here. Various industrial groups in India, such as the Tatas, the Birlas, and the Reliance Group, have considerable experience and a good history of operations. They are familiar with the Indian market and can open a lot of doors. Take, for example, AT&T, which already has two joint ventures with the Tata group: AT&T Switching Systems and Trans-India Network Systems. It recently signed a memorandum of agreement with the Birla group to explore telecommunication opportunities in India. In explaining the choice of Birla as partner, which had no prior telecommunication experience, a spokesperson for AT&T replied, "We are comfortable with that because we have the telecom expertise. What we need is somebody who knows how to execute projects in the country, and is well versed with the customer set and customer expectation" (Mitra 1995).

The opportunity to form joint ventures with Indian industrial groups is not restricted to large multinational corporations alone. Even smaller companies can benefit by partnering with a firm within these industrial groups. Take the example of Liebert Corporation, a $500 million company based in Columbus, Ohio that manufactures uninterrupted power supply and environmental control systems. Liebert formed a joint venture (Tata-Liebert) with one of the companies within the Tata Industrial Group. Not only did Liebert benefit by having the backing of the recognized and respected Tata name, but it also had help in overcoming bureaucratic hurdles.

Has Due Diligence Been Used in Investigating the Potential Partner?

More and more, good partners from big industrial groups are difficult to find. "A lot of big industrial groups that have good political contacts and access to capital have their plates full," says the vice president for international planning and development at Liebert (Oldenborgh 1995). So should a foreign investor look for other candidates? Yes, but it should proceed with extreme caution. Other candidates, such as agents or representatives, can be good, but there are chances of being duped into an agreement that may not be advantageous.

It is important to keep in mind that a company that has served as an agent or representative may not necessarily be the best choice for a partner in a joint venture. Some of these agents or representatives, though they may have served as capable "middlemen" in export-import transactions, do not have the necessary experience or resources to fulfill the responsibilities of being a full JV partner. Before forming a joint venture with the Tatas, Liebert's vice president spent two years talking to a Bombay-based company that had served as his firm's representative in India. He finally realized that this company was putting up a good front but barely had enough resources to maintain a full-time office. He said, "I finally discovered that every time I came to visit, they rented a car and a fax machine, returning them as soon as I left." This happened despite the fact that the vice president had lived in India for some time.

Beyond assessing whether an agent or representative has adequate resources, foreign investors should gauge whether there is compatibility in business philosophy. For instance, before it formed its partnership with the Birla group, AT&T had a distributorship agreement with another company, Bharati Telecom, in India. It decided to leave Bharati for the Birla group because, according to an AT&T spokesperson, "With the Birlas, we feel very comfortable. We share the same philosophies for integrity and customer focus" (Mitra 1995).

In exploring all possible sources of background information on a potential partner, non-competing firms may be a good place for a foreign investor to start. Existing partnerships with non-competing firms may not only serve as sources of information but also as springboards in forming future partnerships. When the $1.7 billion Duracell Corporation was contemplating forming a joint venture with the Poddar group in India, it talked to the Gillette Company first, which was already involved in an ongoing joint venture with Poddar. "Gillette shared a lot of information with us, because they have a similar distribution pattern and we're non-competing," said the vice president of manufacturing for international development at Duracell (Oldenborgh 1995). Eventually, Gillette introduced Duracell to the Poddar group, resulting in a joint venture.

> "Long-term thinking and patience are probably two of the most crucial ingredients for successful managers—local or expatriate—in India."

PERSONNEL DECISIONS

The personnel decisions made by a foreign investor can have a crucial impact on the firm's bility to deal with local challenges as well as its overall chances of business success. An investor wishing to do business in India should focus on four factors: (a) choosing managers who have the right temperament; (b) dedicating personnel exclusively to government work; (c) providing appropriate pre-departure training for managers; and (d) providing adequate infrastructure support in India for them.

Choosing Managers with the Right Temperament

Some firms have chosen expatriate employees of Indian origin to head their operations in India. These managers have the dual advantage of knowing the company and the country culture. However, as the president of AT&T India—himself an expatriate of Indian origin—maintains, "Having an Indian is not as important as having someone with the right outlook, someone who really likes India, because there are lots of frustrations, delays, and a different work ethic" (Abdoolcarim 1994).

Long-term thinking and patience are probably two of the most crucial ingredients for successful managers—local or expatriate—in India. It may take much more time to negotiate and implement a project than initially anticipated. Take AES Corporation, which wanted to build a power plant in the state of Orissa. The project manager had initially anticipated being in India for six to nine months. But after almost a year and a half, AES had gone through various rounds of renegotiations in the power purchase agreement, seeking government approvals on everything from capital costs to technical design, and was still far from completing the project. A senior executive at GE said, "You've got to be prepared mentally to work in a challenging, not-so-streamlined environment [in which] certain inefficiencies such as low productivity, [poor] transport, and power shortages will take a few years to iron out. You have to . . . stay three years before life gets exciting" (Abdoolcarim 1994).

Dedicate Personnel Exclusively to Government Work

Having one person taking care of government work is a worthwhile expense. This is especially true initially, when the company is just starting off. Bry-Air, a $20 million maker of industrial drying equipment from Sunbury, Ohio, has been conducting business in the Indian subcontinent for two decades. But it still employs one person full-time to handle government paperwork. Though on the surface this expense may seem a bit unnecessary, it ends up saving many costly delays and interruptions. The person dedicated to taking care of government work helps establish the requisite contacts and becomes a "known face" in government circles. Moreover, other managers are free to pursue more value-added activities.

Provide Appropriate Predeparture Training

Many organizations provide some sort of pre-departure expatriate training to aid their effectiveness in India. Courses focus on the cultural, social, and business customs of the country and try to prepare managers for a smoother transition. This helps in creating better-adapted managers who have greater chances of business success. Often, however, what has been taught in these courses, though generally correct, may not equip managers very well for their particular assignment. For instance, the managing director of Goodyear India learned some Hindi before he left. But then he was posted in Madras, where the language of choice is Tamil. "I'd been taking lessons in Hindi. But I'm totally lost in Madras," he said (Bansal 1994).

Many other subtle differences may not be covered in these courses but are nonetheless very important for cultural adaptation. For example, one of the first culture shocks is the adjustment to the Indian work-clock, which begins around 9:30 a.m. rather than 7:30 or 8:00, when most expatriates are accustomed to beginning work. The dress code is another source of concern. Expatriates may not know what to expect, partly because there is no rigid dress code in Indian business circles. Awareness of other subtleties, such as the preference for evasive rather than direct refusals for invitations or the custom of showing up a few minutes late for parties, may also help expatriate managers avoid embarrassing situations. Not knowing the decorum for any one situation may not be damaging, but taken together such subtleties can become progressively frustrating. Offering training courses that focus on these subtleties, along with some generalities, can result in better prepared managers.

Provide Adequate Infrastructure Support for Managers

It takes time for expatriates and their family members to adjust to the inconveniences of daily living, such as inadequate water and power supply, traffic snarls, and erratic telephone lines. Adjusting to these nonwork-related issues sometimes takes the biggest toll on expatriates. For example, "living out of a suitcase" for many months has become an unwelcome reality for many expatriates. In some cities, such as Bombay, inadequate housing combined with steep rents has forced expatriates to live in hotels until suitable accommodations are found.

Many expatriates also find that their social circle is considerably narrowed. Social events may be restricted to business lunches and embassy dinners, so spouses may also have problems adjusting. Though such cities as New Delhi have formed network groups to help families adjust to Indian living, others have no such provisions. It may be difficult to find the right schools for the children of expatriates. Lack of privacy at home because of live-in help may cause additional strain for some.

All of these irritants tend to extract a toll on expatriate managers. This in turn may limit their effectiveness on the job and hamper their ability to deal with work-related hurdles. In speaking about his posting in India, the principal economist with the Canadian International Development Research Center warned that "companies now have to seriously consider providing adequate infrastructure to their expatriate employees" (Bansal 1994).

Free market reforms have greatly enhanced the attractiveness of foreign investment in India. Despite such great progress and potential, however, the maze of bureaucracy may greatly increase business costs and frustrations for foreign investors and their executives. Though it is difficult to avoid red tape completely, investors can leverage their major decisions to reduce the anguish of dealing with bureaucratic hurdles. We suggest a three-pronged strategy—the right choices in location, joint venture partner, and personnel—for tackling bureaucratic hurdles and improving the chances of business success.

References

"$130 Billion Investment Proposed," *India Abroad*, May 5, 1995, p. 22.

Z. Abdoolcarim, "India's Power Unleashed," *Asian Business*, February 1994, pp. 18-22.

M.S. Ahluwalia, "India's Quiet Economic Revolution," *Columbia Journal of World Business*, Spring 1994, pp. 6-12.

P. Banks and G. Natarajan, "India: The New Asian Tiger?" *Business Horizons*, May-June 1995, pp. 47-50.

S. Bansal, "The Flatfoots Try to Find their Feet," *Business World*, July 13-16, 1994, pp. 148-151.

J.F. Burns, "India Now Winning U.S. Investment," *The New York Times*, February 6, 1995, pp. C1,C5.

A. Jayaram, "A Sorry State," *Business World*, May 18-31, 1994, pp. 24-26.

S. Joglekar, N. Sriram, T. Raman, K.G. Kumar, A. Panneerselvan, M. Bose, P. Ramnath, M. Shenoy, and D. Purokayastha, "The Ten Best States for Business," *Business India*, June 6-19, 1994, pp. 54-65.

J. Khalizadeh-Shirazi and R. Zagha, "Economic Reforms in India: Achievements and the Agenda Ahead," *Columbia Journal of World Business*, Spring 1994, pp. 24-31.

U.L. Lechner, "India is Elbowing Into China's Limelight," *Wall Street Journal*, January 12, 1995, p. A11.

N. Mitra, "AT&T Joins with Birla in Telecom Venture," *India Abroad*, January 13, 1995, p. 26.

K.S. Nayar, "States Compete for Investors' Money," *India Abroad*, February 10, 1995, p. 26.

M.V. Oldenborgh, "India: Better than China," *International Business*, January 1995, pp. 48-51.

T. Thomas, "Change in Climate for Foreign Investment in India," *Columbia Journal of World Business*, Spring 1994, pp. 32-40.

S. Tyagi, "The Giant Awakens: An Interview with Professor Jagdish Bhagwati on Economic Reform in India," *Columbia Journal of World Business*, Spring 1994, pp. 14-22.

N. Vaghul, "Liberalization of the Financial Markets in India," *Columbia Journal of World Business*, Spring 1994, pp. 42-48.

Sanjiv Kumar is an assistant professor of management and **Leena Thacker-Kumar** is an assistant professor of government, both at the University of Houston-Downtown in Houston, Texas.

How Management Deals with Environmental Forces

- Market Assessment and Analysis (Articles 27 and 28)
- Marketing Internationally (Articles 29 and 30)
- Export and Import Practices and Procedures (Articles 31–33)
- East-West Relations (Articles 34–36)
- Financial Management (Articles 37 and 38)
- Production Systems (Articles 39 and 40)
- Labor Relations, Policies, and Management (Articles 41 and 42)
- Strategic Management and Organization Design (Articles 43 and 44)
- Controlling and Staffing (Articles 45–47)
- Trends and New Directions (Article 48)

Managers of international organizations have to deal with a changing and varied global environment. To be successful, managers cannot just sit back and wait for things to happen. Rather, they need to be proactive in their approach to the problems and opportunities associated with doing business on an international basis, and they need to find partners who can help them. William Shanklin and David Griffith report on such approaches in "Crafting Strategies for Global Marketing in the New Millennium."

One of the major tools that managers have to help their organizations become successful on the global stage is marketing, and in particular, marketing analysis. Managers need to realize that while all markets have certain similarities, they are all different in their own way and each can pose different problems, as outlined in "Troubles Ahead in Emerging Markets." Many practices are different and many hurdles exist. In sales, communicating with customers can be difficult and demanding, even in an "integrated" market such as Europe.

An easy way for a firm to get into international trade is through import/export channels. Often, when a small firm first starts to engage in international trade, it is not due to any deliberate decision of its own part. Instead, the firm may place an advertisement in an industrial magazine, or have a booth at a trade show, or be featured in an article on the news. As a result, one day it happens to get an order from someone outside its domestic market. It may be a very small order that merely says, "Send us one of these; we would like to look at it!" That first small order is then frequently followed by a much larger order, and the small domestic firm suddenly finds itself doing business abroad. This can happen on either side of the equation, as an importer or an exporter. As time passes, the company's foreign business grows at a faster rate than does its domestic business, especially if it in-

volves one of the more rapidly developing economies, and soon, a significant amount of business is being done overseas.

An especially difficult area for firms has been China, Eastern Europe, and the former Soviet Union. Certainly there is great opportunity in these markets, but there is also great risk. Many people in these societies simply do not know how to operate in a developing capitalist system. Commercial laws have not been developed, and an understanding of the fundamental aspects of capitalism has not been achieved by much of the population, including important government officials, as well as quasi capitalists, such as factory managers. International managers must be prepared for setbacks and disappointments before they will be able to experience success, as S. R. Nair points out in "Doing Business in China: It's Far from Easy."

The monetary problem has always been of particular concern in international trade. Currency trading and fluctuations cause managers sleepless nights and terrible days. Some currencies of the developing world, in particular, are difficult to deal with. The rewards can be very high, but, unfortunately, so can the risks. Managers who engage in world trade need to develop a strong financial management system to deal with the financial aspect of their global business if they are going to be successful.

An additional factor that needs to be considered is that of production. A world economy means not only worldwide customers but worldwide production. To be competitive, organizations must be able to produce worldwide and to coordinate production for the greatest advantage. With the introduction of the North American Free Trade Agreement (NAFTA), firms in North America are not just American, Canadian, or Mexican, but North American, with an entire continent as their backyard. Even in Asia, organizations are seeking opportunities for production that lie off

the beaten paths of Hong Kong and Singapore, as described in "The Discreet Charm of Provincial Asia."

Organizations that are going to produce, distribute, and sell overseas must realize that they cannot do this without workers, the people who perform the necessary tasks for the organization's success. Generally speaking, labor relations are very different outside the United States. The relationship between union and management in Germany, for example, frequently involves a highly cooperative arrangement. On the other hand, in some less developed countries, child labor is common, and a living wage, let alone benefits, is as rare as a union organizer. This does not mean that organizations from developed countries should emulate all these practices, but, instead, that they should select the best aspects.

International managers must learn to combine all these parts of the new global business environment. They must plan strategically to make good use of marketing, production, finance, and labor. They must learn to control this highly diverse and sometimes contentious brew by using the most modern management technologies available. Controlling a business on an international scale is certainly not easy, and new systems will be needed in the future for managers to be successful. Perhaps even

new approaches to exactly what constitutes a company need to be considered, as presented in "A Company without a Country?"

In conclusion, there are many challenges facing managers in the international environment. But, fortunately, they have at least some of the knowledge they need to deal with these challenges. The task will not be easy, and new problems and opportunities are certain to arise in the future. Managers will have to develop the necessary new tools to solve the problems and grasp the opportunities for success in the ever-changing international business environment.

Looking Ahead: Challenge Questions

What are some things marketers can do to market more effectively on the international level?

Doing business in the former Soviet Union and Eastern bloc is difficult, but it is possible. What are some things that can be tried when doing business in this part of the world?

The challenge for managers is a changing international environment. How can managers strategically plan for success in the future?

Shock Therapy

The peso's crash in 1994 shattered Mexico's economy but has caused many changes and boosted exports to record highs.

**Richard Zelade and
Carolina Esquenazi-Shaio**

Mexico's business climate is now much more optimistic than a year and half ago when the country fell into one of its worst economic crises ever. The 50 percent decline of the peso in December 1994 was followed by an inflation rate that topped 50 percent and interest rates skyrocketing to 60 percent. Thousands of businesses were forced to close down.

An estimated 1.8 million jobs were lost during 1995; the official unemployment rate reached 6.4 percent, double pre-crisis levels. Industrial output fell 10 percent, domestic consumption 14 percent, retail sales about 21 percent and wholesale sales 16.6 percent. Purchases of consumer durables fell 47 percent in first nine months of last year, and although inflation hit 51.97 percent, the price of food, medicine and clothing rose by 60.57 percent. Public investments fell by 32.5 percent in first 9 months, according to Mexico's Finance Ministry, while private investment dropped by 29.4 percent and overall gross fixed investment dropped by 30 percent, according to the Heritage Foundation.

"In some cities, 10 percent of the businesses closed during the first two months of the crisis, and over 250,000 workers lost their jobs. The impact of the economic crisis is beyond any recent experience in the United States. All these [negative] developments hit the Mexican middle class as well as the lower groups," observes Dr. Frank D. Bean, professor of sociology and director of the Population Research Center at the University of Texas at Austin.

Fortunately 1996 won't be so bad. As Mexican finance minister, Guillermo Ortiz, told U.S. bankers and brokers in December 1995, "I'm not saying there will be a boom. The recovery will be gradual." But a recovery it is.

Mexican gross domestic product (GDP) is forecast to grow 2 percent this year, with most growth expected in the fourth quarter. Mr. Ortiz predicts 3 percent growth if there are no new instabilities, a far cry from last year's economic contraction of between 6 and 8 percent. In the first quarter of 1996, GDP fell 1 percent, which was taken as good news because the Mexican government had expected a 3 percent drop.

After so many shock waves, the economy now is more open and competitive, and many investors are buoyed by the Mexican Bolsa de Valores (stock market) index's recent record highs. Mexican stocks are up 25 percent (in dollars) this year and interest rates are now at their lowest level since devaluation. Fluctuating primary interest rates rose to nearly 90 percent in early 1995, but had dropped to 45 percent by year's end and have continued declining. The interest rate for Mexico's benchmark 28-day Treasury bills, which determine interest rates for Mexican companies, have been descending since April to reach 26 percent at press time.

Key economic indicators such as retail automobile sales, cement consumption, and the Industrial Production Volume Index appear to have hit bottom and are now slowly rising, but they are still far below pre-1994 devaluation levels. During the speech mentioned earlier, Mr. Ortiz pointed out that in October 1995, 85,000 new jobs were created, compared to losses of 85,000 to 90,000 jobs each month from January through July 1995. He also predicted that exports would cool off in 1996 to about half the 1995 rate, but predicted that they would contribute 1.4 percent to Mexico's economic growth this year, almost half of his original forecast of 3 percent.

U.S. EXPORTS TO MEXICO

JANUARY-MARCH 1996
(In Millions of U.S. Dollars)

INDUSTRY	$US	% Change
1. El Machine: Sound/TV Equipment	3,031	15.43
2. Machinery	1,581	4.82
3. Vehicles, Not Railway	1,243	28.74
4. Plastic	828	19.99
5. Special Other	517	7.42
6. Iron or Steel Products	411	44.12
7. Cereals	399	135.82
8. Paper, Paperboard	372	9.75
9. Mineral Fuel, Oil, Etc.	348	3.64
10. Optic (NT8544); Medical Instrument	338	18.47
TOTAL	13,001	16.52

SOURCE: GLOBAL TRADE INFORMATION SERVICES

U.S. IMPORTS FROM MEXICO

JANUARY-MARCH 1996
(In Millions of U.S. Dollars)

INDUSTRY	$US	% Change
1. El Machine: Sound/TV Equipment	4,067	0.39
2. Vehicles, Not Railway	3,470	58.12
3. Machinery	1,760	13.96
4. Mineral Fuel, Oil Etc.	1,354	-3.89
5. Optic (NT8544); Medical Instrument	566	7.76
6. Vegetables	510	-14.74
7. Special Other	487	3.06
8. Woven Apparel	460	19.43
9. Furniture and Bedding	397	16.74
10. Knit Apparel	269	52.21
TOTAL	16,691	11.45

SOURCE: GLOBAL TRADE INFORMATION SERVICES

In a radio interview last month, Mr. Ortiz repeated his forecast of a slow recovery, predicting that Mexico's domestic consumption might not recover to pre-devaluation levels until at least 1998. His caution was buttressed by a government report on consumer demand: retail sales fell 17.5 percent in March from the same period a year ago, while wholesale prices declined 21.8 percent. April's inflation rate was just under 3 percent, according to the Bank of Mexico, which had forecast an annual inflation rate of only 12 percent for 1996.

Silver Lining

Yet not all was bad news last year. Mexico had a trade surplus of $7.09 billion compared to a trade deficit of $18.46 billion in 1994, its first trade surplus since 1989. In January 1996, exports rose 12 percent to $7.7 billion and imports rose 8 percent from the average monthly level of November and December to $6.9 billion, giving it a trade surplus of $779 million. Mexican exports have grown by 30 percent, primarily due to the devalued peso. Despite the crash, the country is still the United States' third-largest and fastest-growing export market, according to the Department of Commerce.

While Mexico's overall economy may still be in a recession, the border areas—especially Baja California—are doing well due to a rise in foreign investment in the region's maquiladora industry. *Maquiladora* is the term used to describe the production-sharing operations along the U.S.-Mexican border. The region around Tijuana alone has almost full employment in its 615 maquiladoras, and these account for one-fourth to one-third of the area's total employment base, with most of the industry being in television manufacturing. Another 30,000 workers cross the border into San Diego daily to work, and there has also been an increase in tourism because of the lower prices.

Enterprises like maquiladoras, along with Mexican/foreign joint ventures, have largely survived the economic crisis. Reflecting this strength, U.S. exporters with familiar products who do business with Mexican firms that can still pay are also doing well. Live Earth Biodynamics Inc. of Gilbert, AZ, reportedly sold more than 60,000 tons or organic fertilizer to the Mexican government in 1995.

Mexican businesses from a broad range of industries have found success through their international links. For instance, the steel industry is not a large part of the Mexican economy, but through its forced privatization in the early 1990s some companies were able to upgrade standards and modernize technology to compete in the international market, allowing for their survival.

The long-term picture is certainly looking brighter. Cumulative direct foreign investment now is estimated

Learning from Mistakes

Back in 1982 the Mexican economy was closed and U.S. exports suddenly decreased about 40 percent. That was the year of Mexico's last great economic crisis. Mexico's 1982 debt crisis then moved to Brazil and the rest of Latin America. It threatened U.S. financial markets and led to what was called the "lost decade"—almost 10 years of protectionism, negative growth, instability, and political and social unrest. This time, things are different. Mexico is opening up its economy instead of closing it down, and whereas in 1982 inflation went out of control and stayed out of control for several years, this time it has been reigned in. Mexico took only a few months to return to the global capital markets.

at $56.1 billion, compared to $42.4 billion at the end of 1993, when NAFTA was passed. In December, 100 major foreign companies announced that they would invest $6.3 billion in their existing operations in Mexico over the course of 1996, demonstrating how attractive the country has become for manufacturers since the peso's devaluation. This is a 53 percent increase from 1995. For many of these investors, Mexico is less of a market and more of an "export platform" due to its low wages and raw material costs.

U.S. companies are expected to lead foreign investment in 1996 with $3.57 billion, a 40 percent increase. Asian companies are anticipated $1.18 billion in investment. Europe will invest $1.15 billion, up 26 percent. In terms of industries, $1.44 billion is expected to be invested in automotive facilities, $1.1 billion in electric and electronic plants, $913 million in chemical and petrochemical sites, $893 million in telecommunications and $694 million in agriculture-related projects.

Analysts agree that further deregulation and trade liberalizations are needed, and the biggest challenge is for domestic companies that produce for the decimated domestic market.

One area that economists see as a good way to achieve growth is to liberalize the oil industry, but the energy plan announced in February for the next five years is again acting on Mexico's traditionally anti-market approach. Although Petroleos Mexicanos (Pemex) believes the oil concern will attract $63 billion in foreign investment in petrochemicals, power plants and natural gas companies, no private investment is allowed in the upstream exploration, production and refining of oil, which may put off many potential investors.

Nevertheless, privatization is continuing, especially in the infrastructure segment. Airports are being privatized, although the government is still deciding which to sell first. One of the upcoming projects on the block is the privatization and rebuilding of Mexico City's airport. In addition, Mexico's railroad system will soon be looking for buyers and upgrades. On the first day of 1997, the telephone industry will be opened for privatization.

Mexico has also kept up with debt payments. The country has paid over $700 million in interest and fees to the United States from the Clinton administration's rescue package. Offered a $20 billion line of credit, Mexico has used $12.5 billion and repaid $2 billion. The bulk of the Mexican debt to the United States is yet to come, being due between 1998–1999.

Financial Maneuvers

In the face of its sudden economic crisis, Mexico avoided full-fledged chaos by lowering inflation through an immediately implemented austerity program and continuation of the North American Free Trade Agreement (NAFTA).

Mexico has almost completely abolished the short-term debt instruments that started the crisis and has embarked on an economic stabilization program that includes cutting government spending and privatizing key industries. It plans to allow private and foreign investment in railroads, communications, natural gas distribution, petrochemicals, airports, and power plants among others. The telecommunications industry has been opened to foreign participation, and joint ventures with MCI, Bell Atlantic and other U.S. companies have already been announced.

Indeed, Mexico's foreign reserves have risen from $6.1 billion in 1994 to $16.0 billion as of May this year. Its tight monetary policy since the crisis helped bring inflation down from a peak of 8 percent monthly in April 1994 to about 3 percent this April.

Mexico is reducing its deficit and tightly controlling the money supply, but because GDP growth figures are slow, economists worry about a rise in interest rates, which is seen as necessary to boost the peso but could slow down economic recovery. Foreign reserves are low and the banking system could be in some danger due to bad loans.

At the same time that the Mexican stock market was hitting new highs in mid-May, the Mexican government was announcing a major plan to shore up the country's rickety banking system and help domestic homeowners whose mortgage payments have skyrocketed. Under the program, which will cost at least $3 billion, the government will pay up to 30 percent of many households' monthly mortgage payments.

Most Mexican banks are not providing loans at present because of a chronic scarcity of funds and the large number of outstanding debts. Interest rates are currently so high that they are attracting few borrowers, and a scarcity of both local and foreign currency has not helped. Credit card interest rates soared to over 100 percent in 1995, and some businesses are paying 60 to 80 percent interest on loans. Such lack of capital obviously leads to stalled growth.

Original NAFTA treaty terms specified foreign control of up to 9 percent of all Mexican bank capital in 1994, rising to a 15 percent limit by 2000. President Ernesto Zedillo's administration allowed an increase in foreign ownership. Total bank capital controlled by U.S. and Canadian banks (combined) can now be up to 25 percent of combined capital of all Mexican banking firms in 1995.

Crafting Strategies For Global Marketing In The New Millennium

William L. Shanklin and David A. Griffith

O ne way to provoke an animated conversation among top executives of multinational companies is to broach the issue of whether a standardized or localized approach to world markets is superior. Advances in communication technologies are giving new life to this old debate and must change conventional thinking in an increasingly information-oriented world economy. To a Dunn & Bradstreet or a Lloyds of London, the demarcation between domestic and international business is disappearing as new and improved means of communicating and conducting business from afar make a client in Paris virtually as close as one down the street.

In his 1995 bestseller *The Road Ahead*, Microsoft cofounder Bill Gates coined the phrase "friction-free capitalism." It describes the Internet's capacity for directly connecting worldwide buyers and sellers, or their computer surrogates acting as agents, and thereby enabling them to share information, negotiate with one another, and transfer funds. As the need for middlemen and other intermediaries is reduced or eliminated, a friction-free exchange between buyer and seller takes place. Innumerable services or intangibles can be tailored to suit individual customer needs—call it mass customization—and offered instantaneously without regard to constraints imposed by time and space.

FOUNDATIONS FOR CORPORATE STRATEGY

T he starting point for formulating corporate strategy is for upper-echelon executives to determine what the organization's main appeal will be to customers. A differential competitive advantage originates from this pro-

cess. In the popular book *The Discipline of Market Leaders*, authors Michael Treacy and Fred Wiersema (1995) masterfully explained why identifying a corporation's major "value discipline" is tantamount to being a first cause of how a company evolves:

Choosing to pursue a value discipline is not the same as choosing a strategic goal. A value discipline can't be grafted onto or integrated into a company's normal operating philosophy. It is not a marketing plan, a public relations campaign, or a way to chat up stockholders. The selection of a value discipline is a central act that shapes every subsequent plan and decision a company makes, coloring the entire organization, from its core competencies to its culture. The choice of value discipline, in effect, defines what a company does and therefore what it is.

Treacy and Wiersema's research and experiences as consultants have led them to conclude that market leaders perfect at least one of three principles—or, put differently, deliver at least one of three primary benefits to customers: operational efficiency (lowest costs), customer intimacy (exceptional service), or product leadership (tech-

> The Global Strategy Matrix can be used to brainstorm ideas and plumb the four issues critical to operating in a dynamic world economy.

From *Business Horizons*, September/October 1996, pp. 11-16. © 1996 by the Foundation for the School of Business at Indiana University. Reprinted by permission.

nological superiority). Companies whose strategic recipe calls for excellence in all three—to be all things to all customers—typically reap mediocre results because of the trade-offs involved. Of course, companies vigorously pursuing their chosen principle do not abandon the other two. Gateway Computer may have built its reputation on low prices made possible by direct selling, but it does not give short shrift to customer service and product development.

This concept of the pivotal strengths of corporate leaders is similar to what many executives and academicians call "core competencies." These underlying capabilities of an organization enable management to offer potential and current customers low-priced products and services, or inordinate customer service, or cutting-edge technological solutions to problems or needs.

Our contention is that the idea of core competency or value discipline is the missing theoretical link for resolving the longtime debate about whether a standardized or localized marketing strategy is superior in doing business globally. This dispute has simmered because there is no universal right answer. The appropriate international marketing strategy for a specific company is contingent on its major core competency. What works well for a cost-driven firm will yield poor results for a corporation focused on customer service.

Once top management adopts a guiding principle, the implementation or "how to" phases of the decision, both domestically and abroad, become easier. Management knows better whether the multinational can standardize its marketing programs in a one-size-fits-all tack to foreign markets or whether it will be required to adapt strategies to local conditions as dictated by differences in culture and buying behavior. Incipient communication technologies are increasing management's capabilities to experiment with innovative strategies.

SEGUE FROM VALUE DISCIPLINE TO GLOBAL MARKET STRATEGY

Executives in multinationals have wrestled for years with the issue of whether marketing strategy is best standardized (globalized), regionalized, or localized. The task is one of estimating when a particular strategy, combined with the firm's main core competency, has a high probability of producing a potent mixture. The right strategy for a company offering lowest prices would be wrong for one with a reputation for superb personal attention to customer needs. Rolls Royce customers would not accept the standardized marketing programs associated with cost-driven automobile manufacturers.

Standardization proponents have steadfastly adhered to believing that as a result of worldwide television broadcasting and expanded international travel, consumers are becoming more homogeneous in terms of their needs and preferences. The payoff that standardization promises comes from economies of scale and brand-image congruency. IBM launched its first global advertising campaign hoping to capitalize on standardization advantages and begin rebuilding its image. Coca-Cola and 3M have relied on Olympic sponsorships to convey a universal image.

Champions of a regionalization strategy counter that the pervasiveness of customer segmentation strategies within domestic markets demonstrates the difficulty of treating the entire world as a homogeneous market. Regionalization is a popular strategy for the European marketplace. British Petroleum treats Europe's retail gasoline market as a single unit by standardizing equipment and products. However, geographical sections of the world have enough in common that nation-by-nation segmentation is unnecessary. Executives embracing regionalization try to straddle a theoretical fence by ascribing to tenets of both standardization and localization.

Devotees of extreme decentralization of marketing efforts, or localization, demur. In their view, both standardized and regionalized marketing strategies are embedded in the oversimplification that the world population is becoming homogeneous. Ergo, cultural differences—the alleged Achilles heel in the homogenization argument—cannot be ignored because of their overwhelming impact on consumer behavior. The crux of the objection centers on a key question: If marketing strategy adaptations are necessary for customers in different geographic regions of the same country, are not comparable customer accommodations warranted among nations?

Localization is a compelling geographic strategy, but it carries the downside risk of confusing customers. Profits turned to losses for British fashion retailer Laura Ashley when management clouded the company's image by offering dissimilar product lines and running inconsistent advertising messages. The firm printed three versions of its mail order catalogue, each with a vastly different style theme, for British, European, and American markets.

Even staunch advocates of these avenues for doing international business concede that the strategies are not unalloyed. Though theoretically dissimilar ideas, they are pragmatically mixed. A company can no more be wholly standardized than it can be completely localized. Each strategic approach incorporates characteristics of the others. Multinationals lean toward standardization, or regionalization, or localization, rather than dealing in absolutes.

DIRECTIONS FOR GLOBAL STRATEGY

What is referred to in the **Figure** as the Global Strategy Matrix depicts combinations of core competencies (based on cost, customer service, or innovation) and geographic approaches to international marketing (standard, regional, or local). Six congruent and three incongruent combinations are portrayed. The rationale for asserting either congruence or incongruence is twofold. First, blending each strategy combination either does, or does not, make sense theoretically when operational considerations are weighed. For example, the control and centralization required for a low-cost approach meshes well with the universal one-size-fits-all strategy, whereas cost-driven uniformity and value-added localization work at cross purposes.

Second, the matrix is compelling from a strictly "show me" empirical standpoint as well. Examples of leading multinationals combining the six conceptually compatible combinations are plentiful, whereas few or no incidences can be adduced in support of the three incompatible aggregations.

Five managerial guidelines for formulating and executing multinational strategies are directly deducible or can be inferred from the Global Strategy Matrix. Each one meets the litmus test of being consistent and logical in the abstract and being amply supported by corroborating corporate experiences.

1. Standardization is required for cost-based competition.

Standardizing enhances a company's odds of achieving a formidable competitive advantage through economies of scale, thus exporting a cost-based core competency. By leveraging both mass production and distribution, leading cost-based multinationals have been able to perform in a superlative manner.

Cases-in-point of synergistic combinations range from large-scale retailing to petroleum. Toys 'R' Us has clearly demonstrated the potency of a standardized approach in conjunction with a cost-based competency. Many experts believed it was unwise for Toys 'R' Us to enter Japan because of the time-honored distribution system and deeply ingrained buying behavior patterns. Toys 'R' Us spurned the conventional wisdom, however, and was able to capitalize on its core competency of efficient distribution, thereby extending the success it had experienced in Canada and Europe.

Multinationals Royal Dutch/Shell and Coca-Cola have coupled their cost-based efficiencies with a standardized marketing strategy. Although

Figure
Global Strategy Matrix

GEOGRAPHIC APPROACHES	CORE COMPETENCIES		
	Cost Based	Customer Based	Innovation Based
Standardization	Toys 'R' Us Royal Dutch/Shell Coca-Cola		Ciba-Geigy Gillette Hewlett-Packard
Regionalization	Procter & Gamble	Nestlé	Intel
Localization		WPP Group Roadway Cable & Wireless	

Coca-Cola makes minor modifications to its marketing programs, mainly in formula adaptations to suit divergent tastes, the overall strategy is boilerplate. Royal Dutch/Shell decentralizes operations but focuses on image consistency across markets. By fitting marketing strategy to its core competency, each firm has fostered an enviable performance record.

A multinational with a competitive advantage that derives from harvesting efficiencies of scale and being the lowest-cost vendor has no realistic choice but to standardize its offerings across world markets. Toys 'R' Us's low-cost edge would immediately begin to erode if its management were to introduce elements of Sotheby's philosophy of catering to carriage-trade customers.

2. Localization is the best avenue for firms seeking to get closest to customers.

The decision is cast in stone for any multinational that bases its fortunes on mastering a philosophy of "different strokes for different folks." Global companies that choose to sell to customers in narrow or even singular niches are, ipso facto, drawn to localization. No other strategy can offer the definitive matching of offerings to needs that will entice customers to pay select prices.

The well-known marketing services company WPP Group enhances customer service to supply a local touch to loyal patrons around the world. Cable & Wireless offers specialized equipment to meet the needs of some 18 countries and makes itself more useful by providing its customers with expert technical advice. The transportation company Roadway charted a path of global differentiation by furnishing customized logistical advice to its largest patrons. In this way, Roadway has managed to escape being just another "me-too" provider in a worldwide commodity business.

Enterprises that have developed and burnished their reputations by routinely exceeding customer expectations use idiosyncratic consumer preferences as a beacon for guiding strategy. Any movement toward a one-size-fits-all approach takes these firms off course. In fact, the cost savings of standardization is fool's gold for multinationals whose advantage lies in close customer relationships. The idea of a McKinsey & Company being able to systematize its counsel for clients throughout the world to garner cost efficiencies is quickly dismissed. Trade-off strategies need to be undertaken with utmost care and consideration; top management may literally be betting the company's future on the decision.

> "The deciding factor in aggregating nations to comprise a marketing region is the degree to which the countries share a common cultural bond."

3. Competing as a product leader in global markets requires standardization.

A company widely admired because of its long-standing product leadership depends on its capability to provide an ongoing stream of state-of-the-art products or services. Established technical pillars such as Ciba-Geigy, Gillette, and Hewlett-Packard are able to command premium prices by trading on their perceived scientific prowess and first-mover market introduction strategies. Consistent track records in commercializing products that surpass buyers' stipulations separate them from the pack.

The competitive advantage of technological leaders comes from their capacity for developing leading-edge, uniform products and commercializing them quickly around the globe. Centralized product-to-market decisions are necessary for developing offerings that meet international needs, controlling the timing of commercialization, and conveying a consistent global image. Alfred Zeien, Gillette's chairman and CEO, articulates a standardized strategy for global markets: "I'm going to sell the same palette of products, made in the same factory from employees of the same training program" (Koselka 1994).

4. A Goldilocks strategy can be a profitable compromise.

Intel embarked on a pan-European advertising strategy for its Pentium processor with the goal of identifying with regional interests and maintaining its hold on the market. Gordon Moore, cofounder and chairman of Intel, speaks of a "Goldilocks strategy" to denote his preference for moderately complicated technologies: "The key [is] the right degree of difficulty. Too easy, you get competition too soon. Too hard, you run out of money before you get it done" (Lenzer 1995). Moore's penchant for choosing the middle course, like Goldilocks in the fairy tale, accounts for Intel's choice of regionalization over standardization and localization.

Regionalism is compatible with any of the three core competencies. Whereas Intel blends a regional tack with product leadership, Procter & Gamble intertwines a regional approach with a low-cost strategy, and Nestlé combines it with the customer-intimacy value discipline.

A Goldilocks strategy will most likely be chosen whenever a multinational has a product line that necessitates some degree of adaptation for customers. It precludes the strict standardized approach of a ConAgra, yet does not require the company to incur the incremental costs of a country-by-country accommodation. The deciding factor in aggregating nations to comprise a marketing region is the degree to which the countries share a common cultural bond.

5. Beware greener-grass escapism.

This is the most fundamental lesson of all: Competitive strength or weakness is portable. A company that has mastered a strategy of low cost or customer service or technological leadership in its home country has a leg up on expanding internationally. British-based retailer Marks & Spencer cloned its thriving low-cost, high-assortment strategy throughout Europe. But when it veered from this formula when purchasing Brooks Brothers and entering the United States, trouble ensued. A firm brilliant in low-cost competition became confused when operating a venerable, carriage-trade haberdashery that tailored military uniforms for Lt. Colonel Theodore Roosevelt in 1898 for his service in the Spanish-American War.

Before top management endeavors to take a company into the international arena, it first needs to demonstrate a sustainable competitive advantage at home. Strengths perfected in a home market can be exported, as can weaknesses.

POWER OF TECHNOLOGY IN CRAFTING NEW-MILLENNIUM GLOBAL STRATEGIES

The Global Strategy Matrix depicts demonstrably profitable combinations of corporate core competencies and geographical marketing strategies. The corollary prescription is that market followers and companies venturing beyond their home borders for the first time should try to achieve the same desirable state of affairs. The implication is, say, that K mart should imitate Wal-Mart—which is easier said than done or else there would be a host of Wal-Mart clones.

Multinational executives contemplating global strategy in terms of the possible synergies between core competencies and geographical approaches can benefit only if they have the ability to do something about what they conclude. Auspiciously, the burgeoning power of technology means that the potential for improving a firm's competitive position may be greater than ever in history. Technological progress is once again putting lie to the conventional wisdom of what is practicable.

A critical distinction in evaluating the degree of potential (or the size of the opportunity) for applying technology to embellish competitive position is the dichotomy between tangible and intangible commercial offerings. Services whose core benefits to customers derive from a vendor that processes transactions or provides information are characteristic of the industries most vulnerable to sweeping change. These are most amenable to the friction-free capitalism that bypasses middlemen and puts the buyer and seller in direct contact. Customers of accounting, advertising, insurance, publishing, and a host of other information services can conveniently do business with vendors, no matter the respective geographical locations and time zones.

Even a small company that basically sells transactions and information can quickly gain an international presence; a marginal global player can, with alacrity, rise to prominence. An on-line, Internet version of *Business Horizons* would immediately become a ubiquitous global publication without its management having to painstakingly arrange for distribution in country after country. Likewise, a small mail-order firm in Maine can master one-on-one customer marketing on a worldwide basis by using the latest in voice and information technologies.

Modern communications capabilities are blurring the difference between global and domestic business. Indeed, as the turn of the century approaches, the exchange of information among individuals knows few earthly geographical constraints. "Telemedicine" now enables physicians who are hundreds or thousands of miles away to "examine" patients through teleconferencing and diagnostic equipment, just as NASA doctors monitor the health of astronauts in deep space. In the legal arena, one can now bypass attorneys and incorporate a business using the Internet, in an hour or so, for about $50. In education, distance learning allows children in isolated locations access to the latest in knowledge presented by renowned instructors.

Skillfully deploying technology is often the modus operandi for both standardization and mass customization by the same firm. A number of leading multinationals have employed communication technologies to mix seemingly incongruent strategies and become more dominant. IKEA, Carrefour, and Kraft have all harnessed technology to reap cost advantages and to better identify and understand their customers in order to customize offerings. By using bar-code scanning data and computerized demographic data, management has been able to differentiate both product lines and promotion appeals for local market tastes.

A prominent illustration of new technologies enlarging strategic potentialities is the automobile industry, which has always flopped in its efforts to build a world car on a common platform that appeals to drivers around the globe. Ford executives are convinced that advanced technologies in communications, product design, and engineering have solved the problems of satisfying regional and national tastes in automobiles. After the biggest reorganization in Ford's history, known as Ford 2000, the inner components of its cars sold globally will be the same, but the outer look will be fitted for customer preferences in more than 200 markets. Ford estimates that it can save upwards of $4 billion annually from volume purchasing and reduced duplication of activities. This figure would more than double Ford's profits from automobile operations. If Ford pulls off this *tour de force*, it will offer the most competitively priced cars that closely meet the preferences of drivers, wherever they may reside.

> "Modern communications capabilities are blurring the difference between global and domestic business."

On the other hand, it is important to recognize that, in a myriad of industries, there are practical limits to what technology can accomplish. In sectors of commerce that deal in physical products or provide services that are not based on information transactions, communication technologies can improve operating efficiencies but cannot replace the core benefits offered. Telecommunications equipment and the Internet cannot move oil from Oman to France, convey medicine from Indianapolis to hospitals in Jordan, ship grain from Kansas to Russia, or house American tourists in London. Additionally, a potpourri of factors—capital, economies of scale, vast experience, and brand franchise—working in favor of a Royal Dutch/Shell or a Coca-Cola are usually too formidable for smaller firms to overcome, regardless of a challenger's ingenuity in trying to gain a differential advantage.

However, communication technologies and an increasingly fact- and data-oriented global economy have meant that the status quo is vulnerable like never before in industries where furnishing knowledge, delivering entertainment, and processing data are their *raison d'etre*. These are precisely the intangible activities comprising a profusion of high-growth, sunrise markets that will lead the world economy into the new millennium. Further, they are activities that give vendors almost immediate entrée to global markets. A peripatetic international executive can carry a briefcase containing software that is worth more than numerous shiploads of new automobiles entering New York Harbor—software that can be sent around the world, while avoiding customs checkpoints, via the Internet at recipients' preferred times and venues.

Except where the market leader makes a string of serious blunders, creative application of communication technologies offers the best means for followers to unseat kingpins in information-oriented industries where entry barriers are not insurmountable. Because the rules for success in business have changed with the advent of remarkable technologies, few market leaders are safe and most followers are not irrevocably condemned to be also-rans.

Bill Gates wrote that not a single precedent can be cited in which a computer company has been the industry leader in two successive eras. Speaking of the future, Gates expressed his concern for Microsoft that history will repeat itself:

> The Internet is the seed corn of a lot of things that are going to happen, and there are so many parallels to when Paul [Allen] and I were involved in the beginnings of the PC. We said back then, 'Don't DEC and IBM know they're in deep trouble?' Here we are staring at the same kind of situation. (Goldblatt 1995)

The Global Strategy Matrix can be employed by executives to brainstorm ideas and think about four issues that are critical in a dynamic world economy:
- What is the company's targeted or ideal core competency—lowest costs, product leadership, exceptional customer attentiveness, or a combination of two of these?
- Which strategic approach to global marketing would be most complementary with the competency in fostering synergy—standardization, regionalization, or localization?
- What global strategy will allow the company to stay ahead of or leapfrog competitors?

- How might technology be brought to bear to gain or magnify a core competency in domestic and international operations?

These inquiries can never be answered satisfactorily once and for all because strategy formulation is a dialectical process. Today's synthesis is replaced tomorrow by somebody's revolutionary approach. The never-ending task for a current leader is to embellish its position against ingenious competitors.

By contrast, market followers and entrepreneurs seek to change the rules of the game by applying technologies to undercut a leader's current advantages. A small biotechnology firm could catapult itself to become a renowned global product leader with a cure for AIDS, just as Sam Walton from Bentonville, Arkansas parlayed state-of-the-art ordering and logistics systems into a low-cost, global juggernaut of a retailer.

The terse philosophy of the infamous American frontier character "Doc" Holliday captures the precarious situation for global leaders and the vast come-from-behind opportunities for innovative market followers and entrepreneurs: "There is no normal life, there's just life."

References

B. Gates, N. Myhrvold, and P. Rinearson, *The Road Ahead* (New York: Viking Penguin, 1995).

H.Goldblatt, "Bill Gates And Paul Allen Talk," *Fortune*, October 2, 1995, pp. 68-82.

R. Koselka, "'It's My Favorite Statistic,'" *Forbes*, September 12, 1994, p. 172.

R. Lenzer, "The Reluctant Entrepreneur," *Forbes*, September 11, 1995, pp. 162-166.

T. Parker-Pope, "Laura Ashley's Chief Tries To Spruce Up Company That Isn't Dressing For Success," *Wall Street Journal*, September 22, 1995, pp. B1 & B4.

A. Taylor III, "Ford's Really Big Leap At The Future: It's Risky, It's Worth It, And It May Not Work," *Fortune*, September 18, 1995, pp. 134-144.

M. Treacy and F. Wiersema, *The Discipline Of Market Leaders* (Reading, MA: Addison-Wesley, 1995).

William L. Shanklin is a professor of marketing and entrepreneurship in the Graduate School of Management at Kent State University, Kent, Ohio, where **David A. Griffith** is a Ph.D. candidate.

Asia's Next Tiger?

Vietnam is fraught with promise and peril for marketers.

by Clifford J. Shultz II and William J. Ardrey IV

Vietnam has come a long way since the 1986 decision by the Communist Party (CPV) to implement *Doi Moi*, or economic renovation. Its economy is humming along with near-double-digit growth rates and foreign investors line up to fund the choice projects for Vietnam's expansion. Abroad, Vietnam has achieved stable relations with its neighbors, reduced its military expenditures, and forged foreign policy successes with the Association of Southeast Asian Nations (ASEAN), the United States, and China.

These macroeconomic and foreign policy trends have spawned a boom economy. The Vietnamese government wants—indeed, desperately needs—this boom to continue, and Vietnamese consumers are increasingly unlikely to accept anything less than full integration into the global economy. As economic reforms create more wealth in Vietnam, more and more Vietnamese consumers are shifting from the grind of daily subsistence to the joys of consumption.

If Vietnam continues its drive to modernize, promising opportunities for marketing firms will continue to emerge. But peril accompanies this promise and marketing managers must have a keen awareness of the many factors that can predict success or failure in Vietnam.

War Wounds

Say the word "Vietnam" and myriad images come to mind. For most Americans, it evokes recollections of grisly war footage and boat people; for younger Americans, it conjures up Hollywood's depictions of the war. Rarely does one think of present-day Vietnam, a country of enormous natural wealth and limitless potential. Its natural assets include timber, fisheries, vast oil and gas reserves, a coastline longer than the one extending between Seattle and San Diego, and fertile soil that has enabled Vietnam to become the third-largest rice producer in the world. The nation's cultural wealth includes the traditions and historical sites of 4,000 years of national identity. Its people are industrious, cheerful, and very keen to join the consumer society. Yet Vietnam still struggles to be seen as a *country*, not a war.

Recently, Vietnam has been able to attract significant private investment capital and multilateral aid; the Ministry of Planning and Investment received license applications for $5.4 billion in

EXECUTIVE BRIEFING

Vietnam has evolved from one of the worst performing economies in Asia during the early 1980s, to winning the Euromoney Best Managed Economy Award in the '90s. Foreign investors, betting that Vietnam was serious about its economic reforms, rushed to penetrate this market. Some succeeded, many failed. Vietnam must now respond to the challenge of rising expectations by foreign investors while delivering increased variety and quality of goods demanded by its people. The transition from a command to a market economy continues to lurch forward, creating a promising but perilous marketing environment.

1995 and hopes to exceed $6 billion in 1996. With development aid came more private business. The World Bank financed a $2 billion highway and infrastructure project that brought big American companies such as Caterpillar, Morrison Knudsen, and others to Vietnam. Total investment of over $520 million from U.S. companies alone flowed into Vietnam by the end of 1995.

Forward-thinking marketing managers look at Vietnam as a promising market; with 74 million consumers, it is the 13th largest in the world. Whether one is selling earth movers or soft drinks, airplanes or cosmetics, Vietnam is already a burgeoning market with considerable purchasing power. In 1994, the United States was a virtual nonplayer; by 1996, it was the sixth-largest investor. Nevertheless, Vietnam is not an "easy" market, nor is it one that lends itself to simple replications of successful strategies used in other parts of Southeast Asia or China. Vietnam is a market of inexplicable contradictions of the good-news, bad-news sort.

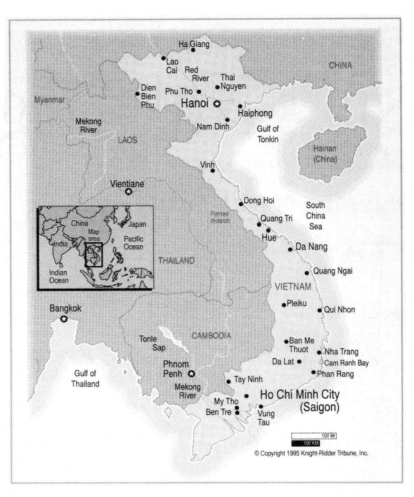

© Copyright 1995 Knight-Ridder Tribune, Inc.

First, the Bad News

With all the hype over opportunity in Vietnam, it's easy to forget that this economic change is quite recent. Once isolated and totally dependent on dwindling aid from the Soviet-controlled Council for Mutual Economic assistance, Vietnam was unable to tap into Western capital and know-how until its withdrawal from Cambodia in 1989. In addition, as a result of the U.S.-led embargo and poor central economic planning at home, Vietnam still has an annual per-capita income under $400. And even though the *Doi Moi* policy has been successful to date, Vietnam's small but growing middle class counts on annual incomes of less than half the $2,600 of their upwardly mobile neighbors in China.

Vietnam remains a poor country with a physical, legal, and economic infrastructure that is still undergoing a massive overhaul. Economic reform was undertaken in reaction to the utter failure of the command economy to survive without Soviet assistance, not as part of a master plan for development as envisioned by other Asian "tiger" states. This overhaul was and still is administered by CPV and any ambition for doing business in Vietnam must consider that the country will continue to be a single-party state. Accordingly, regulations, laws, and licenses continue to be issued and enforced at the discretion of the CPV, which despite the reform movement, is not altogether comfortable promoting "market socialism," the term preferred by the CPV to describe a market economy administered in the shadow of socialist ideology. But the reform process does continue to lurch forward, albeit with numerous stops, starts, and more than a few steps backwards.

The result is that Vietnam is similar to a football field with moving goal posts—the rules always seem to change just when one is about to be profitable. This phenomenon is explained partly by bureaucracy, partly by government insecurities about administering a market economy, and partly by corruption. Despite the efforts of Prime Minister Vo Van Kiet to take a personal interest in streamlining licensing agreements and business procedures, generally, the bureaucracy and red tape in Vietnam remain daunting. So, while license applications for investment continue to grow, actual investment by foreign corporations in approved projects fell over 40% in the first half of 1996. Some foreigners have become especially wary of joint ventures with Vietnamese firms (usually state-owned), and the Vietnam News Agency has reported a trend toward wholly owned foreign projects.

Besides bureaucratic slowdowns and corruption, the CPV continues to coddle state-run enterprises and Hanoi intends to keep the state sector as the vanguard of the economy. Investment in infrastructure and the fledgling private sector remains relatively small. Virtually all investments to date have been in oil and gas exploration, fisheries, cash exports, or other big-ticket items, with state enterprises serving as the Vietnamese partners.

The private sector grew to more than $300 million in combined capital in 1993, with license applications for private businesses maintaining double-digit growth since 1993. But local private manufacturers complain of excessive taxation, lack of capital and resources, and government favoritism for foreign investments, especially joint-venture projects with the state.

Foreigners looking to create partnerships with a private Vietnamese company must be aware that the private sector receives lots of praise, but few useful resources in Vietnam. The state-run commercial banks, which account for almost 90% of bank assets, are heavily, if not exclusively, geared toward the state enterprise sector. Listings on the long-planned Vietnam Stock Exchange—and the exchange itself—have not yet appeared. Some 50 state firms have been ordered to begin "equitization," gradually selling small stakes into private hands.

Unfortunately, there is no secondary market for these equity stakes. Smaller private companies and foreign joint ventures already prepared for privatization have been discouraged from offering shares, and management buyouts and outright acquisitions have been frowned upon as well. By 1996, 5,000 of the 12,000 state-owned enterprises (SOEs) operating in 1993 were closed or merged as part of *Doi*

Important Political Developments Since 1992

➤ The United States and Vietnam established diplomatic relations in 1995; Vietnam likely will be granted most favored nation status as a trade partner. The latest reports out of both Washington and Hanoi suggest this decision is not likely to be made before the end of 1997.

➤ Vietnam joined ASEAN and is expected to join the Asia Pacific Economic Cooperation (APEC).

➤ Constructive engagement with China, Vietnam's principal rival in the region, resulted in reduced military threats, exchanges of senior delegations, and an 80% increase in bilateral trade.

➤ The Greater Mekong subregion—a trading zone of 200 million consumers from Vietnam, Cambodia, Laos, Thailand, and southern China—emerged. The subregion shares the costs and benefits of regional infrastructure and investment products, lowers trade barriers, and facilitates exchanges of goods and services. Vietnam, at the mouth of the Mekong, serves as the primary conduit to the entire region.

➤ A 50% debt forgiveness negotiation with the Paris Club, and rescheduling and forgiveness of over $750 million in debt with the London Club, allowed Vietnam to tap the Eurobond market for needed capital.

➤ Joint arrangements with Asian and Western governments and banking groups were established to reorganize and to reform Vietnam's ailing financial-services sector.

Moi, but only five small state enterprises have "equitized" to permit private participation.

Medium-size firms also have felt the financial squeeze due to efforts by CPV conservatives to keep all assets in the hands of the state. From 1991-1995, Vietnamese state and private partners were able to attract foreign investors by offering land rights directly to foreign companies as an important part of the local partner's contribution to the capital of a new business venture. Before the controversial Decree 18/CP in February 1995, Vietnamese firms also were able to mortgage land-use rights for loans. And while repeal of this decree is still being debated in the National Assembly, for the time being, land use rights must be leased directly from the state. This places a sig-

Vietnam: The Bad News

➤ Inconsistent and frequently inexplicable policies that hinder all aspects of the transition from a command to a market economy, including the legal, banking, and accounting systems.

➤ Persistent and expanding trade deficits, which ballooned from $60 million in 1992 to $2.2 billion dollars in 1996.

➤ Growing overseas debt.

➤ Burgeoning current account deficit, which hit an estimated 15.1% of GDP in 1995.

➤ Stagnating foreign direct investment (FDI) realizations; while approval rates are soaring, actual realization of the projects is slowing, partly because of the frustrations presented by bureaucracy.

➤ Inefficiencies of state-owned enterprises, as evidenced by little job creation and the failure to create value-added exports.

nificant burden on existing companies and new ventures attracting loans and foreign investments.

Individuals and small firms typically have been left out of plans for financial-services reform. If they can buy shares of equitized firms, they cannot trade them. The 62 foreign banks and bank representative offices in Vietnam are severely restricted in taking Vietnamese dong deposits, especially from Vietnamese citizens. The dong's present exchange rate is approximately 11,000 to 1 U.S. dollar. The Vietnamese government has development plans that require between $40 billion and $50 billion of investment, yet it can reasonably expect only half this figure to come from foreign sources. Government officials must mobilize domestic savings to fund the needed investments in infrastructure and key industries if they want to emulate the Asian tiger economies.

Without banking services from foreign banks, Vietnamese citizens and small private firms are left with the state banking system. This system is set up to serve state enterprises and continues to have serious service delivery problems, such as the inability to clear checks between branches of the same bank. Even for a developing country, Vietnam has a low volume of noncash transactions and difficulty with checks and wire payments. In many cases, foreign firms must pay their employees—and settle payroll tax liabilities—in cash.

Vietnam has one of the lowest deposit rates in the developing world, less than 25% of GDP. (Most countries average 75%, with higher rates in Asia.)

This is not surprising considering that local banks charge for withdrawals, an obvious disincentive to save in the formal banking system. Memories of high inflation and bank failures also impede progress. In the 1980s, state-run banks failed to honor withdrawals, informal credit cooperatives collapsed, and high inflation discouraged saving.

Alternative services and sources of capital have filled the vacuum created by state-bank shortcomings. Informal credit rings are flourishing, with more than $2 billion being hoarded outside the formal banking system in U.S. dollars, gold, or consumer goods such as liquor and durable goods that will hold their value over time. Viet Kieu (overseas Vietnamese) infusions also play a role. Approximately 2 million Viet Kieu bring money into the country and/or send money to families and friends. Some private banks also have been established in Vietnam, with many turning a profit from trade finance. Financial-service reforms, however, still tend to ignore small enterprises and consumers, and the institutions generally are out of step with the standards required by serious players in a global economy.

All of these perils have taken the bloom off Vietnam's rose. Many investors who came with high expectations and hopes for quick results quickly had them dashed and departed Vietnam in search of the next investment Shangri-La. Michael Scown, a partner with Russin and Vecchi in Ho Chi Minh City and a former president of the American Chamber of Commerce in Vietnam, recently shared a growing sentiment among investors: "It has become increasingly apparent that investors will have to set more realistic goals, truly commit to projects and settle in for the long haul."

Now, the Good News

It would be easy for a marketing manager in charge of introducing and/or managing a product in Vietnam to become disheartened by the bad-news scenario. But for every investor who leaves, two more seem to fill the vacuum because the market is so promising. The macroeconomic reforms that resulted from *Doi Moi,* have controlled inflation, freed prices, promoted agriculture and export marketing, spurred foreign investment, and opened domestic markets.

Many of the problems in Vietnam are simply growing pains, which the central government is working to remedy. And, after a decade of reforms, the direction, if not the pace of *Doi Moi,* remains focused on economic growth and expansion. Moreover, Vietnamese authorities increasingly are attempting to facilitate the foreign investment process. "We have shifted toward a market economy," says Tran Quang Nghiem, chairman of the Government Price Committee. "Now, we must modernize. This requires establishing a modern, integrated marketing, finance, and accounting system throughout the country and with links to external markets." To those ends legal, tax, and financial reforms have been proposed, and many desirable projects have had their license procedures "fast tracked" by the government. The economy continues to grow, inflation remains low, and some early foreign investors have begun to generate returns.

Recent political developments also should make investors optimistic. Vietnam has been at the heart of a region dominated for centuries by brutal conflict, but the climate in the last five years has arguably fostered progress on a sustainable peace and more-predictable economic growth than any time in the past 50 years.

Improved relations with the United States and China have been critical to Vietnam's economic success. Vietnam faces few external constraints on growth and can continue to reduce military spending in favor of infrastructure investment. Vietnam now boasts of trading relationships with over 100 nations. Once contentious with most countries outside the former Soviet bloc, Le Van Bang and Ha Huy Thong, Vietnam's ambassador to the United States and deputy consul, respectively, have on more than one occasion informed us that Vietnam's current foreign policy is to "get along well with everyone."

Vietnam continues to capitalize on its successful mix of domestic reforms and openness to foreign investment. Even though the country started its reform process nearly a decade after China, the Vietnamese have been able to catch up in the areas of agricultural reform, price reform, currency devaluation, and healthy growth rates for GDP and foreign investment. Similar to China, the Communist Party has remained in command, with the role of guiding the economy along the road to "marketization." In this regard, CPV is functioning much more like the single-party "capitalist" states in the region than the Stalinist regimes of the cold war. The

Asian Development Bank and other sources predict 9%-10% annual growth rates, single-digit inflation rates, and exponential growth in consumption.

Marketing Environment

The bureaucracy can frustrate the most determined investors and the CPV does not yet fully embrace the private sector but, on balance, the macroeconomic and political changes coupled with pent-up consumer demand make a compelling argument for investment in Vietnam. Indeed, precisely because of the current uncertainty of the market, opportunities abound if investors understand the unique dynamism that is Vietnam. Investors who wait for optimal conditions will miss the proverbial boat. But where, exactly, are the opportunities right now?

Infrastructure

Because Vietnam is in the process of rebuilding a nation, there are many opportunities in infrastructure development. Seaports, airports, highways, water treatment facilities, buildings, dams, power stations, and other foundations to support a modern

---

Vietnam: The Good News

▶ Annual GDP over the last five years has averaged 8.2%.

▶ Inflation has dropped from 487% in 1986 to 12.4% in 1995, mainly attributable to tough government budgets.

▶ Agricultural production has risen 7% annually and industrial production has jumped 13%-15% annually since 1988.

▶ Reorientation of trade to a market-style economy doubled exports between 1992 and 1995.

▶ Registered imports are up; unregistered imports smuggled in from Southern China and Thailand via Cambodia are *way* up.

▶ FDI licensing approvals totaled $18 billion at the end of 1995, up 97% in 1995 alone.

▶ Overseas direct assistance pledges remain healthy, with $2 billion pledged at the latest donor conference held in November 1995 in Paris.

EXHIBIT 1

Household possessions of durables

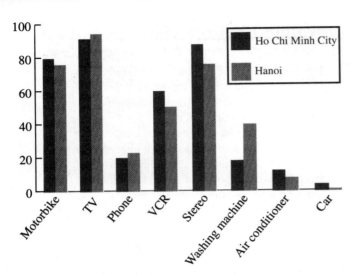

Source: 1996 raw data provided by SRG Vietnam

economy are being built or refurbished. Goods and services that abet the process—construction, telecommunications, and transportation supplies and equipment—are in huge demand, and investors have access to multilateral aid to fund the projects.

Export Markets

Many government policies, including tax breaks and export processing zones, encourage investors to initiate operations that facilitate export growth and development. Imports of heavy equipment, for example, often are duty free. Petroleum and minerals, aquaculture, and agriculture also are viable industries. Vietnam is beginning to demonstrate the ability to produce quality products in low-tech, labor-intensive, value-added industries such as textiles and furniture. With a redoubled effort to establish technology parks and R&D centers, and a commitment to maintain low wages, Vietnam hopes to compete in high-tech industries within a decade.

Consumer Markets

All types and brands of consumer products and services are rapidly diffusing throughout Vietnam. Popular brands familiar to Americans are beginning to dominate the clothing, electronics, household goods, and recreational beverage markets. Foreign brands are equated with quality and prestige, and consumers are willing to pay price pre-

miums for them. This trend, while generally positive, also has some drawbacks because even though brand names are very popular among Vietnamese, brand *authenticity* is a secondary consideration. Consequently, one drawback is a booming brand-piracy industry, whereby the Vietnamese manufacture or distribute counterfeit items. Brands associated with pop culture, Disney characters, Ray Ban sunglasses, and Nike are just a few examples of popular trademarks that are frequently victimized.

A second drawback is concern by the CPV and domestic manufacturers that Vietnamese products are being squeezed out of the marketplace. Consequently, domestic producers have called on the government to protect industries such as cigarettes, beverages, detergents, and paper. The success of foreign products has been accompanied by a crackdown on "social evils" such as karaoke bars and many types of outdoor advertisements. While the government has not expected demand for popular brands or non-Vietnamese ideas to disappear, it has taken steps to avoid cultural disintegration and complete dominance by foreign products. For example, the government stipulates that ads for foreign products include copy in the Vietnamese language.

Government rhetoric, however, cannot affect the reality that the consumer is now king in Vietnam. Truly, there is no stopping or even slowing this revolution. Rising incomes, exposure to popular culture, product availability, and limited opportunities for other forms of recreation are making shopping and consumption popular pastimes. More specifically, trends affecting the shift toward a consumer culture include five basic factors: urbanization, family dynamics, emerging middle and upper classes, a foreign invasion, and the youth movement.

Urbanization. Vietnam is still an agrarian society with 80% of the population living in the countryside, but there is large-scale migration to the cities. This migration is the result of economic growth and opportunities afforded by extensive foreign investment in Hanoi, Ho Chi Minh City, Danang, Can Tho, Hue and Haiphong, and special economic zones such as Vung Tau. As part of this urbanization process, Vietnamese are increasingly exposed to the new consumption ethos found in the cities.

Family dynamics. Large families continue to share small houses, with urban households typically consisting of more than seven members. Although each family member earns only a few hundred dollars each year, household income more than exceeds expenses. Children live at home until marriage, contributing to the family income in addition to their own needs. Viet Kieu family members also contribute significantly by sending money or gifts. So, while individual purchasing power is modest, pooled resources by families create purchasing clout.

Emerging classes. Millions of Vietnamese now have disposable income. Official figures in Hanoi and Ho Chi Minh City indicate incomes now often approach and exceed $1,000, respectively. Our personal interviews indicate much larger, unreported and untaxed pockets of wealth springing up throughout Vietnamese cities. A middle and even a small upper class is emerging. Many consumers or households now can afford relatively expensive items such as motorcycles, televisions, VCRs, stereo equipment, and washing machines; some can afford luxury items of all kinds, including automobiles, villas, and high-fashion products (see Exhibit 1).

Foreign invasion. Many Vietnamese feel under seige with all the new products and advertisements. Furthermore, tourists and expatriates visiting or working in Vietnam bring new ideas, products, expectations, and demands. Hotels, transportation services, discos, newspapers, magazines, golf courses, promotion campaigns, and satellite TV all are intended to meet the needs of this growing "foreigner" market. But Vietnamese also are exposed to these new products, information, ideas, and values and, subsequently, are changing their expectations and demands.

Tabula rasa. The combined impressionable nature of youth and the flood of new ideas and products has created a segment of Generation X consumers in a very short period of time. The *tabula rasa* factor and the sheer size of the youth market is having a profound effect on Vietnamese society. Although still family-oriented and living under the shadow of socialist dogma, more than half of Vietnam's population is under age 20. To these consumers, the Vietnam War and the teachings of Uncle Ho are little more than a history lesson.

But then, who has time for history when one can work for a Western company; save a little money; buy the latest CD, a pair of jeans, and some fake Ray Ban sunglasses; and then cruise Le Loi Boulevard and Dhong Khoi Street on a new Honda Dream motor scooter? Anyone who has spent an evening trying to cross these streets will appreciate the accuracy of this description of the youth market. An affluent population of teenagers in Ho Chi Minh City now has the wherewithal to obtain credit cards from foreign banks and purchase expensive imported consumer goods. In addition to constituting a growing market in their own right, Vietnam's young are becoming opinion leaders for others.

> An affluent population of teenagers in Ho Chi Minh City now has the wherewithal to obtain credit cards from foreign banks and purchase expensive imported consumer goods.

These trends all indicate radical change, rapid market segmentation, and consumer clout. A decade ago there was only one segment: the destitute. Just a few years ago segmentation schemes differentiated consumers on urban-rural and North-South dimensions. More recently, age, access to Western or developed-market Asian ideas and products, one's marketable skills, and disposable income have become factors that predict consumption patterns. Although it should be noted that as in any transforming agrarian economy in which socialism and collectivism were the norm, there is a conservative element, particularly in Northern and rural regions, whose members prefer traditional or local Vietnamese products. Nevertheless, the sweeping trend is a society transforming to a consumer culture, and in the cities this transformation is occurring at an astonishing rate.

'Exit' Interviews

Vietnam is a promising market, but to succeed there, marketing managers must have more than a fundamental understanding of the classic 4Ps of the marketing mix. They must accept that Vietnam is a series of enigmas and seemingly illogical confounds. Management in Vietnam is as much art, nuance, and persuasion as science. We have conducted many exit interviews with investors—literally, interviews with investors at either Tan Son Nhat or Noi Bai airports exiting Vietnam because

EXHIBIT 2

Top five most frequently consumed soft drinks in Ho Chi Minh City

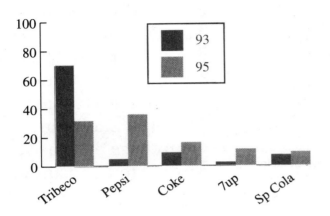

Source: 1996 raw data provided by SRG Vietnam

of failed projects. For the most part, those projects did not fail because of poor market demand for the goods or services, but because managers and investors simply could not come to grips with the arcane conditions of Vietnam's management environment. The emergent themes from those interviews, as well as from the success stories, are factors U.S. managers need to consider.

Move With the Goal Posts

Managers must accept that the goal posts in Vietnam will continue to shift, making it difficult to score. Asian investors and some Europeans seem much more willing to accept this fact and spend considerable amounts of time nurturing relationships with partners and government authorities. (Note too that these two entities are sometimes synonymous.) Consequently, they are able to predict and adjust to goal-post movements. More importantly, they often discover that because of their efforts to nurture relationships, the goal posts haven't moved at all for them.

As a case in point, the country manager for one European brewery was pleased to inform us that his firm would not have to remove or repaint its billboards in response to the social-evils campaign. He attributed this time and cost savings solely to his efforts to maintain a good relationship with government authorities. American investors, however, find

it difficult to work solely on solid relationships and trust and want to ensure that all the legal issues are agreed upon before moving forward. If this strategy were not so counterproductive, it would be comical because the legal codes in Vietnam are either nonexistent or revised continually.

This is not to argue that one should abandon respect for laws and the legal process. To the contrary, understanding Vietnamese laws and Vietnam's legal system is very important. For example, favoritism toward Americans and American brands is a powerful advantage that should not be underestimated. But Tanya Pullin, an attorney for Baker and McKenzie who has practiced in Vietnam, adds that "trademarks in Vietnam mean nothing unless they are registered in Vietnam." Trademark registration begets government protection. Despite problems with brand piracy, the government will crack down by closing bogus plants and fining purveyors of pirated goods *if* the pirated trademarks are registered.

Even the fundamental logic of "best product for the best price" means little in Vietnam. "We went to the Vietnamese government with a proposal for a new cement formula that was 30% better and 30% cheaper," says James Reany of International Trade Resources. "We even used Vietnamese laboratories to 'convince' them of our product's superiority. To make a long story short, there's a lot of building going on in Vietnam, but we're not part of it yet." So, investors and managers constantly struggle to balance home-country laws, Vietnamese laws, and social forces in addition to managing the marketing mix.

The moving goal posts make Vietnam an exceptionally challenging market. But there are good, recent examples of large and small firms that have figured out how to score. PepsiCo, typically second in market share in the cola wars around the globe, arrived in Vietnam five hours after the U.S. embargo was lifted. The company thoroughly researched all relevant aspects of the market and, in so doing, determined demand and found an optimal partner and appropriate manufacturing sites. PepsiCo kept the initial investment low, established quality controls, offered professional training and cash resources, and effectively used *Su Lua Cua The He Moi* ("The choice of a new generation") as Pepsi's promotional tag line.

In one year, this joint venture, in which PepsiCo holds 30% equity, had sales revenues of $33 million and a profit of $2.5 million. In two years, Pepsi outpaced local producer Tribeco to become the dominant brand in southern Vietnam (see Exhibit 2). In the process, PepsiCo solidified its relationship with the government by paying $6 million in taxes and employing 1,200 people. Procter & Gamble, Colgate-Palmolive, and the Coca-Cola Co. also are enjoying success. Companies providing a product or service that consumers can pay for *now* are doing well.

Small-firm success stories also are being written by a number of young, energetic entrepreneurs from the United States who are targeting newly emerging niche markets. From bamboo production and real-estate brokerage to trading companies and language centers, these pioneers are making a mark in Vietnam. They all have some common threads: low overhead, flexibility, an ability to see opportunities where others only saw stumbling blocks, target focus, enthusiasm, and a sense of adventure. And they all made a total commitment: They moved to Vietnam, immersed themselves in the environment, learned the language, and made discoveries that enabled them to leverage their skills. Upon reflection, we concluded that the successful large multinationals exhibited many of these traits as well.

Pick the Right Location

Managing business affairs from outside Vietnam generally proves to be an unsuccessful strategy. Precisely where one should locate in Vietnam depends on the product line, target market and strategic interests, but a local presence and some official support are crucial. Ho Chi Minh City (formerly Saigon) is the largest, most cosmopolitan urban center and Vietnam's commercial hub. Given that it has only been part of a socialist economy since 1975, it also has a population more familiar with free enterprise. Not surprisingly, it is usually favored by foreign investors. (By the way, Saigon is still the preferred term among locals, but marketers would be well-advised to speak of Ho Chi Minh City when dealing with government authorities.)

There are other locations, however, that should not be overlooked. The Vietnamese government is eager to develop the North and the countryside, and often offers incentives to foreigners interested in investing in these areas. The Coca-Cola Co.'s decision to establish a joint venture in the North, for example, has helped to overcome its comparatively slow start in Vietnam and is considered a factor in Coke's popularity in the northern part of the country. Moreover, while the urban sprawl of Ho Chi Minh City may make it an attractive con-

sumer market, rent and wage increases may make it less desirable for manufacturing. Consequently, special development zones such as Haiphong or Vung Tau, which also happen to be ports, may be more attractive sites for factories.

Research the Market

Market research has been and always will be important in Vietnam. But because of proliferating products/promotions and growing consumer sophistication, the dynamics of the market—and the research requirements—have changed considerably during the past three years. For many Vietnamese, attitudes and beliefs have changed. Understanding how they have changed is instrumental in determining how to manipulate the marketing mix.

Second, the competition across product categories has become much more intense.

> Market research has been and always will be important in Vietnam.

These changes collectively shape how one might now administer, for example, a promotions campaign. Unlike the early 1990s, the battle for many segments now is being fought on differentiation rather than awareness. Furthermore, where simple outdoor advertisements and P-O-P materials once sufficed, many managers will now have to consider the importance of other variables in the marketing communications mix.

Several market-research and advertising firms have established operations in Vietnam, but there still is no substitute for sending multiskilled employees there to examine market conditions thoroughly and to determine the viability of the product or service offering as well as the appropriate management of pricing, distribution, and promotion.

Invest in the Vietnamese People

No matter how great the demand for a product or service, if the organization to manage it is going to be larger than a mom and pop operation, employee selection, training, and management are critical. Fortunately, the pool size and quality of applicants for many jobs have increased impressively in the past three years. Younger Vietnamese are scrambling to learn English, computer skills, and marketing. Only three years ago, we were hard-pressed to find anyone who could operate a computer *and* speak English well. We found no one who had both of these skills plus a customer orientation. By comparison, we have associates who recently placed an ad in a Ho Chi Minh City newspaper for a clerical position that required some customer contact and received 1,500 applications—more than 200 of whom met or exceeded the qualifications.

> The Vietnamese have earned a reputation for being hard workers and as a population they enjoy one of the highest literacy rates in Asia.

The Vietnamese have earned a reputation for being hard workers and as a population they enjoy one of the highest literacy rates in Asia; they are also very keen to learn contemporary business practices and often prefer to work for American companies. The work force is still lacking middle managers, however, and this problem can only be remedied with substantial investments in corporate-sanctioned training.

Three More Ps

The initial reforms in Vietnam favored only well-capitalized or well-connected businesses that could build roads, export oil, or generate hard currency. But the country is opening up to marketing enterprises of all sizes and specialties. Vietnam's transformation has created a growing appetite among Vietnamese and the expanding foreign community for all kinds of goods and services. It also has links to other promising markets in the region. For example, its strategic location in the Greater Mekong subregion makes it possible for firms to enter Vietnam as part of a larger plan to market products to the 200 million consumers in this emerging trade bloc.

> Problems especially relevant to Vietnam include the absence of qualified managers, poor infrastructure, and erratic improvements in the legal, tax and accounting systems.

But as promising as the market may be, it is still perilous. Bureaucratic encumbrances and other constraints one would expect to find in any developing economy are inevitable. Problems especially relevant to Vietnam include the absence of qualified managers, poor infrastructure, and erratic improvements in the legal, tax and accounting systems. Rent extractions and other forms of corruption by national and local authorities also are problematic; so too are occasional reactionary movements within the government as Vietnam makes its transition to a market economy. And now competition has become a factor, as many companies struggle to penetrate the market and establish brand dominance.

Any serious marketing manager in Vietnam should add "prudence," "patience," and "persistence" to the classic 4Ps of the marketing mix. In Vietnam, relationships take time to nurture and can be expensive to maintain. Favorable brand and company images must be built and cared for. Good contacts, understanding the market, incremental growth, and sound business practices that address the unique Vietnamese condition will pay off in the long term.

> Good contacts, understanding the market, incremental growth, and sound business practices that address the unique Vietnamese condition will pay off in the long term.

Although the Vietnamese government's policies can be confusing, the government has attempted to address problems that need longer-term solutions. Even with 10% growth rates, however, it will be at least a decade before Vietnam joins the ranks of the tiger economies. But marketers would be well-advised to seize the day. Vietnam will eventually join them, and companies that enter the market now will gain an early foothold as significant players in Vietnam and the region as a whole.

Editor's Note: In April 1996, Cliff Shultz chaired a conference on "Markets and Marketing Opportunities in Vietnam." Cosponsored by the American Marketing Association, Arizona State University West, and the World Trade Center, it brought high-ranking Vietnamese government and business officials together with their American counterparts to address the current marketing environment in Vietnam.

About the Authors

Clifford J. Shultz II is Assistant Professor of Marketing at the Arizona State University West School of Management where he specializes in marketing, consumption, and policy in transition economies. Cliff was the first scholar invited to Vietnam to lecture on consumer research and regularly serves as a Visiting Scholar at Vietnamese universities and research institutes. He holds an MA and PhD from Columbia University and his Vietnam work has been published in the *Columbia Journal of World Business, Business Horizons, Contemporary Southeast Asia, Asia-Pacific Advances in Consumer Research, Marketing News, Journal of Commerce,* and *Research in Consumer Behavior* and is coediting a book on marketing and consumers in East and Southeast Asia. As a consultant for over 15 years, he has helped governments and industries on five continents manage their trade, development, and transition challenges.

William J. Ardrey IV is Senior Vice President and International Policy Analyst at Fiduciary Communications Group in New York. William is a frequent lecturer at the Marketing College of Ho Chi Minh City and has published Vietnam articles in *Business Horizons, Contemporary Southeast Asia,* and *Asian Wall Street Weekly.* He holds a bachelor's degree from the Georgetown School of International Affairs and an MA from Columbia University. He and Shultz have completed a monograph for the United Nations entitled *Enterprise Management in Transition Economies,* and William is currently writing a doctoral dissertation on Financial Services Marketing in Vietnam.

Acknowledgment

The authors wish to acknowledge the ASU FGIA, SRCA, and IIM programs, Nguyen Xuan Que and his associates at the Ho Chi Minh City College of Marketing; Ha Huy Thong, Nguyen Duy Khien; and Tom Vallely and the Harvard Institute for International Development.

Additional Reading

Chapman, Matthew (1996), *Vietnam: Transition Under Threat*, Hong Kong: Peregrine Securities.

Dapice, David O. and Thomas J. Vallely (1996), "Vietnam's Economy: Will It Get and Stay on the Dragon's Trail," research report, Harvard Institute for International Development, Cambridge, Mass.

Shultz, Clifford J. (1994), "Balancing Policy, Consumer Desire, and Corporate Interests: Considerations for Market Entry in Vietnam," *Columbia Journal of World Business*, 29 (Winter), 42-53.

Shultz, Clifford J., William J. Ardrey, and Anthony Pecotich (1995), "American Involvement in Vietnam, Part II: United States Business Opportunities in a New Era," *Business Horizons*, 38 (March-April), 21-7.

Shultz, Clifford J., Anthony Pecotich, and Khai Le (1994), "Changes in Marketing Activity and Consumption in the Socialist Republic of Vietnam," in *Research in Consumer Behavior*, 7, C. Shultz, R. Belk and G. Ger, eds., Greenwich, CT: JAI Press, 225-257.

The opportunities in emerging markets are huge. So are the risks.

TROUBLES AHEAD IN EMERGING MARKETS

by Jeffrey E. Garten

Throughout the 1990s, financial investors, corporate strategists, and political leaders in the United States, Western Europe, and Japan have been intensifying their focus on emerging markets. Such companies as Morgan Stanley, General Electric, and Johnson & Johnson are placing enormous bets on these markets. The Clinton administration's export-promotion strategy is based on the premise that the most promising markets are not in Europe and Japan but in the so-called big emerging markets. And the U.S. approach is mirrored abroad as presidents and prime ministers from France to Japan make pilgrimages to China, India, Brazil, and elsewhere to hawk their countries' wares.

Emerging markets are indeed the new frontier. But like all frontiers, they present a mix of opportunity and risk. The question now is whether businesses and governments in the industrialized world are sober enough about the problems that lie ahead. I do not believe they are. There is considerable evidence indicating that the tides of capital-

Jeffrey E. Garten is dean of the Yale School of Management in New Haven, Connecticut. His new book, The Big Ten: The Big Emerging Markets and How They Will Change Our Lives, *is published by Basic Books. Garten was undersecretary of commerce for international trade in the first Clinton administration and, before that, a managing director of the Blackstone Group, an investment-banking firm.*

ism, which rose so powerfully after the collapse of the Soviet Union, are poised to recede. This reversal may signal much more than the usual ebb and flow of political and economic progress in the developing world, and could amount to a fundamental disruption of the generally upward trajectory in so many countries.

What can governments and businesses in the developed world do in the face of such likely turmoil? The industrial-world member-nations of the Organization for Economic Cooperation and Development (OECD) must ask whether they are pushing enough for growth and trade liberalization. Multinational companies, meanwhile, can no longer leave foreign policy to politicians and bureaucrats. They must develop capabilities that will allow them to anticipate and respond to the upcoming disruptions in emerging markets. And they must remain open to opportunities for cooperation between private and public sectors in those markets. Such cooperation can improve the economic environment and mitigate the risks of doing business in developing countries.

The Clash of Capitalism and Democracy

Emerging markets do represent undeniable commercial opportunities. In the last decade, the ten big emerging markets – Mexico, Brazil, Argentina, South Africa, Poland, Turkey, India, South Korea, the ASEAN region (Indonesia, Thailand, Malaysia, Singapore, and Vietnam),

and the Chinese Economic Area (China, Hong Kong, and Taiwan) – have opened their markets to foreign investment and trade. The gross domestic product of the big emerging markets has been increasing two to three times faster than that of developed countries. At the same time, emerging markets have made genuine progress in reining in deficits and inflation, as well as in selling off bloated state enterprises to private investors. Of course, the measures taken have been uneven, and there is a long way to go in every case, but it is indisputable that Adam Smith's philosophy has won the day.

It should not be surprising, therefore, that long-term projections for market expansion have been optimistic. In 1995, the ten big emerging markets accounted for about 10% of the world's economic output. The U.S. Department of Commerce believes that percentage may more than double over the next two decades, as those countries boost their share of global imports from 19% to 38%. Private capital has been flowing to emerging markets in unprecedented amounts, rising 19% in 1996 to a new high of $230 billion. Enormous potential exists for further expansion: for example, whereas all emerging markets account for 40% of global production, they still represent only 15% of global stock-market value.

Any optimistic reading of the future, however, is based on a critical assumption: the economic reforms that have been so impressive in the 1990s will continue more or less along a straight line. There are good reasons to doubt that developing countries will continue to liberalize at the pace of the last few years. The threat does not lie in a repetition of the financial shocks that have hit emerging markets (such as the peso crisis that struck Mexico in the mid-1990s). Today governments and financial institutions in the OECD are reasonably well equipped to respond to such events. The worrisome problems are of a different order of magnitude—going well beyond the ups and downs of the business cycle, the usual gyrations in countries undergoing difficult transitions, or the episodic political crises that have always characterized such societies.

Something deeper is at play in the late 1990s, the collision of two forces that have not coexisted before in emerging markets: free-market capitalism and democracy. The philosophy of Adam Smith is

world depend on overseas markets for both economies of scale and increasing profits. The countries in the developed world want the jobs at home that come with expanding exports. And many pension-plan investors are banking on the high returns that can result from investing in the developing world.

Threats to Reform

A number of emerging markets already are under severe pressure. In Mexico, the path to progress has some enormous obstacles along its way. True, the economic reforms of the 1980s and 1990s were impressive, even if the government badly mismanaged its currency devaluation at the end of 1994. Today the country appears to be on the road to recovery from the peso crisis: forecasters estimate growth in the range of 4% to 5% for 1997, and the nation's export economy is flourishing. But the current-account deficit is

popular discontent in Mexico, let alone as a vehicle for implementing critical new policies necessary for a rapidly changing economy. The party is in fact resisting change, having recently overturned President Ernesto Zedillo's far-reaching proposal to open and modernize Mexico's political process.

Nevertheless, political change will come–if not peacefully then violently. Already, crime, kidnapping, assassinations, and guerrilla activity are on the rise, signaling both a mounting level of dissatisfaction and the inability of the public sector to maintain order. But even if a more open and representative government emerges, it will lack the experience and the underlying institutions – such as honest courts – to govern effectively in the short run. Initially, that government may be besieged by the accumulated demands of tens of millions of Mexican citizens who have felt disenfranchised. It also will have its hands full cleaning up the old system – getting a grip on widespread criminality and creating a rule of law that all segments of the population can respect.

In light of those pressures, future governments may put off liberalizing the economy and instead concentrate on the immediate welfare of ordinary citizens. A democratic administration could become more nationalistic and more protectionist than the existing oligarchy. It could take many years before Mexico restores its current trajectory, at least in the eyes of foreign companies and governments.

Consider also Indonesia, the largest Muslim nation and the fourth largest country in the world by population. As in Mexico, the political system there may soon be unable to cope with economic and social pressures. By any measure, Jakarta's economic performance has been strong. GDP growth has been on the order of 6% to 7% annually, non-oil exports have been growing, and billions of dollars of foreign investment have poured in. But the country is a powder keg waiting to explode. With the exception of China, no major country is more dominated by autocratic rule than Indonesia. The 75-year-old president Suharto, who has ruled since he came to

Two forces are colliding in the emerging markets of the late 1990s: free-market capitalism and democracy.

giving rise to powerful new pressures that have enriched many, created enormous social changes, and unleashed new political forces. But Thomas Jefferson's part of the equation is not working so well. Democratic structures in many emerging markets are either nonexistent or too weak to ensure the modicum of economic fairness necessary to sustain democratic capitalism. As a result, emerging markets may well lose some of the progress they have made toward regulating markets and creating the rule of law that is essential to any commercial regime.

Moreover, in previous eras of crisis, the companies and governments of the industrialized world essentially wrote off emerging markets and left them to fend for themselves. Now, however, foreign investors, creditors, and governments will not be able to walk away from trouble without damaging themselves. Companies in the industrialized

rising again. Mexico's external debt has grown from 35% of GDP in 1992 to more than 60% in 1996. High interest rates and taxes are strangling the middle class. The banking system borders on insolvency. In the recession of the past two years, 5 million Mexicans have been added to the 22 million citizens (one-fourth of the population) who already live in extreme poverty. And the government estimates that an annual growth rate of 6% is necessary to absorb the 1 million new entrants into the labor force each year—a rate that does not appear to be attainable anytime soon.

Mexico's ability to deal with those daunting problems depends on an effective government. The country has been ruled by the iron fist of the Institutional Revolutionary Party for more than 60 years, but the party has become arthritic and corrupt. It is incapable of acting as a safety valve for the wellspring of power in the mid-1960s in a bloody coup, *is* the political system. The only opposition allowed is government-approved parties that support the president. Any challenge is immediately squelched – by military force if necessary.

Enormous pressures are building below the surface. When the aging president leaves the scene, they are likely to explode. It is difficult to envision a scenario that will contain those pressures when there are no existing political institutions to modulate them aside from the apparatus that Suharto now dominates. The military will want to maintain order. The Chinese minority will want to maintain its wealth. Both will be challenged by the Muslims, who constitute the overwhelming majority of the population; by the labor unions, which have been suppressed; and by the students, whose activism has been outlawed.

In a politically repressive society, change usually does not come gradually; it bursts on the scene. Some recent events are telltale signs of Indonesia's possible fate after Suharto. Last August, for example, when government pressure suppressed the voice of the leader of an opposition party, the largest riots of the past two decades ensued, followed by a brutal military crackdown. Afterward, the government began a systematic persecution of other potential "troublemakers," including the leader of the largest independent labor union. He and several labor and student leaders are currently on trial for subversion, a crime punishable by death. In early 1997, a Muslim mob burned a Chinese temple as well as Christian churches. The alleged cause was a complaint by an ethnic Chinese trader that the call to prayer from a mosque near his home was too loud. The incident highlighted the seething ethnic rivalries and resentments that will play out in the open once Suharto departs. It's difficult to see how economic progress won't suffer.

What about countries that have better track records politically? Several of the big emerging markets have practiced democracy for years, but even those nations are struggling with political pressures stemming from economic change. In India,

for example, Prime Minister P.V. Narasimha Rao's measures in the early 1990s to open the economy astounded outside observers. For nearly half a century, India had been a closed economy wedded to socialism, and its sudden embrace of capitalism stimulated high levels of economic growth and trade as well as an influx of capital from abroad. But in the national elections of 1996, the Indian people jettisoned Rao's government. In its place emerged a coalition of 13 parties – an unwieldy assemblage that includes nearly every major and parochial interest group in the country, from communists to religious extremists.

Such a fractured group will struggle to make the hard political decisions that are necessary to continue economic liberalization – including massive reduction of subsidies, new infrastructure development, and labor reform. If India stands still because of political polarization – in fact, if it doesn't move ahead quickly – it faces a dire situation as popular expectations rise. India has a long way to go to overcome a host of problems such as food production that loses 30% each year to spoilage; an energy distribution system that loses 25% to leakage during delivery; crumbling roads, ports, and airports; and a primitive telecommunications sector. India is falling further behind its Asian rivals in economic reforms, a problem that may jeopardize its ability to attract foreign capital in the future.

Economic pressures also are straining South Korea's politics. No one can deny the progress that this country has made in the past several years on both economic and political fronts, but now it must move out of the ranks of emerging markets to join those that have emerged. It can no longer compete internationally with such countries as China and Brazil, where the costs of doing business are much lower. South Korea must move from a system founded

on paternalism and authoritarianism to one based on democratic values, for there is no other way to unlock the initiative of the Korean people and create an economy flexible enough to cope with rapid technological change.

Nowhere are these challenges more evident than in the need to reform labor laws, which derive from an era when Korea was a military dictatorship. The challenge is to balance the ability of employers to control costs with a system of free collective bargaining. With no experience walking this tightrope, the administration of Kim Young Sam has badly mishandled the task. Last December, it passed legislation making it easier to lay off workers and postponing the right of labor to unionize until the year 2000. The laws were passed in a secret closed session with no public hearings and without the involvement of the political opposition. The unsurprising results were the largest strikes in South Korea's history. Today the government and the unions are still trying to work out a viable long-term settlement.

This bruising struggle is likely to make it more difficult to enact future reforms—reforms that are needed now more than ever. The country's GDP growth is slowing, the current-account deficit is soaring, and the Seoul stockmarket is at its lowest point in several years. Moreover, of all the major emerging markets, South Korea is the most hostile to foreign investment. And in the wake of the prolonged strikes, workers are especially sensitive to the issue of job security—which makes measures to

Many underestimate the impact of the political dimension of change.

open up the economy politically difficult. Such measures, however, are essential if the South Korean economy is to maintain its competitive position.

Other big markets are showing worrisome signs. In South Africa, President Nelson Mandela has not been able to bring about either prosperity or social justice. In fact, political wrangling within the ruling party has rendered it incapable of action, and critics fear that the nation is headed toward anarchy or permanent third-world status. In Brazil, the populist congress is resisting constitutional changes that would enable such reforms as large-scale privatization. In Argentina, unemployment has reached 17%, a level that is severely straining the ability of the ruling party – itself built around the labor movement – to streamline the economy any further. And in Turkey, economic reform has been all but taken off the table amid the election of the first Islamic government in the country's modern history.

Interpreting the Turmoil

There are several ways to account for the mounting pressures in emerging markets. One explanation is that many of the easier economic-reform measures already have been taken. A country's leaders can reduce tariffs from 300% to 50% more easily than they can reduce them from 50% to 5%; similarly, they can sell off the most viable government companies – such as the hard-currency-earning airlines – more readily than they can the money-losing steel plants. That first set of reforms can be enacted quickly: foreign and local investors respond positively, and foreign governments applaud. But the afterglow doesn't last long. Soon the domestic opposition organizes a counterattack, and those who haven't benefited from liberalization measures throw up roadblocks. Ordinary citizens, having heard about the magic of the marketplace, wonder why they can't get hot water or why the phones don't work. And top-level decision makers get worn out fighting battles over such questions.

In many emerging markets, the list of what still needs to be done is long. Market regulation is highly underdeveloped. Rigid labor laws need to be restructured. Limits on prices for energy and telecommunications discourage foreign investment. Government payrolls need to be pared down; at the same time, however, more skilled and experienced people need to be attracted to the bureau-

cracy. Expensive social-welfare policies need to be dismantled and rebuilt. The massive amounts of red tape that still interfere with normal business transactions need to be slashed. And legal systems need to be strengthened.

But by far the biggest reason for anxiety about economic reforms is the political dynamics of the reforms themselves. Those who have embraced emerging markets with enthusiasm have failed to consider a number of factors: the political dimension of change, the difficulty of implementing massive transformation in a short period, and the lack of skills and institutions needed to manage democratic capitalism. In moving toward open political and economic systems simultaneously, emerging markets are on uncharted and precarious ground.

As economic liberalization in emerging markets replaces rigid control, a new more laissez-faire, but more sophisticated, kind of economic and commercial regulation needs to be put in place. Governments need to shrink in size while managing more difficult tasks more effectively – a trick even the leaders in Washington, Bonn, and Tokyo have not yet mastered. In the absence of such a new set of political arrangements, those who held power under

the old regime end up in favored positions under the new one and simply increase their dominance and privileges. In addition, the transition from a command to a market economy brings with it a hiatus of order that invites a serious increase in fraud and corruption. Leaders in emerging markets rarely have the skills and experience to make the transition smoothly.

On the political side, democracies are defined by more than just voting; they also require a complex infrastructure. Without the solid foundations of a professional civil service, a strong independent judiciary, and

arm's-length regulators, the leaders of new democracies can spend all their time dealing with the pressure groups that emerge from an open economy. They cannot attend to the requirements of everyday management, let alone plan for essential long-term investments, and they are unable to deal with the popular demands critical to their legitimacy. Under those pressures, a new democracy sometimes drifts toward weak administrations and deadlock. At other times, the government moves in the opposite direction—toward the very dictatorial systems it replaced. Then comes a popular backlash, which reduces a government's ability to pursue the economic reforms that once constituted its primary mission.

These observations do not apply to every emerging market. Poland, for example, seems to have made an exemplary transition. In seven years, it has created a mature democracy, achieved the highest growth rate in Europe, and reduced the share of GDP stemming from government-owned activity from 100% to 33%. Warsaw did have special advantages: it once had a very sophisticated economy, it has a highly educated population, and it was greatly helped by sitting on Europe's doorstep. Taking another tack, China has managed to combine rigid

In moving to open political *and* economic systems, emerging markets are on uncharted ground.

political control with gradual economic liberalization – perhaps because its system of political control is so highly developed, and because its very size and economic potential is mesmerizing to foreign investors, who have made China the largest destination for foreign capital among emerging markets.

It would be misleading, too, to say that there are no other scenarios for Mexico, Indonesia, South Korea, and India than those described above. Political change in Mexico may come at a slow but steady pace at the municipal or state level. A more conciliatory military group may replace Suharto. South Korea may apply Asian-style discipline and determination, and persevere on the course of economic reform. India may muddle through. In the end, of course, it is not possible to predict with complete confidence the course of such profound and complex transitions.

Still, it is best now to be sober. The prevailing optimistic view of what will happen in key emerging markets underestimates the impact of variables that cannot be measured: frustration about missing out on the boom times and anxiety about the massive changes wrought by foreign investment and technology. Moreover, those who say that Mexico has always had pervasive poverty or that India has always progressed slowly are underestimating both the current pace of global change, which is new, and the impact of seeing and knowing what a better life is all about, which is now more possible than ever because of modern communications. This much is sure: the risks of setbacks in many big emerging markets are escalating. Over time, democracy and free markets can reinforce each other, but the journey will be precarious. And we are entering its most dangerous phase.

Pressure on the Developed World

A slowing of economic reforms in emerging markets would be a disaster for the industrialized world on several counts.

First, powerful trade and investment ties have made the emerging markets essential to the continued economic expansion of industrialized OECD countries. For example, exports have been responsible for about one-third of U.S. economic growth in the past few years, and already the ten big emerging markets account for a greater proportion of U.S. exports than the European Union and Japan combined. Exports to the big emerging markets have been equally important for both Europe and Japan.

The ability to increase exports to emerging markets is all the more important because those markets will be selling a growing amount to industrialized countries. The en-

hanced competitiveness of emerging markets stems from the economic reforms they have already undertaken, as well as from low wage rates and increasing productivity. In the United States, for example, the average hourly wage in 1996 was $17.20. In South Korea, it was $7.40; in Taiwan, $5.82; in Brazil, $4.28; in China, 25 cents. And productivity in these markets will be greatly enhanced because of growing access to Western technology and supervision by foreign managers. To avoid unmanageable trade deficits and the flaring up of protectionist sentiments, the West and Japan will need to offset the likely increase of imports with their own exports. And that can happen only if emerging markets grow at a strong pace.

Second, the developed nations are counting on the growth of emerging markets to help finance pensions for their aging populations. The demographics are well known. People in the industrialized world are living longer, and there are fewer workers to support retirees. Public spending on pensions as a percentage of GDP in OECD countries is projected to soar from 8% in 1990 to more than 15% over the next 25 years. The easiest way to raise the financial returns on workers' savings is to look for a good portion of those returns in those areas where growth will be the fastest. In other words, it means looking for those returns largely in emerging markets.

Third, a slowdown in the growth of emerging markets may lead to destructive competition among governments in the developed world. Encouraged by the boom overseas, multinational companies, often backed by the financing and lobbying of their home governments, have already intensified their competition. Free and fair competition is to be welcomed, but the pressure on companies to win big contracts in emerging markets has led to bribery, violations of OECD trade-financing

agreements, and escalation of political pressure by home governments on those awarding contracts. There is no sign that such competition will let up anytime soon, because the contracts in question are of the utmost national importance to countries suffering from high levels of unemployment. It is not an exaggeration to say that rivalries in this arena are becoming major wedges between countries that were allies during the Cold War. Left unchecked, these contests could create major international tensions.

There also are larger dimensions to economic failures in the developing world. Borders in a number of emerging markets are contested, and civil wars in others are possible. The economic strains caused by slower growth and a reversal of reforms could exacerbate tensions in any of these hot spots. Setbacks in economic development also would hamper the countries' efforts to invest in environmental protection. And continued growth is the only way to boost the livelihood of hundreds of mil-

Multinational companies should not be mere bystanders to change.

lions of people who are living in miserable conditions.

What Can Be Done?

There was a time, just a few decades ago, when the industrialized countries thought they could build democracies and capitalist societies by injecting massive amounts of foreign aid, making trade concessions, and providing technical advice. Following great disappointments with programs such as the U.S. government's Alliance for Progress in Latin America, ambitions about directing such transformations have been greatly deflated. In the last decade, OECD governments have either reduced aid or redirected it toward the poorest countries. The emerging markets in the meantime have entered the mainstream of the world economy, linking their fates not to other government's largesse but to private capital, foreign direct investment, and global trade. In 1990, for example, net financial aid to emerging markets was four times the flow of private capital. By 1996, that ratio was reversed: the flow of private capital was five times that of government aid.

upcoming political decisions. In addition, they can work harder at collecting information about which local businesses are in the best position to survive a prolonged transitional period and might therefore make good partners. Executives can sensitize colleagues and board members to conditions in a particular

institutions of individual developing countries.

Companies also have an opportunity, sometimes in partnership with Western governments or the World Bank, to assist emerging markets in their quest for progress. From Brazil to Thailand, countries need sophisticated technical assistance. Merrill Lynch, for example, is helping public officials in India devise sensible regulatory policy for stock markets. In China, Aetna and Procter & Gamble are helping local schools and universities train and educate leaders who understand how capitalist economies work. In Malaysia, Motorola and Intel have instituted training programs to enhance the skills of local workers. Companies that establish deep local roots and show, by dint of example rather than empty rhetoric, that their strategies are aligned with the long-term goals of the host country stand the best chance of prospering. At the same time, such companies help keep up-and-coming countries on the track of economic and political progress.

In Malaysia, Motorola's and Intel's training programs have enhanced the skills of local workers.

If aid is not the answer, what can governments in the West and Japan do? They will need to manage their economies in a way that keeps the world economy buoyant and conducive to the expansion of trade. That will take some effort. The United States, the European Union, and Japan are all growing at a much slower rate than they have historically, and fiscal contraction is everywhere in vogue. Meanwhile, enthusiasm for trade liberalization seems to be waning; there is little appetite for new rounds of trade negotiations.

As for multinational companies, they should not be mere bystanders to political and economic change abroad. They can take steps to prepare for trouble. For example, they can apply higher discounts on earnings projections and diversify their activities rather than gamble on any one country or region. Managers can engage in serious contingency planning in order to cope with political and economic turmoil in emerging markets. They can improve their efforts to gather information on economic and social trends as well as on

country or region so that new developments do not take them by surprise and cause ill-advised knee-jerk reactions.

Astute human-resource management also can make a difference. For the most part, plenty of capital is available to facilitate entry into the emerging markets. What is often lacking are managers who know how to operate amid uncertainty and instability – managers who appreciate local politics and cultures and can build the relationships that not only enhance today's sales but also act as a safety valve in turbulent times. How to recruit, develop, and train managers who can operate in emerging markets is the key question. Companies should make their best effort to obtain highly adaptable men and women from the local scene. In addition, they should learn as much as possible about the mistakes that other multinational companies have made. Finally, it is essential that companies provide courses to their managers on the history and the political and economic

To be sure, no one can predict exactly how economies and regimes will develop. The emergence of so many capitalist economies within a few years is unprecedented and holds great opportunities – as well as equally great risks. In the 1980s, experts failed to see the rise of Japan or that of the Asian tigers. They failed to predict the collapse of Mexico, Brazil, and Argentina in the 1980s or the implosion of the Soviet Union. When it comes to the future of big emerging markets, however, enough warning signals are flashing. The penalty for not recognizing them will be severe.

Throughout most of Mexico unemployment is 30%.
In Tijuana it's maybe 2%.

Maquiladora-ville

Damon Darlin

A Samsung
maquiladora
in Tijuana
**The Korean
company
plans to
invest
almost $800
million by 1999.**

PHOTOGRAPH BY AMY ETRA

SCRAWNY DOGS still cross dusty streets in Tijuana, but they no longer dare dawdle. Forget *The Treasure of the Sierra Madre*. These streets are paved two-laners, and the dogs are dodging semis laden with locally produced color TVs.

In a generally depressed Mexico, Tijuana is booming. "Anyone who wants a job can get one here," says Rafael Carrillo Barron, president of Grupo Carrillo, a major Tijuana real estate company.

In a great wave of internal migration, Mexicans from the interior are moving north to jobs in and around Tijuana that pay four times Mexico's minimum wage of 25 pesos ($3.40) a day. Tijuana's population, growing about 7% a year, now numbers 1.5

million. The price of improved industrial land in Tijuana is about 25% higher than just across the border in San Diego.

What's behind the boom? The Tijuana region has become the TV-set capital of the world. Japanese- and Korean-owned factories here use low-cost Mexican labor to produce almost 10 million sets a year, or about 30% of the TVs sold in the U.S.

Korean companies, among them Samsung, Hyundai and LG Electronics, have invested $650 million in the Tijuana area just in the last 15 months. Japanese companies, including Sony and Sanyo, are expanding their component and assembly plants to the tune of $400 million.

Tijuana boasts no fewer than 560

maquiladora factories, where Mexican workers turn imported components into finished sets to be sold mostly across the border; to encourage investment, the Mexican government lets manufacturers import duty-free the components they need to build for export.

Unlike Juarez, Nuevo Laredo and other border towns, Tijuana has the especially good fortune to abut San Diego, one of the more pleasant U.S. big cities. Managers and engineers can live there comfortably and commute to work in plants across the border.

With prosperity come problems. Tijuana's economic success is straining the region's already overburdened infrastructure. More than 88%

of all goods transported to Mexico are moved by truck, but no expressway connects San Diego and Tijuana. Trucks waiting for customs clearance and inspection at the border sometimes back up for 5 miles as U.S. Customs people search diligently for illegal drugs and illegal aliens.

Tijuana businesses cope with these problems as best they can. Sanyo, for example, installed a video camera on a tower above its U.S. operations so managers can monitor the length of the line and dispatch employees more efficiently when they see the line shortening. But such drawbacks in part could cancel out the advantages of cheap and plentiful Mexican labor. Denis Ossola, Matsushita Television Co.'s senior vice president, says the congestion could lead Matsushita to expand farther east, along the Mexican border in Texas. Tijuana officials fear others would follow. That alarms California, too, which benefits mightily from the Tijuana boom.

Sony, for example, has spent $140 million on its assembly plant in Tijuana, but $400 million on the U.S. side for engineering and high-technology operations. The San Diego area benefits from high-paying, high-tech jobs.

Feeling the heat, California and Tijuana officials are working together to improve transportation. One plan would reopen a set of railroad tracks running east from San Diego, through Northern Baja and then looping back up into the U.S. to connect to Southern Pacific lines running to eastern markets. Cost: as much as $124 million. Another project would build a modern port in Ensenada, south of Tijuana, and link the port to California with a rail line. Cost: at least $300 million.

Private investors are planning a toll road for commuters to the Mexican border, but a U.S. interstate highway connector for trucks still lacks state funding. Says Neil Whitely-Ross of the San Diego Economic Development Corp.: "We are trying to convince legislators that everyone benefits from our trade with Mexico."

Despite its boom, much of Tijuana is not a pretty place. New-home construction has collapsed under the weight of Mexico's postdevaluation 35%-plus interest rates. With no room for families, single adults trek north and live in *chozas*—shanty towns that continue to spread across Tijuana's hills. The *chozas* now stretch a third of the way to Tecate, 25 miles east of Tijuana.

Given the terrible living conditions, it's no surprise that absenteeism is a serious problem in the *maquiladoras*. Young Moo Kwon, president of Samsung's Tijuana TV operations, sighs when asked if Tijuana could lead Mexico toward becoming another economic tiger, and points to rampant absenteeism. Kwon struggles to get his plant's absenteeism rate down to 3.5%, an excellent rate locally, though his superiors in Seoul were mystified why it couldn't go much lower. Kwon tries to explain to them that in devoutly Catholic Mexico, itinerant workers like to be with their families during religious holidays, and, given the housing situation, there is no way they can bring their families to Tijuana.

Thus, during the week before Easter the Tijuana manufacturers wanted to keep the plants running at least until Holy Thursday. No such luck. Workers started heading home on Monday and Tuesday.

But the boom rolls on. Korea's Samsung Electronics has just spent $212 million to build a television and computer-monitor plant in what was an olive grove a year ago. Samsung plans to spend an additional $580 million to expand the plant, which could employ 9,300 people in four years. Officials on both sides of the border are expecting Tijuana to grow into a city with a population of 3 million in 12 years.

Free trade has transformed a once ramshackle place into a city that may grow as large as Chicago is today.

Smaller than Guatemala,
meaner than Serbia.

THE MYTH OF THE CHINA MARKET

By John Maggs

"We've got to be there," said Ron Brown as he led a delegation of American business leaders to China weeks after Bill Clinton's May 1994 about-face on Most Favored Nation status. "Hundreds of thousands of American workers are already depending on these jobs. China will be the engine for growth. It is the pot at the end of the rainbow."

No, it isn't. China is not a major export market for the United States, nor is it likely to be one any time soon. There's more U.S. investment in the Philippines, and almost as much in the Dominican Republic. And the factors keeping U.S. money out of China show no signs of disappearing; many won't be affected by China's eventual submission to the rules of the World Trade Organization, either.

Call it the great China market myth—the idea that everything from human rights violations to weapons sales is worth enduring because glorious riches await us in the People's Republic. But this expectation is a chimera. U.S. exports to China were $11.9 billion in 1996. In Asia alone, China ranks behind Japan, South Korea, Taiwan and Singapore. Boosters insist that exports to China are growing so quickly that these comparisons are irrelevant. But in fact, since 1980, exports to China have risen about 10 percent annually, compared to an overall rise in U.S. exports of about 8 percent per year. Over the past decade and a half, U.S. exports to Brazil, Poland and dozens of other countries have grown faster than exports to China.

In 1996, China's economy grew at a torrid 9.7 percent, but, to the surprise of economists, American exports to China stayed virtually the same. The best explanation for this centers on another factor that mythologists of the China market don't like to mention. To advance internal economic and social goals, China's leaders continue to pull the levers of what remains a command economy. As in 1988, when inflation spun out of control, there's evidence that a 1996 inflation drive was built around the throttling of imports. Because of the large appreciation

of the dollar last year, imports from the United States were the most expensive, and logically the best target.

China's intervention in trade markets goes far beyond the inflation crackdown. American companies say the greatest obstacle to imports is a vast and shifting network of administrative barriers that are manipulated by Chinese bureaucrats. "Trading rights" must be granted to importing companies; and U.S. companies are sometimes told their goods have been barred by secret laws known as "nebu" that they are not allowed to inspect.

U.S. businessmen concede that trade with China depends foremost on what its government decides is best. Joseph Gorman, chairman of auto-parts giant TRW, says he has been trying to sell power-steering equipment in China for years. TRW is the world leader in power steering—Volkswagen, in fact, uses TRW equipment in the cars it assembles in China. Still, "we haven't been able to sell or market there directly," said Gorman. "China has a very detailed plan for the auto sector, and that's pretty much the way it is going to develop."

Since most economists expect China's growth rate to slow, there's every reason to believe that U.S. exports will continue to hover at their 10-percent-a-year growth. This means that exports to China, now only 1.8 percent of total U.S. exports, will remain insignificant for at least a decade. More surprisingly, it also means that, over this decade, a number of Asian countries are likely to outpace China as markets for U.S. exports. In addition to South Korea, Taiwan and Singapore, Malaysia, too, will overtake China in the next two or three years. Thailand, where U.S. exports have been growing 20 percent a year, now imports half as much from the United States as China, but will overtake it early in the new century.

Many true believers in the China market argue that the United States will eventually get its share of imports because, unlike Japan, China has been running a net trade deficit with the world and will continue to do so. "The good news is that China can't keep growing without imports," said Richard Brecher of the U.S.-China Business Council. "They are going to have to run a trade deficit."

Not anymore. On January 10, China announced that its 1996 trade surplus with the world was $12.24 billion.

U.S. exports are the most important index of how the

JOHN MAGGS writes about international business and economics for *The Journal of Commerce*.

United States is benefiting from its economic relations with China. When Clinton talks about China meaning jobs for Americans, those jobs can only be measured in exports. But what about investment? China marketeers argue that, in that arena, there *has* been explosive growth for U.S. business. American companies, they say, are bringing home mega-profits from newly built factories in China.

Again, not nearly. The cumulative amount of U.S. direct investment in China edged up to $1.9 billion at the end of 1995, the last year on record, from $1.7 billion in the end of 1994. That's about 0.5 percent of the total, which is $170 billion. Colombia receives three times as much U.S. investment, despite a guerrilla insurgency, the threat of imminent U.S. sanctions for non-cooperation on drug interdiction and an economy roughly one-tenth the size of China's. In defending free trade, Bill Clinton got laughs when he said that if low wages were the only factor, then U.S. investment would be flooding into the Dominican Republic. But U.S. direct investment in the tiny Dominican Republic was in fact $1.4 billion at last measure, not too far off from China's total. Some China boosters choose simply to disbelieve these statistics, which are compiled by the Commerce Department. "That's ridiculous," huffed Brecher, who faxed back a page of Chinese government data that was heavy on feel-good stats like "number of contracts signed." But even Beijing says the total U.S. investment is only $3 billion, a relative drop in the bucket.

While it's true that China is attracting more foreign investment than any other developing country, the overwhelming majority of that money continues to come from the three traditional sources for China's capital—Japan, Taiwan and Hong Kong. Beyond commonalities of language and culture, proximity is the most powerful factor driving investment patterns, and East Asia's geography will not change. Neither will the giant foreign reserves in these countries shrink very much, especially if they maintain their huge trade surpluses with the West.

Investment banker John Whitehead understands why U.S. investment in China remains so low. "There's a lot of activity lining up partners, but not a lot of money going in," he said. "China remains a relatively untried market and place to do business" for U.S. companies. Whitehead, a former chairman of Goldman, Sachs and deputy Secretary of State, borrowed Alan Greenspan's comment on the Wall Street bubble to describe an "irrational exuberance" among U.S. businessmen over China. Though Whitehead says he allies himself with Henry Kissinger, Alexander Haig and other "friends of China," he has no illusions about its business environment. "There is inherent instability in any dictatorial regime," he said. "In China, central authority is breaking down. Regional leaders have a great deal of authority. There is no legal structure for protecting private property, and the financial structure is uncertain."

With few exceptions, the China deals that fill the newspapers are agreements in principle, years away from actual investment. Many never come off. That's what happened with the Lippo Group's investment, brokered by Clinton fund-raisers, to build a $1 billion power plant in China with Entergy Corp. Other deals seem to remain perpetually just around the corner. General Motors announced recently that it was in "final negotiations" for a $2 billion deal to build passenger cars with a Chinese partner in Shanghai. GM officials also announced this deal in October of 1995, and have been talking about it since 1993. A GM spokesman said there was no estimate of when ground would be broken on the plant.

Businessmen say that, in China, "the negotiation begins when the contract is signed." Chinese industrialists never stop demanding concessions, which often include the giveaway of valuable technology. For Chrysler Corporation, the price was too high. China demanded that the company turn over all its manufacturing technology and design secrets in exchange for being allowed to invest $1 billion in a minivan joint venture. "They want us to set them up as a world-class competitor to Chrysler, and pay for it, too," said chairman Robert Eaton.

McDonnell Douglas paid the price, then went out of business waiting for the China market to materialize. After agreeing to build twenty airliners in China, it couldn't sell one. The company was willing to play by China's rules, but then those rules changed: China's newly capitalistic airlines decided that Chinese-built planes would be of poorer quality than those made in Europe. McDonnell Douglas's inability to establish itself as an aircraft manufacturer in Asia was one of the major forces that drove it into its proposed merger with Boeing.

If the GM deal goes through, and GM officials are willing to part with the technology they bring with them to China, other restrictions will still limit the deal's value. In most developing countries, GM starts assembling cars almost entirely with parts manufactured elsewhere, mostly in the United States. Under China's auto development plan, Chinese-made parts will have to comprise 40 percent of the first cars that roll off the line in Shanghai. Within five years, the minimum "local content" will rise to 80 percent, ensuring that the engines, transmissions and other high-value components in these cars will not be exported from the United States. As for the fast-growing China market, auto analysts say that production capacity there will outstrip demand within three years. This suggests that GM and other U.S. companies will need to find other markets for these cars, further displacing exports from the United States.

Above all else, believers in the China market believe in the future. They believe the problems of today will surely disappear tomorrow. They believe that China is opening up to more imports when it is not. They believe that development will inevitably lead to greater fairness in the market when it has not.

Westerners have always seen what they want to see in China, beginning with Marco Polo. You don't have to be a protectionist or a Red-baiter to ask whether U.S. priorities in China have been skewed by this false image. If the United States recognizes that it has less to lose economically, perhaps balancing all its goals in China will be a little easier.

SINCE MARCO POLO TRAVELED HIS FAMED TRADING ROUTES and Bedouins plied the fabled markets at Timbuktu, entrepreneurs have scoured the globe buying goods in one place and selling them in another. Big corporations have long been invested in the $1.3 trillion two-way trading between the United States and foreign countries. But a new era of global commerce is dawning as more American entrepreneurs venture into the import/export business. Now smaller traders—from one-person shopkeepers to mid-sized wholesalers joint venturing with other businesses—are launching out overseas.

When Todd Alexander decided to start a business importing fine Italian wines home to Atlanta in January 1993, he thought the application process would be simple. He got labels of the 60 brands he planned to import, attached a check for the registration costs of each—about $10-$20 per label—and filed the appropriate forms with the state and federal government. The only thing left was to wait for a series of personal and financial background checks to be completed. But what Alexander thought would take three or four months ended up taking nine.

Maybe it was because Alexander, who owns Vendemmia Inc. (which means "harvest" in Italian), was only 26 years old when he applied to become an importer. Or maybe it was because alcohol is one of the U.S. government's most regulated commodities. Whatever the reason, Alexander says he was grilled a hundred different ways. "The hardest part has been the paperwork for the state and federal government," he says. "There are so many forms to fill out and I hate paperwork."

For entrepreneurs looking to export, the lure of much-wanted U.S. goods abroad, from boilers to telecommunications, bring visions of cashing in on the $575 billion in exports.

Whether buying or selling, there are ins and outs for importing or exporting in today's global marketplace

MARJORIE WHIGHAM-DÉSIR

Equally attractive is the export of "intellectual property," a.k.a. technical skills and management training by American consultants and project managers to foreign governments and corporations. On the flip side, U.S. businesspeople who wish to import are usually either seeking to cut product or labor costs, or want to sell exotic items that aren't "made in the U.S.A."

But neither logistics nor language are keeping either side at bay. Thanks to telecommunications, transportation and other high-tech systems, the geographic borders of the world are blurring. Whether you're importing or exporting, you have to develop a market strategy, learn the process and regulations, understand the nuances of culture and customs, and be committed to making it work to be successful internationally.

DETERMINE IF YOUR COMPANY OR PRODUCT IS EXPORT-READY

If you have dreams of taking your company or product global, you first need to assess whether there's even a market abroad for what you have to sell. As a general rule, most American goods are considered wanted and valued overseas—even when similar items are made in that country. But there are a few questions you should ask yourself first: Is my product or service successful domestically? Who buys it and why does it sell well? Is there a foreign market similar to it? Will this make it easier to sell abroad?

You should also make sure your domestic business is strong enough to allow you to spend time developing the international side in both capital and time resources. You should also examine how an international sale will dovetail with your overall business plan and domestic marketing strategy. If you've made a pro-export assessment, then it's time to get some outside opinions.

"Go through any department of commerce," suggests Karen Babino, manager of marketing and business development for TransAtlantic Imports in Atlanta. "The federal and state governments, even in most major cities, have an international desk or affiliation, and in some cases, offices abroad that you can call on," she

explains. When going global, advises Herb Smith, chairman of Smith International Enterprises, a global sourcing import distribution company with offices in Cleveland and Hong Kong, check with your state's economic development office. Many states now have their own international trade offices with field offices located around the world. They can provide help, from finding office space and equipment to information on special assistance programs offered to exporters.

The federal version, the U.S. Export Assistance Center (EAC) can help you assess the international potential for your product. An outgrowth of a joint effort between the Commerce Department, the Small Business Administration and the Export-Import Bank, EACs are one-stop resource centers where entrepreneurs can get expert advice, foreign market research and access to export financing.

EACs are a unit of the Commerce Department's Commercial Services Division, and offer customized services, from an international company profile ($100), which can provide information on prospective trading partners, to customized market analysis ($5,000) of your particular company and product or service. The offices are staffed by Commercial Service officers who can assist in your search.

Part of the EAC's mission is to increase the number of small-and mid-size companies exporting products. There are 19 domestic EAC hub sites around the country: Atlanta; Baltimore; Boston; Charlotte, North Carolina; Chicago; Cleveland; Dallas; Denver; Detroit; Long Beach, California; Miami; Minneapolis; New York City; New Orleans; Philadelphia; Portland, Oregon; San Jose, California; Seattle and St. Louis. They also do on-site counseling for potential exporters, all free of charge.

Private organizations such as Assist International (212-725-3311) can help you get started for a fee, while nonprofit ones like the National Minority Business Council (212-573-2385) of New York City offers free help.

DO YOUR HOMEWORK

Research and identify the best foreign markets for your product or service. This is the basis for your international marketing plan. Assess where the best places are to start and identify a strategy for entering that market. K.L. Fredericks, director of the Harlem office of the EAC, suggests using the

"funnel approach," which means considering all countries as potential customers. From there, she advises using population and demographic studies, U.S. census export statistics, economic reports, domestic and foreign government regulations, political and currency stability assessments, trade barriers or special assistance programs to identify the best potential markets for your product.

Look at the top 25 markets where your product or service is needed. You can create this report using Census Bureau statistics for both imports and exports and by searching through the National Trade Data Bank (NTDB) at federal depository libraries (http://www.stat-usa.gov). The NTDB uses an international "harmonized" coding system to determine how well a product will sell overseas. This system gathers statistics from the product's shipments and ranks it in both total dollars spent and the number of units purchased. "The focus should be on the product, not the country, unless you have a particular expertise," adds Fredericks.

Foreign service officers at Commercial Services offices overseas are also a source of information on a particular product in a given country that can be funneled back to the EAC office. They can also provide a list of distributors in that country.

Even when importing, you need to be aware of the regulations in the foreign country you are buying from and the U.S. Customs and state requirements governing products coming in. Not knowing the process may cost you time in receiving your goods, and money.

That's what happened to Floris Brown last August when she went to Ghana to buy collectibles to sell in her Afrocentric boutique, JGillyard Treasures, in a St. Louis suburb. Although Brown had been to Ghana twice before, like most tourists, she'd always brought her things back home in suitcases. This time, she decided to import the items like a real businessperson and split the shipping costs with another vendor whose husband knew how to import.

But when her partner backed out, Brown was left to handle the shipping process herself. This included getting a shipping container and arranging for its transport to providing the appropriate documentation—including a "bill of lading" describing the cargo and stamped by the exporting country—and an "entry of goods" form filed with U.S. Customs upon arrival.

Fortunately, her Ghanaian hosts were local business owners who knew a shipping agent. "My friends knew the process and that's the only reason I ended up doing this," says Brown. She just managed to get her 1,100 pounds of African statutes and carvings on a ship headed for Savannah, Georgia, the day before she was to return to the U.S. The total cost to transport the shipment, which included the container, shipping costs, terminal handling charges and harbor fees, was about $1,100.

"Basically, I was dependent upon someone else for everything—I'll never do that again. Next time, I'll know what to do myself," she reflects.

Enthusiastic but ill-prepared entrepreneurs like Brown set out into international ventures expecting to do business the way they operate domestically. Rarely does it work the way they envisioned.

"That's why you have to spend time with someone who has done this before," says Karen Mayo, executive director of special projects for the Port of Miami and president of Mayo Communications International, a Miami-based marketing firm.

Had Brown contacted the U.S. Customs Service before leaving home, she could have gotten information on how to import her container, including a list of authorized shipping agents and brokers participating in its Automated Manifest System. She then could have been granted a conditional release of her shipment upon arrival from Ghana and five days before actually landing stateside.

LEARN THE COUNTRY'S CULTURE AND CUSTOMS

Part of doing your homework is understanding the people and their culture. While it sounds all too simple, it will be a linchpin to your success.

"Study your market," advises Fredericks. "Language and customs can be a barrier to trade," she readily points out. People usually do business with people they know or get to know, and feel they can trust with their ideas, time and money. Communication is crucial to that exchange, whether you're exporting or importing.

While international firms may prefer to communicate with American businesses in their native tongue, most expect to communicate in English, the international language for doing business. However, it behooves an American entrepreneur to become familiar with the language, especially in Latin American and European markets, if they expect to win customers.

That's what helped Alexander, now 29, launch Vendemmia Inc (see "Drinking in Profits," Enterprise, September 1996), a $1.2 million Atlanta-based wine distribution business. Fluent in Italian, Alexander loved the culture, its wines and traveling back and forth to the country he first visited as an exchange student in high school.

After college, he got a job working as a management trainee for a New Jersey-based wine distributor. A few years and some experience later, he quit and headed back to Italy on a six-month trip to write a book on Italian wines.

"Halfway through the trip, I decided I was going to import Italian wine because the vintners were unhappy with their U.S. distributors," explains Alexander who says his ability to overcome the language barrier was a huge plus. "Being able to pick up the phone and speak the language allowed me to start as quickly and efficiently as I did."

DEVELOP AN INTERNATIONAL MARKETING PLAN

Now that you've identified your market, you have to determine what your goals are there—sales, market penetration, distribution sources, even the terms and conditions of your sales agreements. You should also include the strategy for financing and capitalizing your efforts. This plan will outline your strategy for entering that market and form the backbone of your international structure.

"You must have the same elements in your international plan that you have in your domestic plan, while allowing for differences in pricing, dis-

tribution and transportation costs," advises Mayo.

The International Trade Administration (800-USA-TRADE; http://www.ita.doc.gov) in the Commerce Department and its partnering agencies, from Agriculture to the Small Business Administration, can also help you identify the specifics your plan should include, such as marketing and pricing strategies.

The plan should address your strategy for distributing your product in that country: indirect, direct or via foreign investment. If you want to import, the process is essentially the same, only done from abroad.

Indirect exporting allows you to sell or distribute your product via a middleman such as a broker or export management or trading company. Direct exporting means your company will sell directly to that foreign consumer or find a local representative on your behalf. Both methods are good options for small businesses just getting into the international market. Exporting via foreign investment entails establishing a physical presence in that country via an office, distribution center, assembly operation or even a manufacturing facility. A variation is selling directly to a foreign company stateside, providing the appropriate sales receipts and letting them take responsibility for getting the product out.

> **Eastmond's $15 million South Bronx factory plans to ship 12 prefabricated boilers to China this year**

That was the case for A.L. Eastmond Inc. and its EASCO Boiler Corp., an industrial boiler manufacturer in Bronx, New York. A few years ago, a Mexico City factory-owner was "visiting the area when someone told him about us," says owner Leon Eastmond. "He contacted us and we sold him a firebox boiler. We built everything here and he arranged for all the transport and shipping," he adds. The risk to Edmond was nil; technically, he sold a product domestically that was bound for export.

Or perhaps you decide to set up a foreign-based distributorship that has ties, if not a partnership, with a foreign-based firm. That's what Smith did when he bought a Hong Kong-based import business from an American firm that distributed "soft goods" to discount stores like Kmart and Dollar General.

"After I bought them, I found out that their one client was in financial trouble and losing its business. I had to develop new business. I also had to find key suppliers over there for things that could be supplied to American businesses," explains the CEO of Smith International.

Smith's business strategy was to create a company that could do business in China via a joint-venture relationship with a Chinese firm. That may be the only way you'll get to do business, particularly in the Far East where foreigners cannot own businesses outright.

Every marketing plan must have a budget and address the financing and the capitalization costs needed to do business abroad. "Most small business owners can't stay away as long to travel far, and the costs and expenses involved are felt to be too much for smaller businesses," explains Joseph Saffell, chairman of the International Business Development Consortium Inc. For that reason, he advises African American entrepreneurs to look closer to home to places like the Caribbean.

"Many businesses say that access to capital to venture into new markets is the main drawback," says EAC's Fredericks. For companies trying to export, there are financing sources and lines of credit through state and federal governmental programs. Such agencies include the SBA for loan guarantees under $800,000 and the Export-Import Bank for deals over that amount.

"In China, they deal with an irrevocable letter of credit," explains Smith. Besides ownership restrictions, Smith says his company is also based in Hong Kong because its currency is pegged to the U.S. dollar, ensuring a stable currency. He advises that once you begin to look at global markets, check with your local domestic bank to find out if it has foreign affiliates or associations so that it can make bank or credit transfers for your firm.

But in smaller developing countries, particularly when importing from cottage-sized crafts-based businesses or small manufacturers, it's often cash-in-advance; without it, many of these vendors cannot even start a project.

KNOW YOUR MARKET

Language may not be the only barrier to building an international business. Often, there is a different style of working in other countries. So, if you're trying to get a product made very quickly, time may be an issue, especially when importing on a deadline. Similarly, in some countries, offering an "incentive" may be expected to get your product in or out.

"A timetable is a major problem in Africa and India," says Alioune Dieng, president of AfritexUSA, a New York-based fabric wholesaler. "You could have agreed to a certain time and not get your goods because time is not seen the same way there. Time means money here in America," says Dieng, who also has suppliers in Pakistan and China.

> **Motherland Imports owner, Twyla Lang-Gordon, learned the hard way that communication is essential to trade**

The perception of what is quality and cultural differences may also affect your product. That's what Twyla Lang-Gordon found out when she began importing "customized" kente cloth to sell to Greek sororities, fraternities and graduating seniors. "I had a friend from Togo whose family owned a kente cloth manufacturing plant. I was able to place an initial order for 40 scarves with them. I mailed a sample scarf along with a cash advance. When they sent back the package, they'd made up the scarves with the lettering going sideways!" she recalls. "I took them to the meeting anyway, and sold out. I told them they could wear it as a belt," she recalls. "They [weavers] were envisioning them as designs and were not familiar with Greek letters at all."

Since then, the Los Angeles-based Motherland Imports has moved its operations from Togo to Ghana and gone through several "weaver villages" before finding two that now supply the 5,000–6,000 scarves Lang-Gordon sells annually the way she wants them.

She also realized that she needed a local representative to communicate her needs more effectively and monitor the quality of her product. "You have to have someone over there checking on your product and making sure you're going to get your order," advises Lang-Gordon. It's also the way she communicates with her village factory, since telephones aren't readily available.

BE IN IT FOR THE LONG HAUL

Ultimately, the best advice is to take your time and understand how the international marketplace will fit into your overall business strategy. In fact, if your domestic strategy is strong and your reputation known, you may not have to go out looking for business—the opportunities may come to you.

Eastmond says his company's products are legendary: "We have the fastest turnaround—to build, set up or provide emergency service—of anyone in the country," he says matter-of-factly. That Eastmond can build a complete ready-to-install system at a competitive price has made the $15 million company a favored supplier of contractors and engineers. It's also gotten it the 1994 Manufacturer of the Year award from the MBDA. Having your own Web site also doesn't hurt when searching new markets.

K.L. Fredericks contacted Eastmond about turning EASCO's sights abroad. "The Commerce Department came with a detailed marketing survey of our products and their potential market in China," explains Eastmond and his director of marketing, Omor Igiehon. "The Chinese have a $1 billion annual boiler market." It is also typical of the $220 billion in large-scale projects scheduled to begin in BEM (big emerging market) countries by 2000.

EASCO is now considering an export deal to China for 12 of its boilers, in a range of sizes, to supply heat and hot water for apartment buildings that will house 50-1,000 families in Beijing. To make the deal, Eastmond may partner with a New York-based Chinese firm that wants to be its representative there. The process has taken two years.

But for now, the 70-year-old manufacturing company is proceeding cautiously. "We're negotiating pricing. If we can't make money, I'm not doing it," states Eastmond, who'll ship the units the same way he did to Mexico—ready-to-install and without the responsibility for shipping it. Never one to lay all his eggs in a single basket, Eastmond says the local markets of New York, New Jersey and Connecticut are his "bread and butter." But he's looking to expand nationally and internationally if the deal is right—a move that more 21st century businesses will have to make.

"What businesses must understand is that soon they will no longer have a choice about whether to go international or not, because international is coming to them," says Mayo. "We need to start thinking global because our neighborhood is the world. And the sooner you're ready, the more likely you'll win."

North Korea's economy and ruling cadre
are self-destructing. An East Asian security
nightmare will soon follow, predicts this veteran
observer of the Korean peninsula.

"Compromise increases the risk of war"

An interview with Katsumi Sato by Neil Weinberg

IN THE LATE 1950s and early 1960s Katsumi Sato worked for a Japanese organization helping ethnic Koreans return to communist North Korea. As word filtered back about how life really was in the Workers' Paradise, Sato became one of North Korea's best informed and fiercest critics. Now 68 and the author of four books on North Korea's Stalinist state, Sato is President of Japan's Modern Korea Institute and publishes its magazine, Gendai Korea (Modern Korea), ten times a year.

On Feb. 26 Sato sat down with FORBES to discuss the impending disaster he sees unfolding on the Korean peninsula.

Modern Korea Institute's Katsumi Sato
"I give North Korea a few months or less."

FORBES: Is North Korea now close to collapse?
Sato: It is not close to collapse. It is collapsing. I give it a few months, or less. **North Korea has been more erratic than ever since President Kim Il Sung's death in 1994. In one week last fall, for example, it held a seminar for foreign investors— and sent a submarine full of commandos into South Korea.**
It is not erratic policy. It's an internal power struggle. Since the death of his father, Kim Jong Il has been unable to

take full control. Instead, he has effectively created his own party, with followers who think an open-door economic policy would destroy socialism. But technocrats centered around (recently purged) Prime Minister Kang Song San believe the economy will be destroyed unless the door is opened.

In the midst of this, [Workers' Party of Korea Secretary] Hwang Jang Yop defected Feb. 12 in Beijing and stated clearly that North Korea will be destroyed unless Kim Jong Il is removed. Since it would be a great defeat for Kim Jong Il and his followers not to do anything in response, they have started to remove the reformers by force. After Defense Minister Choe Kwang died suddenly [on Feb. 21], the list of leaders for his funeral included almost no open-door reformers. It means Kim Jong Il is trying to grab power by force with support from within the military.

But Defense Minister Choe also had a very big group of anti-Kim Jong Il military supporters. It is possible that these people will take action that leads to civil war. Is China, which supports the reformers, going to stand by and do nothing? I don't think so.
What is China's long-term objective on the Korean peninsula?
China wants to keep a cushion between itself and South Korea. That means opposing war, since China

knows North Korea would lose and the armed border would move north to the Yalu River.

China already has a sense of crisis due to the 1994 KEDO [Korean Peninsula Energy Development Organization] agreement, which gave the U.S. a foothold in supplying North Korea with fuel oil and light-water nuclear reactors. It symbolizes the U.S. moving into what China thought of as its own turf. What's developing is a race between the U.S. and China for hegemony on the Korean peninsula in the post-Kim Jong Il era.

Since China's main objective is to retain its cushion, it opposes the current purge of reformists by military people who know nothing but war. China will try to check it.
How?
By stopping aid. Or blocking the border. China doesn't have to announce anything. Just close the border and nothing will get into North Korea.
The U.S., like China, still hopes to engineer a soft landing by exchanging aid for less belligerent behavior. Nuclear reactors in exchange for North Korea's promise to stop its nuclear program. What are the chances of success?
Zero. Zero from the beginning. That was the mistake of the U.S. government. The light-water reactors are made

in South Korea. Building them would require 500 to 1,000 South Korean technicians to enter North Korea. The North would never allow such a large exchange of information and so it will find excuses to stop the project.

The U.S. position has been exactly the same as China's. The U.S. thought it could create a soft landing in North Korea with goods and money, but didn't understand the culture and politics. North Koreans don't listen to other people's opinions and don't compromise. What controls people in North Korea is power, period.

How should the U.S. deal with North Korea?

It should have used power from the beginning. When the U.S. started negotiations with North Korea in June 1993, soon after the Clinton Administration came to power, it compromised by saying it would never use nuclear weapons and promising to

help supply two light-water reactors. If instead the U.S. responded to a breakdown in negotiations by sending the Seventh Fleet into the Sea of

Japan, the North would have had to propose further discussions.

Your State Department thinks if it forces North Korea into a corner North Korea will explode. It is the opposite. Compromise increases the risk of war. We gave them rice and it went to the military or high officials. None got to the people's mouths.

How would North Korea's political collapse affect South Korea?

Economic refugees will naturally flow across the military border into South Korea. Once it begins, it will put a tremendous burden on the South Korean economy. If refugees come to Japan as well, all of East Asia will become unstable.

Another thing to watch: The most important statements released by Hwang Jang Yop since his defection are that there are North Korean spies [in the South Korean government]. If names are disclosed, Kim Young Sam's regime could be destroyed.

Doing Business in China:
It's Far From Easy

Despite considerable progress, inflation and corruption remain serious threats.

by S.R. Nair

CHINA is a land of 1,000,000,000-plus potential consumers, a thought that increasingly is tantalizing the imagination of CEOs across America. Yet, there are many horror stories of people who have lost their shirts (and more) in China. A Dec. 10, 1993, article in *The Wall Street Journal* summarized the phenomenon succinctly:

"China's economic transformation, born in a shift to free markets in 1978, is rapidly coming of age—and it has mouths watering throughout the business world.

"It also has stomachs churning. For while some foreigners may be making hay in China, the roll call of dead and dying enterprises there is also tellingly long. China is no sure bet."

The question that is paramount in the minds of China-watchers today is whether it will become politically unstable after aging leader Deng Ziaoping's death. Historically, political volatility has been a rule, rather than an exception, in China. Indeed, today's uncertainty about the future probably is an improvement over the certainty that the future will be unstable. While there undoubtedly will be a power struggle upon Deng's demise, it is highly unlikely that the new leadership can revert to the old ways of a to-

tally communist society. The genie of economic freedom irreversibly is out of the bottle. Whether China can achieve the transition from a communist economy to a market one without going the Russian way is another cause of worry. However, the Chinese are extremely capable of handling their economy and, unlike the Russians, undoubtedly will deregulate one sector at a time, rather than try to do everything at once.

Unless something really drastic occurs (such as a total falling out between China and the Western nations, primarily the U.S.), the odds are that China will fulfill the prophecy attributed to Nostradamus—that this is the century of the yellow race. As the country began to implement quasi-capitalistic policies, many of the inefficiencies in the system were removed and the economy grew at a phenomenal rate. Although there still are

Mr. Nair is a founding partner of Transpacific Industries Corp., a Los Angeles-based firm specializing in setting up ventures in China.

Photos courtesy of S.R. Nair

The amount of commercial activity in the economically transformed China is booming, as evidenced by the thriving downtown area of Dalian.

From *USA Today Magazine*, January 1996, pp. 27-29. © 1996 by the Society for the Advancement of Education, Inc. Reprinted by permission.

many inefficiencies in the system and, by extension, room for growth as these are removed, the economy is expected to grow briskly. By some estimates, China has the world's third largest Gross National Product after adjustment for purchasing power parity. It is predicted to achieve the largest GNP within the next 10 years. According to World Bank projections, in the year 2002, China would have a gross domestic product of $9.8 trillion, compared to $9.7 trillion for the U.S.

Obviously, China no longer can be ignored. Corporate America should—and must—take advantage by investing in China so that, on the one hand, it could export equipment, technology, and expertise and, on the other, penetrate the burgeoning domestic market. If they ignore China, American corporations will have let the opportunity of a lifetime pass and have missed the chance to participate in an event of historic proportions.

China certainly is not an easy place to do business. There are differences in language, culture, and commerce that must be overcome. China also is an expensive place for foreigners. The cost of living in Beijing is roughly equal to that of New York. Rents of offices and expatriate accommodations are prohibitively high. All this often prompts smaller companies to ask themselves whether they can afford to be in China, rather than whether they can afford not to. With their limited resources—both financial and managerial—it is impractical for small and medium-size firms to set up offices in China. Should the smaller companies, therefore, leave China to the McDonalds, GMs, Motorolas, and AT&Ts? The success of scores of small Hong Kong, Taiwanese, Japanese, and American firms indicates that opportunities exist even for some small enterprises.

How does one go about setting up a business in China? There is no simple, straight answer or formula that can be bottled and sold. Each deal or project has to be studied and all elements researched carefully and thoroughly. The following are some generalizations based on personal experience.

The first and most important step is to find the right partner. This is a key element the world over, but absolutely critical in China. On the face of it, there is no dearth of potential partners in China since everyone is trying to make a quick buck and is on the lookout for rich partners and potential ventures. You need to be able to separate the wheat from the chaff and identify the correct person. Who is a "right" partner? The most important measure is broad-mindedness. An open-minded partner will learn as he goes along, and this will make life easier.

When we set up our first joint venture in China to manufacture electronic components, our partner was a factory with facilities that best could be described as primitive. The managers had limited exposure and a mind-set that sought to have a dormitory for the workers to take a nap during the after-

noons. Nevertheless, we sensed that they had the willingness to learn. Convincing them was a difficult task, but achievable. Once convinced, they accepted and adapted. When the factory finally came on line, the workers—despite receiving training at factories in the U.S.—faced a huge learning curve. Because of this, one so-called expert assured us that we had made a mistake in putting up a hi-tech chemical plant; that we would have had a better return on investment if we had started a plant to make bricks. Today, the factory is one of the most profitable and successful plants in the industry in China.

Evaluating partners

When evaluating a potential partner, you should look not only at the individuals, but also at the organization itself since the people you would be dealing with may be changed in the course of negotiations. Therefore, you should be able to fathom whether the company has a stable organization and management structure. Do they have the required clout with government authorities, banks, and financial institutions to arrange for the necessary approvals without any inordinate delay? Does the project have the support and backing of the banks and authorities? Is there an internal power struggle among the key managers? I can assure you from personal experience, the last thing you want is to get caught in the cross fire of a war between managers.

The Chinese have a built-in suspicion of strangers, so initial rounds of discussions often are in the nature of probes. The Chinese say, "The first time we meet, we are strangers; the next time, we get to know each other a little; and the third time, we become friends. Then, we can talk business." In fact, the Chinese often negotiate to develop a relationship, rather than to tie up loose ends. Many foreigners take this to be a sign of disinterest and drop the project even before it can be considered seriously. The familiarization process can be shortened considerably by using a consultant who has done business in China and is familiar to the Chinese.

It generally is accepted that using a consultant with knowledge and experience in China is more cost-effective than setting up an office there. Selecting the correct consultant is a project by itself and there are pitfalls to be avoided. For instance, choosing a Hong Kong Chinese for a project in northern China may be disastrous since there are social, cultural, and linguistic differences between the Hong Kong Chinese and those in the north. It can be extremely dangerous to rely on an influence peddler, as you could face indifference and even animosity if your contact falls out of favor. There are many large consulting companies that recently have set up shop in China. However, it must be borne in mind that more important than the firm is the per-

son. While the Chinese respect a reputation, a familiar face goes further.

Negotiating in China is like an elaborate ritual or game. Negotiations tend to be long-winded, rather than brief and to the point. More often than not, your counterpart will not let you know his true objectives, so you have to play a guessing game. Your patience is likely to be tested sorely. Even when you have to turn your counterpart down, though, it has to be done with politeness and respect! If, in the course of negotiations, your Chinese counterpart feels that he has lost face—not been accorded proper respect—you can kiss the deal goodbye.

The concept of "face" is extremely important to the Chinese. It is vital that any proposal or request must be declined without being abrasive and in a manner that means your counterpart does not lose face. Often, the Chinese will bring up an issue or proposal "officially" (especially with strangers) only after ensuring that it would not be declined.

A few years ago, we were in Wuhan discussing a project. We were meeting our potential partners for the first time, having been introduced through a common friend. We had two days of discussions that didn't seem to get anywhere. The second evening, the president of the company visited our Chinese colleague for an off-the-record conversation. He indicated that he wished to make a proposal, but wanted to ensure that it would be well received by us before "officially" bringing it up in the next meeting.

In another instance, we were negotiating with our Chinese partners the sale of our shares in a joint venture we had set up. Playing the game, we started with an unreasonably high asking price, and our partners began with a ridiculously low offer. After two days of hard bargaining, we felt that we were in the neighborhood of a fair price. At that point, we stuck to our price and insisted that anything less than what we demanded would be loss of face and that we would rather lose all our shares than our face. We closed the deal a few hours later, but I never have stopped wondering whether I should have brought up the "face" argument a few hundred thousand dollars earlier!

The Chinese are not a very litigious people. Most disputes and disagreements are resolved by the parties through "friendly discussions and consultation"—a phrase one gets familiar with rather soon in China—instead of in a court of law. If you are the kind of person who never leaves home without your attorney's number, China isn't the place for you. In China, the legal system is not very well developed and the rule of law is a tenuous concept. This is a source of discomfort for those used to a system where disputes routinely are taken up in a court of law.

Most contracts in China call for arbitration in a third country, but it is a clause rarely employed. While it is important to have as well-defined a contract as possible, it is more fruitful to develop a good relationship with your partners. Having a good partner is more important than having a good lawyer.

Much has been written about the use of connections and corruption in China. As in many other developing countries, they exist and are widespread. Connections get things done in China. There is even a word for it in Chinese—*guanxi*. At one time, we needed to go from Shijiazhuang to Wuhan and couldn't get any plane or train tickets. Our hosts, representing one of the largest factories in the city, were helpless and their influence worthless. Finally, they located a worker in their factory whose husband was employed by a company that supplied some products to the train station. The worker talked to her husband who talked to his contact who talked to the contact at the train station. The result was that we got our tickets.

Corruption is a major problem in modern China. As disparities of wealth increase, corruption and crime become more rampant. Even in Communist China, inequality always was present; some were always more equal than others. The communists had abolished class, but not rank. The disparity in today's China is much greater and more visible. In a country where the per capita GNP is a mere $370, there are people who can afford to spend $3,500 on a meal and $1,000 for a pair of eyeglasses. Conspicuous consumption has come to China in a big way. I even have heard of people eating meals laced with gold dust.

Meanwhile, as society becomes more nonegalitarian, crime is on the rise. Triads, the Chinese Mafia, which were driven out by the communists, have made a comeback and again are well-entrenched. One stands a 50% chance to be propositioned by a prostitute today, whereas three or four years ago, such instances were rare. If you take a cab from the airport, you are almost certain to be overcharged. Public servants seek to augment their incomes by misusing the authority vested in them. The moral fabric of society is becoming increasingly tattered. The tremendous disparity of wealth and the accompanying potential for corruption are destabilizing influences.

Historically, widespread corruption has been one of the primary causes of revolts in China. The Communist Party came to power, in large part, due to the widespread corruption prevalent under the Nationalists. Now, the

cadres are putting their hands in the till with gay abandon. This is one of China's major problems and is at least as important and relevant to its stability as the issue of leadership.

Periodically, the government initiates action to stem corruption. When they do act, the penalties are severe—often execution. Nevertheless, the spread of corruption continues unabated. You may be faced with situations where a little grease in the right palm may seem the easy way out. The temptation must be resisted strongly. In all our years in China, we have not paid a bribe. In our view, it is counterproductive. It makes more sense, in the long term, to locate and deal with partners who are honest and aboveboard.

An American colleague who was the resident engineer on one of our projects told me of one interesting facet of Chinese entrepreneurship: The early entrepreneurs often had some sort of criminal record. There were reasons for this. The Confucian mode of thought looked down on merchants. Therefore, a career in business was not the most sought-after path for China's best and brightest. On the other hand, people with criminal records found it hard to get jobs and had to resort to small business ventures to earn a living. When the economy opened up and developed, many of these small businesses flourished. Attitudes have changed, though. Even the paramount leader has said, "To be rich is to be glorious."

One has to be patient and committed to succeed in China. There are tremendous opportunities that have to be actualized through diligent and intelligent work. The Chinese perception of time is far different from the Western one. The Chinese lack the sense of urgency and do not value time as much. This is very frustrating for a person in whom the "time is money" concept has been ingrained deeply. The Chinese sense this and often use delaying tactics to take advantage. It is unwise to go into a negotiation with a tight schedule, unless you are selling something that the Chinese desperately need. Negotiations will be dragged on in the hope that they could get you to make concessions at the last minute.

I believe that China could not have come as far as it has without communism, which has played an important role in its development. The communists unified the nation, redistributed land, and broke up the entrenched vested interests. The state also has used its unchecked power to enforce policies which, though unpopular, have been good for the

country. For instance, without the authoritarianism of communism, the one-child policy could not have been enforced and China's population could not have been contained the way it was. The system, with all its inherent cruelty and excesses, has been and still is a necessary evil for China.

As the nation and the economy become more developed and open, the leadership—perhaps without any real desire—has become less dictatorial and overbearing. Increasingly, the authorities take a *laissez-faire* attitude so long as one doesn't engage in political activities. For example, despite the efforts of the central authorities to curb credit as part of the fight against inflation, some local authorities continue to finance pet projects. Inflation, like corruption, remains a serious threat.

China is an exciting place to do business. There is much activity and opportunity. However, China is not for those with frail nerves or delicate stomachs.

Talking about stomachs, banquets are an important part of doing business in China. The Chinese insist on wining and dining you. Often, it is an excuse and an occasion for them to have an extravagant meal. They love to treat you to the delicacies of the region. The Chinese seem to eat everything that moves and a lot of things that don't. I believe there exists a restaurant in Guangzhou where all dishes are made with one delicacy—rats! Fortunately for *our* stomachs, we do not have any business in Guangzhou.

In Shijiazhuang, the dishes included camel and duck paws. My hosts became extremely solicitous when they noticed that I was just nibbling at my food. I told them that, although I ate meat, I preferred fish. Well, they beamed, fish is the next dish. Shortly, the waiters ushered in the fish. It was breathing, its body heaving and jaws moving. Even as the fish seemed to stare at me with a "how-could-you?" look, my hosts scooped a spoonful for me. The fish was dead, my hosts assured me, only it was so fresh that one nerve was still twitching.

We never did close that deal. Perhaps my hosts couldn't trust a *gweilo* (a Cantonese term used to mean foreigner—though the literal translation is "foreign devil," it is used without malice or prejudice) who went from being a meat eater to a fish eater to a vegetarian in the course of a single meal.

Doing Business in Vietnam: A Cultural Guide

Esmond D. Smith, Jr. and Cuong Pham

Now that U.S.-Vietnamese diplomatic ties have been restored, many American businesses are hoping to be in on the development opportunities offered by what some analysts consider to be Asia's newest economic "tiger." Structural problems do abound in Vietnam. Its underdeveloped economic infrastructure, a ponderous and pervasive government bureaucracy, and an embryonic legal system are but a few of them. But the country's dynamism lies in its principle asset—its people.

The population of Vietnam is young: 80 percent of its 73 million people are under the age of 40. They are also well educated, with an overall literacy rate approaching 90 percent. In addition, despite two decades of communist "socialism," Vietnamese have retained a strong work ethic and an energetic sense of entrepreneurialism. Add to these facts the current low cost of labor in the country—the average annual per capita income was under $250 in 1994—and it is easy to understand why foreign businesses and investors are pouring into Vietnam.

Competing successfully in Vietnam against other foreign—mostly Asian—businesses will require that American companies make an effort to understand, respect, and, to some extent, adapt to Vietnamese culture. The purpose of this article is to provide some insights into that culture, with a focus on business and interpersonal communications.

THE IMPORTANCE OF CULTURE

Many Americans fail to see the unique set of traits and approaches they bring to international business dealings. Some of these traits are so ingrained in their psyche that they don't even realize they may differ in other cultures. Americans show they are listening respectfully, for example, by staring into the speaker's eyes as he or she talks. In much of Asia, however, including Vietnam, staring directly into a person's eyes is considered discourteous. Respect in such cultures is shown by keeping one's eyes lowered while someone in authority is speaking. Although Vietnamese who are used to dealing with Americans might understand their behavior, an uninformed American might interpret a Vietnamese's lack of eye contact to indicate lack of interest or respect. This small example illustrates the ease with which misunderstandings can occur if both parties fail to study the culturally conditioned behaviors of the other.

> *Patience, formality, small talk, saving face, preserving harmony, giving and receiving gifts—all can spell the difference between success and failure in dealing with the most recent Asian "tiger."*

From *Business Horizons*, May/June 1996, pp. 47-51. © 1996 by the Foundation for the School of Business at Indiana University. Reprinted by permission.

All cultures have developed certain styles, methods, and actions considered appropriate for interpersonal communication. These often vary greatly among cultures, as will be indicated below. Like most Asian cultures, for example, Vietnam is considered to be "high-context" when it comes to communications. In such a culture, the context—situation, place, attitude, non-verbal behavior, and gestures—is more important than the words spoken in a meeting. Americans, on the other hand, are considered "low-context"; words carry the message, and the context in which they are spoken is relatively unimportant. This major difference between the two cultures will have an obvious impact on the communication process itself as well as on the perceptions a person from each culture might carry away from a meeting. By understanding this and other cultural differences, however, American executives can adjust their communication style and behavior appropriately to put their message across.

SOME VIETNAMESE CULTURAL CHARACTERISTICS

Although culture encompasses many areas, we will examine only a few of those relevant to business situations. These include attitudes toward time, personal relationships, individual and group dynamics, gender issues, and age. It should be noted that in most of these areas, Vietnamese attitudes are very different from those of Americans.

Concepts of Time

Like most Asians, the Vietnamese have a more extended concept of time than that of most Americans. The agrarian nature of their traditional society focuses on seasons rather than days or weeks. And this tradition is reinforced by the Confucian tradition of respect for earlier generations. Americans measure time by the clock, Vietnamese by the monsoon.

Although this is changing somewhat, Vietnamese can still be expected to take a longer view of time and be suspicious of the need for urgency in making decisions or culminating a business deal. Patience remains the ultimate Confucian virtue in personal life as well as in business.

Personal Relationships

In Vietnam, propriety and courtesy play a major role in personal relationships. Vietnamese are generally more interpersonally formal than are Americans. This formality decreases the uncertainty surrounding interpersonal contacts in Vietnamese society and is carried over into the business realm for the same reasons. During initial meetings with Vietnamese officials, you can expect little real business to be accomplished. The Vietnamese will concentrate on getting to know you—your background, your expertise, your character. In their high-context communication culture, they will depend heavily on non-verbal clues to assess meaning. By becoming acquainted and establishing a personal relationship with you, they are merely trying to understand you better.

Vietnamese society is comprised of an interconnected network of personal relationships, all of which carry obligations on both sides. These mutual obligations are the underpinnings of social order in Vietnam, so they are taken very seriously. Americans need to understand and be sensitive to the serious nature of what may seem to them to be casual business relations. Failure to do so could easily result in a loss of trust or credibility, with obvious implications for longer-term relationships.

Individual and Group Dynamics

Vietnamese consider themselves part of a larger collective, generally centered on the family or clan. Individual needs are considered subordinate to those of their family or organization. Conformity to familial and social norms is an important goal. Americans, on the other hand, are highly individualistic, believing in the primacy of the individual as a highly valued ideal.

These differences in values and outlook can have significant implications for business transactions. Praising or singling out an individual for attention or to reward in public, for example, is embarrassing to the individual concerned and will likely be counterproductive. Public rewards are best given to groups, not individuals. Although this cultural characteristic may change over time, it remains prudent to proffer individual rewards in private.

The same general rule is even more important when it comes to criticism or censure. Vietnamese culture considers "face," an individual's public image, extremely important. Any overt public criticism or disparaging remarks can result in a loss of face and cause extreme embarrassment. For this reason, criticism is best handled privately and, if possible, indirectly.

In Vietnam, the ultimate goal of all personal interactions is harmony, not discord. Like many Asians, Vietnamese will try to avoid conflict and direct confrontation. A direct refusal or negative answer is considered impolite and crude, often leading Vietnamese to agree to something even when they have no intention of carrying it out. From a Vietnamese perspective, this is not considered to be untruthful; it is simply the means

> "Americans measure time by the clock, Vietnamese by the monsoon."

for maintaining a harmonious relationship. This Vietnamese attribute offers great potential for cross-cultural misunderstandings with Americans, for whom disagreement and negative responses are merely a part of the negotiating process and have nothing to do with interpersonal relationships.

Gender Issues

Vietnamese society is outwardly egalitarian in accord with Marxist ideology, but continues to exhibit paternalistic, male-dominant attitudes in business and most official activities. So when Vietnamese women hold key positions, they are accorded the respect due that position, even if such is not the case in their personal lives.

On the other hand, foreign women professionals are accepted in Vietnam, particularly if they have high status in their company or strong professional reputations. Such individuals will be treated with the respect their position demands. Business women lacking such status will find it harder to be taken seriously in Vietnam.

Attitudes Toward Age

Like other Confucian cultures, Vietnamese believe that respect for the elderly is a cardinal virtue. Age carries experience and wisdom, and in the traditional extended family the word of the father or grandfather is law. This attitude extends into the business arena. The oldest member of a foreign delegation is often treated with great deference, regardless of his official position or rank. Likewise, it is always appropriate for Americans to defer to the older members of Vietnamese groups by being especially respectful and solicitous.

The corollary to this respect for age is a difficulty in taking young people seriously, especially when it comes to having business expertise or making important decisions. Although this attitude may shift as Vietnam is exposed to the relative youth of many American business executives, it should be recognized as an important characteristic of Vietnamese culture.

BUSINESS PROTOCOL IN VIETNAM

With this brief discussion of Vietnamese cultural characteristics as background, some specific advice may now be offered regarding doing business in Vietnam. Some of the more common business situations that arise in the course of visiting Vietnam will be covered. But these suggestions should also serve as a useful background for dealing with Vietnamese business officials elsewhere.

Written Correspondence

Business connections in Vietnam are best established by mail before arriving in the country. Even if you have already met a Vietnamese official or another contact outside Vietnam, it is still best to arrange for a visit and make appropriate business appointments in Vietnam by letter or other correspondence before your arrival. This allows your contact to clear your visit with the appropriate government organs and to set up an appropriate agenda for your trip.

Do not be surprised if a response to your written request is not immediately forthcoming; Vietnam's pervasive government bureaucracy reacts very slowly. A period of several months between a request and a response is not unusual. Your request will be expedited if you give your Vietnamese contacts a good sense of what it is you want to accomplish in Vietnam. This helps reduce uncertainty and any concerns they or the government may have about your intentions.

In written correspondence, adopt a formal style, using the title and full name of your contact, such as Deputy Minister Nguyen Van Tuan. Vietnamese prefer to be addressed by their first or given name, rather than their family name. For example, Mr. Nguyen Van Tuan, a company director, would be addressed as Director Tuan, not as Director Nguyen. Courteous language and a respectful closing—"with warmest regards," "with deepest respect," and so on—are important as well.

> *"Vietnamese want to get to know you as a person before settling down to business."*

Personal Contact

Westerners are generally given a brief handshake upon meeting in business situations. Not everyone uses this gesture, but it is widely understood in business or official situations. When meeting a Vietnamese woman, however, wait for her to extend a hand first. She may simply nod or bow slightly, the most common form of greeting in Vietnam.

As with written correspondence, use titles and first names ("Deputy Minister Cuong") or simply titles ("Thank you, Deputy Director") in conversation. Use of given names should be reserved only for close friends in very informal situations. A common Vietnamese formal greeting is "Chao-Ong" when addressing men and "Chao-Ba" when addressing women, literally meaning "Hello, Mr." or "Hello, Ms."

Business cards are usually exchanged at all first meetings. They are important in Asia because they provide explicit indications of an individual's position and status. Though not absolutely necessary, business cards with one side printed in Vietnamese are appreciated. These can be obtained before leaving the United States.

Making Conversation

Polite conversation and small talk are an important part of establishing relationships in Vietnam. As a high-context culture, Vietnamese want to get to know you as a person before settling down to business. By understanding your background, personality, and interests, they are better able to comprehend your verbal and non-verbal communication, which helps decrease uncertainty and ambiguity in the relationship. This often means that a first meeting—or even the first several meetings—are spent discussing what Americans would consider to be nonproductive topics. Have patience and recognize that their evaluation of you as an individual will bear directly on your success or failure in business dealings.

Personal distance—the physical distance at which people feel comfortable conversing with others—is generally greater in Vietnam than in the West, unless a personal relationship has been well established. Americans generally feel most comfortable about 18 inches away from the person with whom they are speaking. Latin American and Middle Eastern cultures prefer to stand even closer. In contrast, most Asian cultures stay slightly farther away. In addition, Vietnamese do not like to be touched or patted on the back or shoulders in social situations.

Always try to project an appearance of calm and a benign attitude in social or business situations. Never show emotion, and try not to show any evidence of impatience. Keep in mind that in Vietnam, "face" or status is critically important. Belittling or openly criticizing a Vietnamese, even in jest, can cause irreparable damage to a relationship. Likewise, losing your temper or becoming angry causes you to lose "face" and is considered a demonstration of immaturity.

As indicated above, the Vietnamese as a people do not like to say "no" because a refusal implies disrespect and interferes with the harmony of the relationship. They are not being dishonest or devious but are simply demonstrating that they value the relationship more than a mere fact. Understand this and try to phrase your questions to take it into account. For example, rather than asking "Will it be ready by Tuesday?" ask "When will it be ready?" Continuous exposure to Western business methods may eventually change this cultural trait, but such change will likely occur slowly. In the meantime, a negative response can often be inferred from the hesitancy in answering or from a statement such as "It may be inconvenient" or "It will be very difficult." If you sense this, try to rephrase the question in such a way that your respondent will not have to say "no."

When engaging in social conversation, there are certain topics that should be avoided. These include sex, politics, communism, the Vietnam war, religion, and any inference of Vietnamese inferiority in any area. Likewise, jokes and humor usually do not translate well into other cultures and should be avoided in all but the most informal situations. Safe topics for discussion include your own background and hobbies, your family, your counterpart's family, international sports, Vietnamese culture (including literature, poetry, music, and traditions), language, and food. Exchanging information about one's family and personal interests are a key part of the process of establishing relationships in Vietnam and should be expected. Remember, business will be addressed only after these social niceties are observed.

Business Entertainment

Most business luncheons and dinners are held in hotels, restaurants, or government facilities. Usually your host will arrange for a dinner during the early part of your visit. You are expected to reciprocate by arranging for a return dinner, possibly in your hotel or at a well-known restaurant. If no formal dinner is indicated on your itinerary, you should still try to invite your hosts to dinner to show your thanks and appreciation for their arrangements. Business is not usually discussed at dinners, although it may be at luncheons.

Dinner in Vietnam usually consists of several courses, similar to a Chinese banquet. Several dishes will be put on the table and you will be expected to take some from each. Chopsticks are used in Vietnam, but most modern restaurants also have Western eating utensils.

Vietnamese beer or imported wines and liquor are usually served with the meal. It is appropriate for you and your host to exchange toasts, with the host usually going first. Individual toasts can also be expected during the meal. When toasting your host (or when acting as host yourself), stand and raise your glass with both hands in the direction of the senior or oldest Vietnamese present. A flowery but short speech about Vietnam's beautiful scenery, the friendship of your hosts, and prospects for a successful business venture are appropriate. Subsequent toasts may be made and answered from your seat. The end of the meal is usually signaled by a plate of fruit or other sweet dish. After waiting a respectful period after the last course is consumed, the guest is expected to make the first move to leave. Be sure to shake hands with all Vietnamese participants and conclude by thanking your host profusely.

Gifts are expected and should be prepared for presentation during the first day's meeting, either during a break or at the close of the day. You will be expected to bring enough gifts for all of the official participants in your meetings. Such gifts can be small and relatively inexpensive. Tie tacks, pen knives, pictorial books, or similar gifts, made in the United States and preferably inscribed with your company logo, are appropriate. More expensive gifts, such as an inscribed pen and pencil set or a bottle of Western liquor, for example, might be reserved as a departure gift for your hosts. All gifts should be wrapped, but white or black paper should not be used because these colors are associated with death. Vietnamese may or may not open these gifts when they are received; leave the option to them. If the gift is especially expensive or unique, you might suggest that the recipient open it later to preclude embarrassment in front of the group.

You will also receive gifts and should defer to your host as to whether you should open it when received or not. Regardless of when it is opened or what it is, profuse thanks are always appropriate.

This brief survey of Vietnam's culture is meant to be merely an introductory primer for Americans seriously interested in doing business in Vietnam. Many excellent books are available for further study. Our intent, however, is to demonstrate the critical importance of cultural sensitivity and understanding in dealing with Vietnamese. American and Vietnamese cultures have many differing values and customs. To be effective in doing business with Vietnam, Americans must understand the differences between the two and adapt appropriately. If this is done, a long-lasting and mutually beneficial relationship can result.

Esmond D. Smith, Jr. is an assistant professor of international business at Johnson and Wales University in Providence, Rhode Island, as well as a consultant specializing in cross-cultural communications. **Cuong Pham**, a native of Vietnam, is the president of Pham Marketing Network, which provides market research and other business services for companies seeking opportunities in Vietnam, and a business columnist for *Thi Truong Tu Do (Free Market)* magazine.

EARN 20% INVE

Here's why foreign shares are poised to clobber U.S. stocks in '97.

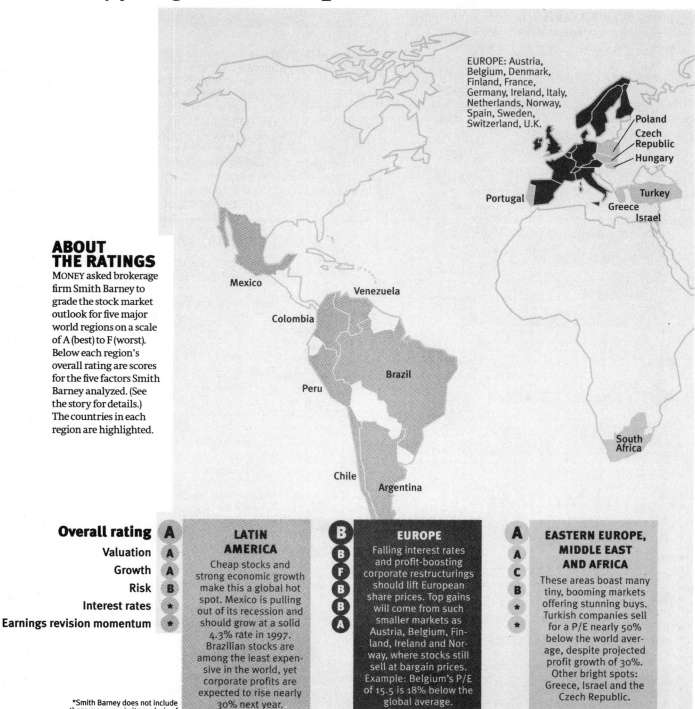

EUROPE: Austria, Belgium, Denmark, Finland, France, Germany, Ireland, Italy, Netherlands, Norway, Spain, Sweden, Switzerland, U.K.

Poland
Czech Republic
Hungary
Portugal
Turkey
Greece
Israel

Mexico
Venezuela
Colombia
Peru
Brazil
Chile
Argentina
South Africa

ABOUT THE RATINGS

MONEY asked brokerage firm Smith Barney to grade the stock market outlook for five major world regions on a scale of A (best) to F (worst). Below each region's overall rating are scores for the five factors Smith Barney analyzed. (See the story for details.) The countries in each region are highlighted.

Overall rating — A
Valuation — A
Growth — A
Risk — B
Interest rates — *
Earnings revision momentum — *

LATIN AMERICA

Cheap stocks and strong economic growth make this a global hot spot. Mexico is pulling out of its recession and should grow at a solid 4.3% rate in 1997. Brazilian stocks are among the least expensive in the world, yet corporate profits are expected to rise nearly 30% next year.

B
B
F
B
B
A

EUROPE

Falling interest rates and profit-boosting corporate restructurings should lift European share prices. Top gains will come from such smaller markets as Austria, Belgium, Finland, Ireland and Norway, where stocks still sell at bargain prices. Example: Belgium's P/E of 15.5 is 18% below the global average.

A
A
C
B
*
*

EASTERN EUROPE, MIDDLE EAST AND AFRICA

These areas boast many tiny, booming markets offering stunning buys. Turkish companies sell for a P/E nearly 50% below the world average, despite projected profit growth of 30%. Other bright spots: Greece, Israel and the Czech Republic.

*Smith Barney does not include these measures in its analysis of the emerging markets.

 Reprinted with special permission from *Money*, Forecast 1997 issue, pp. 98-100, 103, 105-107. © 1997 by Time Inc. Magazine Company.

STING ABROAD

We identify the hot markets—and offer 12 top fund picks.

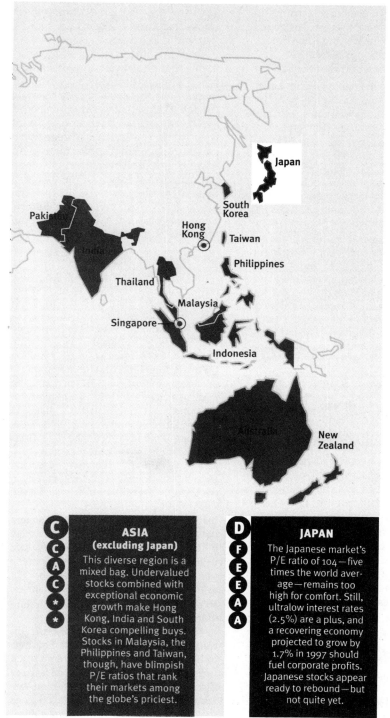

C
C
A
C
*
*

ASIA
(excluding Japan)

This diverse region is a mixed bag. Undervalued stocks combined with exceptional economic growth make Hong Kong, India and South Korea compelling buys. Stocks in Malaysia, the Philippines and Taiwan, though, have blimpish P/E ratios that rank their markets among the globe's priciest.

D
F
E
E
A
A

JAPAN

The Japanese market's P/E ratio of 104—five times the world average—remains too high for comfort. Still, ultralow interest rates (2.5%) are a plus, and a recovering economy projected to grow by 1.7% in 1997 should fuel corporate profits. Japanese stocks appear ready to rebound—but not quite yet.

BY MARK BAUTZ

BET YOU DON'T KNOW THIS: WHILE U.S. stocks have raced ahead 17.5% so far this year, more than a dozen foreign markets—including Brazil, Hong Kong, Ireland and Taiwan—have fared even better. What's more, many investment pros expect international equities to beat U.S. shares handily in 1997. "The coming year looks like one of the best for foreign stocks since the early 1990s," says Douglas Johnson, senior international investment strategist at Merrill Lynch in New York City.

Experts point to three reasons why foreign stocks will shine next year: Corporate profits are revving up overseas, interest rates are heading down, and stocks in many foreign firms are trading at bargain prices. The result, says Henry Frantzen, global chief investment officer at Federated Investors in New York City: "Emerging markets equities could return 30% next year, while Europe could gain 20% or so." By contrast, MONEY chief investment strategist Michael Sivy predicts U.S. shares will plummet 15% before eventually recovering for a meager 7% return for the year.

Moreover, since foreign markets tend to move in different cycles than the U.S. market over periods of five years or longer, international equities can provide a potent defense against downturns in U.S. stocks. A portfolio invested 70% in domestic shares and 30% in foreign stocks, for example, offers comparable returns to an all-American portfolio with about 10% less risk. "Buying foreign shares now gives you some of the world's best companies at extremely cheap prices," says Earl Osborn, a principal at San Francisco investment advisory firm Bingham Osborn & Scarborough, "and you reduce the overall volatility of your portfolio."

Given the ebullient outlook for foreign markets, many advisers urge long-term investors angling for growth to boost their international stake to 20% to 35% of their stockholdings. To uncover the best buys among the world's 44 or so foreign markets, we interviewed more than two dozen international investing experts. We begin by laying out the prospects for five regions around the globe and then focusing on a dozen international stock funds that invest in the countries expected to lead the pack in 1997.

For an overview of the world's markets, MONEY turned to leading international strategist Leila Heckman, managing director of brokerage firm Smith Barney's Global Asset Allocation group. Heckman's forecast for MONEY last year proved to be right on the mark. Her top pick a year ago, Latin America, posted solid gains led by Brazil, up 28% (to Nov. 1); Japan, which Heckman panned, lost 10.8%.

Heckman's 1997 outlook for five major foreign regions appears in the map on pages 98 and 99. To calculate these grades, she and her team of three analysts applied a proprietary forecasting model to 42 countries divided into these five regional groupings: Europe, Japan, Asia excluding Japan, Latin America and Eastern Europe/Middle East/Africa. Heckman based her rankings on five criteria, each of which received separate scores. She then combined the five scores to determine the regions' overall grades of A (best) to F (worst).

The five factors: **stock market valuation** (responsible for 50% of the final grade), taking into account price/earnings ratios based on current and projected corporate profits, and price-to-book ratios (a measure of the market value of the region's stocks compared with the net worth of its companies); **economic growth** (10%), including estimates for projected growth in both gross domestic product (GDP) and export volume; **risk** (10%), which reflects, among other things, the value of a country's currency relative to that of its leading trading partners; **interest rates** (10%), both short and long term; and **earnings revision momentum** (20%), which rewards countries where companies have had the highest percentage of earnings estimates revised upward over the past one and six months.

So where do Heckman and her analysts see the best opportunities in 1997? The emerging markets—especially Eastern Europe and Latin America—along with developed Europe. Here is a profile of each region:

Heckman's top-scoring markets, those in **Eastern Europe/Middle East/Africa**, make up just 3% of the world's stock market wealth (not counting the U.S.) but are nonetheless packed with a bounty of cheap stocks that have superior growth potential. For example, while the regions' forecast earnings growth of 17% and export growth of 7.7% are above the global

STRATEGIST JOHNSON

"I like the emerging markets, where 20%-or-better earnings growth could mean big returns."

average, their average P/E ratio of 14 (based on the most recent 12 months' earnings) is 26% below the global average. Heckman especially favors Turkey and Israel, where forecast P/E ratios are respectively 62% and 31% below the world average of 13.

A 13% run-up in stock prices in **Latin America** this year has made bargain hunting difficult, but you can still scoop up undervalued shares, especially in Brazil and Mexico. For example, in Mexico—which has climbed out of the recession that had kept share prices frozen since 1994—the price-to-book ratio of 1.7 is 19% below the world average and the forecast 1997 P/E ratio of 9 is 31% below the global average.

GDP in Europe is projected to increase just 2.5% next year, but the region's markets figure to enjoy solid gains, thanks to falling interest rates and fatter corporate profits as many countries slog their way out of recessions. Heckman prefers some of the smaller markets, such as Belgium, Finland and Ireland. In Ireland the economy is projected to grow at a 4.9% pace next year, or more than two percentage points faster than Europe overall.

The outlook for **Asia excluding Japan** is decidedly mixed. Despite jitters over China's takeover in July, Hong Kong's estimated P/E of 12 (8% below the world average) and high export growth of 9.2% (33% above) should lead to strong stock gains, as should India's combination of forecast 6.3% GDP growth and below-average P/E ratio of 9. Malaysia and Taiwan, however, are the two priciest world markets that Heckman follows—with forecast P/E ratios 38% or more above the global norm. Cautions Heckman: "In Asia, investors have to pick and choose with extreme care."

As for **Japan**, Heckman is encouraged by the country's low interest rates—10-year bonds yield just 2.5%—and 18% projected corporate profit growth. But even though Japan's market remains 46% below its December 1989 peak, Heckman believes that Japanese stock prices are still high, given their forecast P/E of 37,

which is nearly triple the world average. Thus she rates Japan a "D" and figures stocks there won't take off for another six months or longer.

To profit from this overview, we recommend that you invest in a diversified group of funds that own shares in one or more of our higher-rated regions, as do the dozen below that were recommended by the experts we interviewed. Six of these funds are diversified—three emphasize European stocks, one focuses on Asian equities and two invest in emerging markets securities. In the final section of the story, we highlight six regional funds that specialize in Europe, Latin America and Asia. (For performance data on the funds, see the table.)

DIVERSIFIED FUNDS

Diversified international funds, which typically buy stocks in 20 or more countries to reduce volatility, make an excellent core holding for 50% or more of your international stake. One diversified fund closely aligned with Smith Barney's 1997 forecast is $1.2 billion **Oakmark International,** with a hefty 52% of assets in Europe, 31% in emerging markets (including 14% in Latin America) and just 2% in Japan. Managers David Herro, 36, and Michael Welsh, 33, are long-term investors who like firms that use their excess cash productively— say, to fund profit-generating expansion or to buy back their own stock. One such company is $1.3 billion (estimated 1996 sales) EVC International, a maker of hard plastics that has already bought back nearly 5% of its shares and may purchase another 5% over the next two years. The fund holds a concentrated portfolio of just 55 issues—vs. the 171 average for its peers—in 23 countries. Herro explains: "We don't want to dilute our best ideas."

For a fund that follows the more traditional approach of keeping its holdings in line with those of major foreign stock indexes, Jackson, Miss. financial adviser Tim Medley recommends $5 billion **Vanguard International Growth.** Managed since 1981 by Richard Foulkes, 51, the fund

A DOZEN ROUTES TO BIG GLOBAL GAINS IN '97

The 12 funds below offer a passport to profits in foreign stocks. Six are diversified portfolios, while six others focus on specific regions. The funds are listed in the order that they appear in the story, with our two closed-end choices shown separately.

OPEN-END FUNDS	% gain (or loss) to Nov. 4			Largest regional or country holdings (% of assets)[4]	% maximum sales charge	Minimum initial investment	Telephone (800)
	1996	Three years[3]	Five years[3]				
Oakmark International	20.5	8.2	—	Europe (52), Latin America (14)	None	$2,500	625-6275
Vanguard International Growth	8.5	10.5	11.3	Europe (50), Japan (28)	None	3,000	851-4999
Tweedy Browne Global Value	15.2	12.8	—	Europe (60), Japan (16)	None	2,500	432-4789
Warburg Pincus International Equity	5.4	9.2	10.9	Asia (30), Europe (30)	None	2,500	927-2874
Templeton Developing Markets Trust	15.7	7.3	10.9	Asia (38), Latin America (29)	5.75	100	292-9293
Invesco European Small Company	25.9	—	—	U.K. (32), France (12)	None	1,000	525-8085
Vontobel Eastern European Equity	39.2[1]	—	—	Poland (38), Hungary (31)	None	1,000	527-9500
Scudder Latin America	22.2	5.7	—	Brazil (47), Mexico (26)	None	2,500	225-2470
Colonial Newport Tiger	5.8	8.5	19.7	Hong Kong (47), Singapore (21)	5.75	1,000	248-2828
Guinness Flight Asia Small Cap	5.3[2]	—	—	Hong Kong (41), Malaysia (19)	None	5,000	915-6565
Morgan Stanley EAFE Index	3.3	6.6	7.7				
Morgan Stanley Emerging Mkts. Index	2.5	4.0	9.4				

CLOSED-END FUNDS	Recent price	% premium (or discount)	% gain (or loss) to Nov. 4			Largest regional or country holdings (% of assets)[4]
			1996	Three years[3]	Five years[3]	
Templeton Emerging Markets (EMF)[5]	$17.75	1.0	21.6	8.7	20.4	Asia (48), Latin America (25)
Latin America Equity (LAQ)[5]	16.75	(17.0)	12.5	6.8	13.1	Brazil (29), Chile (23)

Notes: [1]Since inception Feb. 16, 1996 [2]Since inception April 29, 1996 [3]Annualized [4]Asia includes Pacific Basin countries other than Japan. [5]Trades on New York Stock Exchange
Sources: Morningstar, the fund companies.

holds more than 180 stocks in 23 countries with 50% of its assets in Europe, 17% in emerging markets and 28% in Japan. Foulkes seeks overlooked growth companies trading below the value of their future earnings. One example: $20 billion ING, a sleepy Netherlands insurer that Foulkes bought five years ago. The stock has since risen more than 200% yet still trades at a modest P/E of 12.

Investors looking to cash in on small foreign companies selling at discounts to their underlying asset value or earnings potential should consider $1.1 billion **Tweedy Browne Global Value**. The 239-stock fund spreads its holdings over 21 countries (including the U.S., which accounts for 15% of assets) and avoids volatile emerging markets; 52% of its assets are in firms with stock market capitalizations of $1 billion or less. Since small-company stock prices in some European countries have yet to rebound from recession levels, co-manager John Spears says he's finding "the kind of small-company stock bargains we haven't seen in the U.S. in 20 years." One example: Italy's $200 million Franco Tosi, a water distributor that's selling at a 67% discount to its book value.

If you prefer a diversified fund that

FUND MANAGERS HERRO AND WELSH

"We look for out-of-favor stocks that have great prospects for long-term gains."

tilts its mix toward Asian shares, adviser Osborn recommends $3.4 billion **Warburg Pincus International Equity**. Lead manager Richard King, 52, has 22% of assets in smaller Pacific Rim markets such as South Korea and Taiwan and another 29% in Japan. King and his team of four managers look for companies that can capitalize on major economic trends. One such company, says King, is $10 billion DDI Corp., a large player in Japan's rapidly growing (120% annually) cellular-phone industry.

Once you've chosen a core of diversified funds, you may want to expand into emerging markets portfolios, making them 20% to 50% of your foreign hold-

ings. This strategy is especially appropriate for 1997, since most experts pick these developing regions to post the highest returns. Emerging markets funds can take double-digit pratfalls, however, so plan on staying aboard at least five years. Further, be sure to learn how heavily your other international funds are invested in emerging markets so that you don't wind up with too big a stake in these volatile stocks. Oakmark International, for example, recently kept 31% of its assets in developing nations, while Tweedy Browne Global Value had less than 2%.

Tricia Rothschild, international editor of *Morningstar Mutual Funds*, recommends $3.2 billion **Templeton Developing Markets Trust**, managed by 59-year-old Mark Mobius, a 30-year veteran of the global investing scene. Mobius seeks out emerging market stocks that are cheap relative to their peers or their historical trading prices. He has spread his fund's assets among some 491 securities in 32 countries, ranging from Argentina to Zimbabwe. Just under 40% of the fund's assets are in Asia (including a 17% stake in Hong Kong), while another 29% chunk is invested in Latin America, where Mobius likes firms like $11.6 billion Telebras, Brazil's near-monopoly phone company.

Closed-end fund investors now have a rare opportunity to buy Mobius' $290 million **Templeton Emerging Markets** at a bargain price. (Unlike open-end funds, closed-ends trade like stocks on major exchanges, where investor demand determines their share price. As a result, they can sell at a discount or a premium to net asset value—NAV—the per-share value of securities in their portfolios.) Templeton Emerging Markets, which is managed in a similar style to its open-end sibling above, recently traded at just 1% above its NAV, vs. a premium of as much as 37.8% in January 1996. In addition to profiting from gains in the fund's underlying assets, investors have a shot at extra returns if the fund's market price again soars to a blimpish premium.

REGIONAL FUNDS

Aggressive investors may want to shoot for even higher returns by investing, say, 5% to 10% of their foreign stash in one or more of the six regional funds below.

◆ **Europe.** Morningstar's Tricia Rothschild recommends $122 million **Invesco European Small Company**, which invests in small, fast-growing firms. Managers Andy Crossley, 33, and Claire Griffiths, 30, monitor a database of more than 2,600 stocks in 13 countries, searching for ones with market values of less than $1 billion that, for example, have above-average growth potential yet sell at below-average P/E ratios. Recently, 32% of assets were invested in Great Britain.

ADVISER OSBORN

"Many of the world's best foreign companies are selling at extremely attractive prices."

This relatively new fund, launched in February 1995, is off to a blazing start—up 25.9% for the year to Nov. 4. But small stocks can be flighty—the fund dropped 4.7% last July. If you find such a single-month drop scary, you ought to pass on this one.

Emerging Europe is an area that many pros expect to deliver huge gains over the next five years or so. Sheldon Jacobs, editor of the monthly newsletter *No-Load Fund Investor* ($129 a year; 800-252-2042), recommends $56 million **Vontobel Eastern European Equity**, which has the biggest chunk (38%) of its assets in Poland and lesser amounts spread around such countries as Hungary (31%), Russia (14%) and the Czech Republic (6%). The fund, launched in February 1996, is up 39.2% to Nov. 4.

◆ **Latin America.** To invest in Latin America, George Foot, a partner at Newgate Management Associates, a New York City investment adviser, recommends $143 million closed-end fund **Latin America Equity**. Manager Emilio Bassini, 46, spreads his assets among 110 stocks in 10 countries, led by Brazil (29% of assets), where GDP growth is expected to double in 1997 to 5%. Latin American Equity recently traded at 17% less than asset value, far below than its usual 4.3% discount.

Open-end fund investors can choose $630 million **Scudder Latin America**, one of the few Latin America funds that's been around long enough to establish a three-year record. Rather than making bets on specific countries, lead manager Ed Games, 59, looks for companies that invest their excess cash wisely or are market leaders, such as $2.6 billion Companhia Cervejaria Brahma, Brazil's leading beermaker. Lately, he's been

finding the best buys for his 75-stock portfolio in Brazil (47% of assets) and Mexico (26%).

◆ **Asia.** To get a healthy helping of blue-chip stocks in the so-called Asian Tiger countries—including Indonesia, Singapore and South Korea—investors can select top-performing $1.6 billion **Colonial Newport Tiger**. Managers Jack Mussey, 55, and Tim Tuttle, 55, are focused on large companies in the seven markets that have the strongest GDP growth, most predictable earnings and lowest P/E ratios. Hong Kong now accounts for 47% of the fund's assets. Says Tuttle: "Hong Kong is a dynamic economy with a market that's trading at roughly a 25% discount to its Asian peers because of investors' fears about China's takeover in July." Tuttle doubts China will clamp down on Hong Kong's freewheeling capitalism, since Hong Kong's thriving market is China's best source for much needed foreign investment.

Finally, Orleans, Mass. investment adviser John P. Dessauer recommends $14 million **Guinness Flight Asia Small Cap**, which seeks to cash in on fast-growing small companies. Manager Nerissa Lee, 48, has invested 41% of her fund's assets in Hong Kong, where economic growth is forecast at 4% to 5% for 1997, and put a small side bet (4%) on China, a country that's rebounding from recession and is expected to expand at a 10%-plus pace next year. "China and Hong Kong will be the world's fastest-growing economies," says Dessauer. "And Guinness Flight Asia Small Cap has a big stake in the small, rapidly growing companies that should benefit most."

Reporter associate: Paul Lim

Europe In The Global Financial World

ADAPTING TO THE CHALLENGES OF THE THIRD MILLENNIUM

Address by MICHEL CAMDESSUS, *Managing Director of the International Monetary Fund*
Videotaped for presentation at the European Banking and Financial Forum, Prague, Czech Republic, March 19, 1996

I welcome this opportunity to speak to you at the European Banking and Financial Forum — even if it must be from the distance of Washington. If my other obligations had permitted, I would have much preferred to join you and our hosts in Prague. Still, I hope that I will be able to contribute to your discussions. And after all, when talking about globalization, shouldn't we take as a working hypothesis that distance matters less and less?

I have been asked to speak about the challenges of the third millennium and how Europe should prepare to meet them in a world of global financial markets. In fact, this is a key question facing all countries — and it touches on one of the most important aspects of the work of the IMF — helping countries to strengthen their economic policies so that they will be prepared for both the challenges and the opportunities of the global economy.

From my vantage point, I see many opportunities — for Europe and the world. Will Europe be able to seize these opportunities? Well, given that the future is always uncertain — not the least in matters of economics and finance — I ought to be cautious in my remarks. But, in fact, I am quite hopeful about what could be achieved in Europe — and the rest of the world — with good policies, more effective international coordination, and, of course, a lot of persistence and hard work. So let me put aside the circumspection and gravitas expected of the head of an international institution and suggest an outline of the future for Europe and the global economy.

What does the future hold for Europe and the world?

First, there is every reason to expect that the international capital markets will continue to grow larger, more complex and more closely integrated. Further advances in technology, the continued removal of capital controls, the scope for additional portfolio diversification, and the availability of increasing amounts of investment capital as industrial countries, in particular, reduce their fiscal deficits — all of these factors should contribute to the further development of the international capital markets.

Moreover, once EU members move to a single currency — and this, I believe, is both desirable and feasible within the Maastricht timetable for EMU — we can expect to see a broader and deeper European financial market. Many factors will work in this direction, not least of which will be the use of one very strong currency to anchor macroeconomic policy and to denominate European trade and investment; the development of a unified market for government securities issued by EMU members; a large and increasingly dynamic internal market; expanding trade with the rest of the world; and, thanks to further fiscal consolidation, larger amounts of European savings available for investment in Europe and abroad, lower interest rates, and lower risk premia.

I would add that these same developments should help Europe return to the solid growth and higher employment of earlier years. Brighter prospects in the European Union should, in turn, provide further incentives for other European countries — notably those in central and eastern Europe — to complete the structural adjustments required for them to join the EU, as well. Hence, I would not be surprised to see — demanding as the challenge may be — both a wider and a closer European Union.

Second, with more countries pursuing sound policies, and with markets continuing to channel capital into promising investments around the globe, we can expect to see a number of major new players in the international economy. This will be a very positive development, since, with more engines of growth, the world economy could become increasingly resilient. Indeed, there has already been a major shift in the relative economic size of the United States and Asia. Between 1966 and 1988, the relative size of the U.S. economy (measured in terms of purchasing power parities) declined from 27 percent of total world output to 21 percent; while the share of Asia (including Japan) rose from 18 percent to 32 percent. Such shifts are likely to continue during the next century, making todays rankings of a countries economic strength seem as anachronistic as yesterday's debates of North versus South.

I would venture that among the next countries to burst upon the global economy will be a number of the transition economies — countries like the Czech Republic, whose early and determined start on stabilization and reform under the leadership of President Havel and Prime Minister Klaus has paid off in the early resumption of growth and strong capital inflows. In many cases, we will no longer think of these countries as transition economies, for the transition, as such, will be over. Russia, too, has enormous potential, assuming that it perseveres with its strong adjustment program.

From *Vital Speeches of the Day,* May 15, 1996, pp. 450-452. © 1996 by City News Publishing Company, Inc. Reprinted by permission.

Of course, as positive as these developments will be for global prosperity, the world economy will not be risk free. As Mexico illustrated just last year, markets are sensitive to changes in economic fundamentals. Any significant relaxation of policy discipline — and other events that might trigger a shift in market sentiment — will continue to have potentially costly effects. True, the world is now more aware of these risks, and precautions are being taken by the IMF and its members to minimize them. Nevertheless, I think that we can safely warn you that Mexico will not be the last crisis.

In fact, with larger and more closely integrated capital markets, future crises may be still more destabilizing — both for the country immediately concerned and for the world economy at large. This has implications both for Europe and for us in the Fund. As regards to Europe, I would not be surprised if its more prominent role in global financial markets made it feel such crises more keenly in the future than it has in the past! For the Fund, it means we must continue to strengthen our surveillance over country policies and performance, so that emerging problems can be addressed before they become full blown crises. It also means that we must ensure that we have adequate resources to continue fulfilling our mandate: to give confidence to members by making the general resources of the Fund temporarily available to them under adequate safeguards, thus providing them with the opportunity to correct maladjustments in their balance of payments without resorting to measures destructive of national or international prosperity. Here, I was quoting from our Articles of Agreement.

A second risk is that of greater protectionism. As developing countries increase exports — especially in agriculture and basic industry, where many of these countries have, or are likely to develop, a comparative advantage — trade competition will surely intensify. In many industrial countries, the prospect of increased competition, reduced employment in some sectors, and declines in their shares of global output will prompt some to think of globalization in terms of winners and losers. But this will be a very short sighted and ultimately self-defeating point of view. The inevitable changes in relative economic size will not necessarily be detrimental to the countries whose economic weights decline; on the contrary, as long as the global economy continues to expand, even countries with a decreasing share of the total can still enjoy rising levels of domestic income. Of course, the way to achieve this is to ensure that trade continues to be an essential engine of growth. By encouraging countries to specialize production according to comparative advantage, trade will promote a virtuous cycle of increased investment and productivity, leading to a further expansion of world output and trade. It is clear, however, that increasing trade competition will call for permanent structural changes in industrial countries, including more flexible labor markets, better worker training and retraining, and more effective social safety nets.

Finally, you may wonder what kind of international currency arrangements I envision for the next century. To begin with, the continued expansion of world trade, direct foreign investment, and other international capital flows should make the costs of exchange rate misalignments and the benefits of exchange rate stability all the more apparent. Let us hope that the success of EMU will provide the world with some useful lessons on the merits of working hard and paying the necessary price for international monetary stability, as the European countries did. At the same time, however, the emergence of many new players in the international system will probably make policy coordination all the more necessary and demanding, requiring more effective cooperation among the major countries and groups of countries. This latter trend will reinforce the need for the IMF to play a central role in promoting international monetary cooperation and providing the machinery for consultation and collaboration on international monetary problems. And, however strong the world's main currencies turn out to be, perhaps the world will see the need for an even stronger central monetary asset — such as the SDR — to help anchor the international monetary system.

So these are broad outlines of my vision for the future: a more dynamic global economy based on free trade and a high degree of capital mobility; a more dynamic European economy and a more prominent role for Europe in the global financial markets and in the international monetary system following EMU; and greater international monetary cooperation, leading to a more stable international financial system.

No doubt some of you will find this vision too optimistic. I hope that you will be proven wrong! In any event, I assure you — and this we will agree upon — that I have no illusions about the amount of effort that will be required to turn these aspirations into reality. Let me say a few words, then, about what the major requirements are.

First, all countries will need to pursue high quality policies. As I indicated earlier, I see great benefits in a single European currency — for Europe and the world — but EMU is neither a panacea for Europe's problems nor a substitute for fundamental reform. Irrespective of EMU, European countries need to reduce their fiscal deficits — both to ensure a reasonable degree of price stability without overburdening monetary policy, and to allow for adequate levels of investment and growth. Moreover, deficit reduction must be long lasting — both for the health of European economies, and for the sustainability of EMU. Accordingly, European governments need to address, among other issues, the problems of health care and pension costs — an additional structural burden on public finances that will become increasingly onerous with the aging of Europe's population.

At the same time, Europe needs to rethink its present labor market policies. It has become increasingly apparent that the current impediments to job search and job creation not only complicate deficit reduction, they also aggravate the problems of unemployment and low growth, and even undermine the social welfare that these policies were supposed to help protect. Clearly, reform is needed. Moreover, in order for EMU to work well over the longer term, EU members will need to increase both domestic labor market flexibility and international labor mobility within Europe, since exchange rate flexibility will no longer be available to correct competitiveness problems. Tackling these problems now would help boost market confidence, lower interest premia, and thereby facilitate adjustment and convergence.

I have also mentioned my hope for wider European integration. So far, the EU has negotiated Europe Agreements with ten transition economies. All of these countries have made progress in liberalizing, opening, stabilizing, and reforming their economies. But challenges remain, including the need to reduce inflation, reform budgets and social security systems, strengthen the financial sector, and accelerate progress on privatization and enterprise reform. With or without EU membership, these reforms will need to be made. But the prospect of EU membership can help support the transition — by providing a road map, a cooperative framework, and a boost to confidence.

I think enlargement can also help bring positive changes on the other side of the partnership — by acting as a catalyst for the reform of European institutions, including the Common Agricultural Policy. The world must also hope that as the EU evolves and lowers trade barriers vis-a-vis associated countries, it and its non EU trading partners will also lower barriers on a multilateral basis, and thereby contribute to freer world trade.

The development of the financial markets also calls for action to strengthen the soundness of domestic banking systems, by reinforcing internal controls and prudential supervision. At the same time, however more could be done to strengthen the role of the market in ensuring the soundness of financial systems — for example, by encouraging the market to provide high quality and standardized information on financial sector operations and by governments adopting appropriate exit policies vis-a-vis financial institutions. As the markets become more global and interconnected, initiatives such as these would be a useful complement to official oversight.

Finally, a few words on the requirements for greater international financial stability — not just in Europe, but among all the major currencies. If countries want to achieve greater stability — and I do believe that it is in all of their interests to do so — they must work for it. Thus, in addition to pursuing firm domestic policies, countries must also coordinate their policies more effectively. What will this entail? It will entail countries making a greater effort to understand the interests and policies of others. It will involve countries listening more carefully to the judgments of others about their own economic policies. And finally it will require countries to take a more enlightened view of their own national interests — they will have to recognize that taking the interests of other countries into account is in their own self interest.

I hope these remarks will provoke you to think not of what is, but of what should be. I think you will agree that the opportunities are great both for Europe and the world.

The discreet charm of provincial Asia

A new breed of foreign investors is looking on Asia as one big market. They are building their factories ever further away from its teeming cities and relying less on local partners

WITHIN the next few weeks, America's General Motors (GM) will decide whether to build a $500m car plant in Thailand or the Philippines. Both countries are competing fiercely for the factory, which will create thousands of new jobs. Whichever country wins, three things are certain: the factory will not be a joint venture; it will not be built anywhere near the congested capitals of Bangkok or Manila; and 80% of its products will be exported.

The new GM factory is typical of the new sort of foreign investment in Asia. It also vividly illustrates the keenness with which Asian governments are pursuing investors. Both companies and politicians, it seems, now think less about a factory in terms of its local market and more about its regional role serving developing Asia's oft-mentioned "1 billion consumers". Like most transitions, the change is far from instantaneous. All the same, it does seem to have started Asian governments on a race to bring down tariffs and taxes.

In the past, GM's experience as a foreign investor in Asia was fairly typical. To break into a country the car maker usually had to spar with protectionist politicians; once there, it usually invested with a local partner (in some cases, it has had no choice: GM got into China only after agreeing to jump into bed with a Shanghai car factory). Sometimes these partners prove valuable guides; often they are a liability. With its

new factory, GM has decided that it is better off doing the whole thing itself.

That is partly because it will be a different sort of factory making a different sort of car. Elsewhere in Asia, GM has run relatively small joint ventures; its factories in Taiwan and Indonesia each assemble some 20,000 vehicles a year for their domestic markets. The new factory will churn out 100,000 cars a year. Based on GM's German-built Opel models, they will also have to be good enough to be exported anywhere in Asia—even to the fussy Japanese.

Other big car firms are considering a similar approach. Ford and Mazda are already building a $500m factory in the Thai countryside which will manufacture pick-up trucks, many of them for export. Indeed, virtually every big multinational manufacturer in Asia—not to mention most of the more sophisticated overseas Chinese family companies—are looking for ways to "regionalise" their production.

Although these decisions are driven by industrial logic, they are made possible by politics. Five years ago, GM might have found no country in Asia prepared to let in a factory on such terms. Now it has two on the shortlist. This reflects the desire of governments in South-East Asia to react to competitive pressures of their own—particularly the emergence of China and India.

The Association of South East Asian Nations—Brunei, Indonesia, Malaysia, the

Philippines, Singapore, Thailand and Vietnam—is pushing ahead with plans to turn its grouping into a borderless economic zone. The ASEAN members have already agreed to eliminate tariffs on most manufactured and agricultural goods by 2003, and are talking about replacing individual investment rules with a liberal pan-ASEAN one. The pressure for change comes not just from non-Asian manufacturers, but also from the growing number of Asian firms that are keen to invest aggressively in their own backyard.

The main beneficiary of this new harmony among foreign investors and governments is provincial Asia. Most of the first generation of factories were built either in or close to Asia's big cities. That suited governments because they could keep an eye on the investors. Now those governments worry about their capitals becoming overcrowded, and about the widening income gaps between rural areas and urban ones. According to the Thai Farmers Bank, incomes in Bangkok are now around 12 times those in the five poorest rural Thai provinces. According the World Bank, 68% of rural Filipinos live in poverty—double the proportion in urban areas.

Asian governments are offering some of their best deals to investors prepared to go out of town. One of the contenders for GM's factory is Subic Bay, a former American base four hours' drive from Manila, which

Reprinted with permission from *The Economist*, April 27, 1996, pp. 65-66. © 1996 by The Economist, Ltd. Distributed by The New York Times Special Features.

has been transformed into a free port and has already netted $1.2 billion of investment from 200 local and foreign companies. The Philippine government has a list of 20 other preferred provincial outposts including Cebu, another island, which has already attracted some 60 Japanese companies.

Almost nine out of ten investments approved by the Thai Board of Investments last year were in "Zone Three", as it calls the country's rural provinces. Last year the government relaxed restrictions on foreign investment in Zone Three and—with GM in mind—decided to get rid of a 54% local-content rule for all car makers by 1998, some 18 months ahead of the requirements of the World Trade Organisation.

The same trend is visible even in the less developed, ex-communist parts of Asia. In Vietnam, for instance, the southern province of Dong Nai has made a great play of tempting investors away from the commercial hub of Ho Chi Minh City. By allowing 100%-foreign ownership without strings, it has attracted an extra $1.3 billion. In China, where roughly 90% of foreign investment so far has gone into its urbanised coastal strip (particularly Shanghai and the southern province of Guangdong), the Chinese government is trying to lure investors into the interior of the country.

The irony is that, in many cases, foreign companies do not need to be bribed or cajoled into leaving the cities. Even without all the tax breaks, rent-free factories and promises of new roads, rural Asia offers plenty of advantages—especially for the more ambitious projects envisaged by the new wave of investors.

The chief incentive is cost. As Ray Farris,

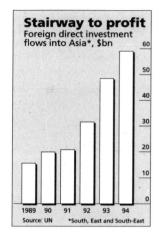

Stairway to profit
Foreign direct investment flows into Asia*, $bn

Source: UN   *South, East and South-East

head of strategic research for Crosby Securities, a Hong Kong-based stockbroker, points out, property prices are considerably lower in the countryside (an important consideration now that factories are getting larger). So is labour. By contrast, the purported advantages that the cities offer in terms of easier access to consumers and better infrastructure seem to lessen by the day. Many big Asian cities are impossible to move around in: one American company reputedly decided not to choose Shanghai as its manufacturing base after it took the visiting chairman four hours to reach the proposed site.

Indeed, it is becoming hard for any place to stay cheap or rural for long. For instance, by offering an environment where operating costs are far lower than in Singapore, Penang, a northern Malaysian island, has succeeded in attracting lots of high-tech firms, such as Hewlett-

Packard, Intel, and Siemens. Now firms are complaining that Penang is too expensive. Seagate Technology, a Californian maker of computer disk-drives, has three plants in Penang, but opened its fourth in January in Ipoh, a town about 90 miles (144km) inland. Komag, another American disk-drive producer with a plant in Penang, is building its new $100m factory in the state of Sarawak, on the island of Borneo.

Another incentive to move yet further into the sticks is the relentless search for talented workers. The provinces often contain fewer educated workers, though the difference can be exaggerated. (Cebu, for instance, produces 2,000 English-speaking engineering graduates every year.) Besides, what foreign investors increasingly want are good basic skills, on top of which they will provide specific training. GM is following the example of Motorola and opening a "university" to accompany its car plant. Once trained, a rural workforce is much less likely to be poached by rivals.

In the provinces, a foreign investor is usually a big fish in a small pond. In many cities foreign investors either have to shout (or pay extortionate amounts) just to be heard. By contrast, bullying local politicians in an area where you employ most of the voters is relatively easy. Even in communist China, provincial officials often turn a blind eye to companies that install their own satellite links in order to bypass the state telephone system. In a country where even ordering a taxi can still be a remarkably complicated experience, such little courtesies can make a foreign investor's life considerably easier.

From major to minor

The world's big oil firms are engaged in an increasingly desperate scramble for giant, low-cost reserves

THE big oil companies—or majors as they like to be known—are a resilient breed. In the 1970s they were booted out of various Middle Eastern countries. They turned to developing oil in remote areas such as Alaska and the North Sea. In the 1980s they suffered a dramatic drop in the oil price. But they survived, and later thrived, by ruthlessly cutting their costs.

Only last week both British Petroleum (BP) and Royal Dutch/Shell, two of the world's biggest oil firms, announced record first-quarter profits. Buoyed by a higher oil price, the American majors also recently recorded impressive first-quarter results. World demand for oil meanwhile is growing healthily at around 2% a year, fuelled by energy-hungry Asian economies.

But is their confidence merited? The oil industry depends for its survival on finding new and profitable reserves. The upstream part of the business (which involves getting the stuff out of the ground) generates most of the profits of the biggest oil companies, and accounts for around three-quarters of the industry's total capital spending. Now it is beginning to look as if there are too many oil companies chasing too few good new oil fields.

The world remains full of oil: in spite of growing demand, proven reserves have increased by around two-thirds since 1970. The difficulty is rather that the countries that contain ample quantities of low-cost oil (and which account for most of the increase in reserves since 1970) are largely inaccessible to western firms.

OPEC countries of the Middle East, for example, sit on over 60% of the world's proven reserves. Yet nationalism runs strong in Saudi Arabia and Kuwait. Neither country will stomach foreign firms exploiting their reserves. Iran and Iraq, by contrast, are eager for foreign investment. But UN sanctions put Iraq out of bounds, and are unlikely to be lifted soon. As for Iran, when Conoco, an American oil firm, last year struck a deal to exploit two Iranian oil and gas fields, Bill Clinton slapped a ban on such contracts.

In the countries of the former Soviet Union, political instability has so far dashed the hopes of western oil firms. In Russia western oil firms have refused to proceed with some $20 billion of contracts until their confused legal and tax status is resolved. A communist victory in next month's presidential elections could delay their investments for much longer.

In Azerbaijan and Kazakhstan several oil majors, including BP, Chevron and Mobil, have signed deals to invest billions of dollars around the Caspian sea. But no one knows when or if the oil will reach its market. Iran, Turkey, America and Russia are bogged down in endless debates over the route of the pipelines needed to export oil from the region.

Many of the oil majors still generate much of their output—and profits—from giant fields discovered decades ago. For example Atlantic Richfield Company (Arco), an American firm, produces around 80% of its oil and gas from North America, principally from reserves in Alaska's North Slope. Four-fifths of BP's oil and gas production comes from North America and Britain, and much of that is from a handful of large fields in Alaska and the North Sea. Mobil, another American firm, may generate around a quarter of its net income from Arun, a single giant gas field in Indonesia.

According to Robin West of the Petroleum Finance Company in Washington DC, production from most of these "crown jewels" is either near its peak, or is already declining. New fields are rarely as large or as profitable. Since the mid-1980s few giant oilfields have been discovered (see chart on next page)—and, though many more smaller fields have been found, they have not delivered the same economies of scale.

Technically, the oil firms are still replenishing resources. A survey of 16 big oil companies by Bear Stearns, an American investment bank, shows that, on average in the decade since 1985, they replaced all the oil and gas reserves they used up. But such statistics conceal two trends. First, many of the reserves have been increased by using expensive new technology either to extend the life of fields or to exploit fields that were previously inaccessible (such as in the deep waters of the Gulf of Mexico).

The other trend is that oil majors are relying increasingly on gas. Fergus MacLeod of NatWest Markets, an investment bank, predicts that the gas production by 15 of the biggest oil firms will rise more than twice as fast as their oil production between 1995 and 2000. Yet most firms would prefer to stick with oil: gas is harder to transport, and usually less profitable to produce.

Ten years ago the world's seven biggest private oil companies spent around 60% of their upstream capital budgets in North America. With North American reserves in decline, they now spend a similar proportion of their budgets overseas. There are still some relatively friendly foreign places where companies can drill for new oil—such as Venezuela and Colombia. But the prices for such contracts are often increasing, particularly because the old established oil majors now face new rivals, including recently privatised giants such as Argentina's YPF.

A senior manager of a European oil giant argues that some American oil firms have recently paid too much for new acreage in several countries, such as Venezuela, because they are so desperate for new reserves. "We are beginning to ask whether the whole game is silly," he complains.

The alternatives

So how else should the big oil companies spend the cash they are now making in ample quantities? Few western oil firms want to diversify, having spent much of the 1980s selling off non-core businesses such as mining and fertilisers. Oil companies are pursuing three options, none ideal.

The first is investing in technology. Techniques such as horizontal drilling have boosted the amount of oil in the deposit that can be extracted to around 60% in some fields, compared with 25% in the 1970s. But technology is no substitute for low-cost reserves. According to the International Energy Agency, production costs in Iran, Iraq, Saudi Arabia and Kuwait are less than $2 a barrel, compared with more than $10 a barrel in the North Sea.

Secondly many oil majors are trying to turn their growing reliance on gas into a virtue. Reserves of gas are more plentiful than oil, they point out, and world demand is expected to increase by around 3% a year. But the gas business is a tough one. The absence of a global gas market compels firms to secure buyers before developing a gas field. Mobil, for example, is now struggling to find buyers for a huge gas field in Qatar—a project essential to its future as the Arun field declines.

Acquisitions are a third option for oil companies that fail to discover reserves of their own. This week directors of Ampolex, an Australian firm with large oil and gas reserves, recommended acceptance of an A$1.78 billion ($1.43 billion) offer from Mobil. Meanwhile Arco recently bought a $340m stake in Lukoil, the Russian oil firm. Both acquisitions raised eyebrows in the industry: Arco's because of the huge risks of investing in Russia, Mobil's because—according to some of its competitors—it is

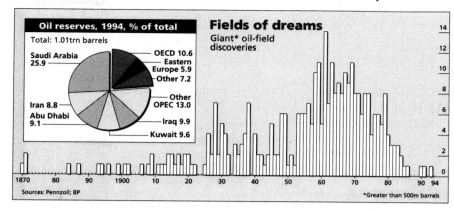

paying a "ridiculous" premium for Ampolex.

Ironically, the oil firms' difficulties in finding profitable new fields may have one consolation: a rising oil price. Growing world oil demand could lift the price early in the next century. That would be terrible news for the world's consumers, but good for the oil companies, whose costlier reserves might become worth developing.

On the other hand, waiting for a third oil-shock does not look like much of a strategy. The best thing for oil firms to do with their profits may be to start paying more of them to shareholders. Otherwise, warns one oilman, "The industry as a whole is going to destroy shareholder value." The trouble is that oil bosses may prefer fruitless and costly searching to presiding over the slow liquidation of their empires.

■ **Global Language Training**

Are Expats Getting Lost in the Translation?

Expatriates can't just get by with English-only anymore. They need to speak their customers' languages—if their business relationships are going to flourish. Here's why all expat programs should include language training, and what can happen if they don't.

By Stephen Dolainski

We all know the image of the ugly American expatriate. It's the business professional who bulldozes his or her way through another country—speaking only English and making everyone around him or her pull out their English phrase books just to keep up.

Although the ugly American image is yet another stereotype that's shattered each and every time a U.S. businessperson goes abroad with a good knowledge of the customer's native language, it's still an image that's perpetuated in the expatriate community and in other business circles. But it shouldn't be. Not knowing the language of the land is a persistent business problem that's holding many professionals back from reaching optimum performance during their trips abroad.

Although English is widely spoken in the global business world, the language of business, as the adage goes, is the language of the customer. Increasingly, that language may not be English.

And as U.S. companies—both big and small—look for new markets outside the major foreign financial centers such as Hong Kong, Paris and Geneva, they're beginning to realize they can't get by with just speaking English anymore. International human resources managers, already facing many challenges associated with relocating employees out of the United States, have the added responsibility of providing some form of language training for outbound expats, a task that may not be high on everyone's priority list.

But it should be—because companies are sending more expats to other countries than ever before, and because a better understanding of a customer's language can translate directly into profit.

Language training for expats is critical to global business success. The globalization process has been responsible for large numbers of Americans sent out of the country to expatriate assignments all over the world. An estimate by the New York City-based National Foreign Trade Council (NFTC) puts the figure at more than 250,000 on overseas assignments currently. According to the survey "Global Relocation Trends, 1995," conducted by the global relocation consulting firm Windham International based in New York City and the NFTC, the number of U.S. expats is expected to grow in the future.

Although these U.S.-based expatriates may bring expertise of their particular business or industry with them on assignment, they often only can communicate it in the English language. And as American companies start turning their attention to China, Mexico, Russia, Malaysia and markets outside the big foreign financial centers, something's surely going to get lost in the translation.

"If Americans spoke other languages the way Norwegians, for example, speak English, we'd take over the world." So says Jack Keogh, the director of client services for Mayflower International Inc.'s relocation division in Carmel, Indiana. In the global business world, U.S. business professionals—monolingual by and large—are at a disadvantage, relying on bilingual secretaries and interpreters to translate for them.

For example, using interpreters may help U.S. expats understand basic conversations with clients, but it won't necessarily help them with the nuances of what their customers are trying to discuss. While interpreters are an important business tool, they also can be another barrier to client relationships. "Your interpreter can have a 20-minute conversation with [your client] and you'll get a four-word answer," says Carrie Shearer, manager of compensation for Caltex Petroleum, a Dallas-based oil company that recently tutored 300 employees in the Thai language before sending them to Thailand.

More than just works are lost, says Robin Elkins, senior manager of Bennett and Associates Inc., a relocation and cross-cultural consultation firm in Chicago that works with *Fortune 500* clients and others. "English may be spoken in the office, in the workplace and in the expatriate community, but it's not always spoken outside those environments," says Elkins.

Employees who are about to go on an expatriate assignment must realize when they accept that assignment in another country where English isn't the norm, that learning the basics of the country's language should be viewed as a direct part of

the assignment—not as a nice add-on skill.

And there's often more than just business at stake. There's also the not-so-small matter of the person simply getting around in the location they're visiting. "If expats can't interact with the locals in the markets and in the streets, they're missing a lot about the thinking and character of the local people," says Elkins. These experiences also influence expats' ability to assess situations back at work, and they'll often make wrong assumptions about people they're managing.

Need Help in Setting Up a Language Training Program?

HR managers who've never set up a language-training program can get some help establishing criteria to evaluate the features and benefits of language-training programs in the "Standard Guide for Use-Oriented Foreign Language Instruction." This seven-page guide is issued by the American Society for Testing and Materials (ASTM) and includes criteria for assessing needs and selecting instructors, descriptions of listening and speaking proficiencies, guides for evaluating instructors' performance and students' progress.

To order the guide, which costs $18, call ASTM customer service at 610/832-9585 or write ASTM, Customer Service, 100 Barr Harbor Drive, West Conshohocken, Penn. 19428. —*SD*

Kevin Murphy, director of international HR for Community Energy Alternatives, Inc., a small Ridgewood, New Jersey-based power producer with 18 expat employees on assignment, says, "Language training is incredibly important. It just makes everything easier.

"In China or Latin America, English isn't the major language, and you're at a tremendous disadvantage if you don't speak the language. So it makes sense to get whoever is going [there] up to speed with the language as soon as possible." Easier said—in any language—than done. But it's vitally important to the success of expatriate assignments.

Language training helps global business relationships thrive. The NFTC estimates that the average one-time cost of an expatriate relocation is $60,000. Corporate language training programs need to contribute to the success of international assignments.

Says Beth Gegner, regional manager in Europe for Blanchard Training & Development Inc., which is based in San Diego, California: "If someone in a foreign country has two vendors, and one speaks the language and the other doesn't, it's almost guaranteed that the one who has the language skill has more of a chance to get the account than the one who doesn't."

Language skills, says Murphy of Community Energy Alternatives, help build the kind of teamwork needed to succeed overseas. "Once you get into a country, and you don't have your act together as a team, you'll find out very quickly that the people in that country will not only steal your lunch, they'll eat it too. So you've got to glue [yourselves] together as a team. Part of that is picking up the language skills."

Cementing business-related communication may be the primary objective, but it's not necessarily the only objective. Knowing the language of the land can also help an expat feel less isolated. Shearer felt that language training was especially important when Caltex sent approximately 300 employees to a rural location in Thailand during the initial stages of building a refinery there. Because of the refinery's remote location, not as many people would speak English as in the capital city, Bangkok.

"You could get by at work without speaking Thai," says Shearer, "but how are you going to converse with the maid or [with a vendor] when you go to the open-air market? There's no way to even look at a coin and know what it is, because Thai is based on Sanskrit and doesn't look [anything] like English."

The good news for Shearer was that she knew about the project in 1994, 18 months in advance. Caltex, which employs approximately 10,000 people worldwide, only has 250 employees in the United States. Many employees who worked on the Thailand project were Caltex workers from South Africa, Australia and other countries.

"A lot of front-end work was being done in Dallas, so we had eight or nine [people of different] nationalities working in Dallas on this project, which made it easier to organize language training for everybody," Shearer explains.

In 1994, she contracted Berlitz to give Thai-language classes to the English-speaking employees and their spouses. A refinery can be a dangerous place, so Caltex employees also were taught to understand Thai vocabulary like "danger," "fire," "watch out," words that might be shouted out in an emergency. "When people are under stress, they're going to speak in their native language [unless trained otherwise]," says Shearer.

Caltex also brought 75 Thai workers to Dallas for technical training before the project commenced. They first were given a six-week, live-in immersion course in English. All together, Caltex ran 30 weeks of training.

Caltex has since decided to set up English-language training in Thailand for workers before they're brought to Dallas for technical training. Knowing what the need is ahead of time helps employees, their managers and HR to plan on which language training program method is best for a given situation.

Typically, before any language training takes place, the expat's personal and professional readiness for the assignment is assessed. But expats aren't the only ones who can benefit from language training. Gegner thinks there's also value in a company training all its employees "on a minimal level" in the language of the foreign companies it does business with. "If delegates visit the United States, they're going to feel much more at home if [workers] here could just say, 'Hello, how are you?' to them."

Helping inbound foreign national employees improve their English skills is another objective of companies like St. Paul, Minnesota-based 3M Co. and Caltex. Most of 3M's tutors are assigned to work with inbound workers already familiar with English but who want "to improve their English skills so they can be more productive on the job in St. Paul," says Margaret Beaubien, 3M's language services administrator.

Tutors are usually employees' spouses, an advantage for inbound workers, says Beaubien, because "our tutors have a knowledge of how 3M works and can field questions from the foreign-service

workers … and we're providing a lot more than language instruction."

> **Learning a language in the in-between moments can be better for many soon-to-be expats than scheduled classes.**

The immersion approach usually works best. Although tutors, classes and other methods are available sources of language training, perhaps the best place to learn a language is in it's homeland, called "total immersion." Because this may not always be a practical option, the next best thing is a simulated immersion program—an environment in which only the target language is spoken and the student is exposed to different accents, three-way conversations, telephone role-playing, and other clearly defined social and business situations. An intensive program like this, which can cost several thousand dollars, might comprise a predeparture three-day crash course emphasizing business and courtesy communication. For the expat who has time, the immersion approach could be the way to go.

Berlitz, based in Princeton, New Jersey, is well-known for its immersion programs. International relocation and cross-cultural consulting firms like Bennett and Associates also offer highly personalized immersion preparation that's tailored to the expat's international assignment.

Ideally, training can continue once the expat is at his or her destination. Bennett and Associates uses its worldwide network of resources to locate qualified tutors. Berlitz operates more

than 320 language centers worldwide. According to Michael Palm, Berlitz's North American marketing manager, curriculum, texts and instructional methods are universal (the centers aren't franchised), offering what might be called a seamless advantage: An expat can begin studying Japanese, for example, at a Berlitz center in America and then once the expat is in the assigned country, he or she can pick it up again on the same page.

Intensive predeparture training, like immersion instruction, however, may not meet a company's needs. Kathy Hoffman, director of international human resources of the Norwalk, Connecticut-based ABB, recalls, "About five years ago, we tried some intensive courses, but reports back from the individuals said they found it better to get trained when they were actually overseas." She agrees that it may be more motivating when you're in the environment and can practice daily, than if you're sitting in a classroom trying to pick up a language. ABB, the U.S. arm of a global engineering group, sends approximately 200 people all over the world each year, most of whom are project workers who don't generally receive language training. Approximately 70 ABB employees, mostly management-level employees, receive foreign-language training once they're in the country, says Hoffman.

But who has time? Many expatriates who are preparing for an international assignment, however, have little or no time for lengthy, intensive language training. That's when HR managers have to intervene with other tactics.

John Freivalds, managing director of JFA, an international public relations firm in Minneapolis, thinks he has a solution: *guerrilla linguistics*—learning several carefully chosen words and phrases, targeted to a country's business culture, that an expat can speak at the appropriate moment to impress locals that he or she knows more about a language and culture than he or she really does.

Although guerrilla linguistics may bring momentary success, the tactic is only temporary and probably works best for someone who has much global experience and speaks several languages.

Self-instructional materials such as audio tapes provide a practical alternative to tutors, classroom study and guerrilla linguistics, according to Jeffrey Norton, president of Guilford, Connecticut-based Jeffrey Norton Publishers Inc., one of the country's largest producers of self-instructional language courses. Learning a language in the in-between moments (between meetings or at lunch) or during off-hours, can be better for many busy soon-to-be expatriates than scheduled classes.

Typically, an HR person is the primary impetus behind employees using self-instructional tapes, Norton notes, and adds that inquiries about such tapes have increased in the last three years. It figures that even if soon-to-be expats can't schedule large blocks of time to learn a new language, they probably can find snippets of time here and there to learn a language.

But beyond these language training methods, there's another longer-term approach and philosophy that companies can adopt for language acquisition.

Make language acquisition a company goal. International human resources professionals might consider making language acquisition more of a global company objective, rather than just a situational tactic.

At 3M's headquarters, what began 30 years ago as informal, lunch-time get-togethers to practice German, has become a well-loved employee tradition and a unique company asset. It's called the "Language Society." In the beginning stages of the society, volunteer teachers were recruited from employee ranks by other employees and classes were formed. Today, at the company's St. Paul location, the Language Society has about 1,000 members who are current or retired 3M employees or immediate family members. Classes in 17 languages, which are taught by a cadre of 70 volunteer teachers, meet once a week for 45 minutes during lunch. There's a nominal fee ($5) to join the society, and 3M supplies texts at cost to members.

Participation in Language Society classes has no official connection with employees' jobs, says Beaubien. Participation is voluntary, and employees are motivated by a variety of personal and professional reasons to study a foreign language.

"We have people who may be working in customer service and who are studying Spanish and they may receive calls from Latin America. They're better able to field those calls," says Beaubien. "3M has also opened a homepage on the

Language Training Improves Global Business at ARCO

Johnna Capitano isn't planning to go to China, but this spring she took a 12-week class in Mandarin Chinese. Now she can exchange greetings in the dialect, and she knows enough to be careful when she uses the Chinese word *ma,* which, depending on the intonation, has different meanings, including horse, mummy and mother.

"It was very challenging, because the tones are difficult to master," says Capitano, a Los Angeles (LA)-based human resources development consultant for ARCO Products Co., the downstream refinery and marketing arm of ARCO. "At times it was very frustrating, not being able to pronounce a word the way the instructor kept repeating it."

But Capitano stuck with it and was one of 10 employees who completed a pilot class in conversational Mandarin Chinese that the company conducted this spring. Twice-weekly classes, which met for 1 1/2 hours at a time, were held at ARCO Products Co.'s two sites in Los Angeles and in Anaheim, California. The company is exploring potential business opportunities in China and has already hosted Chinese delegations on tours of its LA refinery. Capitano will probably be involved in hosting future delegations.

Paula Johnston, ARCO Products' human resources consultant for inter-national projects, set up the pilot language training in response to employees' requests. "Members of our technical team who had been to China to analyze business opportunities found it was difficult to communicate because everything was done through interpreters. We've also had several Chinese delegations visit ARCO, and did everything via interpreters. We thought since we're just looking at opportunities now, why not use the time appropriately and offer Mandarin classes before things heat up?"

Johnston requested bids from three vendors: a university, a consulting firm on the East Coast and Berlitz. Berlitz was selected, Johnston says, "not only on the basis of economics, but [also because] it offers a great deal of flexibility. It's a firm we could utilize not only at the beginning level, but also later for a total immersion program if somebody was actually selected for an assignment, and even in China for follow-up training. [The company offered] continuity and consistency."

Johnston set up classes during work hours at the company's LA refinery site, where Capitano took the class. She also set up a class at the firm's engineering and technology facility in Anaheim so employees wouldn't have to travel. About 28 employees began the classes, but enrollment ultimately dwindled to about 10.

"It was very tough, because some people's schedules were just too busy or they were placed on special projects," explains Johnston. "Some people probably couldn't keep up or just lost interest."

Capitano agrees. "People would get tied up in other projects, and it was difficult to pull away and say, 'Oh, I've got to go to my Mandarin class now.' Employees—and the company —all have to make language acquisition a priority.

"A language isn't easy to learn, especially when it's so different, like Mandarin. It really has to become a work priority that everyone understands," says Capitano.

Johnston is in the process of seeking feedback. Although her impressions, so far, are good, she doesn't want to overplay it. Why? "Because we did lose people for a variety of reasons," she says. Of the people who completed the program, the response, she reports, is "pretty enthusiastic." Although the reports are mixed, learning their customers' language can never be a futile endeavor. Because language training at ARCO hasn't been an afterthought, the wheels of global business are spinning with greater efficiency. —*SD*

Internet, and we're receiving inquiries from all over the world, and, of course, they're coming in different languages. The society is being contacted to translate those messages."

Language training at 3M isn't limited, however, to Language Society classes. Beaubien also manages a tutoring program for outbound and inbound employees, using more than 20 tutors who are either former teachers or hold ESL certification. The decision to receive language tutoring is left up to the individual employee and his or her department manager, says Beaubein.

But not all employees are eager to learn a new language—even if it will benefit them in their jobs.

Motivate expats to know their customers' languages. "It's difficult," says Brian Connelly about the Spanish classes he's currently taking twice weekly after work. Connelly is manager of Pan-American operations for Blanchard Training & Development, a position that will require him to travel several times a year to Latin America. "I work 10 to 12 hours a day, and then go to class two times a week, and try to study in between."

Learning a new language requires time, effort and motivation. With all the responsibilities of an international assignment, it's difficult to take the extra time necessary to learn a new language. It's especially hard if language learning must be reserved for unpaid, after-work hours, even if companies reimburse instructional costs (and generally, they do). More than 60 percent of the companies surveyed by Windham International and the NFTC for the "Global Relocation Trends" survey offer cross-cultural orientation to expats (which generally includes a language training component).

And, according to Elkins, about 80 percent of Bennett and Associates' *Fortune 500* clients offer language training. "But," she says, "not many corporations encourage language fluency. They think they only need enough language to get by, because they'll have a [bilingual] assistant or secretary or have an interpreter."

Shearer of Caltex says that motivation is an "individual thing. You can force people to do something, but you can't force them to learn something." Caltex

didn't require its outbound employees to learn Thai before going to the remote refinery project, and classes were offered after work. Still, about 85 percent of the employees took the training, with 75 percent completing it. A few people did so well, Shearer arranged private tutoring lessons for them, and Caltex paid for it.

What Language Can Cost

If language training is an investment in the success of the expatriate on international assignment, then how much does a good investment cost? That, of course, depends on what kind of training is used, who provides it, where it takes place, how long it goes on and how many employees are participating. Here are a few examples of costs for language training, self-instruction, translation and interpretation:

■ Ten-day immersion program for one individual, including all materials (any language): $4,500.

■ *Guerrilla linguistics*—a written phonetic list of 30 to 40 key terms and phrases: $500-$1,000.

■ Two-part, self-instructional, beginning Japanese course of 24 cassette tapes (30 hours) and two texts: $430.

■ One hour of interpreting time (any language): $325.

■ Twelve-week (48 hours), university extension, intermediate Spanish conversation class: $280.

■ Three-part "executive" Japanese self-instructional course of six cassette tapes (5 1/2 hours) and three texts: $225.

■ "Russian for business" self-instructional program of three cassette tapes (three hours) and phrase book: $65.

■ Document translation: About $.25 per word for translations to or from French, Italian, German or Spanish (FIGS); more for other languages.

—SD

Financial incentive is a tried-and-true motivator, and one that Murphy of Community Energy Alternatives employs. "If you hire a secretary [who knows] stenography, you'll pay that person a little more for [that] skill. So when a person picks up

language skills, I want to be able to give [him or her a reward]." Murphy uses a performance appraisal submitted by the expat's manager that includes a language-skills evaluation. No matter what language a person speaks, everyone speaks the language of money.

Murphy tries to make it as easy as possible for expats at his firm to pick up language skills. He negotiates to purchase a block of time for the year with an outside vendor to provide onsite language training at his company's Ridgewood, New Jersey, headquarters. He schedules classes for employees during work hours. Murphy believes in continuing language training in-country, and negotiates that into his contract as well.

This is the type of long-term approach to language training that companies must adopt for future success in global business.

When all is said and done... As cel phones and the Internet link the Earth's remotest locations, the world grows a little bit smaller. Ironically, American businesses are realizing just how vast and culturally diverse this planet is—and that most of its inhabitants don't speak English.

Says 3M's Beaubien: "It's becoming critical that companies have employees who not only have studied other languages, but also who have received some cultural training and who understand how we can do business with people who are different, how we can work together as productively as possible. That only happens when you understand another culture and the best way to do that, of course, is through language."

As for HR professionals' part: Language training must be an integral part of a company's expatriate program. It can no longer be viewed as just another accent or add on. Because when your client in Mexico says, "Quiero comprar un contrato de un million," (I want to buy a million dollar contract), the last thing you want your expat employee to say is, "Huh?"

Stephen Dolainski is a Studio City, California-based free-lance writer. E-mail laabsj@workforcemag.com to forward comments to the editor.

GLOBAL EXECUTIVE

Getting What You Pay For

Most agree that it's best to hire local people, even at executive level, when setting up shop overseas.

By John Davies

The script is about greed, power, lust and the trouble you can get into if you don't know much about hiring foreign nationals overseas: A promising young computer executive suddenly learns from a factory in Malaysia that his breakthrough product has stopped working. The mystery deepens when a former girlfriend is named his boss, and she moves to eliminate him. In the high-tech battle that follows, the executive breaks into the world of virtual reality to discover how people she hired overseas are leading the firm to disaster.

That's the outline of *Disclosure*, a novel and film that author Michael Crichton says is based on events that occurred at a Seattle computer company.

On the screen, Michael Douglas portrays the bewildered executive, who discovers how quickly years of international effort can go bad. There are no rampaging dinosaurs as in *Jurassic Park*. Incompetent handling of foreign workers proves to be an equally effective monster.

For global executives, it's a cautionary tale.

With the worldwide growth in business, more US executives find themselves assigned to establish or expand overseas operations with foreign nationals, from top executive to assembly line workers, who are best-suited to carry out corporate strategy.

They must decide whether to hire an overseas agent, find a qualified expatriate, bring in a consultant, form a joint venture or employ an executive search firm. They may have to choose from several potential countries to select a base.

What do you want?

A company planning to set up overseas can't do any effective hiring until it has formulated goals and established strategies to meet them. International business advisers at management schools, consulting firms and executive search firms all say that while it may seem elementary, too many companies plunge into overseas hiring without knowing what they want to accomplish.

> "People sometimes think they'll save by sending an expatriate instead of paying the premium to hire a foreign national. It doesn't always work out that way."

"You have to know your objectives and strategy before you start," states A. Paul Flask, managing director in the Chicago office of Korn/Ferry International, the world's largest executive search firm. "Either your own people can figure out the goals, or you can use a consultant, or hire somebody to help you figure out those goals, but you don't want to get an expert at implementation and ask him to figure them out."

Once goals are set, a company has to decide whether its operation will be small enough to deal with a foreign-based representative, who may or may not have other interests to look after, he says. Sometimes, a company is lucky enough to find a joint-venture partner that fits in with US corporate culture and uses the American business to increase its clout or take up slack from otherwise unused capacity.

But a mismatch between agent and company, or between firms, can cause problems as the business grows, Mr. Flask points out. At that point, many companies search their own ranks and may try to establish a foreign office with an expatriate. Others advertise, only to be inundated with hundreds of resumes, mostly from unsuitable people.

Larger companies, however, may turn to executive search firms, sometimes called "headhunters," to find qualified candidates. For a fee of 15 percent to 30 percent of the candidate's first-year salary, a search firm takes a careful look at what a company wants. Researchers then comb though databases of qualified people known to be looking for jobs and then confidentially approach those working for competitors to see if they would be interested. They screen the candidates, verifying their claims, and narrow down the list of candidates.

Mr. Flask, who specializes in emerging markets, contends that when the person sought is to be in charge of an overseas unit, the search may focus on foreign nationals who know the territory they will work. "A fee of $20,000 to $80,000 to hire a foreign national may sound expensive, but when you consider that in Beijing, you're going to pay $13,000 a month in rent to get quarters for an expatriate, having someone who can live in Chinese housing may be a plus," he contends.

Such foreign nationals also don't suffer from the American style in negotiations. "In Asia, things are often done very obliquely," Mr. Flask says. "Americans have to understand they just can't stand up and ask `Am I going to get screwed here?' when they're dealing with Asians. You have to build relationships." An effective top executive for an Asian operation must be bi-cultural.

Rapid growth in Asia also means that there is a shortage of effective and trustworthy, bi-cultural top executives, and American companies will pay a premium to retain them.

In other parts of the world, it may be easier to find a successful foreign manager who is just as much at home within the culture of the US corporation as at home, he suggests. More expensive labor benefits and tougher layoff rules may apply to personnel hired in Europe, but the differences in business culture are not as severe as between the United States and Asia.

"There's still a lot of chauvinism in Europe. For instance, you still have to be careful if you want someone who's calling on Poland not to hire a former enemy. But the problem in Europe is not so likely to be cultural background," Mr. Flask continues.

At the same time, the number of international companies hiring European workers is relatively small compared with the number of foreign companies in Asia hiring Asians. One study estimated that the number of Asians working for foreign companies grew by almost 30 percent per year during the early 1990s.

"There's no doubt that Asia is going to see the largest percentage of growth in the hiring of foreign nationals for at least the next few years," Mr. Flask adds.

Cross-cultural know-how
Others also cited understanding two cultures as the trickiest part of hiring executives and staff in a foreign country. "That's the single biggest problem we have when we try to help

US companies set up offices and hire people in Japan," says Hiroyuki Euguchi, industrial cooperation specialist at the Japan External Trade Representative Office in New York.

American companies usually understand that they must tailor their products for the Japanese market, he explains, but still don't understand Japanese traditional ways of doing business. Without some immersion in Japanese language and culture, they cannot follow standardized formats for carrying on negotiations, such as the junior man-senior man relationship, in which each partner in a negotiating team is expected to fulfill certain roles.

"An American company doing business in Japan has to be able to negotiate with the Japanese. And because negotiations in Japan are not like negotiations in America, foreign hiring is one of the more difficult problems," he claims.

Allen Christian, an international trade specialist in the Japan office at the US Commerce Department, adds that cultural differences, lifetime employment at Japanese firms and the slowdown in Japan's economy have all made it difficult for US firms to hire Japanese workers there.

But he adds that the Commerce Department is also advising would-be exporters that it may be time to reconsider setting up an operation in Japan. A sharp drop in office prices (See *IB*, April 1996) and the growing success of American-made goods in Japan's software, furniture, apparel and sporting goods markets are creating new opportunities.

At the same time, a growing number of Japanese women are looking for jobs and advancement in a society where very few rise to the rank of manager. American firms can take advantage of that combination.

The problem that most US companies encounter when they try to do business in Japan, and elsewhere in Asia, is that potential obstacles are rarely spelled out in law or regulations the way they might be in the United States, the trade specialist indicates.

Instead, Japan relies on a huge bureaucracy that may conceal countless obstacles to product distribution. "They're working on changing that, but the progress is slow," he says.

Hiring Japanese workers away from companies that have traditionally offered lifetime employment isn't difficult for larger US companies with a reputation for treating employees well, but may be hard for smaller ventures without that reputation. Smaller firms often find either a representative or a joint-venture partner.

Mr. Euguchi says he sometimes describes himself as "a gateway to Japan" for companies

seeking information on how to find a Japanese representative or a suitable partner there. The US International Trade Administration also has desk officers who can get smaller companies started.

Hong Kong Ease
If Japan remains a somewhat enigmatic place to do business, the same isn't true in Hong Kong, notes Benjamin Chu of the Hong Kong government's Industrial Promotion Office.

Hong Kong is such a good place for foreign companies to set up business that between a quarter and a third of its workforce of nearly 3 million people are employed by foreign firms. "No one knows the exact number because we treat foreign offices the same way we do domestic offices," he observes.

There is no minimum wage, business taxes are low and employers can hire and fire at will, although some employees may be entitled to severance. Prime sites in downtown Hong Kong can be among the most expensive in the world, but a range of lower-cost property is also available. Foreign companies can hire directly from the market, in contrast to the situation across the border in China, where they must either form joint ventures or accept workers assigned by the government.

With its long history as a British colony, Hong Kong residents typically speak English and represent a part of the Chinese culture most interested in commerce and trade. A large percentage of residents have two or more jobs, creating an affluent consumer group interested in buying western products.

Chinese puzzle
Conditions for hiring workers are a lot more complex across the border in China, claims Jenny Pei, marketing manager at China Business Consultants Group in Chicago. There, companies setting up either representative offices or wholly owned subsidiaries must hire only from government agencies, not from the work force. Only approved joint ventures can hire on their own behalf.

Sometimes, Chinese government officials will search out joint venture partners in the United States, but US companies normally have to search for themselves to find a joint venture. "We do a lot of case studies about prospective joint ventures," she asserts. "Some companies can do it on their own, but a lot of them find having a consultant very helpful." (See *IB* December 1996/January 1997)

Lower inflation and a convertible currency makes China more attractive to US business, but extreme government regulation makes such business development difficult.

"You just cannot imagine the extent to which things are regulated," she says. "China is a planned economy and the government plays a much heavier role than even in Japan — government is in your face anywhere you go. It's not just a different cultural system for negotiating, it's an entirely different economic and political system."

But China shares one thing in common with Japan. Companies that think they've figured out the regulations often discover that they apply to foreigners in a special way. "There's usually some hidden agenda that will make it more difficult for foreign people to do business in China," she comments.

About 75 percent of American businesses in China hire their local employees through joint ventures. As long as they abide by any employment contract they might have signed, those companies can hire and fire freely. For instance, a large US corporation like General Motors, which has 30 operations in China, might face pressure from officials near that plant, but couldn't be forced to keep it running.

"It's no problem to find a place to rent, as long as you're prepared to pay," she adds. A recent survey of the world's 10 most expensive cities to rent office space included Beijing, Shanghai and Guangzhou.

Screening Clout

Once a firm has defined its goals, selected a top executive, chosen a site and established the best form of government, it still must hire lower-level employees. Often, that's left up to the top executive in each country, particularly if he is a foreign national with a superior understanding of the region's labor market. But if an operation is large or will involve employees from a variety of sites, screening tests may still be required.

Mobil Corp. of Fairfax, VA, for example, reports that its personnel managers have developed tests for foreign job applicants. One such test, used for applicants at a job site in Indonesia, helped them evaluate mechanical skills and the ability to learn, things Mobil couldn't always gauge clearly from educational records. The oil company worked with the American Psychological Institute and the UK's Cambridge University to design the test. Its executives said the result was a valid test that accurately measured the skills Mobil sought.

But many companies don't have the time or resources to design their own tests. Medium-sized firms sometimes rely on educational consultants to evaluate job applications. Companies such as World Education Services Inc. in New York City and Evaluation Service Inc. in Albany, NY, screen thousands of applications each year to ensure job candidates are truthful and to give an employer some idea of how a foreign education might compare with a domestic one.

Much of their screening is done for foreign students who want to work in the United States, but such firms can also screen would-be foreign employees. Evaluations may be required to identify foreign-trained job applicants who meet specific standards needed for medical, teaching, scientific or engineering posts.

Employers hiring a foreign staff may also use outside services to verify work experience records, test language fluency for those who will be translating as part of their job, and look into the possibility of criminal violations.

Inquiries about criminal activity are the most difficult to carry out, because some countries either don't permit countries to ask, or are not obligated to say.

Under US immigration law, any foreign employee convicted of even a minor crime might be denied entry into the United States for training or consultation purposes if the possible sentence for the offense exceeded a year. What's more, even foreign employees who have never broken the law in their own country can run into trouble if they made payments that would constitute bribes in the United States.

Legal payments to an adviser involved in a contract award might be a "finder's fee" or a "consulting cost" in some nations, but in the United States these payments constitute violation of the American Foreign Corrupt Practices Act, which may prevent a foreigner from entry to the United States.

In the movie, *Disclosure*, an inexperienced manager faces government pressure to hire more workers in Malaysia. She decides that she can avert a politically motivated labor problem by simply cutting equipment costs and hiring more workers.

To cut costs, she eliminates the air filters that keep dust out of computer drives during assembly, and cuts back on the number of precision mounting machines that ease computer chips into place. Instead, the extra workers push ultra-delicate computer chips into circuitboard sockets with their thumbs. Within days, computer drives are malfunctioning erratically.

"People sometimes think they'll save by sending an expatriate instead of paying the premium to hire a foreign national," observes Mr. Flask at Korn/Ferry. "It doesn't always work out that way."

HUMAN RIGHTS

A COMPANY WITHOUT A COUNTRY?

Unocal says it won't leave Burma, but it may de-Americanize

The U.S. is becoming a distinctly inhospitable place for Unocal Corp. to hang its hat. In March, a federal district court judge in California ruled that the oil and natural-gas company could face trial in the U.S. for human-rights violations in Burma, where it has a $340 million stake in a natural gas project. Then, on Apr. 22, the Clinton Administration imposed sanctions against the rogue state that prohibit further investment by U.S. companies.

Faced with this political pressure at home and drawn by the lure of growth opportunities abroad, the $5.3 billion company is taking a radical step: It is de-Americanizing. Legally, the company is headquar-

tered in El Segundo, Calif. But in company literature, Unocal says it "no longer considers itself as a U.S. company" but a "global energy company." In practice, it is slowly moving assets, research spending, and management to Asia.

On Apr. 21, Unocal opened what it calls a "twin corporate headquarters" in Malaysia. President John F. Imle Jr. and several senior executives will be posted there while CEO Roger C. Beach remains in California. This after it sold off its U.S. refining operations and gas stations to Tosco Corp. in March for $2 billion. Analysts say Unocal may decide to spin off its Asia headquarters into an entirely separate company—and in so

LIGHTNING ROD
Democracy groups say this gas pipeline—a Unocal joint venture—will find the brutal military regime

doing, may be able to bypass U.S. sanctions. "They have structured their operations now so it would be easy for them to pull out of the U.S. if that's what they needed to do," says Jennifer Weinstein, research associate at NatWest Securities Corp.

Unocal says it has no immediate plans to relocate or spin off the international division. Its Burmese operations, the company says, are grandfathered under the sanctions, and 62% of Unocal's revenue is still generated in the U.S., mostly from production in the Gulf of Mexico and Alaska. But two-thirds of its $1.34 billion in capital spending currently goes to Asia—Central Asia, Bangladesh, China, and elsewhere in Southeast Asia—as well as Burma. "Our major focus area for future investment is Asia," Beach wrote in a recent letter to shareholders. In Burma, Unocal owns 28% of a joint venture with France's Total, the Petroleum Authority of Thailand, and Myanma Oil & Gas Enterprise, a state-owned company. The four are investing $1.2 billion to develop a natural-gas field in the Andaman Sea south of Rangoon and a 254-mile pipeline to Thailand set to open in mid-1998. A proposed second pipeline, to Rangoon, could be halted by U.S. sanctions.

Unocal isn't the only U.S. company operating in Burma. Texaco Inc. and Arco Corp. have invested in smaller natural-gas projects. But pressure is mounting against multinationals that deal with the State Law & Order Restoration Council (SLORC), the military junta that has run the country since forcibly taking

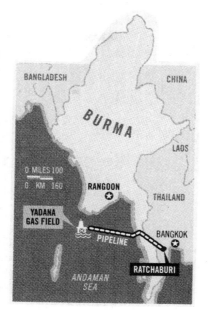

power in 1988. PepsiCo, Philips Electronics, and Motorola, among other U.S. and European companies, have pulled out of Burma in the last year. That leaves Unocal the biggest U.S. player in the country by far—and, so, a magnet for activists.

RUNAWAYS. The anti-SLORC campaign may only drive Unocal closer to divorcing itself from the U.S. Overnight, it could join a growing community that includes Hongkong & Shanghai Banking Corp., which moved to Britain in 1993 ahead of China's takeover of Hong Kong, and ABB Asea Brown Boveri Ltd., which now calls itself a "multidomestic corporation."

Other multinationals will be watching. The human-rights case appears tenuous: Total is building and running the Burma operation, while Unocal is just an investor. But if the trial is heard in the U.S., it could have broad implications for other U.S. companies operating abroad. "It should be a warning that companies should be aware of what any of their government partners are doing," says Robert W. Benson, professor of international human-rights law at Loyola Law School in Los Angeles. Or they should start thinking about a new home.

By Sheri Prasso in New York, with Larry Armstrong in Los Angeles

Asia's Bamboo Network

by

Murray Weidenbaum

and

Samuel Hughes

Ethnic Chinese family businesses based off the mainland of China are the driving force in a new wave of Asian trade, manufacturing, and investment. Quickly becoming a major global power, these overseas Chinese entrepreneurs are weaving a "bamboo network" of complementary business relationships throughout Southeast Asia, tying entrepreneurs, business executives, traders, and financiers together across national boundaries. The private business sector of nearly every Southeast Asian country is dominated by companies owned by overseas Chinese.

Typically, the founders of these businesses possessed little wealth. They built their firms from scratch—working, saving, and reinvesting at prodigious rates. One former student told us of his grandfather who migrated from China to the United States. He took a job in a traditional hand laundry and, after many years of ironing garments, managed to save a very large sum from his modest earnings. He then moved to Hong Kong and invested 50,000 Hong Kong dollars in the rice business, a gutsy move that led to a family fortune now diversified across Southeast Asia.

Today, many small family firms have grown into enormous conglomerates, each of which includes dozens of companies. The total assets of the 500 largest public companies in Asia controlled by overseas Chinese exceed $500 billion. And that excludes the same families' many privately owned enterprises. In Indonesia, for example, Liem Sioe Liong's Salim Group alone is estimated to account for 5 percent of the country's gross domestic product. In Thailand, ethnic Chinese control the four largest private banks, including Bangkok Bank, the region's largest and a key lender to the overseas Chinese community.

Not all of this wealth stays within the home country. Ethnic Chinese are the largest cross-border investors in Thailand, Malaysia, Indonesia, Hong Kong, the Philippines, and Vietnam. In recent years, much of this investment capital has been flowing into the Chinese mainland. Since Deng Xiaoping launched his economic open-door policy in 1978, overseas Chinese have invested more than $50 billion in their motherland, roughly 80 percent of all foreign investment there. To date, members of the bamboo network have formed over 100,000 joint ventures in China.

The tendency of Chinese merchants to establish themselves away from their home country goes back centuries. Much as Americans traditionally migrated to the West, the Chinese moved south into Malaysia, Thailand, and Indonesia. Yet they have remained Chinese in a deep sense. The Confucian tradition is remarkably persistent; it inculcates loyalty to a hierarchical structure of authority, a code of defined conduct between children and adults, and trust among friends. The closely related virtues of pride in work and disdain for conspicuous consumption are especially beneficial to rapid economic growth.

Wary of government, the expatriate Chinese have found that kinship, dialect, or common origin—in a clan, a village, or even a county—provide a basis for mutual trust in business transactions, even ones conducted at great distances. When Taiwan had strict exchange controls, for example, someone in the network would deposit a large sum with a gold shop in Taipei and have a relative withdraw the equivalent from an affiliated gold dealer in Hong Kong.

Shying from publicity, most overseas Chinese take a low profile in the commercial world. Few if any widely known consumer products have a Chinese brand name. Members of the bamboo network mainly make components. They manufacture for others, doing sub-assembly work, wholesaling, financing, sourcing, and providing transportation. Centralized family control and informal transactions minimize company bureaucracy. Key information is obtained in conversation and retained in the heads of the senior managers. In contrast to the typical Western business's many studies and memoranda, the economies of time and effort achieved by the bamboo network are impressive. Money is borrowed from friends on trust. Transactions of great size are often dealt with by common understanding and a note jotted in a diary.

The central institution of these enterprises is the family. Chinese firms are almost always family firms. As the saying goes, "you can only trust close relatives." We came across two cases where the retiring heads of Chinese businesses summoned their eldest sons home to take over. Coincidentally, in both cases, number-one son was a neurosurgeon with a successful U.S. practice. Both dutifully returned to the family business, abandoning medical practice.

Because most overseas Chinese businesses are privately held, little is known about their operations. Nevertheless, some of the larger overseas Chinese firms are publicly held, enabling us to examine them. One classic example is the Formosa Plastics Group, the business empire of Wang Yung-ching, which enjoyed a market capitalization estimated at over $11 billion in 1994. Wang's holdings are centered on the Taiwan-based Formosa Plastics Corporation. Often called "Y.C.", Wang has ten children, each an executive in the family business. His brother, Y.T. Wang, is president of Formosa Chemicals and Fibre, which he runs with Y.C.'s son William. Y.C.'s daughter Cher Wang is president of Everex Systems, a computer manufacturer in California. Another son, Winston Wang, is senior vice president of Nan Ya Plastics. Daughter Charlene Wang and her husband run First International Computer, the world's largest manufacturer of the "motherboards" used to make personal computers.

When starting new businesses, the overseas Chinese are frequently assisted by their compatriots. The Malaysian Lippo Group's founder, Mochtar Riady, received his initial financing from the Indonesian Salim Group's founder, Liem Sioe Liong, who

From *The American Enterprise* magazine, September/October 1996, pp. 68-69. Adapted from *The Bamboo Network: How Expatriate Chinese Entrepreneurs Are Creating a New Superpower in Asia* by Murray Weidenbaum and Samuel Hughes. © 1996 by Murray Weidenbaum and Samuel Hughes. Reprinted by permission of The Free Press, a Division of Simon & Schuster.

obtained his early banking support from the Sophonpanich family of Thailand. At other times, the large overseas Chinese business families join forces to form joint ventures. Indonesia's Salim Group has teamed up with the Kuok family of Malaysia to develop a hotel and golfing resort in Indonesia and a cement factory in Wuhan, China. Both groups have combined with Thailand's CP Group. Stakeholders in the New China Hong Kong Group include Indonesia's Lippo Group, Hong Kong's Li Ka-shing's Group, Singapore's Trade Development Board, Taiwan International Securities, and ten mainland Chinese companies and ministries.

Small enterprises rely on more formal overseas Chinese mutual help associations, typically based on family, clan, common locality in China, or dialect. The associations act like banks through which members can borrow money, trade information, recruit workers, and receive business introductions. They help enforce the "handshake" deals on which much of Chinese business is based. If a business owner violates an agreement, he is blacklisted. This is far worse than being sued, because the entire Chinese network will refrain from doing business with the guilty party. Bankruptcy or dishonesty not only redounds to the individual, but to the entire family and clan.

In the typical ethnic Chinese family firm, there is little separation between owner and management. The head of a Chinese company typically is an all-powerful paterfamilias who entrusts key positions to family members. Within the family, confidence in his judgment borders on the absolute.

Overseas Chinese firms have eschewed traditional business structures in order to capitalize on the weak system of contracting and law throughout Southeast Asia. Core business groups develop varying degrees of ownership in dozens, if not hundreds, of small- to medium-sized businesses. (There is no Chinese equivalent of such complex companies as Sony, Daewoo, or Procter & Gamble.) In turn, many of these businesses maintain cross-holdings with other family-controlled firms. The resulting web of holdings, when combined with the insertion of family members into key management positions, allows the family to maintain ultimate, albeit circuitous, control. This structure provides necessary secrecy and diversification in a region where the threat of governmental expropriation and ethnic discrimination is still pervasive.

Yet there are disadvantages associated with the family-run business. Keeping control within the family almost inevitably restricts the size, or at least the complexity, to which it can grow. That is not so much a problem for low-tech firms, but high-tech companies require sophisticated organizational structures.

The track record of second- and third-generation overseas Chinese managers is mixed. Frequently, these sons and daughters must manage the transition of the family firm from an entrepreneurial start-up to a modern corporation. Family ties can be so strong that incompetent relatives are preferred over outside professionals. The best and brightest Chinese entrepreneurs are trying to

> **The private business sector of nearly every Southeast Asian country is dominated by companies owned by overseas Chinese entrepreneurs, who are quickly becoming a major global power.**

finesse the succession problem by taking their companies public, hiring professional managers, and sending their offspring to Western business schools. Ethnic Chinese firms' most noticeable weakness is a hesitance to enter the world of brand-name goods and mass-marketing. They often need the marketing and design capabilities that a Western company can offer.

What about the future? Great uncertainty clouds the outlook for China, especially after Deng Xiaoping passes from the scene. Through their extensive investments in the mainland, overseas Chinese businesses have exposed themselves to significant risk. At critical junctions, they are likely to exert their powerful influence to ensure the success of China's economic experiment, making them a key factor in the economic development—and ultimately the political transformation—of China and Southeast Asia.

In the most optimistic scenario, the mainland would move to peaceful capitalism, and the bamboo network would then face East to China and the Asian mainland. That combination of forces could enable China to become the major superpower in Asia early in the twenty-first century. By the year 2020, the United States and China would be in a race for the top slot in the world economy. On the other hand, should China destabilize or revert to communism, and mishandle the integration of Hong Kong, the bamboo network will likely face to the West. Overseas Chinese commercial families will develop closer ties with North America and Western Europe. At home, they will emphasize the substantial opportunities in Southeast Asia and Australia. An old saying among overseas Chinese is, "Keep your bags packed at all times."

However China fares, we believe the bamboo network will survive and likely continue on its traditional path of uneven progress amidst setbacks and opportunities. A critical element will be the Western-educated younger generation, who will try to exploit the tremendous possibilities that arise from combining their unique cultural characteristics with modern management and advanced technology. Their potential for success on a global scale is impressive. Yet it is not a foregone conclusion. In every culture, some of the wealthy's offspring merely indulge themselves and dissipate the wealth so painstakingly generated by their ancestors. We know many overseas Chinese business leaders who have this concern.

All in all, the inevitable vicissitudes that the resourceful members of the bamboo network will face in the years ahead will likely serve as challenges that strengthen their resolve and capabilities. Bamboo is the Chinese symbol for durability; it is flexible and constantly developing. In the words of the old saying, "Bamboo bends; it does not break."

....

Weidenbaum is chairman of the Center for the Study of American Business at Washington University in St. Louis, where Hughes served as the John M. Olin Fellow.

When Sexual Harassment Is a Foreign Affair

Sexual harassment can happen between U.S. workers, but in global business situations, it can be even more complex—to identify and to resolve. Here's what you need to know to avoid sexual discrimination liability and increase your company's chances for harassment-free business relationships.

**Wendy Hardman
and Jacqueline Heidelberg**

Scenario #1: Sandra Whitney is on a three-year, career-enhancing assignment in Mexico for her company and finds herself the target of unwanted sexual attention from her new male manager—a citizen of the host country. Whitney complains to a female co-worker (who's also a citizen), but is told this behavior is "normal." When the behavior persists after Whitney has made it clear she isn't interested, she consults with the human resources manager in her host country. She finds there are now laws protecting women from sexual harassment on the job, although she's assured that her company's policy and the U.S. laws will be maintained.

Scenario #2: Connie Bosworth is working on a team with several men from Europe who have been sent to the United States for six months. Bosworth finds these mens' flirtatious language and gestures charming and endearing, but she feels ambivalent because she realizes that if an American man said the same things to her, it wouldn't be acceptable. Are Europeans bound by the same rules?

Sexual discrimination is a little-discussed problem in cross-cultural relationships. Both of the scenarios above, and other tales of sexual discrimination, are realistic for today's multinational companies and the emerging global workplace. In the past five years alone, the number of female expatriates of U.S. companies has more than doubled according to a recent news item in *The Wall Street Journal* on September 5, 1995. New York City-based Windham International, which conducted the survey, predicts the number of expatriate women will reach 20% (of all U.S. expatriates) by the year 2000. In addition, the U.S. workforce is ethnically and culturally more diverse than ever and this trend is expected to continue. As we struggle to understand and negotiate both the subtle and more complicated issues related to sexual harassment in our domestic marketplace, we also must be aware of the added concerns of working overseas with co-workers, customers and vendors of many different nationalities.

To find out what individuals and organizations experience in the international marketplace, we asked several companies to share their stories. As consultants with extensive backgrounds in human resources management and cross-cultural business settings, we also reviewed what has been written on the subject. A key question we posed: "What have you encountered as far as sexual harassment incidents that occurred between people of two different cultures, whether they were employees, customers, vendors or clients?"

While exploring this relatively uncharted territory, several corporate human resources executives from multinational organizations told us we'd have trouble getting any information. Because of the potential liability, and the potential threat to an organization's image, they suggested that candid responses would be scarce. Indeed, the most frequent response we got was that companies had limited experience with the issue, and therefore, they had little to report. The topic of sexual harassment is one that many organizations find difficult to address. And when it's complicated by cross-cultural issues, it becomes even more foreboding.

In fact, several organizations refused to return our calls or stated that they didn't want to participate. Some respondents, including human resources managers at Akron, Ohio-based The Goodyear Tire & Rubber Co. and Chicago-based Amoco Corp., stated they either have had "no incidents" or none that couldn't be handled at the local level.

Is this possible for firms having thousands of employees working both domestically and internationally? Yes, but it's highly unlikely. At Wilmington, Delaware-based E.I. du Pont de Nemours

(DuPont), a company noted for its work in sexual harassment training, there were no reported cases of sexual harassment internationally that have reached HR representatives at the corporate level. Bob Hamilton, a diversity consultant with DuPont, conceded that there may have been some situations, but they would have been handled as close to the front lines as possible. He added that third party cases of sexual harassment aren't rare, but DuPont doesn't keep records of these events.

George Krock, manager of EEO and selection at Pittsburgh-based PPG Industries Inc., told us: "In the last couple of years, there have been four incidents involving employees of PPG: two in North America, one in Asia and one in Europe." Similar numbers were quoted by a senior human resources manager in a large pharmaceuticals company: Approximately one to four sexual harassment complaints are filed each year internationally.

Both of these corporations (typical of an increasing number of multinational organizations) employ tens of thousands of employees outside the United States—although many are citizens of the host country. Philadelphia-based SmithKline Beecham, for example, operates in nearly 80 countries and currently has approximately 250 expatriates. When you consider that there are many more expatriate women these days, the actual number of cases of sexual harassment globally seems surprisingly small. Have we triumphed over sexual harassment in cross-cultural settings? Have employers managed to eliminate "unwelcome conduct of a sexual nature," not to mention ridding their workplaces of "hostile or intimidating environments"? Are individuals in cross-cultural work environments more careful, better informed and generally more respectful of each other?

That's certainly one possibility. More believable, however, is the interpretation by one head of international HR for several financial-service organizations over the last several years. He suggests that companies might not have accurate information to report because employees are cautious about disclosing sexual harassment incidents—particularly when they occur cross-culturally. There are many reasons for this. One is the problem that sexual harassment is often

under-reported, understated or trivialized—regardless of where it occurs or who's involved. Jim Yates, manager of human resources for international operations with Amoco, says another problem may be the desirability of the overseas assignment. "People may not want to jeopardize their jobs," he says. These positions are highly valued, sometimes taking years to attain.

Training employees about cultural differences before international assignments may help avert problems. Craig Pratt, of Craig Pratt and Associates based in Alameda, California, is an investigator of sexual harassment complaints for San Francisco Bay Area companies. Having been an expert witness in 40 sexual harassment court battles over the past four years, he finds that a disproportionate number of cross-cultural sexual harassment complaints involve perpetrators and victims from differing ethnic, racial or national-origin groups. He often has thought about the complexity presented by sexual harassment situations in cross-cultural contexts. His experiences strongly support the idea that when individuals from two different cultures interact, the potential for problems with sexual harassment is greater, not smaller.

Cultural relativism—the notion that ethics, values and behavior are a function of culture—is one way to understand, and perhaps to dismiss, the issue. In fact, all of the HR and international managers we spoke to raised the notion of a cultural context as central to the discussion. Pratt frequently encounters situations which might be better understood (although not necessarily forgiven) when cultural frameworks are considered. What's acceptable in one culture may be disrespectful and confusing in another. What U.S. citizens may construe as sexually provocative or offensive, for example, isn't shared by most—or even many—cultures.

Bill Ferra, director of U.S. management and development services for Heinz USA in Pittsburgh, reports that Europeans think Americans are "crazy" with all of our laws about sexual harassment. Some behaviors that deeply violate norms of U.S. culture may not be perceived as a problem in another cultural context. In many Mediterranean and Latin countries, physical contact and sensuality are a common part of socializing.

For example, one Brazilian senior HR executive was surprised when he was admonished for calling the women at work "girls." While this label was appropriate and acceptable in his native culture, he wasn't aware it was insulting to North American women and could contribute to a "hostile or intimidating work environment" by U.S. standards.

Rudiger Daunke, VP of international HR for Bausch & Lomb Inc. based in Rochester, New York, notes that U.S. citizens proceed carefully in their cross-cultural relationships abroad because of cultural differences. The organizations we surveyed unanimously agreed that the incidence of sexual harassment across cultures can be diminished with adequate cultural preparation of employees. Interestingly, many international companies have such programs in place.

Bill Mossett, vice president and director of employee relations and diversity for SmithKline Beecham, says its program *Managing Transculturally*, is currently being rolled out for managers with assignments in the United States and the United Kingdom. This newly instituted program has both a general component as well as culture-specific information. Theoretically, managers might go through it three or four times during their careers—each time they go on assignment to a different country.

Similarly, Amoco offers its expatriates and spouses a two- to three-day, cross-cultural program. The topics covered include such issues as social behaviors, relationships, titles, dining practices and American perceptions. In addition, once a U.S. expatriate is in the host country, he or she receives another cultural orientation.

While this cross-cultural training is a proactive measure that helps diminish the potential for cultural misunderstandings between men and women, it may be inadequate and limited. None of the programs surveyed includes specific information about sexual harassment or sexual discrimination. Moreover, many U.S. companies don't offer stand-alone sexual harassment training (although it's sometimes included as part of diversity awareness training) for their domestic employees. Such training is rarer still for host-country nationals. One exception, DuPont, reports that as many as 90% of its domestic employees have attended sexual-harassment training. In addition, the company says most of its offshore leaders have participated, as well as its international employees on assignment in the United States. But this is rarely the case.

When sexual harassment training is provided, the content is specific to the laws and customs of the United States, *not* to the international destinations of increasing numbers of employees in multinational companies. The sexual-harassment programs in multinational companies—if they're even offered or required—are for domestic, not international employees. And their focus is local, not global.

Another inadequacy to the cross-cultural preparation for most expatriates is that the courses are usually offered for employees on long-term assignment, not for the occasional visitor or business traveler. One international HR executive says that because of the lack of preparation, the occasional visitor becomes the company's greatest liability. He says: "When [U.S. citizens abroad] aren't culturally sensitive, they may use inappropriate gestures or names that can be perceived as harassment, even when it's not intentional."

One example of a cross-cultural preparation course we encountered is the *Passport/Visa Program* used at Amoco for its international business travelers and U.S. employees who host foreign visitors. The passport section is a fairly generic cross-cultural review, while the visa component is country-specific. The organization has visa programs for countries such as China, Russia, Azerbaijan, Egypt, Trinidad and the United States. HR currently is developing programs for Europe and Latin America. Benefits to the learners include being able to "identify, anticipate, avoid, minimize and resolve areas of potential conflict resulting from cultural differences." The only drawback is brevity—the program is only a half-day course.

Finally, cross-cultural training is designed for employees destined for overseas assignments. But it's rarely an option for domestic employees who'll be interacting with foreigners on a regular basis in their jobs.

Should you define sexual harassment by home- or host-country standards? Even when cultural preparation is adequate, it begs the question of cultural relativism. Should an organization operating in a host country with different customs and moral traditions insist that all behavior be measured according to home-country standards? If men and women have interacted in a certain way for hundreds of years in a culture, who shall judge that certain language or behavior is wrong or *bad*? Sexual harassment is one manifestation of sexual discrimination. Values and behaviors about women's rights aren't as deeply entrenched in many societies as in our own.

Mahbub ul Haq, a United Nations development program team leader and the author of a recent U.N. report cited by *USA Today* on August 29, 1995, states: "There isn't a single society in the world that treats its men and women equally, not even by accident." Undoubtedly, expatriate women face unique problems.

Jim Yates of Amoco echoes a common sentiment about the difficulties women encounter cross-culturally: "In some countries, there are barriers that have affected the ability of females to be fully integrated into a project or team." Another senior HR executive notes: "Particularly in 'macho' cultures, it's strange to interact with women in a professional capacity." In these environments, men may take advantage of women because they're accustomed to relating in traditional ways. Even on the egalitarian ground of the United States, the same problems may arise.

Jane Henderson-Loney, of the Timner Consultant Group in the San Francisco suburb of Clayton, California, describes a Middle Eastern-born man working in the United States who was accused of sexually harassing an American-born woman. She remembers him saying: "In my country, women can't behave like this to men!"

Literature on the subject goes beyond mere sexual discrimination. It supports the view that sexual harassment is common in many countries. The *Harvard International Law Journal* reported in 1992: "Sexual harassment is a pervasive problem in the Japanese workplace." In 1991, *IABC Communication World* reported that in Mexico, "sexual harassment has been recognized as a problem, but is accepted in our culture where many men consider themselves superior over women . . ." The same source reported that a national survey in Australia revealed one in four Australian women suffered from sexual harassment at work. Sexual harassment also is happening in Africa. Pratt says when he read the 1992 deposition testimony by a Nigerian woman in preparation for a sexual harassment case, he concluded that it's common in Nigeria—in fact expected—that male supervisors can have sexual access to female subordinates.

If sexual discrimination, including sexual harassment, is the norm in some cultures, should it be ignored when it occurs?

If sexual discrimination, including sexual harassment, is the norm in some cultures, should it be ignored when it occurs? In the book "Essentials of Business Ethics," edited by Peter Madsen and Jay Shafritz, one respected contributor, Norman Bowie, states that he believes universal ethics do exist that should guide business conduct. However, they often aren't obvious, and may be difficult to decipher. Probably every culture would say it believes in, and upholds, the respect and dignity of every human being. It's hard to imagine a society that would openly condone sexual harassment. "The Essentials of Business Ethics" states: "Such moral rules are not relative; they simply are not practiced universally. ... However, multinational corporations are obligated to follow these moral rules."

In fact, the few incidents of sexual misconduct in international situations that we heard about were frequently resolved once the employees were informed that the women in question were offended by the behavior. Senior HR executives from several companies concluded that these incidents often are caused by lack of awareness of cultural differences—they aren't malevolent in nature. Once an explanation is offered and the woman's perspective is explained, the male (the usual perpetrator) is frequently surprised: He's not aware that his behavior could cause such a degree of anxiety or

uneasiness. The universal ethic—not to offend—seems to transcend the customary behavior and interaction of a particular culture.

On the other hand, perhaps it isn't so innocent or simplistic. In at least two incidents we heard about, the offender was clearly told that his behavior was unacceptable. The Middle Eastern employee accused of sexual harassment was told—in no uncertain terms—that to continue working for his employer he would have to conform to treating women as total equals, or be terminated. Perhaps the explicit or implied threat of losing a job or a contract results in a change in behavior more often than the desire not to offend. The excuse that it was a cultural misunderstanding and totally unintended, may be just that—an excuse.

Regardless of personal values and beliefs, the employees in question were motivated to change their behavior to conform to the standards that were expected by the company. Most of the organizations we interviewed have explicitly stated values and policies regarding sexual harassment that are maintained worldwide. Several senior HR executives emphasized workplaces should be free of harassment for all their employees. PPG Industries' Krock shares a viewpoint that's typical of his HR peers: "[Sexual harassment] isn't only contrary to our U.S. law, it's contrary to the policies established by PPG Industries. ... We don't believe that employees can operate effectively if they don't feel safe."

Consider the legal and business implications of international sexual harassment. Do the laws worldwide, and in the United States, support companies' internal policies against sexual harassment? The U.S. laws that govern sexual harassment are covered under Section 109 for both Title VII of the Civil Rights Act and the Americans with Disabilities Act (ADA). Section 109 addresses two distinct issues: 1) circumstances in which American and American-controlled employers can be held liable for discrimination that occurs abroad; and 2) circumstances in which foreign employers can be held liable within the United States.

If sexual harassment occurs abroad,

American and American-controlled corporations will be covered under Title VII. However, significant interpretation of the law occurs when determining if the company is American-controlled. Section 109 establishes four factors to consider in interpreting whether a company is, or isn't American-controlled. Not all four factors need to be present in all cases:

- Interrelation of operations
- Common management
- Centralized control of labor relations
- Common ownership or financial control of employer and the foreign corporation.

If a workplace is located in the United States, Title VII and ADA apply to a foreign employer when it discriminates within the United States, except when that individual(s) is protected by a *Friendship, Commerce and Navigation* (FCN) treaty. (The FCN treaty grants jurisdiction to one country over another country's corporation, and vice versa.)

In either case, abroad or within the United States, Section 109 doesn't explicitly discuss sexual harassment, although sexual harassment is a part of Title VII. The sexual harassment guidelines that have been issued in this country, increasingly familiar to U.S. employees, have no counterpart in Section 109.

Furthermore, as we mentioned earlier, in most countries there are no laws protecting against sexual harassment in the workplace. A 1992 article published in the *International Labour Review* revealed that in a study of 23 industrialized countries, only nine had statutes that specifically define or mention the term sexual harassment—Australia, Belgium, Canada, France, Germany (Berlin), New Zealand, Spain, Sweden and the United States. The author, Robert Husbands—of the International Labour Organization, based in Geneva, Switzerland—says that the law is in a state of evolution in most of the 23 countries he studied, and that different legal approaches reflect different cultural attitudes and legal systems. In 1994, the European Parliament adopted a resolution to enact legislation obliging employers to "appoint an in-house counselor to deal with cases of sexual harassment." (Belgium is the only European Community country currently with specific legislation on confidential counselors.) This builds on the European

Commission's 1991 Code of Practice to define and combat sexual harassment.

In addition, a November 1992 article in *The New York Times* said: "Legislators in some countries are also reluctant to go too far toward what they see as the desexualization of the United States." When cultures accept and value gender familiarity and unequal roles, it may be difficult to prohibit sexual harassment at work.

The ramifications of sexual harassment when it occurs cross-culturally are more confusing and difficult from both an emotional and legal standpoint. From a business perspective, it's an extremely important area to explore and one that has significant cost implications. With many HR concerns, the human costs of sexual harassment can be high because they directly translate into losses from absenteeism, dissatisfaction and low productivity.

The global nature of the problem adds another cost—expatriate employees are expensive employees. They tend to be high-level and require a great deal of money to support in relocation, schooling their children, tax differences and training, to name just a few. The average expatriate may take approximately $300,000 to replace. When we lose one to a sexual-harassment incident, it's a loss that's costly.

One question mysteriously looms on the horizon of global business: When the practices and laws of two cultures clash, which will apply? This is a question which, apparently, hasn't been widely tested. Perhaps it hasn't even been raised—as some of the organizations we interviewed implied.

It's difficult to believe that a problem that has been so widespread within the United States isn't a problem elsewhere, but the complexities of intercultural socialization blur the lines of what is proper and what is improper. It's HR's job to understand the associated risks when business personnel travel out of—or into—the United States. We also must make training a priority. If our expatriates don't even know which side of the road they'll be driving on when they go abroad on business (or which side of the road their foreign visitors are used to traveling on when they come to the United States), how can we possibly expect them to know what the requirements are regarding intercultural business relationships and the potential for sexually harassing behavior? It's our job to inform our people. Only then can we be sure that the road to international business is a safe one.

■ Global HR Inroads Paved at Conference

HR Pioneers Explore the Road Less Traveled

Human resources professionals whose companies are going global must forge new ground in employment strategy. An expert-laden HR conference helped identify international human resources problems of today and tomorrow— and helped solve them.

Jennifer J. Laabs

ioneers in the new frontier in business—that's what human resources professionals were compared to at the first-ever *Global Business Leadership Through HR* conference, presented by PERSONNEL JOURNAL, October 16-18, 1995 in San Francisco. As the leaders and planners of global human resources strategy, HR professionals were alerted to their unique challenges and opportunities as business continues to forge new markets in a world increasingly without borders.

Settlers, sojourners, travelers, visitors. Whether a company is doing business abroad for the first time, or continually seeking new international markets in which to develop, organizations worldwide are having to carefully plan their personnel strategy in uncharted territory. Personnel strategy has become, by far,

one of the toughest challenges in doing business globally.

HR leaders from around the world converged at PERSONNEL JOURNAL's conference to share problems, information, stories and advice on topics ranging from how to deal with global staffing nightmares, to getting international compensation policies right the first time. They talked about how cultural differences influence how you conduct business. They debated global health-care issues. They discussed worldwide employment-taxation problems. They considered expatriate relocation mistakes. They pondered overseas legal minefields. They shared employee repatriation stories. They commiserated over designing global HRMS systems. They sympathized over assessing performance in a worldwide setting. In a word, they *brainstormed*. It was a three-day think tank for global HR leadership.

Three themes emerged to guide them

into the year 2000 and beyond. Business is becoming more global and HR needs to be at the center of making it happen. Companies need to adapt their practices to other parts of the world, rather than just transplanting American ways. And, finally, HR needs to develop a more complete way to recruit and manage global workers so that individual career paths reflect global expertise and responsibility, and meld from the start with long-term global business strategy. It's a tough job. But HR professionals can—and must—do it. The future of business depends on it.

No doubt about it: HR must be a leader in global business. Allan Halcrow, editor-in-chief and publisher of PERSONNEL JOURNAL, opened the conference with a comprehensive overview of the global business community and HR's role in it. He pointed out that business has become more global, especially for U.S. companies. To date, more than 100,000 U.S. firms are engaged in some type of global venture—with a combined value of more than $1 trillion. And U.S. multinational companies employ almost seven million people outside the United States—people who work in virtually every country in the world.

For example, Colgate-Palmolive operates in 194 countries and receives approximately 70% of its $8 billion in annual revenues from overseas markets. AT&T now has approximately 52,000 employees working overseas in 105 countries. And Bechtel Corp. has more than 30,000 employees working in more than 70 countries.

U.S. multinational companies like these also employ almost 18 million people, representing almost 20% of total U.S. employment. This means one out of every five U.S. workers works for a company with a global presence—and the number is growing by the day.

But globalization isn't just about U.S. companies expanding overseas. Foreign companies also are setting up operations in America. In fact, foreign multinationals employ three million Americans, representing 10% of the U.S. manufacturing work force. Worldwide, at least 37,000 multinational corporations currently are in business. They control more than 200,000 foreign affiliates

and employ more than 73 million people. Information published by the United Nations Conference on Trade and Development states that at the end of 1993, these multinational companies had accumulated assets worth $2.1 trillion dollars.

Economies today know no borders. So, it's no surprise that half of the executives responding to a recent survey by the American Management Association based in New York City believe the single greatest effect on their business will come from the globalization of markets.

As more and more companies rush to become global, more human resources professionals are being asked to navigate international waters—often without the necessary background. And even with experience, they're often learning as they go—because one new global business experience rarely resembles another. The rules change by the country, by the company, by the industry and by the day.

Halcrow pointed out that in the next millennium, the caliber of the people in an organization will be the only source of sustainable competitive advantage available to U.S. companies. Every factor of production, other than work force skills, can be duplicated anywhere around the world. It's all fungible—capital, technology, raw materials and information. The only thing that will distinguish one company from another—indeed one nation from another—will be the quality of its work force. The source of tomorrow's power will be the product of mind work. Says Chuck Nielson, VP of HR at Dallas-based Texas Instruments and a speaker at the conference: "Only one thing differentiates us—our people."

How to get that intellectual property —and keep it—becomes an even greater challenge internationally. And it all falls under the responsibility of HR. Even with the change to having more business units—rather than just HR departments —be responsible for staffing and the basics of personnel management, human resources professionals usually must be the first to forge policies and set standards for these practices when they go abroad, or when they bring intellectual capital here from other parts of the world.

When HR isn't there first, organizations can make huge mistakes in trying to coordinate policies between home and host countries. Just like in the United

States, employees in other countries can be overpaid, underpaid or go on strike. They can be undermotivated, misunderstood and misinformed. And if HR makes mistakes, their firms may have to pick up the pieces by renegotiating terms, reorganizing teams internationally or even completely relocating to other cities or countries if the personnel issues haven't been thought through ahead of time.

From assessing the potential work force in a new country, to deciphering international labor laws, human resources managers often are among the first delegates to have contact with their new foreign partners. Because of this,

Sponsors of the Global Business Leadership Through HR Conference

The *Global Business Leadership Through HR* conference was held October 16th through 18th, 1995 at the Sheraton Palace in San Francisco. Conference sponsors included:

**Chemical Bank
Mayflower International Attache Services
SAP America Inc.**

globalization requires new and higher standards for the selection, training and motivation of people. Organizations are starting to shop globally for talent. So the practices designed to retain good employees also require great scrutiny. The difference between success and failure will depend on how well American organizations learn to manage their global work force.

HR's role is to find ways to maintain those strengths and capitalize on them. We must realize that although we have experienced tremendous success on our own continent, the global marketplace is a whole new world. It's one that requires continuous learning about the big, worldwide picture, as well as focused attention on the details that make a company work.

The U.S. way usually isn't the only—or the best—way. Conference attendees were reminded that Americans often use themselves as the focal point for how the world—and particularly business—works. When doing business in other lands, Corporate America has tried to simply transport U.S.-based HR policies and practices overseas.

Now, HR professionals are universally chanting the following mantra: "HR policies from the United States don't always work elsewhere. HR policies from the United States don't always work elsewhere. HR policies from the United States don't always work elsewhere." Global human resources managers have learned, through much trial and error, that their companies need to adapt their practices to other parts of the world rather than just transplant American ways. As business moves into other countries, we realize we can't use our own egocentric way of looking at people, cultures or employment practices. In fact, our experience with a U.S. work force often gives few clues about how to work with employees internationally. HR managers realize they must start with what's typical in the host country and design policy from there—whether it's compensation, benefits, relocation expense reimbursement or any global employment practice. Just as circles ripple outward when a stone is dropped into a pond, HR policies must first take local practices into consideration, then bounce them off what's possible and practical from the host company perspective.

Shirley Gaufin, VP and manager of worldwide human resources for San Francisco-based Bechtel Group Inc., has solid suggestions for what to do when moving business into countries outside the United States. Bechtel, a 100-year-old engineering and construction company with a presence in 70 countries, suggests that it may seem simple, but the first thing you must do is define your global terminology. For example, Bechtel defines an "expatriate (expat)" as any employee relocated from one country to work in another country, rather than defining it as is done traditionally: an American who's sent abroad. Bechtel defines a "local national" as any employee hired in a country to work in that country. Furthermore, the organization defines a "U.S. expat" as an employee with

U.S. income-tax liability. It designates "international staff" as expats without U.S. income-tax liability. It defines "foreign contract employees" as short-term, expat laborers employed in labor-short areas, such as in Kuwait during the oil fires. And Bechtel doesn't use the term "TCNs"—meaning "third-country nationals"—because of its negative connotation. In the past, a U.S.-based company might have hired an employee with a Swiss passport to work in Germany. We would have called him or her a third-country national. Now, it's better to think of ourselves as one global business community employing various people originating in various countries, and moving them globally as needed.

Bechtel has learned a lot on the global frontier. Gaufin's advice for HR professionals is based on lessons Bechtel has learned the hard way. She suggests you start carefully with a lot of planning. Commit adequate resources. Be culturally sensitive. Know the local labor market. Deploy decision making to the greatest extent possible. And finally, *think globally.*

Thinking globally isn't always easy, especially for HR professionals whose companies have little or no experience in international settings. Speaking at the conference, Richard R. Bahner, global strategy director for AT&T Corp.'s Morristown, New Jersey office, said: "It requires a new mindset." He says human resources managers must go from rule-maker to consultant, from a functional orientation to a business orientation, from a narrow perspective to a broad perspective, from internally focused to customer focused and externally competitive. Overall, HR must go from a reactive stance to a proactive one, and strive to always think outside the box—even though the box in a global business environment is infinitely more complex.

This is exactly the direction the HR department at Levi Strauss & Co. based in San Francisco is taking so that the company is more globally minded in terms of its human resources strategy. Donna Goya, senior vice president, global HR for Levi Strauss, spoke during the conference on how the company's growing global business has affected its human resources opera-

tions. Levi Strauss, which had $6.1 billion in sales in 1994, employs 36,000 workers worldwide, dispersed throughout 53 production facilities and 30 customer-service centers in 46 countries.

Levi Strauss's HR strategy was reformed recently to further align itself with the company's aspirations and values, and to help HR become more of a business partner with the firm's worldwide operations. In fact, says Goya, HR at Levi Strauss has become its own business unit. All staffing and training has moved into its many business units. And HR now is focused on such areas as HR consulting, communications and information services, leadership development, global remuneration and corporate services, such as employee relations.

Although realigning HR is important to being more of a global partner with a company's businesses, perhaps the most important consideration on the road to going global is to never underestimate the power of culture. Allied-Signal Inc.'s Sally Griffith Egan gave her suggestions at the conference on how to adapt to different cultures when going global. Egan, vice president HR services, Allied-Signal Business Services, says that in operating a business overseas, you must respect the nuances of local business culture, yet strive for commonality within your overall corporate culture. While you may start business operations in other countries, don't think of the practices you find there as "foreign." Think of them as simply different from how the United States and other countries do business.

Morristown, New Jersey-based Allied-Signal employs 87,500 workers (26,000 are non-U.S.-based) and has 400 facilities in 40 countries. It operates on the assumption that its worldwide facilities are more similar than different, that intense competition is a global reality, and employees everywhere want dignity, respect and fair treatment. With $12.8 billion in 1994 sales, 38% of which was harvested in foreign markets, it knows whereof it speaks.

U.S. companies impose a huge presence when they go into other countries. In fact, a common theme throughout the conference was that local employees in other countries often have a higher expectation of U.S. corporations than of their own local companies. That means U.S.-based organizations must be careful to educate employees about the company and its policies and practices, and manage expectations. And if HR isn't at the center of this education process, it should be.

Egan advises that to avoid arrogance and achieve total quality in a global culture you must not simply impose a monolithic U.S. business culture upon a local division in another country. You must blend their culture and morés with yours. And you must acknowledge that learning curves exist—both in the United States and abroad. Just as you wouldn't expect employees in the United States to simply *get it* the first time you explain any HR policy to them, don't expect local nationals to understand it on the first try either.

In the performance-management arena, companies need to develop local systems that make sense for the culture and people involved. Using a U.S. grading system doesn't automatically work in another country. For example, Laura M. Simeone, international human resources manager at Cisco Systems Inc. based in San Jose, California, says: "The design of performance management systems needs to be flexible enough to be adaptable for the different needs that countries and cultures have of the system." She adds: "No one size fits all. Flexibility in program design and operation are critical to success."

For example, Gordon R. Finch, international compensation, benefits and corporate relocation director with Burbank, California-based The Walt Disney Company, says in designing job descriptions for workers in countries outside the United States, you must consider (among other things) whether job descriptions are common and culturally acceptable, if they create special issues (such as literally becoming a type of employment contract), if language is an issue (make sure terminology successfully will translate) and if job descriptions are broader than typically described in the home country. (For more information on Disney's international compensation strategy, see the end of this article.)

Again, one home-country policy rarely fits all host countries. And that is doubly true, for example, in teaching managers in local operations abroad how to conduct reviews. "Since culture is such a significant variable in managing and appraising employees, global companies need to provide their managers with training in how culture affects the management process, including the per-

Is Your HR Leadership Thinking Globally?

Sally Griffith Egan, vice president HR services, Allied-Signal Business Service, says asking these questions will help you figure it out.

1. Are you ready to approach a foreign culture with an open mind?

2. How good is the "fit" between your company's domestic culture and the local culture of your operation?

3. Have you allocated sufficient funds for adaptation/translation/ease of travel?

4. What have you done to earn the trust of local employees?

5. Have you given foreign employees good reason to believe that they can rise as far as their talents will take them within your organization?

formance-management process," says Simeone. It must make sense for them, and for you.

Allied-Signal's Egan echoes this advice. "Develop training that's tailored. Adopt local educational methods and adapt materials—translation alone never is enough."

Come full circle: Develop HR systems based on long-term business goals. When jumping into global business territory, it isn't the time to be short-sighted. Experts in globalization agree that while it's excruciatingly difficult to know where the business is going to be five years, one year or even six months down the road, you must plan for future personnel needs as early in the process as possible. And you must also plan careers around those business needs as well.

U.S. companies used to think only in terms of moving U.S. expatriates to other countries for short- or long-term assignments to get new businesses off the ground and on their feet. Now, a new strategy has emerged. Don't send U.S.

expats—or any other expatriates for that matter—into new business ventures abroad on long-term assignments if you can help it. Albert Siu, human resources director, education and development for Hong Kong-based AT&T (China) Co. Ltd., said at the conference: "It's an issue deep in the heart—having local people running companies."

The long-term goal is to have local managers and employees working to make new businesses in other countries flourish. It's the least-expensive way, and overall, perhaps the most productive. Although you'll probably never be completely free from moving employees from one global operation to another (because it helps spread business knowledge around the organization and it helps boost careers), you'll probably want to think in terms of developing managers in the countries in which your business is located. Don't just transplant them. Grow them. General Electric calls it "glocalization"—thinking globally and acting locally.

As AT&T's Bahner said at the conference, "The key to creating a global work force is having the right person, in the right position—regardless of nationality—at the right time." So, how do you do that? He says the business mission, the human development system, the business infrastructure and the compensation strategies must be inextricably intertwined.

Global experts say when you do need to move people from one country to another, make sure they're managed in a "circular" way. That means, develop policies and practices that ensure inpatriates and expatriates are an integral part of the globalization process. Prepare individuals ahead of time for global moves. Pay them fairly while they're on assignment. Make sure their health-care and benefits needs are adequately covered. Prepare them and their families for their new cultural experience. Keep in touch while they're abroad. Make sure you—and they—know where their next assignment is. Help them when it's time to repatriate. Learn from their experience abroad. Don't waste the human resources your company has invested in by losing them to inattention or misplanning.

GE Medical Systems (GEMS), based in Milwaukee, has a comprehensive international career-development and career-management program. More than 50% of GEMS' sales are outside the United States, and it employs 14,000 people worldwide; 51% of them are non-American. Janet A. Nelson, manager HR for GEMS, describes her organization's approach to managing global business and global careers: In keeping with its parent company's strategy of the boundaryless organization, GEMS either runs or has access to (through GE) a global new employee orientation program, an entry-level GE leadership program, a GEMS leadership forum, a global leadership program and GE executive education program. These programs and processes help employees throughout the organization's operations, which span from Milwaukee to Asia, learn how to think globally in business and manage their careers around it.

In addition, GEMS uses the following HR techniques to give expatriates and repatriates a complete exit and re-entry experience as they move about GEMS' worldwide operations: a peer mentor program, pre-departure and cross-cultural workshops, ongoing roundtables for expat support, and an expat peer mentor program. GEMS stays in touch with workers coming and going.

It has to. There's no question—its business depends on it. As GEMS 1993 annual report stated: "You're either the best at what you do, or you won't do it for very long." Companies that don't address HR issues in a complete way will pay for their mistakes at best, in missed opportunities. At worst, they'll pay in closed operations. There's no time, in a 24-hours business-is-open world, for anything less.

If globalization, and your role as an HR professional within it, makes you feel like you're a sojourner in a new land, you aren't alone. It means you're on the right track. If it were easy, it probably wouldn't be worth the effort. But there's money to be made in them 'thar hills, and your company's going to need the right people and HR strategies to move you into peak profitability. While HR road maps may be hard to come by, finding other trailblazers won't be difficult. PERSONNEL JOURNAL is committed to bringing them to you in future global HR leadership conferences and in its ongoing coverage of these issues in the pages of PERSONNEL JOURNAL. It may very well be a small world after all.

Jennifer J. Laabs is the senior writer at PERSONNEL JOURNAL.

One Assignment, Two Lives

Charlene Marmer Solomon

Today's global managers have more to consider than just the expat. International assignments increasingly are turned down or disrupted because of dissatisfied spouses. For the expats' assignments to succeed, HR will have to design helpful programs that make their partners' overseas lives equally meaningful.

To the outside observer, even to friends and acquaintances, Carol Leigh looked fine. But she remembers the day problems began: It was during a small luncheon with six other expat wives. As they sat around the table introducing themselves, every woman gave her name, then her husband's title, then the name of his company. Nothing else.

This was not Leigh's way of doing things. A financial analyst who worked 60-hour weeks, she'd left a thriving career in New York when her husband was offered an international opportunity in Tokyo. Although she wanted to continue working, she quickly discovered the legalities of acquiring a new job internationally were almost insurmountable.

After helping her family settle into school and work, establishing the household and getting into the rhythm of the new city, Leigh realized she needed something more to occupy her time. At first she was happy to explore and meet other expat wives. But, day after day, she began to feel the erosion of her identity; her self-image was so connected to her work (which no one seemed to care about) that she didn't quite feel herself.

Her self-esteem began to suffer and she found herself becoming less confident and a little angry. First, there was the introduction at the luncheon, then cocktail parties at which people talked about work and paid only passing interest to her ideas, then an encounter with a colleague of her husband's who said all she needed was a "good cry." She started to go back to bed in the morning after she'd sent the kids off to school. She began complaining to her husband that they hadn't received the same generous benefits package some of his colleagues had.

And then her friend from New York came to visit. Brimming with news of the office goings-on, delivering gossip about chums, Leigh learned her friend had received a well-deserved promotion. Filled with envy and sorrow at what she had left behind, she increasingly became annoyed about her situation. Why should all the focus be on Jack's career? On his work? Why was he the only one with a paycheck? She knew she could always have her old job back at home, and she began to feel like she was wasting time and wasting away while Jack (and her friends at home) were in high gear. She began to harangue Jack about returning early to the States.

Help spouses find meaning in their lives, too. Carol Leigh isn't unique. Her tale is repeated in various guises by expatriate spouses around the world. She may be a stock broker who's unable to trade on a foreign exchange, an architect who can't work because local customs prohibit women from doing so, or a secretary unable to obtain a work permit. And increasingly, she is a he, a male accompanying partner following his expat wife.

No matter what the reason—or the gender—after the scramble to help their families settle-in settles down, spouses confront an emptiness based on their own lack of routine, lack of network and lack of job. They must create a new life, often with a frequently absent partner and regularly without the prospect of employment for themselves. They face isolation, a loss of identity and diminished self-esteem. This isn't only because they've relinquished their career (or at least paid employment), but also because they encounter stress every day in the new environment—stress that makes them question if they can do anything competently anymore.

The dilemma of expatriate spouses, particularly dual-career spouses, is a growing and difficult one for HR managers. It not only rears its head during the selection of candidates (when many turn down assignments because of the spouse's career), but it also affects the success of the assignment and the ability for spouses and families to successfully repatriate. Consequently, if global managers want to help the Carol Leighs (and the assignments their husbands are on), they're going to have to design practices to help spouses find meaningful ways to spend their time during international assignments. In some cases, this may mean helping the spouse find employment or navigating through a maze of foreign immigration technicalities; in other cases it means helping him or her contact organizations to find out about volunteer work and educational opportunities; in still others it means simply connecting the spouse with a worthwhile network of peers. No easy task with one-size-fits-all solutions. Nevertheless, global HR managers must face this problem, head-on, and attempt to tackle some of these myriad issues with innovative approaches.

"We began to realize that the entire effectiveness of the assignment could be compromised by ignoring the spouse," says Steve Ford, manager of corporate relocations for Hewlett-Packard Co. based in Palo Alto, California. "Lots of things have changed in recent years," he says, "but one of the most significant is the growing percentage of working spouses and a realization that sending a family on a foreign service assignment isn't that simple. The assignment could be unsuccessful because of issues related to greater stress or unhappiness with the spouse (or other family members). And, from the company's point of view, a foreign service assignment is very expensive."

Indeed, statistics support Ford's claim that the number of dual-career couples is growing. The Bureau of Labor Statistics points out that in 1995, more than 65% of all married couples with children were dual-earner families (up 9% in 10 years). Women comprise 46% of the U.S. labor force. Furthermore, simply talk to global HR managers, and they'll tell you the spouse's career is becoming more and more an

FOCUS on Service

Walk into the offices of FOCUS Information Services, and you feel the energy, the bustle of activity all around. An enclave of information, this not-for-profit membership organization (supported by corporate donations and individual memberships) was created for expats of all nationalities living in the United Kingdom. (Other similar organizations are located in Belgium, France and Switzerland). It's purpose: to provide expatriates with the information and support they need while living in a new country to enable them to get the most out of the country immediately.

Looking around at the resources, you can see it's a powerhouse of intelligence. Building on the knowledge of other expatriates (the office alone has a Danish office manager, French marketing manager and Hungarian program director, and abounds with Americans, including Pamela Drobnyk, executive

director), newcomers don't have to spend endless days and weeks trying to locate services, goods, even friends. Seasoned foreign assignees find the center a place to gather with people from similar backgrounds, a place where they can simply congregate with their compatriots or hear their native language with all of its colloquialisms and natural richness. This is exactly what expatriates need. The group has its finger on the pulse of the expatriate community, and tries to adapt to the changing needs. For example, FOCUS increasingly is appealing to men—both employees and accompanying spouses—who may want career support.

FOCUS offers a volunteer-staffed phone line that provides access to a huge database of information; a bulletin board with job openings (expatriates can work in the U.K.); volunteer opportunities; a newsletter; and a reference library of

data about relocation job hunting, cross-cultural wisdom, immigration, child-rearing, traveling and other related topics.

FOCUS is renown for its seminars and networking meetings. Topics respond to critical needs of men and women, and are offered in the evenings as well as during the day to accommodate working people. Topics include: *Relocating to a New Country,* (a five-part workshop); *The Movable Spouse* (how moving affects the spouse as well as the employee, how to adjust and build a professional and private life outside of the family); *Networking in Cyberspace: Bridging the Cultural Gap in Your Office; Long Distance Care Giving; Raising Children Abroad;* and *Global Nomads.*

For other similar organizations, see "Expatriate Resource Services."

—CS

impediment to overseas relocations. In fact, this is the biggest factor when employees refuse to accept an international assignment. They decline because they can't afford to lose the income or they worry it may derail the spouse's career entirely if he or she is out of the workforce for a few years. It's becoming such an important issue that some organizations are beginning to consider redefining the length of assignments so they're much shorter (and thus, less disruptive to a spouse's career), and some

meaningful work, whether that be paid or unpaid:
• Immigration regulations that bar foreigners from working
• Language
• Lack of transferable skills to meaningful available work
• Scarcity of volunteer opportunities
• Cultural barriers that don't allow women to perform certain jobs—paid or voluntary
• Lack of knowledge about educational opportunities.

These services don't have to cost a lot of money. "At the outset, what's most important is a commitment from the company that it's willing to provide some support and acknowledgment that expatriate spouses are an important issue," says Eleanor Haller-Jorden, managing director of Zurich, Switzerland-based Paradigm Group and an authority and frequent lecturer on this topic. An expatriate herself, Haller-Jorden says companies can provide a variety of simple services that address the problem directly. For example, they can consolidate data, creating a clearinghouse of information and resources; they can set up a conference room and phone line for spouses or a small room to serve as a resource library with materials on the local community; they can create a directory of expatriates (especially those who would be willing to speak with newly arrived expatriates). For firms that feel they can get more involved, they can create a job hotline in which project-based jobs are available or they can create a consortium of companies and pool resources in a specific location or within an industry and create a job bank. Moreover, they can always help with acquiring work permits and offering career counseling. Finally, she says, companies could take stock of what they're currently offering and get feedback from expatriates— what's useful and what's not.

Indeed, that's precisely where Shell International, based both in London and The Hague, began its initiative to support spouses. With more than 5,500 expatriates, Shell possibly has the most expatriates of any company in the world. In 1993, the giant oil and petroleum multinational conducted a survey to discover the details of its expatriate community. (Shell International's expatriate spouse policies and the survey will be profiled in an upcoming issue of PERSONNEL JOURNAL.) The company discovered one of the greatest impediments to employees' mobility was their partners' reluctance to move. It also discovered that spouses felt they weren't being utilized enough and their expertise wasn't valued.

Quickly, the company moved into action. Once the main operating companies supported the findings and conclusions, it appointed a Spouse Employ-

You've just sent your expat to the United Kingdom. But did you know you can refer the spouse to FOCUS Information Services (above) in London? There, spouses can utilize myriad resources to help them also find fulfillment while living overseas.

are willing to consider international commuter marriages as alternatives. And these issues will become ever-more complex as greater numbers of men are the accompanying partner.

Already, we see this domestically. The Employee Relocation Council stated that in 1992 women constituted up to 15% of corporate moves (an increase from 5% in 1980). *The Wall Street Journal* estimates approximately 25% of accompanying partners will be males by the year 2000.

Here are some of the obstacles accompanying partners of either gender say they encounter in their quest to find

As daunting as the challenge may seem, companies and their global HR managers know it's critical to tackle these issues, and some are making inroads. Companies such as Hewlett-Packard Co. (HP), Shell International B.V., Medtronic Inc. and Monsanto Co. take a two-pronged approach: First, they help the spouse overcome cultural and emotional hurdles as well as the loneliness of a new location by offering cross-cultural counseling and connecting them with a network of spouses in the host community; and secondly, they offer a variety of options to begin to address the dual-career dilemma.

ment consultant who advises spouses and partners on a broad range of employment issues (either directly or by referral to external agencies). For example, a partner may come to Shell's consultant, Kathleen van der Wilk-Carlton, because he or she has only a vague idea of what's available in a destination country, or the person may have a very defined career path in mind and speak with her about ways to promote that career. Van der Wilk-Carlton first conducts a thorough assessment that will ultimately lead to career planning. Then she helps to either locate employment, aid in work permit acquisition or—when paid employment is impossible—find appropriate educational and volunteer activities that interest the person and help him or her keep on track. This can be very difficult because many expatriates in Shell go from one international location to another, and thus one area may be conducive to paid employment whereas the next destination may have only a few opportunities.

Apart from the area of employment, Shell also recognized the strong desire on the part of expatriate spouses to have greater recognition and contribution to the company. As a result, it created a network of briefing centers for expatriation around the world. It's for the entire expatriate family and it's run by spouses and becoming a spouse information center. The model is in The Hague Center in The Netherlands, which has a paid staff of expatriate spouses as well as volunteers. Each center serves a different community, and thus offers somewhat different activities, but each is generated by the interest of spouses.

Keep support consistent with company culture and values. Hewlett-Packard's Ford concurs with Shell's approach of promoting independence. "My belief is that HP people like to take ownership for their own lives and their own careers. What they want is to have us provide an environment in which they can do that. We try to make people as self-reliant as possible and to allow them to channel their energies in some productive way by giving them ideas and giving them access to counseling, education or whatever," he says. HP prepares for this predeparture

through counseling sessions that explore a variety of opportunities for the spouse.

HP's awareness of the dual-career problem, however, doesn't mean the company will do just anything to solve the problem. Solutions must be consistent with its fundamental principles about foreign assignments and its corporate culture. In keeping with that idea, the company doesn't approve of commuter marriages. "HP has a very strong philosophy about keeping the family

---

Expatriate Resource Services

United Kingdom:
FOCUS Information Services
13 Prince of Wales Terrace
London W8 5PG
171-937-00-50

Belgium:
FOCUS Career Services
Rue Lesbroussart 23
1050 Brussels
2-646-65-30

The Netherlands:
Federation of American Women Clubs Overseas (FAWCO) Resource Center
Schouwweg 65
NL-2243 BH Waffenaar

France:
WICE, 20, Boulevard de Montparnasse
15th arrondissement Paris
1-45-66-75-50

Switzerland:
Paradigm Group
Riedhofstrasse 354
8049 Zurich
41-1-342-3606

U.S.-based resource:
Women On The Move
Fax: 212/369-0238
(Contact: Pamela Perraud)

---

together so we actively discourage commuter relationships in [our] international policies," says Tee Hitchcock, interna-

tional relocation specialist. "In fact, it could be the basis for nonselection of a candidate," she says.

The firm also won't try to replicate the spouse's income. "It's not under consideration," she says. But, she continues, "We understand that asking a family to relocate these days [involves] talking about two-career families, so we try to create policies that reflect that concern." The following are HP's policies that affect dual-career spouses:

• One-day session of spouse-specific training that's either career-related or interest-related (it could be academic or it could be a hobby). Usually the counselor researches beforehand what's available in the host country and also gives contact names.
• Financial assistance for the spouse by which HP shares the cost of all types of educational activities up to $2,000 annually (this can include host-location career-counseling).
• Assistance with resume preparation and payment for visas when work is a possibility in the destination country.
• Three days of cross-cultural counseling and orientation for the whole family that's designed to cover local customs (business and social; history) as well as ways to become more quickly accustomed to the local environment.
• Language training.
• If the spouse is an HP employee, there's often a leave of absence with a guarantee of work upon return.

Obviously, the policies HP developed and implemented demonstrate the value the company places on spouses, whether they're leaving a paid career or not.

HR can channel spouse contributions toward volunteer work. Tamara Homburg is a spouse who took the international relocation as an opportunity to create something exceptional. On assignment with her husband for St. Louis-based Monsanto Co., Homburg was always optimistic and enthusiastic about the international opportunity. The chance to move to Brussels, Belgium with Monsanto came when Homburg, a practicing lawyer, was pregnant with her and her husband's second child and she was eager to take a break in her career. During the first year in Brussels, she taught business law classes. Nevertheless, Homburg (who has been on assignment once before) felt antsy to do more involved and challenging work.

Luck intervened. When Marena Rahusen, the HR manager in Brussels who's responsible for expatriate policies, initiated the idea of a Spousal Sponsor Network and asked for assistance, Homburg's hand shot up as the volunteer to lead the effort. At first, it began as a regular gathering for coffee and sharing of relocation horror stories—things such as learning to use gasoline station pumps, marketing in less than three hours, and other relatively minor situations you laugh at afterward that are " . . . huge events in . . . your life that can move very competent people to tears . . ." These were the basis for lively, continuing discussions.

> # The Spousal Sponsor Network began as a gathering for coffee and sharing of relocation horror stories, such as learning to use gasoline station pumps and marketing in less than three hours.

Soon after, the group decided to formalize the network as a way to be sure newcomers could learn from their experiences. Monsanto provides a place to meet, facilities for group gatherings, postage and copying services. Well-known for its responsive international relocation policies, the company not only attempts to sustain the spouse, but actually recognizes his or her contribution to the company. "We value spouses. In fact, we let them know it's not just

employees' knowledge we value, it's theirs as well," says Carol Jones, global development director for Monsanto. As an example of this belief, Rahusen helped the group begin and maintained a sense of sponsorship and offered resources. But the company wants spouses to assume ownership of the organization. It also pushes for the group to be autonomous to assure it avoids the possibility of spouses being involved in company politics.

Today, the Spousal Sponsor Network has created a databank of families who have lived in Brussels at least a year. These people (both expatriate and local families) must meet specific criteria similar to the core competencies the company identifies for successful, adaptive expats. Before new expats come on the network's house-hunting trip, they receive a package from the Brussels office with a letter from the network describing the program and asking if they'd like to participate.

The family provides a profile (who the kids are, whether they've had previous global assignments, what their interests are) and then they're matched with one of the sponsor families. During the family's house-hunting trip, the sponsor makes contact and invites the newcomers over to their home for dinner during the weekend to become acquainted.

The sponsors actually undergo a competency development workshop so they're able to be helpful to the newcomers, understand the stress they're undergoing, and respect confidentiality. Sponsors are proactive. After an initial needs assessment, sponsors are encouraged to keep in touch with the people and make certain they're doing well. "The whole purpose of the sponsor program was to get people integrated as quickly as possible so they had a network or support group to go to," says Homburg.

Provide financial support and creative employment assistance. Monsanto utilizes financial resources to help spouses identify their transferable skills and assists them with finding opportunities in the host country. The company has a clear dual-career policy with three tiers. One is for predeparture: a one-time dislocation payment that's 33% of the last six months of gross tax-

able earned income. Another tier applies during the assignment: a payment of up to $5,000 of pre-approved expenses for higher education that's career-related (job search assistance, immigration help, travel to the country-of-origin for professional meetings, payment for professional certification fees and professional magazine subscriptions). The third tier is for repatriation: a $1,000 allowance for re-entry job-search assistance, resume preparation, interviewing techniques and skills analysis. These policies apply to people who work full time or part time. They can be self-employed or employed by a company.

Another company that offers financial assistance is Minneapolis-based Medtronic Inc., makers of heart pacemakers and other cardiac-related devices. The firm generates 44% of its revenue from overseas.

Possibly the most innovative way the company recognizes the needs of all the family members of its 25- to 30-member expat group is its Flexible Reimbursement Account. It's a matching account in which the family can spend up to $6,000 per year on personal development and the company will reimburse 50% of that. The policy statement offers examples: Dual-career spouses can use the money for travel expenses to conferences outside the foreign location or for other educational expenses. It also can use the money for any other expense that will make the relocation easier on any family members, such as additional telephone calls home or flying grandparents to see the expatriates. The intent? The company recognizes expatriates have needs in addition to what they would have if they were in the United States. But, clearly, as beneficiaries of money, expats share the expense.

In addition to financial support, Medtronic helps dual-career families by networking with the spouse's company and trying to arrange innovative opportunities. In the past, the company has worked with the spouse's employer to find a position in the same country, to alter the timing of the expat's assignment—speed it up or slow it down—if the spouse's career was positively affected, and to help with work-related legalities such as acquiring visas and paying union dues. Furthermore, Medtronic has attempted to find ways to help the spouse maintain a long-distance relationship with the employer, such as a long-distance telecommuting relationship.

The following key policy features are ways in which Medtronic tries to impact the spouse's experience:

• Flexible Reimbursement Account
• Predeparture cultural orientation for expatriate, spouse and children, if appropriate
• Automobile (including special lease rates if a second car is desired for the spouse)
• Language training prior to and during the assignment
• Outsourced settling-in services to assist expats in finding their way to the bank, the grocery store and other activities of day-to-day life
• On-the-ground, in-country follow-ups by a third-party to be sure the expatriate family is doing well.

The company also has defined ways to improve personnel responsiveness. It comprehensively assesses cultural adaptability for the entire family before the assignment to identify any red flags. It establishes closer ties with expatriates throughout the duration of the assignment by talking with them at specific intervals. At the same time, the company creates a network of global managers at other companies to determine what is state-of-the-art assistance. It also continuously measures the effectiveness of current services. For example, it asks families how useful settling-in services, cultural counseling and predeparture training are to them, and what may be missing.

Monsanto, HP and Shell show that although the dual-career dilemma may be a difficult one, it's not impossible to solve. They're trying to support spouses in so many ways: Helping them identify transferable skills that will assist their adaptation in the destination; encourag-ing career development discussions before relocation; telling them about volunteer and educational opportunities that will further their careers; counseling them about such possibilities as taking a leave-of-absence and returning to the job for specified periods of time during the assignment; providing long-term career counseling and development support; providing names of local spouse centers and counseling facilities; and even exploring collaborations with other global firms for job possibilities.

To be sure, it's not simple. Indeed, it may be one of the most thorny aspects of expatriation. But the needs of the accompanying spouse must be adequately addressed or there may be no assignment at all.

Charlene Marmer Solomon is a contributing editor to PERSONNEL JOURNAL.

Toward Global Convergence

William B. Werther, Jr.

"In the long run, we are all dead," observed British economist John Maynard Keynes. Although speculation about tomorrow is, at best, problematic, three seemingly unconnected undercurrents are converging with nearly the same certainty as Lord Keynes' morbid prediction. One trend is the "global youth culture"; another is "freed markets." Together these two help shape a third pattern, "competitive convergence." All three "megatrends"—as John Naisbitt might have labeled them—are global in consequence. The result will mean a need to further re-think management and marketing in this fast-growing, billion-plus subculture.

These self-reinforcing trends will not mean the "end of history"—though the result may make war, famine, discrimination, and nation-states as uncommon as modern-day crucifixions. And, admittedly, the full force of these trends remains just out of view, somewhere beyond the short time horizons of this decade and just shy of that distant "long run" Keynes spoke of. Nevertheless, an early glimpse of that future is embodied in the McDonald's Generation.

THE MCDONALD'S GENERATION

No hard and fast date marks the start of the McDonald's Generation. For me, it began in 1969. In that year, while baby-sitting an early rising four-year-old, I was watching Saturday morning cartoons during which a McDonald's commercial appeared. At the time, it seemed odd that a sophisticated company like McDonald's would "waste" its advertising dollars on four-year-olds who lacked the wherewithal to buy a Big Mac. That is, it seemed odd until the following Friday evening, when his mother came home from work asking, "Where are we going for dinner?" Faster than an adult could translate her question into the universal statement of "I'm not cooking," it was answered from the back bedroom by a small voice crying, "McDonald's! McDonald's!" Thus was recorded one birth into the McDonald's Generation. A pixel of the picture fell into place, though the sociological shift it suggested went unnoticed because it was only a sample of one.

My generation (early Baby Boomers) and previous ones would have been far less likely to shout "McDonald's!" (or, in my youth, "Howard Johnson's!") in response to a mother's question about dinner. First, it was unlikely that our mothers would be returning from work at dinner time; more likely, they would already have been home making dinner. Second, eating out was seldom the extemporaneous decision it is today, and was more likely reserved for special occasions. Third, and perhaps more telling, my generation and those before it were more likely to be "seen, not heard." "Children don't speak unless spoken to" was a kindly enforced dictum one rarely risked violating with unsolicited outbursts. Simply put, the plea for "McDonald's!" mirrored the culturally significant exodus of mothers from home to the brave new world of paid work.

Also mirrored in that outburst were even more fundamental changes. Whether motivated by guilt or fatigue or the pressure of "Madison Avenue," the parent-centered family changed its orbit and became a child-centered household. This was not true for all homes, and perhaps not even for most, but it represented a significant

> *Before the "long run" arrives for most of us, the foreseeable future will be reshaped in some surprising ways.*

From *Business Horizons,* January/February 1996, pp. 3-9. © 1996 by the Foundation for the School of Business at Indiana University. Reprinted by permission.

beginning. Indeed, a visit to the supermarket on Saturday mornings—then or now, whether in North or South America, Europe or Asia—allows one to eavesdrop on the insistent demands of the grocery-cart set as they are chauffeured down the sugar-coated aisles of today's stores, pre-programmed to "buy" by a ubiquitous electronic media. Or watch their older brothers and sisters in China or Chile as they enjoy the same movies and music in the U.S. and Europe, dress in the same blue jeans, tee shirts, and athletic shoes, stop by the Citibank ATM, and then rush off to Taco Bell, Kentucky Fried Chicken, Pizza Hut, or McDonald's outlets.

A pixel here, a pixel there.

And it is not just the toddlers or teenagers, either. Most professors I know have experienced a student lamenting a low grade with the irrelevant (and seldom true) argument, "But Professor, I was there every day!" Their repetition of that whining mantra suggests that life has taught them to plead long enough and they too can get the grade (or the sugar-coated cereal, or the trip to McDonald's).

FROM MCDONALD'S TO MTV

The 1950s lament "Rock 'n roll will corrupt our youth" has proven to be largely true in the minds of many parents and grandparents. But rock 'n roll has had a much more pervasive impact than even its harshest critics of the 1950s could imagine. Music has served as the battle cry of each post-World War II generation. More impressively, it has become a global language uniting successive generations from Santiago to Miami, Beijing to Moscow, in a common perspective that says: Authority figures are stupid. From parents and police to teachers and timekeepers, they all cling to the outdated and the outmoded.

The "authority figure is wrong" shows up as the central theme of many films aimed at the movie-going youth of the world. Whether in the cinemas of the world's cities or the bicycle-generator-powered VCRs of remote African and Asian villages, the media—the largely English-speaking media—have permeated the globe, molding an increasingly uniform teenage culture. One need only listen to the rock 'n roll of hotel lobbies around the world, watch the satellite movie broadcasts in the room, and then walk out on the streets and observe the Levi- and Nike-clad youth of Los Angeles or Hong Kong, Bombay or Melbourne to see that this is so.

And why not? For most of civilization, cultural values have been transmitted to children by their grandparents, while parents worked in the fields and later in the factories and offices. But with increased urbanization, grandparents play an increasingly trivialized role in the transmission of values. Extended families increasingly give way to nuclear families. This "marginalization" of grandparents and societal values is most noticeable where migration to cities is high, as in the United States and in newly industrialized countries that see migration patterns such as China's 100-million member "floating work force" or Brazil's, Indonesia's, and Nigeria's massive shifts from the countryside to urban slums. Those migration patterns often sever the reinforcing influence of extended families and close-knit communities, replacing them with the anonymity of the city and culture-leveling television.

To some degree, technology has filled the void of grandparents and even mothers as the keeper of the culture. Today, TVs increasingly serve as a combination babysitter and values transmitter. The spread of MTV, videos, and satellite movies around the globe injects previously diverse cultures with a virus of values more common and potent than mere music and dress. It adds a growing uniformity to the values of the "global youth culture." The result? Teenagers today in Seoul and the South Bronx have a commonality of values, tastes, and aspirations that are more similar to each other than to those of their respective grandparents.

Such values and aspirations go beyond the outward symbols of pop music, jeans, Nike shoes, and Big Macs. At a deeper level one finds a greater demand for personal freedom. The traditional anti-authority message aimed at youth in the developed nations for the past couple of generations has gained near-universal distribution. Where once the expectation of freedom was limited to the developed nations, the media have brought this expectation to the developing countries. Even in the oppressive societies of the planet we now see youths stand before tanks or pointed rifles—just as their predecessors did in developed countries a generation earlier by erecting barricades in Paris or being shot at Kent State. At the same time, one can witness among the world's young people a growing acceptance of such issues as women's rights and concern for the ecological consequences of technological advancement. Whether the complaint is the destruction of rain forests or French nuclear testing, spontaneous protests spring up in Chile and Japan, Germany and the United States. There is a greater recognition of Spaceship Earth as our common lifeboat.

The argument here is not that traditional values and aspirations of family, health, and well-being are being discarded. Rather, this era is witnessing the injection of new, widely agreed-upon values of freedom and ecological concern that are permeating the remotest regions of the world and cutting across the most diverse cultures. The pattern is far from universal, but it is moving toward universality.

Such a growing uniformity of culture results from billions of points of contact among young

people and the media every day. Though each interaction is insignificant, the pervasiveness of these contacts is like the combined impact of thousands of tiny pixels in a television: A picture begins to emerge of a separate subculture with implications for management and marketing as well as for governance and global unity.

LOOKING THROUGH THE TRENDLINE

The still fuzzy picture painted above suggests an unheralded and uncoordinated—but nonetheless real—linkage around the globe, uniting in some peculiar ways today's youth, tomorrow's decision makers. Before these young people attain leadership roles, they will reshape organizations, local and global, small and large, public and private. Consider but a few areas of impact:

• "McDonaldized" youths already expect—even demand—greater participation in decisions that affect them at home, in school, and at work, guiding them toward new leadership strategies and behaviors.

• "Empowerment" is not just an active organizational response to competitive pressures. It is also a reaction to a cultural reality shaped by youth-driven expectations of the more egalitarian participation patterns they have encountered in today's less autocratic families and schools.

• Traditional middle-class values of hard work, patience, earnestness, and striving for future rewards may become secondary concerns

when compared with the instant gratification and immense wealth seen every day as a result of lawsuits, lotteries, game shows, sports and entertainment salaries, and the drug deal going down on the corner. Those same middle-class work values don't seem to hold a candle to being "cool" and "accepted." A look at rap music and ghetto-inspired grungy dress, for example, suggests that perhaps for the first time in history, middle-class youths are emulating their lower-class counterparts. Though parallels with the 1960s can be drawn, today's dress code may be more than a fashion statement as it extends across diverse cultures and reaches beyond teenagers to those both younger and older. Such "coolness" and acceptance seldom come from a job—at least not those outside sports and entertainment.

• The growing proportion of out-of-wedlock babies born to middle-class girls (and women) in the United States now stands at 30 percent, following the trend set by the lower classes and the disadvantaged groups a generation earlier. Do these trends suggest that fundamental societal changes may reach all the way into core middle-class values, making changes in dress and musical tastes seem superficial? If something as fundamental as mating practices changes in one generation, can the work ethic be far behind?

• A growing uniformity of values along generational lines leads to different attitudes about attendance, loyalty, and responsibility. Unlike the "work-then-play" values of earlier generations, senior supervisors often report that jobs are seen as an interruption of the younger generation's personal plans, especially when overtime is concerned. Is this merely stereotypical thinking among old timers? Or has the work ethic already shifted?

These implications go on to suggest even more questions:

• With children having children, who transmits societal values besides the media? Though demands for employer-provided child care will continue to grow in countries where these demands have not already been institutionalized, will employers need to be concerned with values education among employees *and* their children? Is business going to face the *in loco parentis* responsibilities that universities gave up in the 1960s?

• As the youth culture spreads around the "global electronic village" (as some view Spaceship Earth), will today's ethnic, tribal, racial, and religious differences loom as large tomorrow? Will one or two more generations of "global culture" ameliorate these ancient differences as national media and mobility have largely smoothed over the regional diversity between North and South in the United States during the last two generations? Are not intergenerational differences *always* resolved in favor of the younger generation, sooner or later?

• If ideas, dress, music, entertainment, sociosexual mores, and values are converted to digitized pixels that freely roam across the borders of even the most repressive political states, how meaningful are those borders? How well will they contain the next generation, now being force-fed by a steady stream of satellite movies, commercials, and rock videos? Will those billion-plus youths of developing countries follow their fathers and older brothers, tracing those electronic beams back toward their origin in search of some fantasy world—an imaginary electronic world that comes closer to science fiction than the reality most of the planet's teenagers now experience? Does anyone know how many young Mexicans have already done so by moving to the world's second largest Mexican city, Los Angeles? Ditto for young Cubans drifting along the Gulf Stream to Miami, the world's second largest Cuban city? London, Amsterdam, Paris, Lisbon, and other European cities are already swelling with youthful immigrants from former colonies, while Lagos, Rio de Janeiro, Santiago, Beijing, Bombay, and other third world cities bulge from migration.

"The emerging picture suggests that markets, once freed, are lifting nation-states onto a faster-track economic growth."

With the possible exception of North Korea (where all televisions and radios only receive the two government-controlled channels), there already exists a McDonald's generation of perhaps a billion pre-teens, teenagers, and young adults, peppered throughout every other country on earth. If that does not constitute a megatrend, move forward 50 years when this cadre embraces those age 70 and under.

THE MACRO TREND: FREED MARKETS

Beginning with the demise of the "Articles of Confederation" that pr[e]ceeded the present-day constitution of the United States, the 13 colonies have grown to become 50 integrated and free American markets. In 1993, the European Economic Community, begun in the late 1950s, transformed itself into the European Union (EU). And beginning in 1994, Mexico's approximately 92 million people joined Canada and the United States in eliminating almost all trade barriers to form another continent-spanning market, the North American Free Trade Agreement (NAFTA).

Recent years have also seen free trade agreements signed between Mexico, Columbia, and Venezuela. Brazil and its neighbors are also dismantling trade barriers. More recently the EU voted to add Sweden, Norway, Finland, and Austria to its membership, with the middle European countries standing in line waiting to join. Likewise, Chile and others are seeking membership in NAFTA. Restated, at the global level we see country-sized pixels clustering together into integrated, free-market collections.

The emerging picture suggests that markets, once freed, are lifting nation-states onto a faster-track economic growth. For example, between 1990 and 1993, Chile pulled one million of its 13 million citizens out of poverty. Though a feat not likely to be duplicated, the Chilean government has achieved this little-known success through free-market inspired growth. By pulling down trade barriers, cutting taxes, stabilizing its government, and redesigning its social security system, Chile stands as a beacon, attracting imitators in adjoining Argentina, Bolivia, and Peru that want to play by similar, macroeconomic rules.

In Chile's case, it took an economically enlightened (albeit politically repressive) military dictatorship to follow the free-market advice of the "Chicago boys"—youthful economists from the University of Chicago and their protégés. Import tariffs fell from 400 percent to 11 percent. Public businesses and services were privatized, ranging from major utilities to city buses and street sweepers. Even social security was converted from the thinly disguised tax and welfare program typical in Europe and North America into a privately administered retirement account. This account allows Chilean workers to send their funds to a choice of for-profit investment firms that report their results to these "micro-capitalist" investors three times a year. Every worker has become an "investor" in Chile's system of developing capitalism, adding to the country's political stability. Ironically, as this Chilean model is exported up the Andes and across the pampas, freed markets find governments giving up economic controls, tariffs, and other impediments to the efficient flow of goods. In other words, governments' involvement in the economies lessens.

As business leaders and entrepreneurs respond, domestically and internationally, to such activity, separate nation-states (usually those nearest) also become increasingly interdependent, lessening the likelihood of war. This story could be repeated using Singapore and its neighbors—Malaysia, Indonesia, and Thailand. Does anyone expect another war among those who comprise the European Union, for example? The resulting prosperity also yields resources to stave off famine. Even in the face of local crop failures, free economies become less dependent upon agriculture as they move up to higher value-added industries and services. Discrimination—within and between countries—lessens, at least to the extent that such discrimination emerges out of poverty and the ignorance it fosters.

In time, the economic interdependencies may overshadow the importance of political units, as has happened with the decline of "states' rights" in the United States and as appears destined to continue among the EU countries. Whether NAFTA and other economic structures evolve into tentative political unions in the long run is uncertain, but ample precedent exists.

YOUTH, FREED TRADE, AND COMPETITIVE CONVERGENCE

The issues of the global youth culture and the expansion of freed trade that have brought the world to its present configuration are obvious to see. Less obvious, but perhaps equally powerful, is a third trend—competitive convergence. Here the argument is straightforward: similarities in macroeconomic and political policies affecting competition have given birth to free trade areas (such as NAFTA), economic union (such as Western Europe), and the General Agreement on Tariffs and Trade (GATT) and its successor, the World Trade Organization. These similarities, combined with a growing uniformity of expectations among the upcoming generation of workers, will lead to a convergence in competitive practices.

Competitive convergence will be driven by competitive necessity. The need to battle stronger and stronger global competitors, which are likely to emerge from larger and larger free markets, will not permit firms to ignore practices that meet

a pragmatic test (does it work?). At the same time, fewer trade barriers will mean that those who do not rapidly adopt global best practices will find fewer "safe" or "home" markets in which to continue their less efficient ways. And with growing homogeneity of values among the young, the cultural, political, and economic roadblocks to global best practices will be dismantled by an ever expanding (and aging) youth culture as it reaches the levers of political and corporate power.

> "The cultural, political, and economic roadblocks to global best practices will be dismantled by an ever expanding (and aging) youth culture as it reaches the levers of political and corporate power."

By way of illustration, consider some preliminary examples of best practices that have been adapted across borders and cultures with increasingly less resistance. Management examples first:

• Just-in-time production and inventory techniques developed in Japan have spread to many U.S. and European businesses, as have time-to-market innovations for new product introductions, such as concurrent engineering.

• Downsizing—the forced reduction in company employment—has remained a predominantly U.S. management approach, restricted by tradition among Japan's large employers and by employment laws throughout most of the EU. However, with Japan's often overstaffed white-collar positions and European employer reluctance to hire new workers, the U.S. competitive advantage in costs, flexibility, and speed is causing Nissan and other large Japanese firms to announce work force reductions that are poorly disguised downsizing efforts. Likewise, EU ministers—in the name of "labor law equalization"—are discussing the politically sensitive revision of restrictive employment laws.

• Continuous quality improvement efforts, largely pioneered by U.S. statisticians before and during World War II, gave Japan a competitive edge that led to adoption by U.S. and European producers. This is evidenced by a look at the U.S. **Malcolm Baldri[d]ge Award and the EU's ISO 9000** standards.

• Flexible manufacturing systems, long used in the Japanese automobile industry to balance production flows with market demand and accelerate model change-over times, are gaining popularity in American factories.

Global best practices extend to marketing and distribution:

• MTV (and its imitators), specializing in English-language rock 'n roll, can be seen even in the jungles of Africa, Asia, and South America, advertising a largely identical parade of products, sometimes even using the original English language ads found in the United States.

• With parents in tow by their four-year-olds, one of the largest McDonald's restaurants can be found in Beijing's Tiananmen Square (ironically located only a few hundred yards from China's major tourist attraction—Mao's crypt).

• Coke and Pepsi battle for the youth market from Shanghai to Chicago, touting to investors the growth potential of the third world.

• Sonae Investments—Portugal's largest group of private companies—proudly counts among its holdings the Pizza Hut franchise for the country.

• Jeans, running shoes, and printed tee shirts are the global youth culture's uniform everywhere, implying a standard dress (and product) configuration for one, global-wide demographic segment.

If there has been one growth industry that accelerated through the global recession of the early 1990s, it is the worldwide explosion of MBA programs—particularly in developing countries. Though not necessarily a "global best practice," similarity of curricula and training in business disciplines seems likely to hasten further the spread of (past and future) competitive best practices.

Admittedly, a handful of anecdotal illustrations do not prove competitive convergence. Nor is the argument being made for some future universality of business practices. German and Japanese business leaders are likely to retain longer planning horizons than their U.S. counterparts; Asian nations are more likely to subordinate personal freedoms to the good of the group; and long-term employment stability is more likely in Japan or Europe than in the United States for the foreseeable future. Nevertheless, evidence for a convergence of global best practices seems strong. Other trends—from computer networking to proliferating international alliances—make competitive convergence appear to be the not-so-invisible hand and sword of competition.

From here on into the future, the evidence for trends is replaced, of necessity, by speculation. Certainly, extending the past 25 years of cultural dispersion, movements toward freed trade, and competitive convergence is—like any extrapolation—dangerous, because it assumes that current conditions will hold in the distant future. Paradoxically, such an assumption is both unlikely *and* the most reasonable basis from which to proceed.

So we plunge into a future where, current conditions suggest, in less than 15 years trade barriers in North America will effectively be gone—probably along with those between Central America, the Caribbean, northern South America, and the Andes countries. The Southern

Cone of Argentina (which has already pegged its currency to the dollar), Brazil (which is trying to), Uruguay, and Paraguay will be even further advanced in eliminating their intra-regional barriers. Perhaps with greater stability in Brazil, these Southern Cone members will already have joined their neighbor, Chile, in affiliation with the descendants of NAFTA—forming a truly hemispheric free trade area of more than half a billion people.

Of approximately equal size, one might imagine a European Union early in the next century that (in various stages of social and economic integration) reaches from Ireland to the Urals, becoming truly pan-European. Assuming some form of Asian free trade area, one might also imagine three billion people stretching from Pakistan through India and Southeast Asia to Indonesia, the Philippines, China, Japan, Korea, and eastern Siberia.

Faced with the prospects of a three-billion member free trade area, it takes only a little more imagination to see a European-oriented North and South America achieving some form of economic free trade (though not necessarily political) arrangement with an enlarged European Union. In fact, geo-political-economic realities may demand the formation of a billion-member free trade area stretching east from the beaches of Hawaii to North America and Europe to the Ural mountains deep in Russia. This Eurocentric trade area may well be needed to offset the staggering possibility of 21st century Japanese technology combining with Chinese entrepreneurship, industriousness, and markets.

At this stage—perhaps within a generation from now and well within the lifetimes of even Baby Boomers—a free trade agreement between the West and the East may become a prudent reality to ensure peace and economic stability for a world of investors and micro-capitalists. Then the economies of the Middle East, Africa, and Oceania (not already affiliated with one or more trading areas) could be folded into a truly global, free trade environment. Presumably, higher standards of living for the then 10 billion or so inhabitants of Spaceship Earth would create additional political freedoms.

Remember, too, the youth trend. Today's teenagers a quarter of a century from now will be the middle-aged business and government leaders who will negotiate these ever-expanding agreements. They, more than any generation in history, will have been nurtured on a world-oriented culture and are more likely to see similarities where their grandparents saw differences. Being less focused on regional or ethnocentric differences, they are likely to view international differences in politics, culture, and economics as unimportant impediments to a more culturally and economically unified planet.

Of course, this scenario and its assumptions

are far from certain. Just as mass production gave rise to the affluence that allowed "mass customization," the backlash to an increasingly uniform, global culture will undoubtedly be the need to reassert individual, even group differences. One need only think of the war in the former Yugoslavia or the French separatist movement in Québec to see centuries old cross-currents vigorously resisting the forces of convergence. Freedom of choice to those not used to it may be a burden to be resisted more than a joy to be embraced. Likewise, when rising expectations are blunted by a stagnant reality that offers little improvement for some and reverses for many, counterrevolutions may arise to reattain some idealized, if not ideal, past. Certainly there are many in the former Soviet Union who would prefer a return to the past over their turbulent adventure into the future. And deeply embedded cultural and religious beliefs will still be communicated by family and community, continuing to resist the modern forces of economic and social convergence well beyond the foreseeable future.

Nor does such an optimistic scenario suggest ten billion people uniformly marching to an identical drum beat. Instead, what is proposed here is that as the drum grows louder, more people will march to its unifying beat. Ten billion pixels will not suddenly snap into focus. Instead they will slowly emerge to reveal a world increasingly devoid of war, famine, bigotry, and oppression—because none of these conditions are particularly favorable for free trade and a world of voters turned micro-capitalists.

The result will not be Utopia. Poverty will exist, even if hunger does not. Social tensions from mass migrations and immigrations will still strain relations between "different peoples," even though these differences will erode under the bombardment of satellite-based TV, telephone, and computer communications. It won't quite be one planet, one people, one culture—one world. But a growing number of people will hold MBAs, not guns. And in this not-so-long run, many of us will defy Keynes' dictum and still be alive to enjoy the fruits of this new millennium—fresh fruits undoubtedly provided by Chilean businesses during the Northern hemisphere's long winters.

William B. Werther, Jr. is the Samuel N. Friedland Professor of Executive Management at the University of Miami's School of Business Administration.

Index

Credits/Acknowledgments

Cover design by Charles Vitelli.

1. The Nature of International Business
Facing overview—Dushkin/McGraw-Hill illustration by Mike Eagle.

2. The International Environment: Organizations and Monetary Systems
Facing overview—© 1997 by PhotoDisc, Inc.

3. Foreign Environment
Facing overview—AP/Wide World photo by Greg Baker.

4. How Management Deals with Environmental Forces
Facing overview—Sony Corporation of America photo. 198—AP/Wide World photo by Robert Horn. 199—*Business Week* map by Ray Vella. 214—FOCUS Information Services photo.

ANNUAL EDITIONS ARTICLE REVIEW FORM

■ NAME: _____ DATE: _____

■ TITLE AND NUMBER OF ARTICLE: _____

■ BRIEFLY STATE THE MAIN IDEA OF THIS ARTICLE: _____

_____

■ LIST THREE IMPORTANT FACTS THAT THE AUTHOR USES TO SUPPORT THE MAIN IDEA:

_____

_____

_____

_____

■ WHAT INFORMATION OR IDEAS DISCUSSED IN THIS ARTICLE ARE ALSO DISCUSSED IN YOUR
TEXTBOOK OR OTHER READINGS THAT YOU HAVE DONE? LIST THE TEXTBOOK CHAPTERS AND
PAGE NUMBERS:

_____

_____

_____

_____

_____

■ LIST ANY EXAMPLES OF BIAS OR FAULTY REASONING THAT YOU FOUND IN THE ARTICLE:

_____

_____

_____

_____

■ LIST ANY NEW TERMS/CONCEPTS THAT WERE DISCUSSED IN THE ARTICLE, AND WRITE A SHORT
DEFINITION:

_____

_____

_____

_____

*Your instructor may require you to use this ANNUAL EDITIONS Article Review Form in any
number of ways: for articles that are assigned, for extra credit, as a tool to assist in developing
assigned papers, or simply for your own reference. Even if it is not required, we encourage
you to photocopy and use this page; you will find that reflecting on the articles will greatly
enhance the information from your text.

We Want Your Advice

ANNUAL EDITIONS revisions depend on two major opinion sources: one is our Advisory Board, listed in the front of this volume, which works with us in scanning the thousands of articles published in the public press each year; the other is you—the person actually using the book. Please help us and the users of the next edition by completing the prepaid article rating form on this page and returning it to us. Thank you for your help!

ANNUAL EDITIONS: INTERNATIONAL BUSINESS 98/99
Article Rating Form

Here is an opportunity for you to have direct input into the next revision of this volume. We would like you to rate each of the 48 articles listed below, using the following scale:

1. **Excellent: should definitely be retained**
2. **Above average: should probably be retained**
3. **Below average: should probably be deleted**
4. **Poor: should definitely be deleted**

Rating	Article	Rating	Article
	1. Growth through Global Sustainability		23. Wanted: Muscle
	2. American Isolationism versus the Global Economy		24. Global Economy, Local Mayhem?
	3. "Globalization and the International Division of Labor: The Role of Europe and the Response of European Companies"		25. Global Deregulation: Deutsche Hegira
			26. Investing in India: Strategies for Tackling Bureaucratic Hurdles
	4. Building Effective R&D Capabilities Abroad		27. Shock Therapy
	5. Back to the Land		28. Crafting Strategies for Global Marketing in the New Millennium
	6. Education and the Wealth of Nations		
	7. World Education League: Who's Top?		29. Asia's Next Tiger? Vietnam Is Fraught with Promise and Peril for Marketers
	8. Balancing Act		
	9. Riding the Dragon		30. Troubles Ahead in Emerging Markets
	10. Challenges in Managing Technology in Transnational Multipartner Networks		31. Maquiladora-ville
			32. The Myth of the China Market
	11. The Great Escape		33. Ship It!
	12. International Banking: Coping with the Ups and Downs		34. "Compromise Increases the Risk of War"
			35. Doing Business in China: It's Far from Easy
	13. International Monetary Arrangements: Is There a Monetary Union in Asia's Future?		36. Doing Business in Vietnam: A Cultural Guide
			37. Earn 20% Investing Abroad
	14. Ignored Warnings		38. Europe in the Global Financial World
	15. Africa's New Dawn		39. The Discreet Charm of Provincial Asia
	16. Global Transfer of Critical Capabilities		40. From Major to Minor
	17. Put Your Ethics to a Global Test		41. Are Expats Getting Lost in the Translation?
	18. Keeping Up on Chinese Culture		42. Getting What You Pay For
	19. American Involvement in Vietnam, Part II: Prospects for U.S. Business in a New Era		43. A Company without a Country?
			44. Asia's Bamboo Network
	20. Political Risk Analysis in North American Multinationals: An Empirical Review and Assessment		45. When Sexual Harassment Is a Foreign Affair
			46. HR Pioneers Explore the Road Less Traveled
	21. The Scourge of Global Counterfeiting		47. One Assignment, Two Lives
	22. Rule by Law		48. Toward Global Convergence

(Continued on next page)

ABOUT YOU

Name _____ Date _____

Are you a teacher? ❏ Or a student? ❏

Your school name _____

Department _____

Address _____

City _____ State _____ Zip _____

School telephone # _____

YOUR COMMENTS ARE IMPORTANT TO US !

Please fill in the following information:

For which course did you use this book? _____

Did you use a text with this *ANNUAL EDITION*? ❏ yes ❏ no

What was the title of the text? _____

What are your general reactions to the *Annual Editions* concept?

Have you read any particular articles recently that you think should be included in the next edition?

Are there any articles you feel should be replaced in the next edition? Why?

Are there any World Wide Web sites you feel should be included in the next edition? Please annotate.

May we contact you for editorial input?

May we quote your comments?

ANNUAL EDITIONS: INTERNATIONAL BUSINESS 98/99

BUSINESS REPLY MAIL

| First Class | Permit No. 84 | Guilford, CT |

Postage will be paid by addressee

Dushkin/McGraw·Hill
Sluice Dock
Guilford, CT 06437